"MEDALS WILL BE WORN"
Wearing Medals Past and Present
1844–1999

"MEDALS WILL BE WORN"

Wearing Medals
Past and Present
1844-1999

by

Lieutenant-Colonel Ashley R. Tinson

1999

First published in Great Britain in 1999 by
Token Publishing, PO Box 14, Honiton, Devon EX14 9YP, UK
Telephone: 01404 46972 Fax: 01404 831895
e-mail: info@medal-news.com website: www.medal-news.com

© Lieutenant Colonel A.R. Tinson and Token Publishing 1999

British Library Cataloguing in Publication Data:
A catalogue record for this book is available from the British Library
ISBN 1 870 192 23 0

Printed in Great Britain by
The Book Company, PO Box 243, Ipswich, Suffolk

Contents

Chapter	Title	Page
	Preface	vii
	Summary of Recommendations	ix
1.	Arguments of Tradition and Typical Problems	1
2.	The Publications and Their Problems	9
	Appendices:	
	1. British Campaign Medals and Clasps	13
	2. Commonwealth and Foreign Campaign Medals and Clasps for British Troops	30
	3. Commemorative Medals in Order of Date	32
3.	1844 to 1913	35
	Appendices:	
	1. From Army Dress Regulations 1900	40
	2. From Army Order 181 of 1902	42
	3. From Army Dress Regulations 1904	44
	4. From Army Order 196 of 1905	46
	5. From Army Dress Regulations 1911	48
	6. From Army Order 246 of 1912	51
	7. From Army Dress Regulations 1911 amended 1913	55
4.	1914 to 1923	59
	Appendices:	
	1. From Army Council Instruction 754 of 1918	63
	2. From Army Council Instruction 1230 of 1918	67
	3. From *London Gazette* dated 22 April 1921	71
	4. From Army Council Instruction 1 of 1923	75
5.	1923 to 1951	79
	Appendices:	
	1. From *London Gazette* dated 22 November 1929	82
	2. From *London Gazette* dated 4 April 1936	87
	3. From *London Gazette* dated 22 February 1941	92
	4. From *London Gazette* dated 11 February 1947	97
	5. From *London Gazette* dated 12 July 1949	103
	6. From *London Gazette* dated 27 July 1951	109

Chapter	Title	Page
6.	1952 to 1995	115
	Appendices:	
	1. From *London Gazette* dated 15 June 1954	119
	2. From *London Gazette* dated 19 April 1955	125
	3. From *London Gazette* dated 14 January 1958	131
	4. From *London Gazette* dated 28 April 1961	137
	5. From *London Gazette* dated 27 October 1964	143
	6. From Army Dress Regulations 1969	150
	7. From *London Gazette* dated 28 October 1983	157
	8. From Army Material Regulations 1995	165
7.	Mentioned in Despatches and Similar Subjects	173
8.	Restricted Wear and the Two Medal Myth	178
9.	Ideas for the Future	185
	Appendices:	
	1. Suggested Order of Wear Using a Logical Sequence	190
	2. Canadian Order of Wear for Their Own Awards	195
	3. Canadian Order of Wear for Their Own Awards with British Orders Awarded pre-1 June 1972	199
	4. Australian Order of Wear for Their Own Awards with British Awards	202
	5. New Zealand Order of Wear (Note—a new range of awards is imminent)	206
	Bibliography	211

Preface

IN the best traditions explained in the TV Series *Yes, Prime Minister* I have decided to put the summary of recommendations first:

    Sir Humphrey—"Where is the one page summary for the Cabinet?"

    Sir Frank as he passed the document over—"Janet and John bit?"

The reasons behind the recommendations do come later in the book, but I hope the summary will provoke thought.

This book is essentially a history of changes which have taken place in the order of wearing Orders, Decorations and Medals over the years. Since I was in the Army it is based on Army Publications and the lists which have appeared in the *London Gazette* since 1921. It shows changes to the order of wear that have taken place, often with reluctance, to reflect popular opinion of the day, in particular the gradual escalation of the position in which other ranks' and native troops' awards appear.

Whatever their human failings, our Royal Family have, over the years, provided an enviable and non-partisan rock, one on which our Society is based. Some in the "Establishment" who act on their behalf and advise may be more interested in trying to maintain the status quo and avoiding controversial proposals than in highlighting outdated customs and practices especially relating to medals. For example many Warrants include provision that the awards, often long service awards, may be "worn by Us, Our Heirs and Successors etc." This is normally only seen by those interested in medals, but to me it always jars. Why should the Sovereign and Heirs be allowed to wear a long service award without earning it? In fact they never do, so why leave this archaic phrase in the Warrants? This book attempts to highlight some deficiencies in relation to awards and to suggest solutions in order to help, in a small way, to avoid these pitfalls in the future.

I feel that changes must be made to keep up with popular opinion, and the Royal Family has often shown that they are aware and can move towards the people when needed. I suspect that their apparent inertia is often more a reflection on their advisers than on their own inclination. In connection with medals this is witnessed by the fact that the Victoria Cross, instituted in 1856 by Queen Victoria, was open to all ranks. In his reign King George V put the suggestion that bravery awards should be given regardless of rank and much more recently Prince Philip made the same suggestion. However, until the 1990s these suggestions got nowhere; now, as a result of former Prime Minister John Major's insistence on reforms, we have a system which has lost some of the wealth of variety of awards when this could have been avoided with a bit more knowledge and imagination. Despite the so-called "classless" system adopted, we now have one where the number of awards, especially to the lower ranks and ordinary citizens, has been diminished. In the Armed Forces few of the MBEs available go to the lower ranks recently made eligible, and the higher classes available in the Orders inevitably go to the upper grades of society.

In the higher echelons of industry, the military, or the civil service senior personnel often receive a knighthood or become companions of orders, and there is more likelihood of alternative awards; Knight Bachelor or KBE for example. Unless the practice of bestowing titles on our leaders, in whatever sphere, is discontinued I cannot see any merit in addressing this part of the honours system. It is too much wrapped up in the constitution and the existence of the House of Lords. If that were to be abolished no doubt "Knights" would also be vulnerable. Unless that happens it is difficult to see what isolated changes might be made to the higher two, or even three, grades of Orders. On the other hand in the majority of cases, for more ordinary people, there is only one reward for merit—the Order of the British Empire, in most cases the MBE. Even in this so-called enlightened age I cannot see a dustman (or are they Refuse Operatives?) however excellent, ever being given an OBE, but why not if they are good enough?

Even the system for the higher echelons is flawed in detail and could be altered with benefit. In most forms of dress only one neck decoration may be worn. So Sir Humphrey Appleby, KCB, CBE may never wear one of these illustrious and expensive awards since both have neck insignia. If awards capable of being worn are given but never displayed except in a glass case, what is the point? Admittedly Sir Humphrey can wear both in miniature on his evening dress, but that is at his own expense while a perfectly good badge sits in its box gathering dust. I have a suggestion on this.

Since Medals in the widest sense are associated with Royalty, regardless of the various Governmental Committees and Departments involved, this is an area where examples of apparent inequality get blamed on the Royal Family and not on their advisers. Unfortunately the system is often lacking and a "them and us" mentality is fostered to the detriment of the Royal Family. In this publication, as well as quoting historical fact, I include my personal reading of the reasons behind some decisions, decisions which I believe were wrong. I also give my suggestions for some changes, most of which would cost nothing. If implemented these might make the public feel that Royalty is progressing into the 21st century, in this respect anyway, right from the start of the new Millennium.

I have been studying the subject of "medals", in the widest sense, for years and over the past three years have been answering the letters on the subject received by the Royal British Legion in London. Answering over a thousand letters has reinforced my earlier views that there is tremendous ignorance of the subject amongst the public. Also, it is an illogical subject much influenced by subjective emotions, ignorance and lack of imagination, often by those in high places.

Those who are denied a medal, and those who feel that one should be created to meet their particular circumstances, are often incensed by lack of response. Many are satisfied when they are given a detailed explanation, but there are three main areas where satisfaction is not present and for which I have great sympathy. One relates to National Service; one concerns the lack of a medal for those in the Canal Zone in Egypt before we pulled out; the last refers to the rules for foreign awards. This last is particularly pertinent as more people are employed in other European countries and our Armed Forces act alongside other NATO and United Nations forces.

I offer my thoughts for solutions to some of these problems and only one would cost the country anything. I hope that some notice might be taken of these suggestions in the cost conscious era we live in and some unhappy citizens made less unhappy.

Finally, to scotch any suspicions of "sour grapes", I would also say that I have been very fortunate in receiving medals during my service and even if all my suggestions here were accepted it would only result in adding a single set of long service post-nominal letters after my name.

A. R. Tinson
Fleet, Hampshire

Summary of Recommendations

The recommendations below are in order of priority based largely on need, ease of implementation, and cost.

- Afford the fourth level bravery/merit awards, mentions and commendations, an appropriate place in the order of wear and display them on their own ribbons.
    Chapter 7.   Cost - Nil.

- Readjust the order of wear to reflect the relative merits of awards for gallantry and for merit regardless of the title of the insignia.
    Appendix to Chapter 9.   Cost - Nil.

- Make use of the OBE, MBE and QCVS to reflect three levels of achievement so that the "ordinary" citizen may share in the structured honours system.
    Chapter 9.   Cost - Nil.

- Permit a much wider use of post-nominal letters to recognise service, especially, voluntary work.
    Chapter 9.   Cost - Nil.

- Revise and re-issue the *London Gazette* lists on wearing awards on a regular basis to give accurate and up-to-date information.
    Chapter 2.   Cost - Negligible.

- Allow holders of multiple neck decorations to wear one at the neck and the rest on the medal bar on the left breast. Also, use the ribbon appropriate to their later wear at the investiture.
    Chapter 1.   Cost - Nil.

- Come to an equitable, better explained, method of displaying "Queen's Commonwealth Awards", and one that applies equally to Royalty and commoner.
    Chapter 1.   Cost - Negligible.

- Permit the acceptance and wear of awards from Foreign Governments on a relaxed and logical basis, one which is the same for all parts of the world.
    Chapter 8.   Cost - Nil.

- Award a General Service Medal for the Canal Zone.
    Chapter 8.   Cost - Significant.

- Try to limit the number of unofficial medals by allowing certain selected ones to be purchased and worn on the official bar behind all other awards including foreign medals.
    Chapter 9.   Cost - Nil.

Chapter 1

Arguments of Tradition and Typical Problems

"MEDALS" is an emotive word, especially to those who feel they have not been properly rewarded for their Services, particularly for Military Service. Two deserving examples are those who feel that National Service should have been recognised by a medal, while others, no less deserving consideration, feel that personnel who served in the uncomfortable, and often dangerous, Canal Zone of Egypt in the early post-war years should have received a General Service Medal.

The former problem has been answered to some extent by an unofficial medal which can be purchased and which is co-sponsored by the Royal British Legion, a proportion of the cost being donated by the makers to the Poppy Fund. It has been tacitly accepted that these, and many other unofficial medals, may be worn either below the official row or on the right lapel. Both these solutions create their own problems.

Where there is no official row, an unofficial one on the left breast takes on the appearance of an official one. If unofficial medals are worn on the right this detracts from the few, and relatively rare, bravery medals which are officially worn on that side, even in uniform. As will be seen these include a number of medals given by revered Societies in connection with Life Saving. In addition the "unofficial" rows often equal, or even outnumber, the official ones to the detriment of the latter. There seems no answer to this as it is most unlikely that banning their wear would be a workable solution. On the other hand, official acceptance for wearing some of the more legitimate ones could alleviate the problem in the future. Such a decision would go against all official arguments in the past, but it would meet a need, and it would merely move the medals to the end of the official row. This would reduce the need for the plethora of unofficial medals. Recognition of awards given by Foreign Governments is dealt with elsewhere, but in the case of purchased medals, for example the National Service Medal, recognition could only be based on the premise that the medals must be purchased, otherwise current holders would have recourse to claim their money back.

In addition to these minor problems the powers that be, while appearing to become embroiled in arguments of great detail regarding medals in general, often seem unable to address the overall problems. For example the most recent list in the *London Gazette* was issued in 1983. Its predecessor was in 1964. Apart from omissions detailed later, the latest list includes for the first time the CGM (Flying), yet this was instituted in 1943.

Before going any further mention needs to be made of the semantics from which the subject suffers. In this book the word "medals" is used in a very general sense. It includes "Orders", "Decorations" and "Medals", but if one tries to define each of these problems do arise. An "Order" includes Orders of Chivalry, but what does that mean? To most people the term probably includes only the ancient rewards originally associated with the concept of the Knights of the Round Table and which entitle the holder to be called "Sir". The *London Gazette* lists get round the problem by the use of the heading—"British Orders of Knighthood, etc.". However, in recent arguments about allowing all gallantry awards to be awarded posthumously it was said that the

Distinguished Service Order (DSO) could not be included because it was an Order of Chivalry. This is a spurious argument. Apart from the understanding of the term as given above King George V, in considering the new awards for the Great War, such as the Military Cross (MC) and Medal (MM), assumed that all would include provision for "bars" for second awards, and he included the DSO. This was accepted, clearly meaning that the DSO fell into the same category as the MC and MM. This order is in one class and no other Orders may be awarded a second time by the addition of a bar. There are, however, other awards, which include "Order" in the title, but are not classified as "Orders of Chivalry". Indeed, in *The Queen's Orders of Chivalry* (1964), Brigadier Sir Ivor de la Bere, Secretary of the Central Chancery from 1945 to 1960, states categorically that the only current official British Orders of Chivalry are the Garter, Thistle, Bath, St Michael & St George, Royal Victorian Order and British Empire. Despite this the argument held and the DSO cannot be awarded posthumously. It can only be suspected that this was more to do with preserving the status quo than with any technical classification. In any case mankind makes the rules and can change them.

This attitude is also reflected in the lists on order of wear, and changes have been hard won, many in battle and the terrible events of 1914-18 which brought demands from the troops for greater recognition for their awards. This led, surprisingly, to their success in having the relative order of wear changed to reflect the importance they attached to, say, a MM related to a Jubilee Medal. This was no small achievement by the "masses". In the current climate, which increasingly questions the value of the Monarchy and the Establishment, authority would be wise to heed history and real take steps to abolish "class" from the order of wear of awards. The steps already taken are far from what needs to be done.

To return to the words used, "Decorations" is used as a collective term for crosses such as the Military Cross, awarded in the past mainly to officers, now open to all ranks. Nonetheless in the past reports on this subject have referred to soldiers being decorated with the DCM or MM, yet these were never included under a heading "Decoration". We also have "Decorations" which are nothing more than long service awards, e.g. the Efficiency Decoration. There is again differentiation here as officers are allowed to put "TD" after their names while soldiers with the Efficiency Medal may not use post-nominal letters. The only argument for this appears to be that officers in the Reserve Forces are subject to military law at all times whereas non-commissioned ranks are not. Again a spurious argument since, when the reserves are embodied, all ranks are full time and subject to the same laws at all times, and all their service counts towards the same long service awards.

Even "Medal" is difficult to define. The obvious description is a circular metal ornament designed to be worn on the chest and suspended from a ribbon. This covers the majority, but some medals are oval, the Air Force Medal and the Efficiency Medal being two examples. Some awards are called medals but are quite ornate in design and by no means fit the definition, such as the Kaiser-i-Hind Medal and the Albert Medal. The former used to be grouped under a collective heading "Orders given only in India". The long service "Decorations" already mentioned are also ornate and cannot be described as medals. Some "medals" are given other titles, such as the Air Efficiency Award.

All these complications make it very difficult to categorise awards. The *London Gazette* listings of the order of wear have collective titles which underline these difficulties. Some of these difficult entries are shown without a collective title. For example the Indian Order of Merit (Military) falls between the headings "British Orders of Knighthood, etc." and "Decorations". It is so positioned that it falls into neither category. Later in the lists the categories are allowed to become even sloppier. The Royal Family's Long and Faithful Service Medals appear under the collective title "Jubilee, Coronation and Durbar Medals" while the final collective title of "Efficiency and Long Service Decorations and Medals" gathers a gaggle of dubious (only in the sense of this argument) Good Shooting and Independence Medals. Lack of attention to the actual contents under the Jubilee, etc., title led to a badly worded amendment to Dress Regulations 1969 where the Queen's Silver Jubilee Medal was added to the end of the group. This would have been correct if the heading had been accurate, but as worded the amendment put the new medal after the Royal "Long and Faithful Service Medals", clearly not the intended position.

So there are considerable problems which are totally avoidable, but only if those making the rules can address the problem without being blinded by the details and the decisions made by their predecessors.

Examples of the blinkered approach taken are related to so-called "Civilian" bravery awards, though they may also be awarded to members of the Armed Forces. At the beginning of the 1939-45 War we had a number of awards which were available for rewarding civilian gallantry. These, in order of wear and prestige, were the Albert Medals (AM), often referred to as the Civilian VC, the Edward Medals (EM) and the Empire Gallantry Medal (EGM). This should have been adequate as the AMs covered two grades of gallantry on land and sea, i.e. four awards. The EM covered two grades of gallantry in the mines and in industry, again actually four awards. The EGM was for any brave act (not in the face of the enemy). However, with the bombing of civilian targets it was considered that new awards were needed and the George Cross (GC) and George Medal (GM) were instituted in 1940. For reasons never explained the EGM, bottom of the 1939 bravery pile, was exchanged for the GC while the AMs and EMs were not so exchanged until 1972, and then only after years of campaigning. The logical step in 1940 would have been to utilise the GC to replace the two top "civil" bravery awards, the Albert Medal in Gold and the Edward Medal in Silver, and thereafter discontinue their award.

Matters were further complicated in 1958 when an attempt was made to increase the "Civilian" bravery awards to four levels, in line with the "Military" awards. What is now called the third level of award in the Civilian sphere was filled by introducing a gallantry emblem to be worn on the ribbons of the Order or Medal of the British Empire. This was not retrospective, so the many given the Order or Medal in earlier years, even if the citation was clearly for gallantry, remained unrecognised. The major drawback of this arrangement is best illustrated in terms of Military awards. The range of awards available was George Cross (GC), George Medal (GM) and Queen's Commendation for Brave Conduct. Within this list the various classes of the Order of the British Empire fall between the GC and GM. However the British Empire Medal (BEM) comes between the GM and Queen's Commendation. So the "new" award immediately took on the role of both second level and third level awards entirely depending on the status (rank) of the recipient. Added to this, the grades of the Order itself were awarded based on the rank of the recipient. So a Lieutenant Colonel could only become an Officer (OBE), and a Colonel or Brigadier only a Commander (CBE), yet a Sergeant could only get a BEM. There was one award of a CBE for Gallantry—Canadian Brigadier J. A. Dextraze, OBE, CD, with United Nation forces in the Congo received a gallantry CBE in circumstances where one might think that he ought to have been considered for a DSO.

As time went by it was inevitable that bars were awarded for BEMs, but there is no provision for bars to the Order and promotion within the Order is based on rank, not second acts. At first the gallantry emblem was worn on the ribbon even if the recipient was promoted in the Order for merit. So an OBE for gallantry later becoming a KBE would wear the gallantry emblem on the KBE, though it was never stated how this should be done. Since then the evolved answer has been that those in the Order, subsequently promoted, may wear both insignia. So a person getting an MBE for gallantry and later the OBE for merit wears two identical ribbons, one with the gallantry emblem. On the other hand someone getting the BEM for gallantry and again later for gallantry or merit wears one ribbon with the gallantry emblem and a rosette indicating the bar without signifying whether it was for merit or gallantry. All this should have been foreseen from the start, but was apparently overlooked. The real solution came in 1974 when the system was scrapped in favour of a new medal - the Queen's Gallantry Medal (QGM) —which should have been the answer from the beginning, but its position in the order of wear left much to be desired. It is the third level of gallantry award and should have equated to the Military Cross or Military Medal. Initially it was placed just above the BEM. Now the MM has been discontinued it should rank with the MC group of awards, in fact it lies 27th after the ARRC (last of the MC grouping) in the 1983 list.

Instructions regarding the wear of, for example, a gallantry MBE with a meritorious OBE, were promulgated to individuals but not in general until about 1983. The first intimation of the permission to wear the two insignia came to the public at large in the *London Gazette* of 1983, many years after the changes were made. Admittedly there are few civilians who are affected, but this does not alter the fact that publication of the method of wearing medals is painfully slow and the general level of ignorance of the rules is not surprising.

It is curious too that one set of letters after the name could relate to three different awards. It could be that an MBE (Military Division) for Gallantry, subsequently promoted to OBE (Military Division) later retires to civilian life in a high managerial position and is promoted to CBE (Civil Division). He or she would wear the civil ribbon followed by the military ribbon, unadorned, then the military ribbon with gallantry emblem but use the only letters CBE after his or her name. This is in contrast to the early awards of the Order and Medal of the British Empire. The Pamphlet on Military Honours and Awards, 1960, included a note against the Order of the British Empire stating "On promotion to a higher class in a different Division, the insignia of the lower class shall be returned to the Registrar of the Order *UNLESS* awarded for Military Service in the 1914–18 War, when the ribbons and insignia of both classes may be worn together, and both sets of post-nominal initials used."

Another major problem area lies in the region of Commonwealth awards instituted by the Queen. Up to the list of 1961 there was no great difficulty in this area. The few awards peculiar to Commonwealth countries were included in the "British" list of order of wear and "Foreign" awards came at the end. The particular problem this has given rise to in relation to some long service awards, and even now how it impinges on Mentions in Despatches and Queen's Commendations, is dealt with elsewhere.

Apart from these difficulties there was no problem, but since that time the complexity has increased both for us and for our former Empire, at least for that part which remains under the Monarch. Although not alone, Canada, Australia and now New Zealand have instituted their own system of awards and all the new ones are instituted by their Queen, who is also our Queen. Canada began to develop its system in 1972, Australia and New Zealand followed in 1975 though in the latter's case the process is only just reaching completion. Both Canada and Australia issued lists for their order of wear which had to take into account the existing British "Imperial" awards which many of their citizens already held. In Canada they have now issued a further list of purely Canadian awards effective from 1972 while retaining the original list for pre-1972 awards. That this is an embarrassment to them is evidenced by the fact that both countries now have two positions for wearing, say, an MBE. Those who received it in "imperial days" wear it in amongst their own set of awards. If they receive it as a result of a recent attachment to British forces it is worn last, as a foreign award by order date of award. As a matter of interest at least one Australian and one Canadian received the MBE for their work with us during the Gulf War. The current order of wear for all three countries is shown in the appendices to Chapter 9. In the case of New Zealand this does not yet include some of their new range of awards and is included mainly to show the relative positions of the Order of New Zealand and Queen's Service awards.

The 1983 *London Gazette* listing met this challenge for British citizens, after nearly a decade of deliberation, by introducing a new category—"Honorary Membership of Commonwealth Orders (instituted by the Sovereign)". They get over the fact that this title should also have included "Decorations and Medals" by a note which begins "The general rule is that non-British insignia should be worn after all British Orders, decorations and medals and in the order of the dates on which they were conferred." It goes on to allow a higher precedence if the occasion demands this, something which applies in practical terms to neck decorations of Orders, such as the Orders of Canada or Australia, when it might be diplomatic to wear their insignia before, or instead of, ours. It becomes more difficult and very costly, if not impossible, when applied to awards mounted with others on the left breast.

This is a solution, but not a good one and other matters do need to be addressed. Continuing with the Australian example, there are medals which were "Imperial" when they were instituted, but nonetheless were not actually British awards. The Vietnam Medal is a case in point and was awarded to a number of British citizens in the Australian and New Zealand forces; at least one being awarded the MBE for his services in Vietnam. Some of these people subsequently joined, or rejoined, the British forces. They wore their Vietnam Medal amongst British campaign medals, but what is the status of the Vietnam Medal now? Does it now become "honorary" and move to the end of the row?

Honorary membership of an order has always been said, in relation to this country's awards, to bring with it its post-nominal letters but no right to a title. In fact the use of the citizen's post-nominal letters may also be banned in his or her own country. Although Bob Geldoff can use "KBE" in England he probably cannot do so in Ireland. He cannot call himself "Sir" anywhere. This position should be clarified for the new "honorary" class of Commonwealth award holders as many entitle the holders to post-nominal letters in the country giving the award. Up to the present the initials "QSO" (Queen's Service Order) have been commonly used by British holders of this New Zealand award. Prince Philip and Prince Charles both hold this order and wear it first on their medal bar, before all other medals. Both have the Order of Australia and use the post-nominal letters "AC QSO" and "AK QSO" respectively, after their British (more senior) letters. They show no signs of changing even though the rules changed fifteen years ago and these letters are included in the most recent Service Lists. Although it is arguable that, as members of the Royal Family, they are somehow different to others, they are not the only British recipients of these orders. At least one other "QSO" is shown in the Army List today. So is this now "Honorary"? Should it be worn last?

Quite apart from the holders of honours of this nature awarded before the 1983 innovation, this is no theoretical problem. Major S. T. W. Bridge, King's Royal Hussars, was awarded the Canadian Medal of Bravery (MB) in Croatia. So far no Army List has been produced since his award and it will be interesting to see if he is allowed "MB" after his name when a new list is published.

One final thought on this subject. The Victoria Cross has been adopted by Canada, Australia and New Zealand in their own honours systems. Except for the wording on the Canadian scroll ("Pro Valore" instead of "For Valour") these VCs are identical to ours, but they are separate and discrete awards. This came about because veterans in all these countries held this particular award in great esteem and demanded its retention. Although perhaps unlikely, it is not inconceivable that some wandering soldier could follow the example of his Vietnam forerunners and join the Canadian, Australian or New Zealand Forces for a campaign, win their VC, and then return to the British Forces. Under the present rules his VC would be honorary and worn almost last. In 1948, when Indian VC holders wore their Independence Medal before their British VCs, there was an outcry in our Press. How will the Commonwealth Press and people react to us "degrading" their highest award? This might give added fuel to "Republicanism".

It would not be impossible to compile a list which included every "Queen's" award, both British and from "Royal" Commonwealth countries, so that this type of thing is avoided and all "Queen's" awards given their proper relative positions. Difficult, perhaps, but not impossible. The stumbling block would probably be in overcoming the problem which seems to be cast in concrete and is abhorrent to our thinking, that of placing stars and medals ahead of Orders and crosses. Yet this is a hurdle which must be addressed, as it has in the past with the Kaisar-i-Hind Medal. For example, the relationship of the relative values of the MBE and GM needs review. The Appendix 1 to Chapter 9 giving the suggested future order of wear shows their relative positions according to levels of award.

One other stupidity in relation to our awards and which incurs unnecessary cost, is the display of neck awards. Although, in relative terms, few are awarded, they are given with a full sized ribbon of a suitable length to allow the award to be placed over the head of the recipient during an investiture complete with hook and eye fastening. The ribbon is sewn into position through a ring designed to support the badge from a ribbon of that width and strength, and the ribbon is carefully folded into its case. Although awards to females are normally in the form of a bow, those in the Armed Forces receive dual-purpose badges made for both bow and neck display, so these have to be considered.

The widths of ribbons including those of the lowest class in the Order are:

KCB	2 in	DCB	1.75 in	CB	1.5 in.	
KCSI	2 in	—	—	CSI	1.5 in.	
KCMG	2 in	DCMG	1.75 in	CMG	1.5 in.	
KCIE	2 in	—	—	CIE	1.5 in.	
KCVO	1.75 in	DCVO	1.75 in	CVO	1.5 in.	LVO/MVO 1.25 in.
KBE	1.75 in	DBE	1.75 in	CBE	1.75 in	OBE/MBE 1.5 in.

On uniform, when ribbons alone are worn, the width used is that of the right-hand column in each case. Miniature width ribbons are all about 0.375 in wide.

All very logical but the instructions for wear are that this ribbon is replaced by a "miniature" width ribbon on all occasions with one exception—the Army in Service Dress or its equivalent. Though even this appears to have changed; in a recent newspaper photograph both Prince Charles and General Sir Rupert Smith wore their neck badges of the Order of the Bath from miniature ribbons. All other male recipients, including the Army in Mess Dress, adopt the miniature ribbon. When ribbons alone are worn the CVO and CBE ribbons are the wrong width to be utilised for this purpose, so the length carefully sewn and awarded at the investiture is of no practical value to most recipients. The suspension rings on the full-sized insignia are too big for miniature ribbons and these, in turn, are not stiff enough adequately to hold up a full-sized decoration. The impression when these are worn is poor. The easy solution would be to wear the issued ribbon at all times. It should be awarded at investitures using a length, perhaps with Velcro-type fastenings, so that it can be worn thereafter without alteration. This would save the country and recipient wasted money.

Until the introduction of the CBE, the only third class of an order worn at the neck was the CVO. The rules for most forms of dress, including all forms of civilian clothes, preclude wearing more than one neck badge. This means that eminent persons rewarded twice at the level of Companionship or above can rarely wear their second costly insignia. It would seem sense in this case to permit the second and subsequent (i.e. junior) "neck" insignia to be worn on the medal bar with other medals as used to be the case.

In the *London Gazette* there seems to be a fixation regarding categorising the lists into collective titles which do not fit the bill. As has been said earlier there is the "etc." with the "Orders of Knighthood"; a medal under "Orders given only in India" which is a heading that does not include the IOM (Civil); "Jubilee etc." includes long service awards and "Long Service etc." includes a number of unrelated medals. In addition some awards fit nowhere and are so placed that they are their own heading, though not in capitals—Badge of Honour is an example. The latest listing in Material Regulations 1995 goes even further and creates after "War Medals" a new heading of "Alliance Medals" listing United Nations (UN) and Economic Community (EC). This contradicts the text and the individual instructions on these medals, both of which place them amongst, not after, British Campaign Medals.

In many lists, though not in the *London Gazette* itself, relating to the order of wear the word "precedence" has become common in the title. This is misleading as the order of precedence, at least in the United Kingdom, includes the relative importance of numerous ennobled and titled persons or appointments. Naturally this has to include those with titles connected with Orders but the list is mainly to determine the relative importance of Dukes, Earls, Judges, Bishops and the like. It is not directly connected with medals. Nevertheless the inclusion of "precedence" as related to the order of wear of medals does cause problems. Certain individual Australian servicemen were denied British awards for which they had not only been recommended, but also had approved in the last Vietnam War honours list. This was because the Australian honours system had just been introduced so they were to get Australian honours instead. However this was not implemented and the case is still causing concern. The reason being that The Australian Gazette uses in its title the word "precedence". As a result, by inadequate logic coupled with the later British decision to cease award of the military bravery medals, the MM has been equated with an Australian Commendation for Gallantry. This is entirely due to the relative positions of precedence (wear) which are Australian Star of Gallantry (SG), MC, Australian Medal for Gallantry (MG), MM and Commendation for Gallantry. The illogical argument runs that the MM is now the MC which must equate to the next up Australian gallantry award (SG) whereas the MM was much lower in precedence. Therefore the MM must relate to the Commendation. This, of course, puts stress on the word "precedence" and ignores the fact that the MC, MM and MG are all third level awards whereas the Commendation is a fourth level award. Those concerned have rightly refused the award and are campaigning for the award of the MG.

The most sensible way to deal with this would be to reassess the entire listing in the light of the actual purpose of each award, not the theoretical notion that an overall "Orders, Decorations and Medals" division with subdivisions will suffice. That the VC and GC should take pre-eminent positions is universally accepted. The problem of the higher "Orders" has already been mentioned and is so tied in with our way of life, the House of Lords and so on that it is a subject on its own and is ignored here. The awards worn on the medal bar on the left breast are those which impact on most people and these are the ones addressed here. This, in practical terms, means the VC and GC and everything from the DSO onwards. Rather than becoming embroiled in semantics it is probably best to use the word "awards" for all these and then classify them in the light of their purpose.

First amongst these are awards for bravery, leadership and merit. This order of importance is probably universally accepted, if only because the VCs/GCs are already given pride of place. There may be those who would want to argue the relative positions for the three categories but this should be a minor matter. The most equitable method would appear to relate levels of effort within these categories, rather as it is now the fashion to speak of a VC as the first level of bravery and the mention in despatches as the fourth. Considered in this way, with similar "levels" for merit, the awards could be grouped to list like level with like. This would mean overcoming the hurdle of wearing medals before or amongst Orders and Crosses. Once this is accepted it should be easy to relate all the Queen's awards across the Commonwealth. So far as Queen's awards in the Commonwealth are concerned there seems no problem in categorising awards by "level" but allowing each nation to wear its own awards first. Thus a British individual with an Australian Star of Gallantry (SG) and a British Conspicuous Gallantry Cross (CGC), both second level awards, would wear them in the order CGC, SG whereas an Australian with the same combination would reverse the order of wear to SG, CGC.

For the remainder there may be considerable differences of opinion. It seems logical, and defensible, to list British awards in order of the degree of endeavour needed to earn them. This would put commemorative medals well to the rear, though this position may not please some people regarding Coronation and Jubilee medals. Nonetheless these have diminished in value in today's world. They are awarded on a meagre ration, yet in a haphazard way. It has been said that one cavalry regiment allocated these medals on the basis of walking a horse, with a medal on the saddle, round the ranks and where the medal fell off the nearest soldier got the medal. This may be apocryphal but it reflects what many feel about these awards. In this light they deserve to go to the back. Likewise Independence Medals depend on the luck of the draw in being posted to a country just as independence is given; the actual preparatory work might have been done by the person who left before Independence.

Based on the above and coming after awards for actual bravery or merit, an order in line with the popular perception of relative importance would be:

- Second - Awards for campaign service.
- Third - Awards for peacekeeping service.
- Fourth - Awards for long service.
- Fifth - Awards commemorating events such as Coronations and Independence.
- Sixth - Commonwealth and Foreign awards in the current order subject to the discussions already stated regarding Queen's Commonwealth awards.

These groupings would, in fact, cover all the awards currently listed, though there would be some reallocation in detail. A full listing is suggested in a later chapter but these headings would allow all the gallantry and meritorious awards to be treated in the light of what they were given for rather than the status of those to whom they were awarded.

Chapter 2

The Publications and Their Problems

SINCE the Army is the Service most involved with medals, the research for this book has been largely confined to Army publications and to the *London Gazette* which took up the publication for the order of wear in 1921. The *London Gazette* has continued to publish these lists periodically on behalf of the Central Chancery of the Order of Knighthood. Unfortunately these lists are very infrequent and often omit entries which one has every expectation of seeing. The latest *London Gazette* list was published in 1983, sixteen years ago and nineteen years after the previous list in 1964! The next is just beginning in preparation.

Since 1983 the Honours system has undergone major changes, though admittedly some of these, such as extra posthumous awards and classless eligibility, are not normally subjects of these lists. However, additions since 1983 include the Conspicuous Gallantry Cross (1995); the Accumulated Campaign Service Medal (1994); the Northern Ireland Home Service Medal (1996); the Ambulance Service (Emergency Duties) Long Service and Good Conduct Medal (1996); the Hong Kong Disciplined Services Medal (1986); a complete change in the Mentioned in Despatches and Queen's Commendations field (1994); not to forget five Independence Medals of which at least three are Queen's awards. So a further list is well overdue. The fact that a new Order to replace the Order of the British Empire is rumoured, and new Regular and Reserve tri-Service Long Service Medals are in the pipeline now, does not excuse this tardiness. Also, every new medal has its position in the order of wear specified at the time it is announced. It should not be difficult to produce a list consolidating this quite frequently. All the inter-Governmental and inter-Departmental arguments must have been decided before each announcement of the new medals, so where is the difficulty in issuing a new list? A clerk could do it.

In addition to this the lists are incomplete; a notable feature from the beginning. They include or omit awards on a basis defying logic and betraying ignorance of the subject. Indian Orders, Gallantry and Police awards, not given since 1948, remain in the lists whereas the equivalent Burma awards were deleted after appearing only in 1941 and 1947. The Canada Medal, long since overtaken by another in the new Canadian list of awards, and, it is understood, never actually awarded to anyone, is still shown in 1983. The Soldiers', Sailors' and Airmen's Association Long Service Medal which was approved by the Queen in 1969 and, in SSAFA regulations is shown as being worn after the Voluntary Medical Service Medal, does not appear.

The list of war and campaign medals is no more accurate. The 1983 list states:

Campaign Stars and Medals for service during the First World War, 1914-19, should be worn in the following order: 1914 Star, 1914-15 Star, British War Medal, Mercantile Marine War Medal, Victory Medal, Territorial Force War Medal, India General Service Medal (1908) (for operations in Afghanistan, 1919). Campaign Stars and Medals awarded for service in the Second World War, 1939-45, should be worn in the following order: 1939-45 Star, Atlantic Star, Air Crew Europe Star, Africa Star, Pacific Star, Burma Star, Italy Star, France and Germany Star, Defence Medal, Volunteer Service Medal of Canada, War Medal 1939-45, Africa Service Medal of the Union of South Africa, Indian

Service Medal, New Zealand War Service Medal, Southern Rhodesia Service Medal, Australia Service Medal.

The order of wearing of the Africa General Service Medal (1902), India General Service Medal (1908), Naval General Service Medal (1915), General Service Medal (Army and Royal Air Force) (1918) and India General Service Medal (1936) will vary, and will depend upon the dates of participation in the relevant campaigns. A General Service Medal, 1962, was instituted by The Queen in 1964. A Pakistan General Service Medal was instituted by King George VI in 1951. A Sierra Leone General Service Medal was instituted by the Queen for award from 1961.

This is all very well as far as it goes but note that the following post-war campaign medals are omitted: Queen's Korea Medal (1951); United Nations Service Medal (Korea) (1951); United Nations Medal for Service in the Congo (ONUC) (1962 revamped in 1966); United Nations Medal for Service in Cyprus (UNFICYP) (1964); Vietnam Medal (1968); South Atlantic Medal (1982). Although the Vietnam Medal was for Australian and New Zealand personnel, it is in fact what the Australians term "Imperial" and so falls into the same category as the Pakistan and the Sierra Leone General Service Medals instituted by our Sovereign.

As well as these the following have been added since 1983 through Defence Council Instructions or have involved British participation: Gulf Medal (1991); Vietnam Logistic and Support Medal (1992) (Australian); NATO Medal (1994); European Community Observer Mission Medal (1992); Western European Union Mission Service Medal (1996). Also many, if not all, the following have been awarded to British servicemen. The United Nations Medals for Service with: the Disengagement Observer Force (Golan Heights) (UNDOF) (1974); the Assistance Mission in Rwanda (UNAMIR) (1995); the Angola Verification Mission (UNAVEM III) (1995); the Protection Force (former Yugoslavia) (UNPROFOR) (1993); the Transitional Assistance Group (Namibia) (UNTAG) (1990); the Iraq-Kuwait Observer Mission (UNIKOM) (1992); the Referendum Mission in Western Sahara (MINURSO) (1990); the Advanced Mission in Cambodia (UNAMIC) (1991); the Transitional Authority in Cambodia (UNTAC) (1992); Operations in Mozambique (ONUMOZ) (1992); Special Service Medal (UNSSM) (1992); Observer Mission in Georgia (UNOMIG) (1993); Confidence Restoration Operation (UNCRO) (1995); Preventative Deployment Force (UNPREDEP) (1995); Transitional Administration for Eastern Slavonia, Baranja and Western Sirmium (UNTAES) (1996); Mission of Observers in Prevlaka (UNMOP) (1996). A full list of campaign medals and clasps, both by title and earliest date of participation, is included with details of foreign campaign medals to British servicemen and commemorative and independence medals in appendices to this Chapter. On this subject there is hardly a "precedent" which cannot be found. In the early days when permission to wear seemed easier to obtain, the difference was less easy to determine between "English" awards, those given by various overseas Companies which were, in effect, local Governments' for India and Africa, and those which were indeed "foreign". For this reason some of the decisions to put medals in the "English" Appendix 1 as opposed to the "foreign" Appendix 2 are arbitrary. In addition to the recent campaign medals in Appendix 1 the Rhodesia Medal and Accumulated Campaign Service Medal have been included. In the order of wear the former is placed at the head of the independence medals, out of date order, but it has the unusual distinction of carrying on its ribbon a mentioned in despatches emblem if awarded. Until this award this distinction was given only for campaign medals. The latter comes immediately after the MSM but it is in fact a sort of extended campaign medal and so deserves inclusion in the appendix. Medals are listed in order of the date of their first campaign. Except for the two world wars the listing is not in order of wear and many early awards were not instituted until well after the campaign for which they were awarded.

The omissions mentioned earlier are quite serious ones from listings issued under the heading of so august a body as the Central Chancery for Orders of Knighthood. They do not inspire confidence in the compiler's awareness of the subject, at least beyond the almost unchanged portion regarding Orders. Apart from any arguments about the status of United Nations and similar awards, i.e. those other than actual British awards, the 1983 omissions include five medals which bear the Queen's head on the obverse. Also left out is the United Nations Service Medal with bar "Korea" which, in the original Army Order, was stated to have been accepted as a Queen's award to be worn with British awards by date of participation in the campaign. This definition has been absent from the more recent Defence Council Instructions dealing with United Nations Service Medals but the ruling as to their position in the order of wear, and that of NATO and European Community Medals, remains the same—they are treated as if they were British Campaign Medals. The Korean War should merit its own mention, as for 1914-18 and 1939-45. The UN medal was awarded to both those in Korea and those outside, e.g. in Japan, and it could, therefore, be earned before the Queen's Medal by anyone who worked with the UN in Japan before going to Korea. So the order of wear might, therefore, be UN then Queen's Medal though this arrangement was not allowed by the original Army Order on the subject.

The first *London Gazette* with a list showing the order of wear was published dated 22 April 1921. Before that references to the subject appeared in Queen's Regulations, Army Orders, Army Dress Regulations and Army Council Instructions. Since 1921 the list includes Clothing Regulations, Dress Regulations for Officers, Material Regulations as well as the periodic addition of new awards published in Ministry of Defence Orders and Instructions. The current National authority must be considered to be the *London Gazette* listings as the others are derived from these.

Inevitably, due to the long delays between *London Gazette* lists, military regulations in one form of another have to fill the gaps and some are incorrect. For example, an amendment in 1976 to Dress Regulations for Officers, 1969, misplaced the Queen's Gallantry Medal, putting it just after the George Medal and the now discontinued Police and Fire Service Gallantry Medals.

Another point worth mentioning here is that the DCI relating to the Accumulated Campaign Service Medal (ACSM), given for three years of General Service Medal operational service from 1969, suffered from a deficiency in the mathematics department. Bars are awarded for additional periods of three years. Each bar is denoted on the ribbon alone by a silver rosette. Four silver rosettes are replaced by one gold rosette. This must be to overcome the problem of lack of space, mentioned in Dress Regulations and decreeing that four or more rosettes on the various territorial efficiency awards are to overlap. The DCI on the ACSM gives examples up to six clasps represented by one gold and two silver rosettes. It then says that "This sequence will be followed until nine clasps are denoted by three gold rosettes. A further announcement will be made in the event that holders of the ACSM become eligible for a tenth clasp."

Of course, three gold rosettes would indicate twelve clasps and before that stage is reached the holder will have passed the eleven clasps point represented by two gold and three silver rosettes, total five. So crisis point for overcrowding is either reached at the eleven clasps point or is not reached until the fifteen clasps point when six rosettes, three of each metal, have to be fitted to the ribbon. Although this would mean forty-eight years operational service it is not, perhaps, impossible in the Northern Ireland context where we have already reached the twenty-nine year point from the start of the current "troubles".

Full listings expanding on the various publications referred to in the text, thus avoiding footnotes explaining certain aspects, are included at the end of the chapter in which they receive comment. These are in date order and designated as appendices to the chapter concerned. An indication is given of the entries affected by change from the previous list. A "+" shows an addition and a "-" a deletion (included in brackets to indicate what was deleted). A "*" shows there is either a change of position or some significant change in title.

The post-nominal letters shown in these appendices are those applying at the time of the publication. They do not include any that were authorised at a later date. Post-nominal letters were first consolidated and indicated in the *London Gazette* of 19 April 1955. All those shown in earlier lists are related to the Warrants and customs and traditions of the time, they do not appear in the published lists of the order of wear.

A full list of the publications used in this book, the bibliography, including all known military publications authorising recent medals is given at the end of the book.

Appendix 1 to Chapter 2

British Campaign Medals and Clasps

Full Title of Medal

Clasp [if any]	Earliest date awarded	Latest date awarded
Naval General Service Medal 1793-1840		
Nymphe, 18th June, 1793	18/06/1793	18/06/1793
Crescent, 20th Oct., 1793	20/10/1793	20/10/1793
15th March, 1793	15/03/1793	15/03/1793
Zebra, 17th March, 1794	17/03/1794	17/03/1794
17th March, 1794	17/03/1794	17/03/1794
Carysfort, 29th May, 1794	29/05/1794	29/05/1794
1st June, 1794	01/06/1794	01/06/1794
Romney, 17th June, 1794	17/06/1794	17/06/1794
Blanche, 4th Jan., 1795	04/01/1795	04/01/1795
Lively, 13th March, 1795	13/03/1795	13/03/1795
14th March, 1795	14/03/1795	14/03/1795
Astraea, 10th April, 1795	10/04/1795	10/04/1795
Hussar, 17th May, 1795	17/05/1795	17/05/1795
Thetis, 17th May, 1795	17/05/1795	17/05/1795
Mosquito, 9th June, 1795	09/06/1795	09/06/1795
17th June, 1795	17/06/1795	17/06/1795
23rd June, 1795	23/06/1795	23/06/1795
Dido, 24th June, 1795	24/06/1795	24/06/1795
Lowestoffe, 24th June, 1795	24/06/1795	24/06/1795
Spider, 25th August, 1795	25/08/1795	25/08/1795
Port Spergui	17/03/1796	17/03/1796
Indefatigable, 20th April, 1796	20/04/1796	20/04/1796
Santa Margarita, 8th June, 1796	08/06/1796	08/06/1796
Unicorn, 8th June, 1796	08/06/1796	08/06/1796
Southampton, 9th June, 1796	09/06/1796	09/06/1796
Dryad, 13th June, 1796	03/06/1796	13/06/1796
Terpischore, 13th Oct., 1796	13/10/1796	13/10/1796
Lapwing, 3rd Dec., 1796	03/12/1796	03/12/1796
Minerve, 19th Dec., 1796	19/12/1796	19/12/1796
Blanche, 19th Dec., 1796	19/12/1796	19/12/1796
Amazon, 13th Jan., 1797	13/01/1797	13/01/1797
Indefatigable, 13th Jan., 1797	13/01/1797	13/01/1797
St. Vincent	14/02/1797	14/02/1797
Nymphe, 8th March, 1797	08/03/1797	08/03/1797
San Fiorenzo, 8th March, 1797	08/03/1797	08/03/1797
29th May, 1797	29/05/1797	29/05/1797
Camperdown	11/10/1797	11/10/1797
Phoebe, 21st Dec., 1797	21/12/1797	21/12/1797
Mars, 21st April, 1798	21/04/1798	21/04/1798
Isle St. Marcou	06/05/1798	06/05/1798
Lion, 15th July, 1798	15/07/1798	15/07/1798
Nile	01/08/1798	01/08/1798
Espoir, 7th Aug., 1798	07/08/1798	07/08/1798
12th Oct., 1798	12/10/1798	12/10/1798
Fisgard, 20th Oct., 1798	20/10/1798	20/10/1798
Sybille, 28th Feb., 1799	28/02/1799	28/02/1799
Telegraph, 18th March, 1799	18/03/1799	18/03/1799
Acre, 30th May, 1799	30/05/1799	30/05/1799
9th June, 1799	09/06/1799	09/06/1799
Schiermonnikoog, 12th Aug., 1799	12/08/1799	12/08/1799
Arrow, 13th Sept., 1799	13/09/1799	13/09/1799

British Campaign Medals and Clasps (cont)

Full Title of Medal

Clasp [if any]	Earliest date awarded	Latest date awarded
Naval General Service Medal 1793-1840 (cont)		
Wolverine, 13th Sept., 1799	13/09/1799	13/09/1799
Surprise with Hermione	25/10/1799	25/10/1799
Speedy, 6th Nov., 1799	06/11/1799	06/11/1799
Courier, 22nd Nov., 1799	22/11/1799	22/11/1799
20th Dec., 1799	20/12/1799	20/12/1799
Viper, 26th Dec., 1799	26/12/1799	26/12/1799
Harpy, 5th Feb., 1800	05/02/1800	05/02/1800
Fairy, 5th Feb., 1800	05/02/1800	05/02/1800
Peterel, 21st March, 1800	21/03/1800	21/03/1800
Vinciego, 30th March, 1800	30/03/1800	30/03/1800
Penelope, 30th March, 1800	30/03/1800	30/03/1800
Capture of Désiré 8th July, 1800	08/07/1800	08/07/1800
29th July, 1800	29/07/1800	29/07/1800
Seine, 20th August, 1800	20/08/1800	20/08/1800
29th Aug., 1800	29/08/1800	29/08/1800
27th Oct., 1800	27/10/1800	27/10/1800
Phoebe, 19th Feb., 1801	19/02/1801	19/02/1801
Egypt	08/03/1801	02/09/1801
Copenhagen, 1801	02/04/1801	02/04/1801
Speedy, 6th May, 1801	06/05/1801	06/05/1801
Gut of Gibraltar, 12th July, 1801	12/07/1801	12/07/1801
21st July, 1801	21/07/1801	21/07/1801
Sylph, 28th Sept., 1801	28/09/1801	28/09/1801
Pasley, 28th Oct., 1801	28/10/1801	28/10/1801
27th June, 1803	27/06/1803	27/06/1803
4th Nov., 1803	04/11/1803	04/11/1803
4th Feb., 1804	04/02/1804	04/02/1804
Scorpion, 31st March, 1804	31/03/1804	31/03/1804
Beaver, 31st March, 1804	31/03/1804	31/03/1804
Centurion, 18th Sept., 1804	18/09/1804	18/09/1804
Acheron, 3rd Feb., 1805	03/02/1805	03/02/1805
Arrow, 3rd Feb., 1805	03/02/1805	03/02/1805
San Fiorenzo, 14th Feb., 1805	14/02/1805	14/02/1805
4th June, 1805	04/06/1805	04/06/1805
Phoenix, 10th Aug., 1805	10/08/1805	10/08/1805
Trafalgar	21/10/1805	21/10/1805
4th Novr. 1805	04/11/1805	04/11/1805
St. Domingo	06/02/1806	06/02/1806
Amazon, 13th March, 1806	13/03/1806	13/03/1806
London, 13th March, 1806	13/03/1806	13/03/1806
Pique, 26th March, 1806	26/03/1806	26/03/1806
Sirius, 17th April, 1806	17/04/1806	17/04/1806
16th July, 1806	16/07/1806	16/07/1806
Blanche, 19th July, 1806	19/07/1806	19/07/1806
Anson, 23rd August, 1806	23/08/1806	23/08/1806
Arethusa, 23rd August, 1806	23/08/1806	23/08/1806
Curacoa, 1st Jan., 1807	01/01/1807	01/01/1807
2nd Jan., 1807	02/01/1807	02/01/1807
Pickle, 3rd Jan., 1807	03/01/1807	03/01/1807
21st Jan., 1807	21/01/1807	21/01/1807
19th April, 1807	19/04/1807	19/04/1807
Hydra, 6th August, 1807	06/08/1807	06/08/1807
Comus, 15th August, 1807	15/08/1807	15/08/1807
Louisa, 28th Oct., 1807	28/10/1807	28/10/1807

British Campaign Medals and Clasps (cont)

Full Title of Medal

	Earliest date awarded	Latest date awarded
Clasp [if any]		
Naval General Service Medal 1793-1840 (cont)		
Carrier, 4th Nov., 1807	04/11/1807	04/11/1807
Ann, 24th Nov., 1807	24/11/1807	24/11/1807
13th February, 1808	13/02/1808	13/02/1808
Sappho, 2nd March, 1808	02/03/1808	02/03/1808
San Fiorenzo, 8th March, 1808	08/03/1808	08/03/1808
Emerald, 13th March, 1808	13/03/1808	13/03/1808
Childers, 14th March, 1808	14/03/1808	14/03/1808
Stately, 22nd March, 1808	22/03/1808	22/03/1808
Nassau, 22nd March, 1808	22/03/1808	22/03/1808
Off Rota, 4th April, 1808	04/04/1808	04/04/1808
Grasshopper, 24th April, 1808	24/04/1808	24/04/1808
Rapid, 24th April, 1808	24/04/1808	24/04/1808
Redwing, 7th May, 1808	07/05/1808	07/05/1808
Virginie, 19th May, 1808	19/05/1808	19/05/1808
Redwing, 31st May, 1808	31/05/1808	31/05/1808
Seahorse with Badere Zaffer	06/07/1808	06/07/1808
10th July, 1808	10/07/1808	10/07/1808
11th Aug., 1808	11/08/1808	11/08/1808
Comet, 11th August, 1808	11/08/1808	11/08/1808
Centaur, 26th August, 1808	26/08/1808	26/08/1808
Implacable, 26th August, 1808	26/08/1808	26/08/1808
Cruizer, 1st Nov., 1808	01/11/1808	01/11/1808
Amethyst wh. Thetis	10/11/1808	10/11/1808
28th Nov., 1808	28/11/1808	28/11/1808
Off the Pearl Rock, 13th Dec., 1808	13/12/1808	13/12/1808
Onyx, 1st Jan., 1809	01/01/1809	01/01/1809
Confiance, 14th Jan., 1809	14/01/1809	14/01/1809
Martinique	02/02/1809	10/02/1809
Horatio, 10th Feb^y., 1809	10/02/1809	10/02/1809
Supérieure, 10th Feb^y., 1809	10/02/1809	10/02/1809
Amethyst, 5th April, 1809	05/04/1809	05/04/1809
Basque Roads, 1809	12/04/1809	12/04/1809
Recruit, 17th June, 1809	17/06/1809	17/06/1809
Pompee, 17th June, 1809	17/06/1809	17/06/1809
Castor, 17th June, 1809	17/06/1809	17/06/1809
Cyane, 25th and 27th June, 1809	25/06/1809	27/06/1809
L'Espoir, 25th and 27th June, 1809	25/06/1809	27/06/1809
Bonne Citoyenne with Furieuse	06/07/1809	06/07/1809
7th July, 1809	07/07/1809	07/07/1809
14th July, 1809	14/07/1809	14/07/1809
25th July, 1809	25/07/1809	25/07/1809
27th July, 1809	27/07/1809	27/07/1809
29th July, 1809	29/07/1809	29/07/1809
28th Aug., 1809	28/08/1809	28/08/1809
Diana, 11th Sept., 1809	11/09/1809	11/09/1809
1st Nov., 1809	01/11/1809	01/11/1809
13th Dec., 1809	13/12/1809	13/12/1809
Anse la Barque, 18th Decr., 1809	18/12/1809	18/12/1809
Guadaloupe, Jan.-Feb., 1810	01/01/1810	28/02/1810
Cherokee, 10th Jan., 1810	10/01/1810	10/01/1810
Scorpion, 12th Jan., 1810	12/01/1810	12/01/1810
Thistle, 10th Feb., 1810	10/02/1810	10/02/1810
13th Feb., 1810	13/02/1810	13/02/1810

British Campaign Medals and Clasps (cont)

Full Title of Medal

Clasp [if any]	Earliest date awarded	Latest date awarded
Naval General Service Medal 1793-1840 (cont)		
Surly, 24th April, 1810	24/04/1810	24/04/1810
Firm, 24th April, 1810	24/04/1810	24/04/1810
Sylvia, 26th April, 1810	26/04/1810	26/04/1810
Royalist, May and June, 1810	01/05/1810	30/06/1810
1st May, 1810	01/05/1810	01/05/1810
Spartan, 3rd May, 1810	03/05/1810	03/05/1810
28th June, 1810	28/06/1810	28/06/1810
Amanthea, 25th July, 1810	25/07/1810	25/07/1810
Banda Neira	09/08/1810	09/08/1810
Staunch, 18th Sept., 1810	18/09/1810	18/09/1810
Otter, 18th Sept., 1810	18/09/1810	18/09/1810
Boadicea, 18th Sept., 1810	18/09/1810	18/09/1810
27th Sept., 1810	27/09/1810	27/09/1810
Briseis, 14th Oct., 1810	14/10/1810	14/10/1810
4th Nov., 1810	04/11/1810	04/11/1810
23rd Nov., 1810	23/11/1810	23/11/1810
24th Dec., 1810	24/12/1810	24/12/1810
Lissa	13/03/1811	13/03/1811
Anholt, 27th March, 1811	27/03/1811	27/03/1811
Arrow, 6th April, 1811	06/04/1811	06/04/1811
4th May, 1811	04/05/1811	04/05/1811
Off Tamatave, 20th May, 1811	20/05/1811	20/05/1811
30th July, 1811	30/07/1811	30/07/1811
2nd Aug., 1811	02/08/1811	02/08/1811
Java	04/08/1811	18/09/1811
Hawke, 18th August, 1811	18/08/1811	18/08/1811
20th Sept., 1811	20/09/1811	20/09/1811
Skylark, 11th Nov., 1811	11/11/1811	11/11/1811
Locust, 11th Nov., 1811	11/11/1811	11/11/1811
Pelagosa 29th Nov., 1811	29/11/1811	29/11/1811
4th Dec., 1811	04/12/1811	04/12/1811
Victorious wh. Rivoli	22/02/1812	22/02/1812
Weasel, 22nd Feb., 1812	22/02/1812	22/02/1812
Griffon, 27th March, 1812	27/03/1812	27/03/1812
Rosario, 27th March, 1812	27/03/1812	27/03/1812
4th April, 1812	04/04/1812	04/04/1812
Growler, 22nd May, 1812	22/05/1812	22/05/1812
Northumberland, 22nd May, 1812	22/05/1812	22/05/1812
Malaga, 29th May, 1812	29/05/1812	29/05/1812
Off Mardoe, 6th July, 1812	06/07/1812	06/07/1812
Sealark, 21st July, 1812	21/07/1812	21/07/1812
1st Sept., 1812	01/09/1812	01/09/1812
17th Sept., 1812	17/09/1812	17/09/1812
29th Sept., 1812	29/09/1812	29/09/1812
Royalist, 29th Dec., 1812	29/12/1812	29/12/1812
6th Jan., 1813	06/01/1813	06/01/1813
21st March, 1813	21/03/1813	21/03/1813
Weasel, 22nd April, 1813	22/04/1813	22/04/1813
April and May, 1813	29/04/1813	03/05/1813
29th April, 1813	29/04/1813	29/04/1813
2nd May, 1813	02/05/1813	02/05/1813
Shannon wh. Chesapeake	01/06/1813	01/06/1813
St. Sebastian	01/08/1813	30/09/1813
Pelican, 14th August, 1813	14/08/1813	14/08/1813

British Campaign Medals and Clasps (cont)

Full Title of Medal

    Clasp [if any]

	Earliest date awarded	Latest date awarded
Naval General Service Medal 1793-1840 (cont)		
Thunder, 9th Oct., 1813	09/10/1813	09/10/1813
Gluckstadt, 5th Jan., 1814	05/01/1814	05/01/1814
Cyane, 16th Jan., 1814	16/01/1814	16/01/1814
Venerable, 16th Jan., 1814	16/01/1814	16/01/1814
Eurotas, 25th Feb., 1814	25/02/1814	25/02/1814
Hebrus with L'Etoile	27/03/1814	27/03/1814
Cherub, 28th March, 1814	28/03/1814	28/03/1814
Phoebe, 28th March, 1814	28/03/1814	28/03/1814
8th April, 1814	08/04/1814	08/04/1814
19th April, 1814	19/04/1814	19/04/1814
6th May, 1814	06/05/1814	06/05/1814
24th May, 1814	24/05/1814	24/05/1814
The Potomac, 17th Aug., 1814	17/08/1814	17/08/1814
3rd and 6th September, 1814	03/09/1814	06/09/1814
14th December, 1814	14/12/1814	14/12/1814
Endymion wh. President	15/01/1815	15/01/1815
Gaieta, 24th July, 1815	24/07/1815	24/07/1815
Algiers	27/08/1816	27/08/1816
Navarino	20/10/1827	20/10/1827
Syria	01/11/1840	30/11/1840
Military General Service Medal 1793-1814		
Egypt	02/03/1801	02/09/1801
Maida	04/07/1806	04/07/1806
Roleia	17/08/1808	17/08/1808
Vimiera	21/08/1808	21/08/1808
Sahagun	21/12/1808	21/12/1808
Sahagun and Benevente	21/12/1808	01/01/1809
Benevente	01/01/1809	01/01/1809
Corunna	16/01/1809	16/01/1809
Martinique	30/01/1809	24/02/1809
Talavera	27/07/1809	28/07/1809
Guadaloupe	01/01/1810	28/02/1810
Busaco	27/09/1810	27/09/1810
Barrosa	05/03/1811	05/03/1811
Fuentes d'Onor	05/05/1811	05/05/1811
Albuhera	16/05/1811	16/05/1811
Java	14/08/1811	26/08/1811
Ciudad Rodrigo	08/01/1812	19/01/1812
Badajoz	17/03/1812	16/04/1812
Salamanca	22/07/1812	22/07/1812
Fort Detroit	16/08/1812	16/08/1812
Vittoria	21/06/1813	21/06/1813
St. Sebastian	17/07/1813	08/09/1813
Pyrenees	28/07/1813	02/08/1813
Chateauguay	26/10/1813	26/10/1813
Nivelle	10/11/1813	10/11/1813
Chrystler's Farm	11/11/1813	11/11/1813
Nive	09/12/1813	13/12/1813
Orthes	27/02/1814	27/02/1814
Toulouse	10/04/1814	10/04/1814

British Campaign Medals and Clasps (cont)

Full Title of Medal

Clasp [if any]	Earliest date awarded	Latest date awarded
Army of India Medal 1799-1826		
Allighur	04/09/1803	04/09/1803
Battle of Delhi	11/09/1803	11/09/1803
Assaye	23/09/1803	23/09/1803
Asseerghur	21/10/1803	21/10/1803
Laswarree	01/11/1803	01/11/1803
Argaum	29/11/1803	29/11/1803
Gawilghur	15/12/1803	15/12/1803
Defence of Delhi	08/10/1804	14/10/1804
Battle of Deig	13/11/1804	13/11/1804
Capture of Deig	11/12/1804	23/12/1804
Nepaul	01/10/1814	31/03/1816
Kirkee	05/11/1817	05/11/1817
Kirkee and Poona	05/11/1817	16/11/1817
Poona	11/11/1817	16/11/1817
Seetabuldee and Nagpore	26/11/1817	16/12/1817
Seetabuldee	26/11/1817	27/11/1817
Nagpore	16/12/1817	16/12/1817
Maheidpoor	21/12/1817	21/12/1817
Corygaum	01/01/1818	01/01/1818
Ava	01/01/1824	31/12/1826
Bhurtpoor	17/01/1826	18/01/1826
Waterloo Medal	16/06/1815	18/06/1815
South Africa Medal 1834-53	01/01/1834	31/12/1853
First China War Medal	05/07/1840	29/08/1842
Second China War Medal 1857-60		
China 1842	05/07/1840	29/08/1842
—	25/05/1857	05/11/1860
Fatshan 1857	25/05/1857	01/06/1857
Canton 1857	28/12/1857	05/01/1858
Taku Forts 1858	20/05/1858	20/05/1858
Taku Forts 1860	21/08/1860	21/08/1860
Pekin 1860	13/10/1860	24/10/1860
Candahar, Ghuznee and Cabul Medal	01/10/1841	31/10/1842
Ghuznee and Cabul Medal	01/10/1841	31/10/1842
Jellalabad Medal	12/11/1841	07/04/1842
Defence of Kelat-i-Ghilzie Medal	01/02/1842	30/05/1842
Candahar Medal	01/05/1842	31/05/1842
Cabul Medal	15/09/1842	15/09/1842
Scinde Campaign Medal (Meeanee and Hyderabad)	17/02/1843	24/03/1843
Scinde Campaign Medal (Meeanee)	17/02/1843	17/02/1843

British Campaign Medals and Clasps (cont)

Full Title of Medal Clasp [if any]	Earliest date awarded	Latest date awarded
Scinde Campaign Medal (Hyderabad)	24/03/1843	24/03/1843
Gwalior Campaign Star (Maharajpoor)	29/12/1843	29/12/1843
Gwalior Campaign Star (Punniar)	29/12/1843	29/12/1843
Sutlej Campaign Medal (Each medal bore the name of the first action with clasps for subsequent actions)		
Moodkee	18/12/1845	18/12/1845
Ferozeshuhur	21/12/1845	21/12/1845
Aliwal	28/01/1846	28/01/1846
Sobraon	10/02/1846	10/02/1846
New Zealand Medal	01/01/1845	31/12/1866
New Zealand Medal 1845-46	01/01/1845	31/12/1846
New Zealand Medal 1845-47	01/01/1845	31/12/1847
New Zealand Medal 1846	01/01/1846	31/12/1846
New Zealand Medal 1846-47	01/01/1846	31/12/1847
New Zealand Medal 1847	01/01/1847	31/12/1847
New Zealand Medal 1848	01/01/1848	31/12/1848
Punjab Campaign Medal		
—	07/09/1848	21/02/1849
Mooltan	07/09/1848	22/01/1849
Chilianwala	13/01/1849	13/01/1849
Goojerat	21/02/1849	21/02/1849
New Zealand Medal 1860	01/01/1860	31/12/1860
New Zealand Medal 1860-61	01/01/1860	31/12/1861
New Zealand Medal 1860-63	01/01/1860	31/12/1863
New Zealand Medal 1860-64	01/01/1860	31/12/1864
New Zealand Medal 1860-65	01/01/1860	31/12/1865
New Zealand Medal 1860-66	01/01/1860	31/12/1866
New Zealand Medal 1861	01/01/1861	31/12/1861
New Zealand Medal 1861-63	01/01/1861	31/12/1863
New Zealand Medal 1861-64	01/01/1861	31/12/1864
New Zealand Medal 1861-65	01/01/1861	31/12/1865
New Zealand Medal 1861-66	01/01/1861	31/12/1866
New Zealand Medal 1862-66	01/01/1862	31/12/1866

British Campaign Medals and Clasps (cont)

Full Title of Medal

Clasp [if any]	Earliest date awarded	Latest date awarded
New Zealand Medal 1863	01/01/1863	31/12/1863
New Zealand Medal 1863-64	01/01/1863	31/12/1864
New Zealand Medal 1863-65	01/01/1863	31/12/1865
New Zealand Medal 1863-66	01/01/1863	31/12/1866
New Zealand Medal 1864	01/01/1864	31/12/1864
New Zealand Medal 1864-65	01/01/1864	31/12/1865
New Zealand Medal 1864-66	01/01/1864	31/12/1866
New Zealand Medal 1865	01/01/1865	31/12/1865
New Zealand Medal 1865-66	01/01/1865	31/12/1866
New Zealand Medal 1866	01/01/1866	31/12/1866
Indian General Service Medal 1854-95		
North West Frontier	03/12/1849	22/10/1868
Pegu	28/03/1852	30/06/1853
Persia	05/12/1856	08/02/1857
Umbeyla	20/10/1863	23/12/1863
Bhootan	01/12/1864	28/02/1866
Looshai	09/12/1871	20/02/1872
Perak	02/11/1875	20/03/1876
Jowaki 1877-8	09/11/1877	19/01/1878
Naga 1879-80	01/12/1879	31/01/1880
Burma 1885-7	14/11/1885	30/04/1887
Burma 1887-89	01/05/1887	31/03/1889
Sikkim 1888	15/03/1888	27/09/1888
Hazara 1888	03/10/1888	09/11/1888
Chin Lushai 1889-90	15/11/1889	30/04/1890
Hazara 1891	12/03/1891	16/05/1891
NE Frontier 1891	28/03/1891	07/05/1891
Samana 1891	05/04/1891	25/05/1891
Hunza 1891	01/12/1891	22/12/1891
Baltic Medal	01/03/1854	31/08/1855
Crimea Medal		
Sebastopol	11/09/1854	09/09/1855
Alma	20/09/1854	20/09/1854
Balaklava	25/10/1854	25/10/1854
Inkermann	05/11/1854	05/11/1854
Azoff	25/05/1855	22/09/1855
Indian Mutiny Medal 1857-58		
—	10/05/1857	30/12/1858
Delhi	30/05/1857	14/09/1857
Defence of Lucknow	29/06/1957	22/11/1857
Relief of Lucknow	01/11/1857	30/11/1857
Lucknow	01/11/1857	31/03/1858
Central India	01/01/1858	30/06/1858

British Campaign Medals and Clasps (cont)

Full Title of Medal

Clasp [if any]	Earliest date awarded	Latest date awarded
Canada General Service Medal 1866-70		
Fenian Raid 1866	31/05/1866	07/06/1866
Fenian Raid 1870	26/05/1870	30/06/1870
Red River 1870	14/05/1870	24/08/1870
Abyssinian War Medal 1867-68	04/10/1867	19/04/1868
Ashanti War Medal		
—	09/06/1873	04/02/1874
Coomassie	05/01/1874	04/02/1874
South Africa Medal		
1877	26/09/1877	31/12/1877
1877-8	26/09/1877	13/11/1878
1877-8-9	26/09/1877	02/12/1879
1878	01/01/1878	13/11/1878
1878-9	01/01/1878	02/12/1879
1879	11/01/1879	02/12/1879
—	11/01/1879	01/09/1879
Second Afghan War Medal 1878-80		
Ali Musjid	21/11/1878	21/11/1878
Peiwar Kotal	02/12/1878	02/12/1878
Charasia	06/10/1879	06/10/1879
Kabul	10/12/1879	23/12/1879
Ahmed Khel	19/04/1880	19/04/1880
Kandahar	01/09/1880	01/09/1880
Kabul to Kandahar Star	09/08/1880	31/08/1880
Cape of Good Hope General Service Medal 1880-97		
Transkei	13/09/1880	15/05/1881
Basutoland	13/09/1889	27/04/1881
Bechuanaland	24/12/1896	30/07/1897
Egypt Medal 1882-89		
Alexandria 11th July	11/07/1882	11/07/1882
Tel-el-Kebir	13/09/1882	13/09/1882
Suakin 1884	19/02/1884	26/03/1884
El-Teb Tamaai	29/02/1884	13/03/1884
El-Teb	29/02/1884	29/02/1884
Tamaai	13/03/1884	13/03/1884
The Nile 1884-85	01/08/1884	07/03/1885
Abu Klea	17/01/1885	17/01/1885
Kirbekan	10/02/1885	10/02/1885
Suakin 1885	01/03/1885	14/05/1885
Tofrek	22/03/1885	22/03/1885
Gemaizah	20/12/1888	20/12/1888
Toski	03/08/1889	03/08/1889
North West Canada Medal 1885		
—	24/04/1885	28/05/1885
Saskatchewan	24/04/1885	28/05/1885
Royal Niger Company Medal 1886-97		
Nigeria 1886-97	01/01/1886	31/12/1897
Nigeria	01/01/1886	31/12/1897

British Campaign Medals and Clasps (cont)

Full Title of Medal

Clasp [if any]	Earliest date awarded	Latest date awarded
East and West Africa Medal 1887-1900		
1887-8	13/11/1887	02/01/1888
Witu 1890	17/10/1890	27/10/1890
1891-2	29/12/1891	02/02/1892
1892	08/03/1892	25/05/1892
Liwondi 1893	01/02/1893	31/03/1983
Witu August 1893	07/08/1893	13/08/1893
Juba River 1893	23/08/1893	25/08/1893
Lake Nyassa 1893	01/11/1893	30/11/1893
1893-94	16/11/1893	11/03/1894
Gambia 1894	23/02/1894	13/03/1894
Benin River 1894	01/08/1894	30/09/1894
(M'wele 1895 or 1895-6 on rim of medal)	01/01/1895	31/12/1896
Brass River 1895	17/02/1895	26/02/1895
1896-98	27/11/1896	27/06/1898
Niger 1897	06/01/1897	26/02/1897
Benin 1897	06/02/1897	07/08/1897
Dawkita 1897	28/03/1897	28/03/1897
1897-98	01/09/1897	31/08/1898
1898	01/01/1898	31/12/1898
Sierra Leone 1898-99	18/02/1898	09/03/1899
1899	01/02/1899	31/05/1899
1900	04/01/1900	08/05/1900
British South Africa Company's Medal 1890-97		
(Except for 1890 each medal bore the name of the first action with clasps for subsequent actions)		
Mashonaland 1890	01/06/1890	12/09/1890
Matabeleland 1893	16/10/1893	24/12/1893
Rhodesia 1896	24/03/1896	31/12/1896
Mashonaland 1897	24/03/1896	31/10/1897
Central Africa Medal 1891-1898		
—	01/07/1891	30/06/1894
Central Africa 1894-98	01/01/1894	30/04/1898
India Medal 1895-1902		
Defence of Chitral 1895	03/03/1895	19/04/1895
Relief of Chitral 1895	07/03/1895	15/08/1895
Punjab Frontier 1897-98	10/06/1897	06/04/1898
Malakand 1897	26/07/1897	02/08/1897
Samana 1897	22/08/1897	02/10/1897
Tirah 1897-98	02/10/1897	06/04/1898
Waziristan 1901-2	23/11/1901	10/03/1902
Ashanti Star 1896	07/12/1895	17/01/1896
Sudan Medal 1896-97	07/06/1896	02/09/1898
British North Borneo Punitive Expedition Medal 1897-98		
Punitive Expedition	01/07/1897	31/12/1897
Punitive Expeditions	01/01/1898	31/01/1898
East and Central Africa Medal 1897-99		
Uganda 1897-98	20/07/1897	19/03/1898
Lubwa's	23/09/1897	24/02/1898
1898	12/04/1898	03/10/1898
Uganda 1899	21/03/1899	02/05/1899

British Campaign Medals and Clasps (cont)

Full Title of Medal

Clasp [if any]	Earliest date awarded	Latest date awarded
Transport Medal		
S Africa 1899-1902	01/01/1899	31/12/1902
China 1900	10/06/1900	31/12/1900
African General Service Medal 1902		
B.C.A. 1899-1900	01/08/1899	31/12/1900
N. Nigeria	01/07/1900	30/09/1901
Uganda 1900	03/07/1900	31/10/1900
Jubaland	16/11/1900	30/04/1901
Gambia	01/01/1901	31/03/1901
S. Nigeria	01/03/1901	31/05/1901
Lango 1901	24/04/1901	24/08/1901
Somaliland 1901	22/05/1901	30/07/1901
Aro 1901-1902	15/11/1901	23/03/1902
Somaliland 1902-04	18/01/1902	11/05/1904
N. Nigeria 1902	01/02/1902	30/11/1902
S. Nigeria 1902	15/06/1902	30/12/1902
S. Nigeria 1902-03	07/07/1902	08/06/1903
East Africa 1902	04/09/1902	25/10/1902
N. Nigeria 1903	29/01/1903	27/07/1903
S. Nigeria 1903	04/02/1903	05/12/1903
N. Nigeria 1903-04	23/12/1903	12/03/1904
S. Nigeria 1903-04	23/12/1903	12/03/1904
Jidballi	10/01/1904	10/01/1904
S. Nigeria 1904	12/01/1904	03/06/1904
East Africa 1904	13/02/1904	17/03/1904
N. Nigeria 1904	01/03/1904	31/10/1904
S. Nigeria 1904-05	15/11/1904	27/02/1905
S. Nigeria 1905-06	01/01/1905	31/12/1906
Kissi 1905	27/03/1905	28/06/1905
East Africa 1905	31/05/1905	09/10/1905
S. Nigeria 1905	10/10/1905	18/10/1905
Nandi 1905-06	18/10/1905	06/07/1906
N. Nigeria 1906	14/02/1906	24/04/1906
West Africa 1906	09/06/1906	17/02/1907
East Africa 1906	18/06/1906	19/07/1906
Somaliland 1908-10	19/08/1908	31/01/1910
West Africa 1908	11/12/1908	31/12/1908
West Africa 1909-10	02/11/1909	27/05/1910
East Africa 1913	17/06/1913	07/08/1913
East Africa 1913-14	15/12/1913	31/05/1914
East Africa 1914	02/04/1914	07/07/1914
Shimber Berris 1914-15	19/11/1914	09/02/1915
Nyasaland 1915	24/01/1915	17/02/1915
East Africa 1915	04/02/1915	25/05/1915
Jubaland 1917-18	23/07/1917	24/03/1918
East Africa 1918	20/04/1918	19/06/1918
Nigeria 1918	11/06/1918	31/07/1918
Somaliland 1920	21/01/1920	12/02/1920
Kenya	21/10/1952	17/11/1956
Queen's Mediterranean Medal	11/10/1899	31/05/1902

British Campaign Medals and Clasps (cont)

Full Title of Medal

Clasp [if any]	Earliest date awarded	Latest date awarded
Queen's South Africa Medal		
—	11/10/1899	31/05/1902
Natal	11/10/1899	11/06/1900
Cape Colony	11/10/1899	31/05/1902
Rhodesia	11/10/1899	25/05/1900
Relief of Mafeking	11/10/1899	17/05/1900
Defence of Mafeking	13/10/1899	17/05/1900
Defence of Kimberley	14/10/1899	15/02/1900
Talana	20/10/1899	20/10/1899
Elandslaagte	21/10/1899	21/10/1899
Defence of Ladysmith	03/11/1899	28/02/1900
Belmont	23/11/1899	23/11/1899
Modder River	28/11/1899	28/11/1899
Relief of Ladysmith	15/12/1899	28/02/1900
Tulela Heights	14/02/1900	27/02/1900
Relief of Kimberley	15/02/1900	15/02/1900
Paardeberg	17/02/1900	26/02/1900
Orange Free State	28/02/1900	31/05/1902
Dreifontein	10/03/1900	10/03/1900
Wepener	09/04/1900	25/04/1900
Transvaal	24/05/1900	31/05/1902
Johannesburg	29/05/1900	31/05/1900
Diamond Hill	11/06/1900	12/06/1900
Laing's Nek	02/06/1900	09/06/1900
Wittebergen	01/07/1900	29/07/1900
Belfast	26/08/1900	27/08/1900
South Africa 1901	01/01/1901	31/12/1901
South Africa 1902	01/01/1902	31/05/1902
British North Borneo Medal Tambuan 1899-1900		
Tambuan	01/01/1899	31/12/1900
Ashanti Medal		
—	31/03/1900	25/12/1900
Kumassi	31/03/1900	15/07/1900
Third China War Medal 1900		
—	10/06/1900	31/12/1900
Defence of the Legations	10/06/1900	14/08/1900
Relief of Pekin	10/06/1900	14/08/1900
Taku Forts	17/06/1900	17/06/1900
King's South Africa Medal		
South Africa 1901	01/01/1901	31/12/1901
South Africa 1902	01/01/1902	31/05/1902
Tibet Medal		
—	13/12/1903	23/09/1904
Gyantse	05/05/1904	06/07/1904
Natal Rebellion Medal		
—	08/02/1906	03/08/1906
1906	08/02/1906	03/08/1906

British Campaign Medals and Clasps (cont)

Full Title of Medal

    Clasp [if any]

	Earliest date awarded	Latest date awarded
Indian General Service Medal 1908-35		
North West Frontier 1908	14/02/1908	31/05/1908
Abor 1911-12	06/10/1911	20/04/1912
Afghanistan NWF 1919	06/05/1919	30/09/1919
Waziristan 1919-21	01/10/1919	20/12/1921
Mahsud 1919-20	18/12/1919	08/04/1920
Malabar 1921-22	20/08/1921	25/02/1922
Waziristan 1921-24	21/12/1921	31/03/1924
Waziristan 1925	09/03/1925	01/05/1925
North West Frontier 1930-31	23/04/1930	22/03/1931
Burma 1930-32	22/12/1930	25/03/1932
Mohmand 1933	28/07/1933	03/10/1933
North West Frontier 1935	23/02/1935	15/10/1935
Naval General Service Medal 1915-62		
Persian Gulf 1909-1914	19/10/1909	01/08/1914
Iraq 1919-20	01/07/1920	17/11/1920
NW Persia 1920	10/08/1920	31/12/1920
Palestine 1936-39	19/04/1936	03/09/1939
SE Asia 1945-46	03/09/1945	30/11/1946
Bomb-Mine Clearance 1945-53	03/09/1945	28/04/1953
Bomb and Mine Clearance 1945-56	03/09/1945	31/12/1956
Minesweeping 1945-51	03/09/1945	30/09/1951
Palestine 1945-48	27/09/1945	30/06/1948
Malaya	16/06/1948	31/07/1960
Yangste 1949	20/04/1949	31/07/1949
Bomb and Mine Clearance Mediterranean	01/01/1955	31/12/1960
Cyprus	01/04/1955	18/04/1959
Near East	31/10/1956	22/12/1956
Arabian Peninsula	01/01/1957	30/06/1960
Brunei	08/12/1962	23/12/1962
1914 Star	05/08/1914	22/11/1914
5th Aug : 22nd Nov 1914	05/08/1914	22/11/1914
1914-15 Star	05/08/1914	31/12/1915
British War Medal 1914-19	05/08/1914	01/07/1920
Mercantile Marine War Medal	05/08/1914	11/11/1918
Allied Victory Medal	05/08/1914	01/07/1920
Territorial Force War Medal	05/08/1914	11/11/1918
British North Borneo Medal Rundum 1915-16		
Rundum	01/01/1915	31/12/1916
General Service Medal (Army and RAF) 1918-62		
S. Persia	12/11/1918	22/06/1919
Kurdistan	23/05/1919	18/06/1923
Iraq	10/12/1919	17/11/1920
N.W. Persia	10/08/1920	31/12/1920
Southern Desert: Iraq	08/01/1928	03/06/1928
Northern Kurdistan	15/03/1932	21/06/1932
Palestine	19/04/1936	03/09/1939

British Campaign Medals and Clasps (cont)

Full Title of Medal

Clasp [if any]	Earliest date awarded	Latest date awarded
General Service Medal (Army and RAF) 1918-62 (cont)		
Bomb & Mine Clearance 1945-49	09/05/1945	31/12/1949
Bomb & Mine Clearance 1945-56	03/09/1945	10/11/1956
South East Asia 1945-46	03/09/1945	30/11/1946
Palestine 1945-48	27/09/1945	30/06/1948
Malaya	16/06/1948	31/07/1960
Cyprus	01/04/1955	18/04/1959
Near East	31/10/1956	22/12/1956
Arabian Peninsula	01/01/1957	30/06/1960
Brunei	08/12/1962	23/12/1962
Indian General Service Medal 1936-39		
North West Frontier 1936-37	25/11/1936	16/12/1937
North West Frontier 1937-39	16/12/1937	31/12/1939
1939-45 Star		
—	03/09/1939	02/09/1945
Battle of Britain	10/07/1940	31/10/1940
Atlantic Star		
—	03/09/1939	08/05/1945
Air Crew Europe	03/09/1939	05/06/1944
France and Germany	06/06/1944	08/05/1945
Air Crew Europe Star		
—	03/09/1939	05/06/1944
Atlantic	03/09/1939	08/05/1945
France and Germany	06/06/1944	08/05/1945
Africa Star		
—	10/06/1940	12/05/1943
North Africa 1942-43	23/10/1942	12/05/1943
8th Army	23/10/1942	12/05/1943
1st Army	08/11/1942	12/05/1943
Pacific Star		
—	08/12/1941	02/09/1945
Burma	11/12/1941	02/09/1945
Burma Star		
—	11/12/1941	02/09/1945
Pacific	11/12/1941	02/09/1945
Italy Star	11/06/1943	08/05/1945
France & Germany Star		
—	06/06/1944	08/05/1945
Atlantic	06/06/1944	08/05/1945
Defence Medal	03/09/1939	02/09/1945
Canada Volunteer Service Medal		
—	03/09/1939	01/03/1947
Silver with maple leaf	03/09/1939	01/03/1947
War Medal	03/09/1939	02/09/1945

British Campaign Medals and Clasps (cont)

Full Title of Medal Clasp [if any]	Earliest date awarded	Latest date awarded
Africa Service Medal 1939-43	03/09/1939	13/05/1943
India Service Medal 1939-45	03/09/1939	02/09/1945
New Zealand War Service Medal 1939-45	03/09/1939	02/09/1945
Southern Rhodesia Service Medal 1939-45	03/09/1939	02/09/1945
Australia Service Medal 1939-45	03/09/1939	02/09/1945
South African Medal for War Services 1939-46	06/09/1939	15/02/1946
The Newfoundland Volunteer War Service Medal	03/09/1939	03/09/1945
Pakistan General Service Medal		
Kashmir	01/01/1948	?
United Nations Service Medal		
Korea	27/06/1950	27/07/1954
Queen's Korea Medal	02/07/1950	27/07/1953
United Nations Medal for Service in the Congo	10/07/1960	30/06/1964
Sierra Leone General Service Medal		
Congo	26/01/1962	28/02/1963
General Service Medal 1964-		
Borneo	24/12/1962	11/08/1966
South Vietnam	24/12/1962	28/05/1964
Radfan	25/04/1964	31/07/1964
South Arabia	01/08/1964	30/11/1967
Malay Peninsula	17/08/1964	11/08/1966
Northern Ireland	14/08/1969	Current (1998)
Dhofar	01/10/1969	30/09/1976
Lebanon	07/02/1983	09/03/1984
Mine Clearance—Gulf of Suez	15/08/1984	15/10/1984
Gulf	11/11/1986	28/02/1989
Kuwait	08/03/1991	30/09/1991
N. Iraq & S. Turkey	06/04/1991	17/07/1991
Air Operations Iraq	19/09/1991	Current (1998)
United Nations Medal for Service in Cyprus		
Numerals	27/03/1964	Current (1998)
Vietnam Medal	29/05/1964	27/01/1973
Vietnam Logistics & Support Medal	29/05/1964	27/01/1973
Accumulated Campaign Service Medal	14/08/1969	Current (1998)
Royal Ulster Constabulary Service Medal	01/01/1971	Current (1998)
United Nations Medal for Disengagement Observer Force		
Numerals	31/05/1974	Current (1998)

British Campaign Medals and Clasps (cont)

Full Title of Medal

Clasp [if any]	Earliest date awarded	Latest date awarded
Rhodesia Medal	01/12/1979	20/03/1980
South Atlantic Medal 1982		
—	02/04/1982	14/06/1982
Rosette	02/04/1982	14/06/1982
United Nations Special Service Medal		
UNOCHA (Afghanistan)	01/01/1989	31/12/1990
Former Yugoslavia	03/07/1992	12/01/1996
United Nations Medal for the Transitional Advisory Group Namibia		
Numerals	01/04/1989	31/03/1990
Gulf Medal 1990-191		
—	02/08/1990	07/03/1991
2 Aug 1990	02/08/1990	02/08/1990
16 Jan – 28 Feb 1991	16/01/1991	28/02/1991
United Nations Medal for the Iraq-Kuwait Observation Mission		
Numerals	03/04/1991	Current (1998)
United Nations Medal for Western Sahara. (Mission des nations unies pour le referendum dans Sahara Occidental)		
Numerals	01/09/1991	Current (1998)
United Nations Medal for the Advance Mission in Cambodia		
Numerals	01/11/1991	31/03/1992
United Nations Medal for the Protection Force (Yugoslavia)		
Numerals	01/03/1992	30/07/1995
United Nations Medal for Transitional Authority in Cambodia		
Numerals	01/03/1992	31/09/1993
Western European Union Mission Service Medal		
Former Yugoslavia 1992	22/07/1992	?
European Community Monitor Mission Medal	27/07/1992	30/06/1993
United Nations Medal for Operations in Mozambique		
Numerals	01/12/1992	31/12/1994
United Nations Medal for Operations in Georgia		
Numerals	01/08/1993	Current (1998)
United Nations Medal for Assistance Mission in Rwanda		
Numerals	02/08/1994	22/11/1994
United Nations Medal for the Preventive Deployment Force (Former Yugoslavia)		
Numerals	01/03/1995	Current (1998)
United Nations Medal for Confidence Restoration Operation (Former Yugoslavia)		
Numerals	01/03/1995	31/01/1996
United Nations Medal for the Angola Verification Mission III		
Numerals	15/04/1995	15/07/1995

British Campaign Medals and Clasps (cont)

Full Title of Medal

                                            Earliest   Latest

                                            date   date

          Clasp [if any]   awarded   awarded

North Atlantic Treaty Organisation Medal
    Former Yugoslavia   01/07/1995   Current (1998)

United Nations Medal; for the Transitional Administration for Eastern Slavonia, Baranja and Western Sirmium (Former Yugoslavia)
    Numerals   01/01/1996   Current (1998)

United Nations Medal for the Mission of Observers in Prevlaka (Former Yugoslavia)
    Numerals   01/01/1996   Current (1998)

Appendix 2 to Chapter 2

Commonwealth and Foreign Campaign Medals and Clasps for British Troops

Full Title of Medal Clasp [if any]	Earliest date awarded	Latest date awarded
Ghuznee Medal	21/07/1839	23/07/1839
Turkish Crimea Medal	20/09/1854	22/09/1855
Khedive's Egyptian Star 1882	16/07/1882	14/09/1882
Tokar 1308H	19/02/1891	19/02/1891
Khedive's Egyptian Star 1884	19/02/1884	26/03/1884
Tokar 1308H	19/02/1891	19/02/1891
Khedive's Egyptian Star 1884-86	26/03/1884	07/10/1886
Tokar 1308H	19/02/1891	19/02/1891
Khedive's Egyptian Star (1887 & 1889)		
—	01/01/1887	31/12/1889
Tokar 1308H	19/02/1891	19/02/1891
Hunza Nagar Badge 1891		
Burma 1889-92	16/04/1892	18/04/1892
Lushai 1889-92	11/01/1889	08/06/1892
Chin Hills 1892-93	19/10/1892	10/03/1893
Kachin Hills 1892-93	03/12/1892	03/03/1893
Waziristan 1894-95	22/10/1894	13/03/1895
Khedive's Sudan Medal 1896-1908		
—	30/03/1896	23/09/1896
Firket	30/03/1896	07/06/1896
Hafir	19/09/1896	19/09/1896
Abu Hamed	15/07/1897	02/09/1898
Sudan 1897	15/07/1897	06/11/1897
The Atbara	08/04/1898	08/04/1898
Khartoum	02/09/1898	02/09/1898
Ghedaref	07/09/1898	26/12/1898
Gedid	22/11/1899	24/11/1899
Sudan 1899	01/01/1899	31/12/1899
Bahr-el-Ghazal 1900-02	13/12/1900	28/04/1902
Jerok	11/02/1904	03/03/1904
Nyam-Nyam	01/01/1905	31/05/1905
Talodi	25/05/1905	17/06/1905
Katfia	01/05/1908	02/05/1908
Nyima	01/11/1908	21/11/1908
Sudan Medal		
—	09/02/1910	20/01/1922
Atwot	09/02/1910	04/04/1910
S Kordofan 1910	10/11/1910	19/12/1910
Sudan 1912	12/10/1911	12/04/1912
Zeraf 1913-14	18/12/1913	20/02/1914
Mandal	01/03/1914	10/04/1914

Commonwealth and Foreign Campaign Medals and Clasps for British Troops (cont)

Full Title of Medal Clasp [if any]	Earliest date awarded	Latest date awarded
Sudan Medal		
Mongalla 1915-16	01/01/1915	14/03/1916
Miri	13/04/1915	12/06/1915
Darfur 1916	01/03/1916	31/12/1916
Fasher	15/05/1916	23/05/1916
Lau Nuer	27/02/1917	25/04/1917
Nyima 1917-18	05/04/1917	21/02/1918
Atwot 1918	13/03/1918	25/05/1918
Garjak Nuer	13/05/1919	26/04/1920
Aliab Dinka	08/11/1919	06/05/1920
Nyala	26/09/1921	20/01/1922
Darfur 1921	26/09/1921	22/11/1921
Malay Active Service Medal	31/08/1957	15/09/1963
Ghana Congo Medal		
Congo	01/07/1960	30/06/1964
Kenya Campaign Medal		
(North Eastern Kenya)	12/12/1963	30/11/1967
Oman General Service Medal		
Dhofar	23/05/1965	30/06/1976
Oman As Sumood Medal	23/05/1965	02/12/1975
Oman Peace Medal		
Operational Award	23/05/1965	01/07/1984
—	01/07/1976	17/11/1985
Iraq Flood Rescue Medal	01/01/1966	01/01/1966
Malaysian General Service Medal	11/08/1966	?
Brunei Service Medal	12/08/1966	Current (1998)
Czech Peacekeeping Medal	01/01/1997	01/01/1997

Appendix 3 to Chapter 2

Commemorative Medals in Order of Date of Event (Not Order of Wear)

Full title of Medal	Date of occasion
Queen Victoria's Jubilee Medal in Gold, 1887 clasp "1897"	21/06/1887 20/06/1897
Queen Victoria's Jubilee Medal in Silver, 1887 clasp "1897"	21/06/1887 20/06/1897
Queen Victoria's Jubilee Medal in Bronze, 1887 clasp "1897"	21/06/1887 20/06/1897
Queen Victoria's Police Jubilee Medal, 1887 clasp "1897"	21/06/1887 20/06/1897
Queen Victoria's Diamond Jubilee Medal for Lord Mayors and Lord Provosts in Gold, 1897	20/06/1897
Queen Victoria's Diamond Jubilee Medal for Mayors and Provosts in Silver, 1897	20/06/1897
Queen Victoria's Diamond Jubilee Medal in Gold, 1897	20/06/1897
Queen Victoria's Diamond Jubilee Medal in Silver, 1897	20/06/1897
Queen Victoria's Diamond Jubilee Medal in Bronze, 1897	20/06/1897
Queen Victoria's Diamond Jubilee Police Medal 1897	20/06/1897
Queen Victoria's Commemoration Medal, 1900 (Ireland)	03/04/1900
King Edward VII's Coronation Medal for Lord Mayors, Lord Provosts, Mayors and Provosts 1902	09/08/1902
King Edward VII's Coronation Medal in Silver, 1902	09/08/1902
King Edward VII's Coronation Medal in Bronze, 1902	09/08/1902
King Edward VII's Police Coronation Medal in Silver	09/08/1902
King Edward VII's Police Coronation Medal in Bronze	09/08/1902
King Edward VII's Delhi Durbar Medal 1903 in Gold	01/01/1903
King Edward VII's Delhi Durbar Medal 1903 in Silver	01/01/1903
King Edward VII's Delhi Durbar Medal 1903 in Bronze	01/01/1903
King Edward VII's Police Medal, 1903 (Scotland)	11/05/1903
King Edward VII's Visit Commemoration Medal in Silver 1903 (Ireland)	31/07/1903
King Edward VII's Visit Commemoration Medal in Bronze 1903 (Ireland)	31/07/1903

Commemorative Medals in Order of Date of Event (Not Order of Wear) (cont)

Full title of Medal	Date of occasion
Union of South Africa Commemoration Medal 1910	31/05/1910
King George V's Coronation Medal 1911	22/06/1911
Clasp "Delhi"	12/12/1911
King George V's Police Coronation Medal 1911	22/06/1911
King George V's Commemoration Medal 1911 (Ireland)	07/07/1911
King George V's Delhi Durbar Medal 1911 in Gold	12/12/1911
King George V's Delhi Durbar Medal 1911 in Silver	12/12/1911
King George V's Delhi Durbar Medal 1911 in Bronze	12/12/1911
King George V's Silver Jubilee Medal 1935	06/05/1935
King George VI's Coronation Medal 1937	12/05/1937
India Independence Medal	15/08/1947
Pakistan Medal	01/01/1948
Ceylon Police Independence Medal (1948)	01/01/1948
Ceylon Armed Forces Inauguration Medal	01/01/1950
Queen Elizabeth II's Coronation Medal 1953	02/06/1953
Ghana Republic Commemorative Medal	01/07/1960
Nigeria Independence Medal	01/10/1960
Sierra Leone Independence Medal	27/04/1961
Jamaica Independence Medal	06/08/1962
Uganda Independence Medal	09/10/1962
Uniformed Services Malaysia Medal (Singapore)	16/09/1963
Malawi Independence Medal	06/07/1964
Royal Brunei Malay Regiment Inauguration Medal	31/05/1965
Iran Coronation Medal	01/01/1966
Guyana Independence Medal	26/05/1966
Canadian Centennial Medal	01/01/1967
Fiji Independence Medal	01/01/1970
Papua New Guinea Independence Medal	16/09/1975
Queen Elizabeth II's Silver Jubilee Medal 1977	06/02/1977

Commemorative Medals in Order of Date of Event (Not Order of Wear) (cont)

Full title of Medal	Date of occasion
Gilbert Islands Independence Medal	01/01/1978
Ellis Island Independence Medal	01/05/1978
Solomon Islands Independence Medal	07/07/1978
Zimbabwe Independence Medal (Silver)	01/12/1979
Zimbabwe Independence Medal (Bronze)	01/12/1979
Vanuatu Independence Medal	28/08/1980
St Christopher Nevis Independence Medal	01/01/1983
Swaziland Independence Medal	01/01/1983
Papua New Guinea 10 year Independence Medal	16/09/1985
New Zealand 1990 Commemoration Medal	01/01/1990
Commemoration Medal for the 125th Anniversary of Confederation 1992 (Canada)	01/01/1992
Belize Defence Force 15th Anniversary Medal	05/02/1993
New Zealand Suffrage Centennial Medal 1993	19/09/1993
Unitas Medal (South Africa)	01/07/1994

Chapter 3

1844 TO 1913

THE first medal to be instituted in a modern context, ignoring Orders and Gold Medals for senior commanders in the field and some very early campaign medals including a few to the East India Company, was the Waterloo Medal 1815, instituted in 1816. This concept of campaign medals for all ranks was due to a suggestion by the Duke of Wellington. After this, in 1830, there came the Long Service and Good Conduct Medal (Army); the naval version of this in 1831; and the Meritorious Service Medal and the Medal for Distinguished Conduct in the Field followed in 1845. It was not until 1847, after heated discussion in Parliament and largely as a result of the efforts of the Duke of Richmond, that the Army General Service Medal was produced covering campaigns from 1801 to 1814. The naval equivalent was instituted in the same year for engagements from 1793 to 1840. Other campaign medals were instituted around that time and the current system has evolved from these beginnings.

The first mention of "medals" in Army Regulations is to be found in Queen's Regulations 1844 where a "Silver Medal with gratuity to non-commissioned officers and soldiers" is mentioned as having the Royal Arms and "for Long Service and Good Conduct" on the reverse. In fact the "Royal Arms" was a trophy of arms on the obverse of the medal.

The regulations had been expanded by 1859 to mention also the Medal for Meritorious Service with annuity for "Serjeants"; and "The Medal for Distinguished Conduct in the Field, Crimea" with gratuity for non-commissioned officers or soldiers. A directive from the War Office, Circular 1171 of 4 December 1854, stated that the Long Service and Good Conduct and the Meritorious Service Medals could be awarded, with gratuity, to men for bravery in the field. The latter was restricted to Serjeants but the former was open to Serjeants, Corporals and Privates with gratuities of fifteen pounds, ten pounds and five pounds respectively. It seems this did not find favour, for reasons to be repeated over the years. Five days later (9 December 1854) a vigorous article appeared in the *Naval and Military Gazette* pressing for a special medal for bravery and stating what is held to be Army opinion of the time "The man who was foremost in the charge and he who kept guard over the baggage, are decorated alike".

Queen's Regulations 1868 began to detail the method of wear by laying down that medals were worn only on the tunic; the ribbon was not to exceed one inch unless the number of clasps necessitated a longer one; the ribbons should be stitched to the coat or attached by a plain buckle without ornament. It also laid down that on undress uniform the ribbon only was to be worn and must not exceed half an inch in length. Up to this time medals had been worn to individual, or perhaps Regimental, tastes, often in a diamond pattern for four.

These Queen's Regulations also include the first regulations from the Foreign Office giving the guidelines for accepting and wearing foreign awards. Basically Orders could be accepted, with permission, only if the individuals were in the service of the foreign power and the award was in consequence of active and distinguished service before the enemy. No titles were to be adopted and permission was needed from the Queen after the War Office had a chance to comment. The regulations went on to exclude the Royal Guelphic Order of Hanover which, it said, was not foreign and was a "personal favour" bestowed on British subjects by the British Sovereign. The regulations regarding foreign medals continued to the effect that the Field Marshal the Commander-in-Chief or Lord of the Admiralty were permitted to give permission to wear these but only if the military or naval services were performed by command of, or with the sanction of, Her Majesty. No permission was required if the medal was not to be worn.

Queen's Regulations 1873 repeated the above and added that "Medals awarded by a Society for bravery in saving human life are, if specially authorised, to be worn on the right breast".

In Queen's Regulations 1881 the first of the lists of order of wear was included. It laid down that military decorations and medals were to be worn on the left breast and the buckles of the third class of the Order of the Bath and of St. Michael and St. George were to show. It appears that the term "Decorations" at that time was used to include "Orders" but to exclude "Medals". The latter title probably included the Victoria Cross. Also, it should be noted that the third class of orders were, at that time, worn on the medal bar on the left breast. Hence the reference to the buckle showing, this was usually a rectangular metal piece with two to four prongs worn centrally on, or at the top of, the ribbon or sometimes in both places. QR 1881 also said that medals were worn over the sash and under the pouch belt. What this meant was not explained but presumably the sash was the one worn by officers in full dress. In later regulations it is amplified by adding "worn by Scottish regiments". The QR continued with the order of arrangement which was:

1. English decorations.
2. English medals.
3. Foreign decorations.
4. Foreign medals.

Various notes and comments stated that the Victoria Cross, when suspended from the bar, came immediately after the badge of the Order of the Indian Empire. This would mean the third class or Companionship badge. The Medal for Distinguished Conduct in the Field was worn after the appropriate war medal and the Long Service and Good Conduct Medal and Medal for Meritorious Service came last. Whether this "last" actually included foreign awards was not specified. At that time one, not both, of these long service medals could be worn; the Long Service and Good Conduct Medal being returned on award of the Meritorious Service Medal. Best shots and life saving medals, if sanctioned, were worn on the right breast. Again it was not stated if this meant the Queen's Medal for Shooting, instituted in 1869, or the many "regimental" medals awarded and worn in profusion by some "shots" of the day, especially those in the Militia, Yeomanry and so on.

The regulations went on to give details of when knights were to wear their insignia and said that "KCB, KCSI, KCMG wear, in full dress, ribands of the Order over the collar of the tunic on all occasions when the Sovereign is present, the Sovereign is represented, or birthday, State occasion, Levee, Drawing Room and Ball". It also went on to state the provision that "Miniatures may be worn in undress by officers or the ribbons alone".

Queen's Regulations 1883 repeated this but instructed knights to wear the ribbons inside the tunic with two inches showing to suspend the badge. They also stated that ribbons were not to overlap and if necessary should be worn in two rows.

Queen's Regulations 1889 again gave the order of wear that was now:

- English decorations.
- Jubilee medals.
- English medals.
- The Order of St. John of Jerusalem in England.
- Foreign decorations and medals.

The notes included the same provisions for the VC, DCM and Long Service/Meritorious Service medals as were in QRs 1881.

In 1890 an Army Order (241) directed that ribands alone were to be worn with mess dress or undress by officers. Ribands of the Knights Grand Cross and Knights Companion were not to be worn; the Companion width was to be worn instead. It also banned wearing miniatures with uniform. However, these could be worn with evening dress (plain clothes) in the presence of the Royal Family, etc.

Queen's Regulations 1891 added notes to the effect that the Jubilee medals were worn before all English medals and the Order of St. John of Jerusalem in England (given a Royal Charter in 1888) after all English medals.

Army Dress Regulations 1891 consolidated most of the foregoing into one document omitting only the reference to miniatures. It stated that the Queen's Jubilee Medal was to be worn after English decorations and the badges of the Order of St. John of Jerusalem in England after English medals. In 1894 a new footnote was added to say that the Volunteer Officers' Decoration was to be worn immediately after English medals and before the Order of St. John of Jerusalem in England.

Queen's Regulations for 1892 and 1893 add nothing to the foregoing but apply to "men"; there is no mention of officers.

Queen's Regulations 1894 also stated that "The Volunteer Officers' Decoration will be worn immediately after English medals and before the Order of St. John of Jerusalem" and specifically mentioned that Royal Humane Society medals could be worn in uniform when authority was issued.

In 1895 the Albert Medals were added after the VC and the wording makes clear that "last" did indeed mean that the Long and Meritorious Service medals came after foreign awards. In 1898 soldiers are referred to the Dress Regulations for Officers regarding wearing medals. In 1899 soldiers who were in possession of the Long Service and Good Conduct Medal were permitted to retain it, but not wear it, if they subsequently received the Meritorious Service Medal

Dress Regulations for 1900 add a few details in that ribbons are one and a quarter inches wide; buckles of the third classes of the Bath and St. Michael and St. George are still to show; stars of foreign orders are worn on the right or left according to the custom of the country concerned; the stars of the Garter and Thistle are worn on the left. Also the rules for miniatures are unchanged except that the miniature is not worn if the order is worn round the neck. This last provision would apply in the main to Knights of the various orders, so a "double" Knight (KCB and KCMG) would need three sets of miniatures to allow for him wearing one or other or neither of his neck decorations. Not very practical, but probably not a great problem at the time. However one further complication had recently been added in that the new (1896) Royal Victorian Order had a third class (Commander) which was worn at the neck and took precedence over the older third classes. This was to reappear as a problem in connection with the Order of the British Empire much later on in 1917.

It is of note that, in all the foregoing instructions up to 1900, the position of wear for the Distinguished Service Order, instituted in 1886, is left to conjecture. The Royal Warrant of 1886 for the DSO places it after a Companion of the Order of the Indian Empire; this was amended in 1902 to place it after the Royal Victorian Order. After that it falls into the lists quoted in this book.

In Dress Regulations 1902 we see the first real signs of popular opinion being imposed. The earlier major conflicts, Crimea, China and Indian Mutiny had been remote and the issue of medals was in its infancy. The South African (Boer) War of 1899-1902 was closer to home as it involved large numbers of volunteers. This enhanced public interest and probably inspired the move of the Medal for Distinguished Conduct in the Field from behind the campaign medal for which it was awarded, to being ahead of all campaign medals. One other change was notified in Army Order 250 of 1902 permitting recipients of the Long Service and Good Conduct Medal to retain and wear it if they were subsequently awarded the Meritorious Service Medal.

Dress Regulations 1904 added little to the general instructions except to say that the first earned clasp on a campaign medal was to be worn nearest to the medal. The order of wear was expanded a little but the main innovation, following the spirit of the previous changes to the DCM, was that the Victoria Cross moved from its position after the various Orders to a prime place at the head of the order of wear. In addition the Distinguished Service Order moved above the fifth class of the Royal Victorian Order, probably for similar reasons to the VC and DCM moves. New additions included the Order of Merit, Imperial Service Order, Kaisar-i-Hind Medal, Colonial Auxiliary Forces long service awards and Board of Trade Medals for Saving Life at Sea. There were a few less significant amendments but they include a massive jump in position for the Albert Medals and Volunteer Officers' Decoration from behind to before the commemorative (Jubilee, etc.) medals. Although never distinguished in the order of wear there were three grades of Kaisar-i-Hind Medals, gold and silver, originally 1st and 2nd classes from 1900, with bronze added in 1933.

Army Order 196 of 1905 saw the Order of St. John of Jerusalem in England leap from last place to one place ahead of the newly added Conspicuous Service Cross (later becoming the Distinguished Service Cross) before the Albert Medals. The naval Conspicuous Gallantry Medal was placed, for the first time, just before the DCM and the Medal of the Order of St. John moved up one from behind to ahead of war medals. The Royal Victorian Medals and a few long service medals made their debut.

Dress Regulations 1911 consolidated the earlier position although the Imperial Service Order moved up the scale to a position between the DSO and MVO (5th Class). Otherwise the new regulations merely added the Territorial Decoration and Territorial Efficiency Medal plus the Naval Good Shooting Medal which was given for ships gunnery practices and was a rare award. It also added the Badge of the Order of the League of Mercy (established in 1899 by Royal Charter and wound up in 1947) in a surprising position immediately ahead of the Conspicuous Gallantry Medal. Certain other changes were made to the instructions for wear. The 1900 ruling, that miniatures could not be worn when the full sized Orders were worn, was rescinded. The position for wearing the buckles of the Companions of the Bath and St. Michael and St. George were specified as half way down the riband. There is also considerable detail regarding what could be worn with specific forms of dress and on what occasions. The instructions also included some information about wearing broad ribands, collars, stars and neck decorations. Collars are limited to wearing one at a time and are not worn with other insignia of the same Order. Broad ribands are also limited to one and worn over the right shoulder, except for the Garter and Thistle, which are worn over the left shoulder. The instructions on neck decorations are confusing and seem to say that one should be worn in Review Order, but two could be worn if the owner felt like it. How this was to be achieved was not detailed. Notes, which still appear today almost unchanged, are included regarding the wear of a higher class of a lower order before a lower class of a higher order; and that the Indian Order of Merit is unconnected with the Order of Merit. This last note was necessary because the Indian Order of Merit was originally known in India as simply "The Order of Merit".

Queen's Regulations 1912 stated that the only non-military medals allowed for wear in uniform were the Albert Medal, Edward Medal, Board of Trade Medal for Saving Life at Sea on the left; and the Royal Humane Society Medal and the Stanhope Gold Medal on the right. Army Order 17 of 1912 added the Royal National Life Boat Institute Medals on the right.

Army Order 246 of 1912 brought further additions, several stemming from the Indian Empire. For the first time the Order of British India and Indian Order of Merit (Military) appeared, and were joined by the Kaiser-i-Hind Medal, after the MVO (5th class) and before the Order of St. John of Jerusalem. There was a considerable upheaval in that the Albert Medals and Board of Trade Medal for Saving Life at Sea, moved abruptly downwards to come after both War medals and the newly added Polar Medals. The Conspicuous Service Cross also moved down to come after the Conspicuous Gallantry Medal. The Volunteer Officers' Decoration, its Colonial equivalents and the Territorial Decoration all moved to or joined the long service awards towards the end of the list and a number of new long service awards joined this group. Other new arrivals included the Constabulary Medal (Ireland), Edward Medals, Indian Order of Merit (Civil), Indian Distinguished Service Medal, King's Police Medal all placed between the Albert Medals and long service awards. The Naval Long Service and Good Conduct Medal joined the list after its Army counterpart and the Meritorious Service Medal moved down to come after both these medals. Also certain adjustments were made at the tail end of the list including splitting positions for the silver and bronze versions of the Royal Victorian Medals. All these were promulgated into Dress Regulations for 1911 by Army Order in 1913 when the Royal Red Cross was added to the list immediately after the Royal Marine (sic) Meritorious Service Medal. At that time the Royal Red Cross consisted of one grade only.

This completed the changes which took place before the Great War and it is of note that the really significant alterations all relate to an enhancement of the appreciation of the rewards for soldiers generally, including Indian soldiers, as opposed to the previous preoccupation with senior officers. There is also the introduction of recognition of civilians with the acceptance of the Albert and Edward Medals for civilian gallantry, together with other awards such as the King's Police Medal, into the order of wear; although this recognition suffered a blow in their downward move in 1912. It is noteworthy too that the commemorative medals, Jubilee, Durbar, Royal Visits and Coronation, remain in a prominent position ahead of War medals and Polar medals. They were considered to be Royal gifts, much more than today, and as such to be treasured. So they got a prime position which, for most recipients would be first in their row.

Appendix 1 to Chapter 3

From Army Dress Regulations 1900

Titles	Post-nominals
Knight of the Most Noble Order of the Garter	KG
Knight of the Most Ancient and Most Noble Order of the Thistle	KT
Knight of the Most Illustrious Order of St. Patrick	KP
Knight Grand Cross of the Most Honourable Order of the Bath	GCB
Knight Grand Commander of the Most Exalted Order of the Star of India	GCSI
Knight Grand Cross of the Most Distinguished Order of St. Michael & St. George	GCMG
Knight Grand Commander of the Most Eminent Order of the Indian Empire	GCIE
Knight Grand Cross of the Royal Victorian Order	GCVO
Knight Commander of the Most Honourable Order of the Bath	KCB
Knight Commander of the Most Exalted Order of the Star of India	KCSI
Knight Commander of the Most Distinguished Order of St. Michael & St. George	KCMG
Knight Commander of the Most Eminent Order of the Indian Empire	KCIE
Knight Commander of the Royal Victorian Order	KCVO
Commander of the Royal Victorian Order	CVO
Companion of the Most Honourable Order of the Bath	CB
Companion of the Most Exalted Order of the Star of India	CSI
Companion of the Most Distinguished Order of St. Michael & St. George	CMG
Companion of the Most Eminent Order of the Indian Empire	CIE
Member of the Fourth Class of the Royal Victorian Order	MVO
Member of the Fifth Class of the Royal Victorian Order	MVO
Victoria Cross	VC
Companion of the Distinguished Service Order	DSO
Queen Victoria's Jubilee Medal, 1887 (Gold, Silver & Bronze)	
Queen Victoria's Jubilee Medal, 1897 (Gold, Silver & Bronze)	
Albert Medals (Sea & Land 1st & 2nd Class)	

From Army Dress Regulations 1900 (cont)

Titles   Post-nominals

War Medals in order of date of award

Medal for Distinguished Conduct after the campaign medal
for which it was awarded

Order of St. John of Jerusalem in England (All Classes)

Medal for Meritorious Service

Medal for Long Service and Good Conduct (Army)

Volunteer Officers' Decoration   VD

Foreign Orders (by date of award)

Foreign Decorations (by date of award)

Foreign Medals (by date of award)

Appendix 2 to Chapter 3

From Army Order 181 of 1902

Change Titles	Post-nominals
Knight of the Most Noble Order of the Garter	KG
Knight of the Most Ancient and Most Noble Order of the Thistle	KT
Knight of the Most Illustrious Order of St. Patrick	KP
Knight Grand Cross of the Most Honourable Order of the Bath	GCB
Knight Grand Commander of the Most Exalted Order of the Star of India	GCSI
Knight Grand Cross of the Most Distinguished Order of St. Michael & St. George	GCMG
Knight Grand Commander of the Most Eminent Order of the Indian Empire	GCIE
Knight Grand Cross of the Royal Victorian Order	GCVO
Knight Commander of the Most Honourable Order of the Bath	KCB
Knight Commander of the Most Exalted Order of the Star of India	KCSI
Knight Commander of the Most Distinguished Order of St. Michael & St. George	KCMG
Knight Commander of the Most Eminent Order of the Indian Empire	KCIE
Knight Commander of the Royal Victorian Order	KCVO
Commander of the Royal Victorian Order	CVO
Companion of the Most Honourable Order of the Bath	CB
Companion of the Most Exalted Order of the Star of India	CSI
Companion of the Most Distinguished Order of St. Michael & St. George	CMG
Companion of the Most Eminent Order of the Indian Empire	CIE
Member of the Fourth Class of the Royal Victorian Order	MVO
Member of the Fifth Class of the Royal Victorian Order	MVO
Victoria Cross	VC
Companion of the Distinguished Service Order	DSO
Queen Victoria's Jubilee Medal, 1887 (Gold, Silver & Bronze)	
Queen Victoria's Jubilee Medal, 1897 (Gold, Silver & Bronze)	

1844-1913

From Army Order 181 of 1902 (cont)

Change	Titles	Post-nominals
+	King Edward's Coronation Medal, 1902	
	Albert Medals (Sea & Land 1st & 2nd Class)	
*	Medal for Distinguished Conduct in the Field	
	War Medals in order of date of award	
	Order of St. John of Jerusalem in England (All Classes)	
	Medal for Meritorious Service	
	Medal for Long Service and Good Conduct (Army)	
	Volunteer Officers' Decoration	VD
	Foreign Orders (by date of award)	
	Foreign Decorations (by date of award)	
	Foreign Medals (by date of award)	

Key to "Change"
"+" = *addition*   "- (??)" = *deleted from this list*   "*" = *change of position/title.*

"Medals Will Be Worn"

From Army Dress Regulations 1904

Change	Titles	Post-nominals
*	Victoria Cross	VC
	Knight of the Most Noble Order of the Garter	KG
	Knight of the Most Ancient and Most Noble Order of the Thistle	KT
	Knight of the Most Illustrious Order of St. Patrick	KP
	Knight Grand Cross of the Most Honourable Order of the Bath	GCB
+	Member of the Order of Merit	OM
	Knight Grand Commander of the Most Exalted Order of the Star of India	GCSI
	Knight Grand Cross of the Most Distinguished Order of St. Michael & St. George	GCMG
	Knight Grand Commander of the Most Eminent Order of the Indian Empire	GCIE
	Knight Grand Cross of the Royal Victorian Order	GCVO
	Knight Commander of the Most Honourable Order of the Bath	KCB
	Knight Commander of the Most Exalted Order of the Star of India	KCSI
	Knight Commander of the Most Distinguished Order of St. Michael & St. George	KCMG
	Knight Commander of the Most Eminent Order of the Indian Empire	KCIE
	Knight Commander of the Royal Victorian Order	KCVO
	Commander of the Royal Victorian Order	CVO
	Companion of the Most Honourable Order of the Bath	CB
	Companion of the Most Exalted Order of the Star of India	CSI
	Companion of the Most Distinguished Order of St. Michael & St. George	CMG
	Companion of the Most Eminent Order of the Indian Empire	CIE
	Member of the Fourth Class of the Royal Victorian Order	MVO
	Companion of the Distinguished Service Order	DSO
*	Member of the Fifth Class of the Royal Victorian Order	MVO
*	Albert Medals (Sea & Land; Classes I & II (Gold & Bronze))	
+	Board of Trade Medal for Saving Life at Sea	
*	Volunteer Officers' Decoration	VD

From Army Dress Regulations 1904 (cont)

Change	Titles	Post-nominals
+	Colonial Auxiliary Forces Officers' Decoration	
+	Kaisar-i-Hind Medal (Classes I & II)	
+	Companion of the Imperial Service Order	ISO
	Queen Victoria's Jubilee Medal, 1887 (Gold, Silver & Bronze)	
	Queen Victoria's Jubilee Medal, 1897 (Gold, Silver & Bronze)	
+	Queen Victoria's Commemoration Medal, 1900 (Ireland)	
	King Edward's Coronation Medal, 1902	
	Medal for Distinguished Conduct in the Field	
	War Medals in order of date of award	
+	Medal of the Order of St. John of Jerusalem in England	
	Medal for Meritorious Service	
	Medal for Long Service and Good Conduct (Army)	
+	Volunteer Long Service Medal	
*	Order of St. John (All Classes)	
	Foreign Orders (by date of award)	
	Foreign Decorations (by date of award)	
	Foreign Medals (by date of award)	

Key to "Change"
"+" = *addition*   "- (??)" = *deleted from this list*   "*" = *change of position/title.*

Appendix 4 to Chapter 3

From Army Order 196 of 1905

Change	Titles	Post-nominals
	Victoria Cross	VC
	Knight of the Most Noble Order of the Garter	KG
	Knight of the Most Ancient and Most Noble Order of the Thistle	KT
	Knight of the Most Illustrious Order of St. Patrick	KP
	Knight Grand Cross of the Most Honourable Order of the Bath	GCB
	Member of the Order of Merit	OM
	Knight Grand Commander of the Most Exalted Order of the Star of India	GCSI
	Knight Grand Cross of the Most Distinguished Order of St. Michael & St. George	GCMG
	Knight Grand Commander of the Most Eminent Order of the Indian Empire	GCIE
	Knight Grand Cross of the Royal Victorian Order	GCVO
	Knight Commander of the Most Honourable Order of the Bath	KCB
	Knight Commander of the Most Exalted Order of the Star of India	KCSI
	Knight Commander of the Most Distinguished Order of St. Michael & St. George	KCMG
	Knight Commander of the Most Eminent Order of the Indian Empire	KCIE
	Knight Commander of the Royal Victorian Order	KCVO
	Commander of the Royal Victorian Order	CVO
	Companion of the Most Honourable Order of the Bath	CB
	Companion of the Most Exalted Order of the Star of India	CSI
	Companion of the Most Distinguished Order of St. Michael & St. George	CMG
	Companion of the Most Eminent Order of the Indian Empire	CIE
	Member of the Fourth Class of the Royal Victorian Order	MVO
	Companion of the Distinguished Service Order	DSO
	Member of the Fifth Class of the Royal Victorian Order	MVO
*	Order of St. John (All Classes)	
+	Conspicuous Service Cross	CSC

1844-1913

From Army Order 196 of 1905 (cont)

Change	Titles	Post-nominals
	Albert Medals (Sea & Land; Classes I & II (Gold & Bronze))	
	Board of Trade Medal for Saving Life at Sea	
	Volunteer Officers' Decoration	VD
	Colonial Auxiliary Forces Officers' Decoration	
	Kaisar-i-Hind Medal (Classes I & II)	
	Companion of the Imperial Service Order	ISO
	Queen Victoria's Jubilee Medal, 1887 (Gold, Silver & Bronze)	
	Queen Victoria's Police Jubilee Medal, 1887	
	Queen Victoria's Jubilee Medal, 1897 (Gold, Silver & Bronze)	
	Queen Victoria's Police Jubilee Medal 1897	
	Queen Victoria's Commemoration Medal, 1900 (Ireland)	
	King Edward's Coronation Medal, 1902	
+	King Edward's Police Coronation Medal, 1902	
+	King Edward's Durbar Medal, 1903 (Gold, Silver & Bronze)	
+	King Edward's Police Medal, 1903 (Scotland)	
+	King's Visit Commemoration Medal, 1903 (Ireland)	
+	Conspicuous Gallantry Medal	
	Medal for Distinguished Conduct in the Field	
+	Royal Victorian Medal (Silver and Bronze)	
*	Medal of the Order of St. John of Jerusalem in England	
	War Medals in order of date of award	
	Medal for Meritorious Service	
	Medal for Long Service and Good Conduct (Army)	
+	Militia Long Service Medal	
+	Imperial Yeomanry Long Service Medal	
	Volunteer Long Service Medal	
	Foreign Orders (by date of award)	
	Foreign Decorations (by date of award)	
	Foreign Medals (by date of award)	

Key to "Change"
"+" = addition   "- (??)" = deleted from this list   "*" = change of position/title.

Appendix 5 to Chapter 3

From Army Dress Regulations 1911

Change	Titles	Post-nominals
	Victoria Cross	VC
	Knight of the Most Noble Order of the Garter	KG
	Knight of the Most Ancient and Most Noble Order of the Thistle	KT
	Knight of the Most Illustrious Order of St. Patrick	KP
	Knight Grand Cross of the Most Honourable Order of the Bath	GCB
	Member of the Order of Merit	OM
	Knight Grand Commander of the Most Exalted Order of the Star of India	GCSI
	Knight Grand Cross of the Most Distinguished Order of St. Michael & St. George	GCMG
	Knight Grand Commander of the Most Eminent Order of the Indian Empire	GCIE
	Knight Grand Cross of the Royal Victorian Order	GCVO
	Knight Commander of the Most Honourable Order of the Bath	KCB
	Knight Commander of the Most Exalted Order of the Star of India	KCSI
	Knight Commander of the Most Distinguished Order of St. Michael & St. George	KCMG
	Knight Commander of the Most Eminent Order of the Indian Empire	KCIE
	Knight Commander of the Royal Victorian Order	KCVO
	Commander of the Royal Victorian Order	CVO
	Companion of the Most Honourable Order of the Bath	CB
	Companion of the Most Exalted Order of the Star of India	CSI
	Companion of the Most Distinguished Order of St. Michael & St. George	CMG
	Companion of the Most Eminent Order of the Indian Empire	CIE
	Member of the Fourth Class of the Royal Victorian Order	MVO
	Companion of the Distinguished Service Order	DSO
*	Companion of the Imperial Service Order	ISO
	Member of the Fifth Class of the Royal Victorian Order	MVO

1844-1913

From Army Dress Regulations 1911 (cont)

Change	Titles	Post-nominals
	Order of St. John (All Classes)	
	Conspicuous Service Cross	CSC
	Albert Medals (Sea & Land; Classes I & II (Gold & Bronze))	
	Board of Trade Medal for Saving Life at Sea	
	Volunteer Officers' Decoration	VD
+	Territorial Decoration	
	Colonial Auxiliary Forces Officers' Decoration	
	Kaisar-i-Hind Medal (Classes I & II)	
	Queen Victoria's Jubilee Medal, 1887 (Gold, Silver & Bronze)	
	Queen Victoria's Police Jubilee Medal, 1887	
	Queen Victoria's Jubilee Medal, 1897 (Gold, Silver & Bronze)	
	Queen Victoria's Police Jubilee Medal, 1897	
	Queen Victoria's Commemoration Medal, 1900 (Ireland)	
	King Edward's Coronation Medal, 1902	
	King Edward's Police Coronation Medal, 1902	
	King Edward's Durbar Medal, 1903 (Gold, Silver & Bronze)	
	King Edward's Police Medal, 1903 (Scotland)	
	King's Visit Commemoration Medal, 1903 (Ireland)	
+	King George's Coronation Medal, 1911	
+	King George's Police Coronation Medal, 1911	
+	King's Visit Police Commemoration Medal, 1911 (Ireland)	
+	King George's Durbar Medal, 1911 (Gold, Silver & Bronze)	
+	Badge of the Order of the League of Mercy	
	Conspicuous Gallantry Medal	
	Medal for Distinguished Conduct in the Field	
	Royal Victorian Medal (Silver and Bronze)	
	Medal of the Order of St. John of Jerusalem in England	
	War Medals in order of date of award	
	Medal for Meritorious Service	

From Army Dress Regulations 1911 (cont)

Change Titles   Post-nominals

        Medal for Long Service and Good Conduct (Army)

        Militia Long Service Medal

        Imperial Yeomanry Long Service Medal

        Volunteer Long Service Medal

+   Territorial Efficiency Medal

+   Medal for Good Shooting (Naval)

        Foreign Orders (by date of award)

        Foreign Decorations (by date of award)

        Foreign Medals (by date of award)

Key to "Change"
"+" = addition   *"- (??)" = deleted from this list*   *"*" = change of position/title.*

Appendix 6 to Chapter 3

From Army Order 246 of 1912

Change	Titles	Post-nominals
	Victoria Cross	VC
	Knight of the Most Noble Order of the Garter	KG
	Knight of the Most Ancient and Most Noble Order of the Thistle	KT
	Knight of the Most Illustrious Order of St. Patrick	KP
	Knight Grand Cross of the Most Honourable Order of the Bath	GCB
	Member of the Order of Merit	OM
	Knight Grand Commander of the Most Exalted Order of the Star of India	GCSI
	Knight Grand Cross of the Most Distinguished Order of St. Michael & St. George	GCMG
	Knight Grand Commander of the Most Eminent Order of the Indian Empire	GCIE
	Knight Grand Cross of the Royal Victorian Order	GCVO
	Knight Commander of the Most Honourable Order of the Bath	KCB
	Knight Commander of the Most Exalted Order of the Star of India	KCSI
	Knight Commander of the Most Distinguished Order of St. Michael & St. George	KCMG
	Knight Commander of the Most Eminent Order of the Indian Empire	KCIE
	Knight Commander of the Royal Victorian Order	KCVO
	Commander of the Royal Victorian Order	CVO
	Companion of the Most Honourable Order of the Bath	CB
	Companion of the Most Exalted Order of the Star of India	CSI
	Companion of the Most Distinguished Order of St. Michael & St. George	CMG
	Companion of the Most Eminent Order of the Indian Empire	CIE
	Member of the Fourth Class of the Royal Victorian Order	MVO
	Companion of the Distinguished Service Order	DSO
	Companion of the Imperial Service Order	ISO
	Member of the Fifth Class of the Royal Victorian Order	MVO
+	Order of British India	OBI
+	Indian Order of Merit (Military)	IOM

From Army Order 246 of 1912 (cont)

Change	Titles	Post-nominals
*	Kaisar-i-Hind Medal (Classes I & II)	
	Order of St. John (All Classes)	
	Queen Victoria's Jubilee Medal, 1887 (Gold, Silver & Bronze)	
	Queen Victoria's Police Jubilee Medal, 1887	
	Queen Victoria's Jubilee Medal, 1897 (Gold, Silver & Bronze)	
	Queen Victoria's Police Jubilee Medal, 1897	
	Queen Victoria's Commemoration Medal, 1900 (Ireland)	
	King Edward VII's Coronation Medal, 1902	
	King Edward VII's Police Coronation Medal, 1902	
	King Edward VII's Durbar Medal, 1903 (Gold, Silver & Bronze)	
	King Edward VII's Police Medal, 1903 (Scotland)	
	King's Visit Commemoration Medal, 1903 (Ireland)	
	King George V's Coronation Medal, 1911	
	King George V's Police Coronation Medal, 1911	
	King's Visit Police Commemoration Medal, 1911 (Ireland)	
	King George V's Durbar Medal, 1911 (Gold, Silver & Bronze)	
	Medal for Distinguished Conduct in the Field	
*	Conspicuous Gallantry Medal	
*	Conspicuous Service Cross	CSC
	War Medals in order of date of award	
+	Arctic Medal 1815-1855	
+	Arctic Medal 1876	
+	Antarctic Medal 1901-1903	
+	Constabulary Medal (Ireland)	
*	Albert Medals (Sea & Land; Classes I & II (Gold & Bronze))	
*	Board of Trade Medal for Saving Life at Sea	
+	Indian Order of Merit (Civil)	IOM
+	Edward Medal (1st & 2nd Classes)(Silver and Bronze)	EM
+	Indian Distinguished Service Medal	

1844-1913

From Army Order 246 of 1912 (cont)

Change	Titles	Post-nominals
+	King's Police Medal	
	Medal for Long Service and Good Conduct (Army)	
+	Naval Long Service and Good Conduct Medal	
*	Medal for Meritorious Service	
+	Indian Long Service and Good Conduct Medal (for Europeans of Indian Army)	
+	Indian Meritorious Service Medal (for Europeans of Indian Army)	
+	Royal Marine Meritorious Service Medal	
+	Indian Long Service and Good Conduct Medal (for Native Army)	
+	Indian Meritorious Service Medal (for Native Army)	
*	Volunteer Officers' Decoration	VD
*	Volunteer Long Service Medal	
+	Volunteer Officers' Decoration (for India & the Colonies)	VD
+	Volunteer Long Service Medal (for India & the Colonies)	
*	Colonial Auxiliary Forces Officers' Decoration	
+	Colonial Auxiliary Forces Long Service Medal	
*	Medal for Good Shooting (Naval)	
	Militia Long Service Medal	
	Imperial Yeomanry Long Service Medal	
	Territorial Efficiency Medal	
*	Territorial Decoration	
+	Special Reserve Long Service and Good Conduct Medal	
+	Decoration for Officers of the Royal Naval Reserve	RD
+	Decoration for Officers of the Royal Naval Volunteer Reserve	VD
+	Royal Naval Reserve Long Service and Good Conduct Medal	
+	Royal Naval Volunteer Reserve Long Service and Good Conduct Medal	
+	Union of South Africa Commemoration Medal	
*	Royal Victorian Medal (Silver)	

From Army Order 246 of 1912 (cont)

Change Titles   Post-nominals

+   Imperial Service Medal

*   Medal of the Order of St. John of Jerusalem in England

+   Badge of the Order of the League of Mercy

*   Royal Victorian Medal (Bronze)

        Foreign Orders (by date of award)

        Foreign Decorations (by date of award)

        Foreign Medals (by date of award)

Key to "Change"
"+" = addition   *"- (??)" = deleted from this list*   *"*" = change of position/title.*

Appendix 7 to Chapter 3

From Army Dress Regulations 1911 amended 1913

Change	Titles	Post-nominals
	Victoria Cross	VC
	Knight of the Most Noble Order of the Garter	KG
	Knight of the Most Ancient and Most Noble Order of the Thistle	KT
	Knight of the Most Illustrious Order of St. Patrick	KP
	Knight Grand Cross of the Most Honourable Order of the Bath	GCB
	Member of the Order of Merit	OM
	Knight Grand Commander of the Most Exalted Order of the Star of India	GCSI
	Knight Grand Cross of the Most Distinguished Order of St. Michael & St. George	GCMG
	Knight Grand Commander of the Most Eminent Order of the Indian Empire	GCIE
	Knight Grand Cross of the Royal Victorian Order	GCVO
	Knight Commander of the Most Honourable Order of the Bath	KCB
	Knight Commander of the Most Exalted Order of the Star of India	KCSI
	Knight Commander of the Most Distinguished Order of St. Michael & St. George	KCMG
	Knight Commander of the Most Eminent Order of the Indian Empire	KCIE
	Knight Commander of the Royal Victorian Order	KCVO
	Commander of the Royal Victorian Order	CVO
	Companion of the Most Honourable Order of the Bath	CB
	Companion of the Most Exalted Order of the Star of India	CSI
	Companion of the Most Distinguished Order of St. Michael & St. George	CMG
	Companion of the Most Eminent Order of the Indian Empire	CIE
	Member of the Fourth Class of the Royal Victorian Order	MVO
	Companion of the Distinguished Service Order	DSO
	Companion of the Imperial Service Order	ISO
	Member of the Fifth Class of the Royal Victorian Order	MVO

From Army Dress Regulations 1911 amended 1913 (cont)

Change Titles	Post-nominals
Order of British India	OBI
Indian Order of Merit (Military)	IOM
Kaisar-i-Hind Medal (Classes I & II)	
Order of St. John (All Classes)	
Queen Victoria's Jubilee Medal, 1887 (Gold, Silver & Bronze)	
Queen Victoria's Police Jubilee Medal, 1887	
Queen Victoria's Jubilee Medal, 1897 (Gold, Silver & Bronze)	
Queen Victoria's Police Jubilee Medal, 1897	
Queen Victoria's Commemoration Medal, 1900 (Ireland)	
King Edward VII's Coronation Medal, 1902	
King Edward VII's Police Coronation Medal, 1902	
King Edward VII's Durbar Medal, 1903 (Gold, Silver & Bronze)	
King Edward VII's Police Medal, 1903 (Scotland)	
King's Visit Commemoration Medal, 1903 (Ireland)	
King George V's Coronation Medal, 1911	
King George V's Police Coronation Medal, 1911	
King's Visit Police Commemoration Medal, 1911 (Ireland)	
King George V's Durbar Medal, 1911 (Gold, Silver & Bronze)	
Medal for Distinguished Conduct in the Field	
Conspicuous Gallantry Medal	
Conspicuous Service Cross	CSC
War Medals in order of date of award	
Arctic Medal 1815-1855	
Arctic Medal 1876	
Antarctic Medal 1901-1903	
Constabulary Medal (Ireland)	
Albert Medals (Sea & Land; Classes I & II (Gold & Bronze))	
Board of Trade Medal for Saving Life at Sea	
Indian Order of Merit (Civil)	IOM

From Army Dress Regulations 1911 amended 1913 (cont)

Change	Titles	Post-nominals
	Edward Medal (1st & 2nd Classes)(Silver and Bronze)	EM
	Indian Distinguished Service Medal	
	King's Police Medal	
	Medal for Long Service and Good Conduct (Army)	
	Naval Long Service and Good Conduct Medal	
	Medal for Meritorious Service	
	Indian Long Service and Good Conduct Medal (for Europeans of Indian Army)	
	Indian Meritorious Service Medal (for Europeans of Indian Army)	
	Royal Marine Meritorious Service Medal	
+	Royal Red Cross	
	Indian Long Service and Good Conduct Medal (for Native Army)	
	Indian Meritorious Service Medal (for Native Army)	
	Volunteer Officers' Decoration	VD
	Volunteer Long Service Medal	
	Volunteer Officers' Decoration (for India & the Colonies)	VD
	Volunteer Long Service Medal (for India & the Colonies)	
	Colonial Auxiliary Forces Officers' Decoration	
	Colonial Auxiliary Forces Long Service Medal	
	Medal for Good Shooting (Naval)	
	Militia Long Service Medal	
	Imperial Yeomanry Long Service Medal	
	Territorial Efficiency Medal	
	Territorial Decoration	
	Special Reserve Long Service and Good Conduct Medal	
	Decoration for Officers of the Royal Naval Reserve	RD
	Decoration for Officers of the Royal Naval Volunteer Reserve	VD
	Royal Naval Reserve Long Service and Good Conduct Medal	
	Royal Naval Volunteer Reserve Long Service and Good Conduct Medal	

From Army Dress Regulations 1911 amended 1913 (cont)

Change   Titles   Post-nominals

        Union of South Africa Commemoration Medal

        Royal Victorian Medal (Silver)

        Imperial Service Medal

        Medal of the Order of St. John of Jerusalem in England

        Badge of the Order of the League of Mercy

        Royal Victorian Medal (Bronze)

        Foreign Orders (by date of award)

        Foreign Decorations (by date of award)

        Foreign Medals (by date of award)

Key to "Change"
"+" = addition   "- (??)" = deleted from this list   "" = change of position/title.*

CHAPTER 4

1914 TO 1923

THE sheer magnitude of the conflict during the Great War brought about many changes to our system of honours. Not only was there a need for more awards, there was also a total change in public perceptions and attitudes after the war. The ordinary man who had taken such risks, and suffered so many casualties, wanted recognition of his efforts. The active part taken by women, unprecedented, both at home and abroad, needed recognition. The new dimension of the air demanded acknowledgement. "Native" troops, from India and the Colonies, had contributed bravely and steadfastly alongside British troops who recognised their worth as never before. All these factors had a marked effect on medals; in the scope available, in the numbers awarded, and in the relative importance one to another as reflected in the order of wear. Much of what follows is extracted from a Military Secretary's report on the subject made in 1920 which fully described both the development of various awards in the nineteenth century and the particular problems and solutions during the war.

In 1914 the awards generally available for war service connected with the British Army were:

Victoria Cross	All ranks
Order of the Bath	Majors and above
Distinguished Service Order	All officers
Distinguished Conduct Medal	All other ranks
Meritorious Service Medal	Sergeants
Royal Red Cross	Nurses

The Royal Navy had a similar list with the addition of the Conspicuous Service Cross, which had always carried the right to "CSC" after the name and was available for Warrant Officers and subordinate officers. In October 1914 this name changed to Distinguished Service Cross and the eligibility was altered to be Naval and Marine officers of the relative rank of Lieutenant Commander and below. In 1915 the letters "DSC" were permitted after the names of recipients.

The size of the conflict demanded that additional awards be made available. The Military Cross was instituted in December 1914 but the letters "MC" were specifically banned; this was the first official recognition that others such as "VC" and "DSO" were already in use. This ruling did not find favour, possibly due to the "DSC" used by the Royal Navy, and was reversed in 1916. However, it was not until Army Order 13 of 1918 that the "privilege" was extended to all similar distinctions including the RRC, ARRC, DCM and MM.

In 1915 a special statute extended the scope of the Order of St. Michael and St. George, normally for Colonial services, for award for "services during the present War" on exactly the same terms as the Order of the Bath. In November 1915 a second class was added to the Royal Red Cross for nurses who would become "Associates". At that time this award, although confined to women, was not just for executive nurses as there was no other reward for the associated administrative services. The institution of the Order of the British Empire in 1917 changed this situation and the Royal Red Cross was then awarded for nursing services alone, the First Class for fully trained nurses and the Second Class for all others performing executive nursing services actually in connection with the sick and wounded.

The Military Medal was instituted in March 1916. Initially restricted to non-commissioned officers and men it was later opened to Warrant Officers and to women. The Royal Navy and Royal Marines were ahead of the Army in this respect as their equivalent, the Distinguished Service Medal, had been instituted in 1914.

The institution of the Order of the British Empire in 1917 gave rise to a number of problems. It was in a single Division, which meant that all awards were regulated, recorded and published by the Home Office. Lists were published in alphabetical order, regardless of the circumstances of the award or whether the recipient was military or civilian. In addition although it was the junior Order it followed the precedent of the Royal Victorian Order whereby the third class badge was worn at the neck. In the other older Orders, the third class was worn on the left breast and, until now, the third class of the Royal Victorian Order, despite its "youth", had been regarded as senior to the other third classes. The solution to this particular problem was to move all third classes to the neck and decree the order of wear for this particular area to be—CB, CMG, CVO, DSO, MVO (4th), OBE, ISO, MVO (5th), MBE.

This could be termed cosmetic and real problems remained concerning both the new Order and the older awards. Of those available only the Victoria Cross and Military Medal were specifically for services under fire. The statutes for the DSO, MC and DCM had no such limitation and awards were being made to those in rear areas to the chagrin of those at the sharp end. However, except for the Meritorious Service Medal, limited to Sergeants, there was no other existing award available for merit until the Order of the British Empire was instituted in 1917. At the end of 1916 plans for the new Order were sufficiently advanced to allow the issue of instructions that the DSO, MC and DCM were to be restricted for specified services in the forward areas. The Order of the British Empire would deal with the others. But this it did not, mainly due to the lack of a clear military link as already discussed.

This led to consideration of the idea of dividing the DSO and MC into two classes with different ribbons, or added emblems to the ribbons, to denote whether they were for "fighting" or "non-fighting" services. The Army Council did not support this solution and it was shelved. The problems remained and in June 1918 a Conference of both staff and regimental officers, under the Military Secretary, addressed it again. Should there be two classes of DSO and MC? If so should they be retrospective to past wars? If adopted should the distinction be in the ribbon or an emblem on the existing ribbon? The Conference was strongly of the opinion that the proposal was unworkable and it recommended that the "fighting awards" should be restricted to "Services in action" which included "under fire" and enemy action such as bombardment and air raids. This was virtually in operation already so no changes were necessary.

However, the Conference did recognise the other problem of the Order of the British Empire having no military links. It recommended that there should be a Military Division under Military control with awards notified in lists identifying them as being for military services. This was accepted by the Army Council and approved by the King. It came into effect in August 1918 with the new rules and the addition of a red stripe on the ribbon of the Military Division. All earlier awards to those who became eligible for the Military Division were automatically transferred to the new division.

Before turning to the orders of wear published in 1918 there were some other visible changes made during the Great War in connection with ribbons and bars. Originally the Army Long Service and Good Conduct Medal and the Meritorious Service Medal had identical ribbons which were plain crimson. The Victoria Cross had a similarly coloured plain ribbon for the Army, while the Royal Navy used blue for both the VC and their Long Service medal. So it will be seen that a number of soldiers and sailors, especially early in the war, would have one ribbon which might be that for merit or long service but could easily be confused with a VC. To overcome this both the medal ribbons for the Army were altered to crimson with white edges in 1916 while in 1917 the Meritorious Service Medal had an additional white stripe added centrally. A similar change was made in the Royal Navy and white edges were added to the Long Service ribbon, also in 1916. In 1917 it was decided that the VC ribbon when worn alone would carry a miniature representation of the cross at the centre. Originally this had been added in 1916 to denote a bar but the change in 1917 meant that the holder of a VC and bar would, in future, wear two miniatures on the ribbon when worn alone.

The formation of the Royal Air Force in 1918 also gave rise to new awards in the form of the Distinguished Flying Cross and Medal and the Air Force Cross and Medal. These all had horizontal stripes to begin with but practical difficulties led to these being quickly changed to diagonal stripes.

The blue ribbon for the Naval VC was dropped in 1918 in favour of the Army crimson for all three services. In 1921 the Naval Conspicuous Gallantry Medal ribbon was altered to white with blue edges from equal blue, white, blue; i.e. the same as the Distinguished Service Cross though narrower.

The problem of second and subsequent awards also arose during the terrible fighting of the war. Before the war the Victoria Cross (1855), Albert Medals (1867/1877), Edward Medals (1907/1909), and Distinguished Conduct Medal (1881) had provision for "bars" from the years shown. The other awards, both those instituted during the War and earlier, had provision for bars made as follows:

Conspicuous Gallantry Medal	1916
Distinguished Service Medal	1916
Military Cross	1916
Military Medal	1916
Indian Distinguished Service Medal	1917
Royal Red Cross 1st Class	1917
Distinguished Service Order	1918
Distinguished Flying Cross	1918
Air Force Cross	1918
Distinguished Flying Medal	1918
Air Force Medal	1918

Although individual Warrants, etc., specified the order in which newly instituted awards were to be worn, no wartime publications on the order of wear have been traced until the issue of Army Council Instruction 754 of July 1918. This added all the war-time awards, largely in the expected order of wear, but with some features which clearly did not satisfy the climate of the day. The additions were the CI; CH; Order and Medal of the British Empire; DSC (formerly the CSC but now among the "officers' crosses"); MC; DFC; AFC and their counterparts as medals. The Albert Medals regained their position just after the Order of St. John.

However, the most contentious area obviously lay in the fact that the Jubilee, etc., medals retained their position not only ahead of the war and polar medals but also before all the bravery awards for "other ranks". That this did not satisfy the troops is evident in that Army Council 1230 of November 1918, published only four months later, made only one change and placed the Jubilee, etc., medals after "other ranks'" bravery awards, war medals, polar medals and the civilian bravery awards. This was a major alteration, and would have been unthinkable had it not been for the impact of the war on society. However, the instruction was somewhat marred by adding a note to the effect that officers should not go to the expense of changing their ribbons until they needed renewal anyway! This gave a strong impression that the move of these "Royal" medals was not to the liking of, at least, some people in the War Office, though to be fair this was the type of concession which was not unknown in that period. The changes prevailed and the first National list in the *London Gazette* in 1921 incorporated only three new alterations. It placed the Indian Distinguished Service Medal immediately after the AFM and before war medals; previously it had languished behind the Edward Medals, and some other civilian awards as well as the war and polar medals. The *London Gazette* also recorded the move of the Territorial Efficiency Medal from immediately before, to immediately after the Territorial Decoration. Finally it added the new Special Constabulary Medal among the long service awards. In the Army this order was confirmed by Army Council Instruction 1 of 1923 which made no changes except to add the Coast Life Saving Volunteer Corps Long Service Medal immediately before the Special Constabulary Medal. However, one other change was quietly made in the area now termed "political correctness". The long service and meritorious awards to the Indians changed from "for Native Army" to "for Indian Army". Quite a big alteration in thinking at that time which must have come about both from the events of the war and from rising Indian demands for independence.

In connection with War Medals the order of wear was first laid down in ACI 522 of 1919 as being 1914 Star, 1914-15 Star, British War Medal, Mercantile Marine War Medal, and Victory Medal. This was changed in ACI 751 of 1920 to make the two stars alternatives and add the Territorial Force War Medal and the Indian General Service Medal 1908 for Afghanistan 1919 to the end of the list. These particulars about War stars and medals did not appear in the list in the *London Gazette* of 1921.

One other instruction issued, presumably as a result of the number of foreign awards exchanged at high level, was contained in War Office letter 0137/9638(QMG 7) of 2 June 1921. This restricted the number of stars of orders permitted to be worn to four. As can be seen from the photograph of Mutiny VCs, this could have been a problem earlier but the wide use of Service Dress must have exacerbated the difficulties of fitting more stars into the space available. Old War Office files also contain letters enquiring about the status of foreign awards. One questioned that of the United States Army Distinguished Service Medal. It is an ornate medal with enamelling and normally awarded to senior officers, usually Generals. The decision on this was to treat it as a "decoration" not a "medal". The old problem of semantics again.

This concluded the alterations directly consequent on the war and showed a remarkable surge in the influence exerted by public opinion. It is of interest to note the total number of awards given during the war:

All Military Orders, Decoration, Medal and promotions

1914	1915	1916	1917	1918	1919	1920	Total
409	5,421	29,537	52,073	65,917	77,492	2,400	233,249

To this must be added 6,604 from India and 17,134 "in connection with the War" making a grand total of 256,987.

Mentioned in Despatches (not included above) alone amounted to

1914/15	1916	1917	1918	1919	1920	Total
9,407	22,991	36,137	33,054	37,948	1,545	141,082

This brings the overall total number of awards to 398,069.

Appendix 1 to Chapter 4

From Army Council Instructions 754 of 1918

Change	Titles	Post-nominals
	Victoria Cross	VC
	Knight of the Most Noble Order of the Garter	KG
	Knight of the Most Ancient and Most Noble Order of the Thistle	KT
	Knight of the Most Illustrious Order of St. Patrick	KP
	Knight Grand Cross of the Most Honourable Order of the Bath	GCB
	Member of the Order of Merit	OM
	Knight Grand Commander of the Most Exalted Order of the Star of India	GCSI
	Knight Grand Cross of the Most Distinguished Order of St. Michael & St. George	CMG
	Knight Grand Commander of the Most Eminent Order of the Indian Empire	GCIE
+	The Imperial Order of the Crown of India	CI
	Knight or Dame Grand Cross of the Royal Victorian Order	GCVO
+	Knight or Dame Grand Cross of the Most Excellent Order of the British Empire	GBE
+	Member of the Order of the Companions of Honour	CH
	Knight Commander of the Most Honourable Order of the Bath	KCB
	Knight Commander of the Most Exalted Order of the Star of India	KCSI
	Knight Commander of the Most Distinguished Order of St. Michael & St. George	KCMG
	Knight Commander of the Most Eminent Order of the Indian Empire	KCIE
	Knight Commander of the Royal Victorian Order	KCVO
+	Knight or Dame Commander of the Most Excellent Order of the British Empire	KBE/DBE
	Companion of the Most Honourable Order of the Bath	CB
	Companion of the Most Exalted Order of the Star of India	CSI
	Companion of the Most Distinguished Order of St. Michael & St. George	CMG
	Companion of the Most Eminent Order of the Indian Empire	CIE
*	Commander of the Royal Victorian Order	CVO

From Army Council Instructions 754 of 1918 (cont)

Change	Titles	Post-nominals
+	Commander of the Most Excellent Order of the British Empire	CBE
	Companion of the Distinguished Service Order	DSO
*	Member of the Fourth Class of the Royal Victorian Order	MVO
+	Officer of the Most Excellent Order of the British Empire	OBE
	Companion of the Imperial Service Order	ISO
	Member of the Fifth Class of the Royal Victorian Order	MVO
+	Member of the Most Excellent Order of the British Empire	MBE
*	Member of the Royal Red Cross	RRC
*	Distinguished Service Cross	DSC
+	Military Cross	MC
+	Distinguished Flying Cross	DFC
+	Air Force Cross	AFC
+	Associate of the Royal Red Cross	ARRC
	Order of British India	OBI
	Indian Order of Merit (Military)	IOM
	Kaisar-i-Hind Medal (Classes I & II)	
	Order of St. John of Jerusalem in England (All Classes)	
*	Albert Medal (Sea & Land; Classes I & II (Gold & Bronze))	AM
	Queen Victoria's Jubilee Medal, 1887 (Gold, Silver & Bronze)	
	Queen Victoria's Police Jubilee Medal, 1887	
	Queen Victoria's Jubilee Medal, 1897 (Gold, Silver & Bronze)	
	Queen Victoria's Police Jubilee Medal, 1897	
	Queen Victoria's Commemoration Medal, 1900 (Ireland)	
	King Edward VII's Coronation Medal, 1902	
	King Edward VII's Police Coronation Medal, 1902	
	King Edward VII's Durbar Medal, 1903 (Gold, Silver & Bronze)	
	King Edward VII's Police Medal, 1903 (Scotland)	
	King's Visit Commemoration Medal, 1903 (Ireland)	
	King George V's Coronation Medal, 1911	

1914-1923

From Army Council Instructions 754 of 1918 (cont)

Change	Titles	Post-nominals
	King George V's Police Coronation Medal, 1911	
	King's Visit Police Commemoration Medal, 1911 (Ireland)	
	King George V's Durbar Medal, 1911 (Gold, Silver & Bronze)	
	Medal for Distinguished Conduct in the Field	DCM
	Conspicuous Gallantry Medal	CGM
+	Distinguished Service Medal	DSM
+	Military Medal	MM
+	Distinguished Flying Medal	DFM
+	Air Force Medal	AFM
	War Medals (in order of date)	
	Arctic Medal 1815-1855	
	Arctic Medal 1876	
	Antarctic Medal 1901-1903	
	Constabulary Medal (Ireland)	
	Board of Trade Medal for Saving Life at Sea	
	Indian Order of Merit (Civil)	IOM
	Edward Medal (1st & 2nd Classes)(Silver and Bronze))	EM
	Indian Distinguished Service Medal	IDSM
	King's Police Medal	
*	Long Service and Good Conduct Medal	
	Naval Long Service and Good Conduct Medal	
	Medal for Meritorious Service	(MSM)
	Indian Long Service and Good Conduct Medal (for Europeans of Indian Army)	
	Indian Meritorious Service Medal (for Europeans of Indian Army)	
	Royal Marine Meritorious Service Medal	
	Indian Long Service and Good Conduct Medal (for Native Army)	
	Indian Meritorious Service Medal (for Native Army)	
	Volunteer Officers' Decoration	VD

From Army Council Instructions 754 of 1918 (cont)

Change	Titles	Post-nominals
	Volunteer Long Service Medal	
	Volunteer Officers' Decoration (for India & the Colonies)	VD
	Volunteer Long Service Medal (for India & the Colonies)	
	Colonial Auxiliary Forces Officers' Decoration	
	Colonial Auxiliary Forces Long Service Medal	
	Medal for Good Shooting (Naval)	
	Militia Long Service Medal	
	Imperial Yeomanry Long Service Medal	
	Territorial Efficiency Medal	
	Territorial Decoration	
	Special Reserve Long Service and Good Conduct Medal	
	Decoration for Officers of the Royal Naval Reserve	RD
	Decoration for Officers of the Royal Naval Volunteer Reserve	VD
	Royal Naval Reserve Long Service and Good Conduct Medal	
	Royal Naval Volunteer Reserve Long Service and Good Conduct Medal	
	Union of South Africa Commemoration Medal	
*	Royal Victorian Medal (Gold and Silver)	
	Imperial Service Medal	
+	Medal of the Order of the British Empire	
	Medal of the Order of St. John of Jerusalem in England	
	Badge of the Order of the League of Mercy	
	Royal Victorian Medal (Bronze)	
	Foreign Orders (in order of date of award)	
	Foreign Decorations (in order of date of award)	
	Foreign Medals (in order of date of award)	

Key to "Change"
"+" = addition   "- (??)" = deleted from this list   "*" = change of position/title.

Appendix 2 to Chapter 4

From Army Council Instructions 1230 of 1918

Change	Titles	Post-nominals
	Victoria Cross	VC
	Knight of the Most Noble Order of the Garter	KG
	Knight of the Most Ancient and Most Noble Order of the Thistle	KT
	Knight of the Most Illustrious Order of St. Patrick	KP
	Knight Grand Cross of the Most Honourable Order of the Bath	GCB
	Member of the Order of Merit	OM
	Knight Grand Commander of the Most Exalted Order of the Star of India	GCSI
	Knight Grand Cross of the Most Distinguished Order of St. Michael & St. George	GCMG
	Knight Grand Commander of the Most Eminent Order of the Indian Empire	GCIE
	The Imperial Order of the Crown of India	CI
	Knight or Dame Grand Cross of the Royal Victorian Order	GCVO
	Knight or Dame Grand Cross of the Most Excellent Order of the British Empire	GBE
	Member of the Order of the Companions of Honour	CH
	Knight Commander of the Most Honourable Order of the Bath	KCB
	Knight Commander of the Most Exalted Order of the Star of India	KCSI
	Knight Commander of the Most Distinguished Order of St. Michael & St. George	KCMG
	Knight Commander of the Most Eminent Order of the Indian Empire	KCIE
	Knight Commander of the Royal Victorian Order	KCVO
	Knight or Dame Commander of the Most Excellent Order of the British Empire	KBE/DBE
	Companion of the Most Honourable Order of the Bath	CB
	Companion of the Most Exalted Order of the Star of India	CSI
	Companion of the Most Distinguished Order of St. Michael & St. George	CMG
	Companion of the Most Eminent Order of the Indian Empire	CIE
	Commander of the Royal Victorian Order	CVO

From Army Council Instructions 1230 of 1918 (cont)

Change Titles   Post-nominals

    Commander of the Most Excellent Order of the British Empire   CBE

    Companion of the Distinguished Service Order   DSO

    Member of the Fourth Class of the Royal Victorian Order   MVO

    Officer of the Most Excellent Order of the British Empire   OBE

    Companion of the Imperial Service Order   ISO

    Member of the Fifth Class of the Royal Victorian Order   MVO

    Member of the Most Excellent Order of the British Empire   MBE

    Member of the Royal Red Cross   RRC

    Distinguished Service Cross   DSC

    Military Cross   MC

    Distinguished Flying Cross   DFC

    Air Force Cross   AFC

    Associate of the Royal Red Cross   ARRC

    Order of British India   OBI

    Indian Order of Merit (Military)   IOM

    Kaisar-i-Hind Medal (Classes I & II)

    Order of St. John of Jerusalem in England (All Classes)

    Albert Medal (Sea & Land; Classes I & II (Gold & Bronze))   AM

* Medal for Distinguished Conduct in the Field   DCM

* Conspicuous Gallantry Medal   CGM

* Distinguished Service Medal   DSM

* Military Medal   MM

* Distinguished Flying Medal   DFM

* Air Force Medal   AFM

* War Medals (in order of date)

* Arctic Medal 1815-1855

* Arctic Medal 1876

* Antarctic Medal 1901-1903

* Constabulary Medal (Ireland)

From Army Council Instructions 1230 of 1918 (cont)

Change	Titles	Post-nominals
*	Board of Trade Medal for Saving Life at Sea	
*	Indian Order of Merit (Civil)	IOM
*	Edward Medal (1st & 2nd Classes)(Silver and Bronze)	EM
*	Indian Distinguished Service Medal	IDSM
*	King's Police Medal	
	Queen Victoria's Jubilee Medal, 1887 (Gold, Silver & Bronze)	
	Queen Victoria's Police Jubilee Medal, 1887	
	Queen Victoria's Jubilee Medal, 1897 (Gold, Silver & Bronze)	
	Queen Victoria's Police Jubilee Medal, 1897	
	Queen Victoria's Commemoration Medal, 1900 (Ireland)	
	King Edward VII's Coronation Medal, 1902	
	King Edward VII's Police Coronation Medal, 1902	
	King Edward VII's Durbar Medal, 1903 (Gold, Silver & Bronze)	
	King Edward VII's Police Medal, 1903 (Scotland)	
	King's Visit Commemoration Medal, 1903 (Ireland)	
	King George V's Coronation Medal, 1911	
	King George V's Police Coronation Medal, 1911	
	King's Visit Police Commemoration Medal, 1911 (Ireland)	
	King George V's Durbar Medal, 1911 (Gold, Silver & Bronze)	
	Long Service and Good Conduct Medal	
	Naval Long Service and Good Conduct Medal	
	Medal for Meritorious Service	(MSM)
	Indian Long Service and Good Conduct Medal (for Europeans of Indian Army)	
	Indian Meritorious Service Medal (for Europeans of Indian Army)	
	Royal Marine Meritorious Service Medal	
	Indian Long Service and Good Conduct Medal (for Native Army)	
	Indian Meritorious Service Medal (for Native Army)	

From Army Council Instructions 1230 of 1918 (cont)

Change	Titles	Post-nominals
	Volunteer Officers' Decoration	VD
	Volunteer Long Service Medal	
	Volunteer Officers' Decoration (for India & the Colonies)	VD
	Volunteer Long Service Medal (for India & the Colonies)	
	Colonial Auxiliary Forces Officers' Decoration	
	Colonial Auxiliary Forces Long Service Medal	
	Medal for Good Shooting (Naval)	
	Militia Long Service Medal	
	Imperial Yeomanry Long Service Medal	
	Territorial Efficiency Medal	
	Territorial Decoration	
	Special Reserve Long Service and Good Conduct Medal	
	Decoration for Officers of the Royal Naval Reserve	RD
	Decoration for Officers of the Royal Naval Volunteer Reserve	VD
	Royal Naval Reserve Long Service and Good Conduct Medal	
	Royal Naval Volunteer Reserve Long Service and Good Conduct Medal	
	Union of South Africa Commemoration Medal	
	Royal Victorian Medal (Gold and Silver)	
	Imperial Service Medal	
	Medal of the Order of the British Empire	
	Medal of the Order of St. John of Jerusalem in England	
	Badge of the Order of the League of Mercy	
	Royal Victorian Medal (Bronze)	
	Foreign Orders (in order of date of award)	
	Foreign Decorations (in order of date of award)	
	Foreign Medals (in order of date of award)	

Key to "Change"
"+" = addition   "- (??)" = deleted from this list   "*" = change of position/title.

Appendix 3 to Chapter 4

From *London Gazette* dated 22 April 1921

Change	Titles	Post-nominals
	Victoria Cross	VC
	Knight of the Most Noble Order of the Garter	KG
	Knight of the Most Ancient and Most Noble Order of the Thistle	KT
	Knight of the Most Illustrious Order of St. Patrick	KP
	Knight Grand Cross of the Most Honourable Order of the Bath	GCB
	Member of the Order of Merit	OM
	Knight Grand Commander of the Most Exalted Order of the Star of India	GCSI
	Knight Grand Cross of the Most Distinguished Order of St. Michael & St. George	GCMG
	Knight Grand Commander of the Most Eminent Order of the Indian Empire	GCIE
	The Imperial Order of the Crown of India	CI
	Knight or Dame Grand Cross of the Royal Victorian Order	GCVO
	Knight or Dame Grand Cross of the Most Excellent Order of the British Empire	GBE
	Member of the Order of the Companions of Honour	CH
	Knight Commander of the Most Honourable Order of the Bath	KCB
	Knight Commander of the Most Exalted Order of the Star of India	KCSI
	Knight Commander of the Most Distinguished Order of St. Michael & St. George	KCMG
	Knight Commander of the Most Eminent Order of the Indian Empire	KCIE
	Knight Commander of the Royal Victorian Order	KCVO
	Knight or Dame Commander of the Most Excellent Order of the British Empire	KBE/DBE
	Companion of the Most Honourable Order of the Bath	CB
	Companion of the Most Exalted Order of the Star of India	CSI
	Companion of the Most Distinguished Order of St. Michael & St. George	CMG
	Companion of the Most Eminent Order of the Indian Empire	CIE
	Commander of the Royal Victorian Order	CVO

"Medals Will Be Worn"

From *London Gazette* dated 22 April 1921 (cont)

Change	Titles	Post-nominals
	Commander of the Most Excellent Order of the British Empire	CBE
	Companion of the Distinguished Service Order	DSO
	Member of the Fourth Class of the Royal Victorian Order	MVO
	Officer of the Most Excellent Order of the British Empire	OBE
	Companion of the Imperial Service Order	ISO
	Member of the Fifth Class of the Royal Victorian Order	MVO
	Member of the Most Excellent Order of the British Empire	MBE
	Member of the Royal Red Cross	RRC
	Distinguished Service Cross	DSC
	Military Cross	MC
	Distinguished Flying Cross	DFC
	Air Force Cross	AFC
	Associate of the Royal Red Cross	ARRC
	Order of British India	OBI
	Indian Order of Merit (Military)	IOM
	Kaisar-i-Hind Medal (Classes I & II)	
	Order of St. John of Jerusalem in England (All Classes)	
	Albert Medal (Sea & Land; Classes I & II (Gold & Bronze))	AM
	Medal for Distinguished Conduct in the Field	DCM
	Conspicuous Gallantry Medal	CGM
	Distinguished Service Medal	DSM
	Military Medal	MM
	Distinguished Flying Medal	DFM
	Air Force Medal	AFM
*	Indian Distinguished Service Medal	IDSM
	War Medals (in order of date)	
	Arctic Medal 1815-1855	
	Arctic Medal 1876	
	Antarctic Medal 1901-1903	

From *London Gazette* dated 22 April 1921 (cont)

Change	Titles	Post-nominals
	Constabulary Medal (Ireland)	
	Board of Trade Medal for Saving Life at Sea	
	Indian Order of Merit (Civil)	IOM
	Edward Medal (1st & 2nd Classes)(Silver and Bronze)	EM
	King's Police Medal	
	Queen Victoria's Jubilee Medal, 1887 (Gold, Silver & Bronze)	
	Queen Victoria's Police Jubilee Medal, 1887	
	Queen Victoria's Jubilee Medal, 1897 (Gold, Silver & Bronze)	
	Queen Victoria's Police Jubilee Medal, 1897	
	Queen Victoria's Commemoration Medal, 1900 (Ireland)	
	King Edward's Coronation Medal, 1902	
	King Edward's Police Coronation Medal, 1902	
	King Edward's Durbar Medal, 1903 (Gold, Silver & Bronze)	
	King Edward's Police Medal, 1903 (Scotland)	
	King's Visit Commemoration Medal, 1903 (Ireland)	
	King George's Coronation Medal, 1911	
	King George's Police Coronation Medal, 1911	
	King's Visit Police Commemoration Medal, 1911 (Ireland)	
	King George's Durbar Medal, 1911 (Gold, Silver & Bronze)	
	Long Service and Good Conduct Medal	
	Naval Long Service and Good Conduct Medal	
	Medal for Meritorious Service	(MSM)
	Indian Long Service and Good Conduct Medal (for Europeans of Indian Army)	
	Indian Meritorious Service Medal (for Europeans of Indian Army)	
	Royal Marine Meritorious Service Medal	
	Indian Long Service and Good Conduct Medal (for Native Army)	
	Indian Meritorious Service Medal (for Native Army)	
	Volunteer Officers' Decoration	VD

From *London Gazette* dated 22 April 1921 (cont)

Change	Titles	Post-nominals
	Volunteer Long Service Medal	
	Volunteer Officers' Decoration (for India & the Colonies)	VD
	Volunteer Long Service Medal (for India & the Colonies)	
	Colonial Auxiliary Forces Officers' Decoration	
	Colonial Auxiliary Forces Long Service Medal	
	Medal for Good Shooting (Naval)	
	Militia Long Service Medal	
	Imperial Yeomanry Long Service Medal	
*	Territorial Decoration	
	Territorial Efficiency Medal	
	Special Reserve Long Service and Good Conduct Medal	
	Decoration for Officers of the Royal Naval Reserve	RD
	Decoration for Officers of the Royal Naval Volunteer Reserve	VD
	Royal Naval Reserve Long Service and Good Conduct Medal	
	Royal Naval Volunteer Reserve Long Service and Good Conduct Medal	
+	Special Constabulary Medal	
	Union of South Africa Commemoration Medal	
	Royal Victorian Medal (Gold and Silver)	
	Imperial Service Medal	
	Medal of the Order of the British Empire	
	Medal of the Order of St. John of Jerusalem in England	
	Badge of the Order of the League of Mercy	
	Royal Victorian Medal (Bronze)	
	Foreign Orders (in order of date of award)	
	Foreign Decorations (in order of date of award)	
	Foreign Medals (in order of date of award)	

Key to "Change"
"+" = addition   "- (??)" = deleted from this list   "*" = change of position/title.

Appendix 4 to Chapter 4

From Army Council Instruction 1 of 1923

Change	Titles	Post-nominals
	Victoria Cross	VC
	Knight of the Most Noble Order of the Garter	KG
	Knight of the Most Ancient and Most Noble Order of the Thistle	KT
	Knight of the Most Illustrious Order of St. Patrick	KP
	Knight Grand Cross of the Most Honourable Order of the Bath	GCB
	Member of the Order of Merit	OM
	Knight Grand Commander of the Most Exalted Order of the Star of India	GCSI
	Knight Grand Cross of the Most Distinguished Order of St. Michael & St. George	GCMG
	Knight Grand Commander of the Most Eminent Order of the Indian Empire	GCIE
	The Imperial Order of the Crown of India	CI
	Knight or Dame Grand Cross of the Royal Victorian Order	GCVO
	Knight or Dame Grand Cross of the Most Excellent Order of the British Empire	GBE
	Member of the Order of the Companions of Honour	CH
	Knight Commander of the Most Honourable Order of the Bath	KCB
	Knight Commander of the Most Exalted Order of the Star of India	KCSI
	Knight Commander of the Most Distinguished Order of St. Michael & St. George	KCMG
	Knight Commander of the Most Eminent Order of the Indian Empire	KCIE
	Knight Commander of the Royal Victorian Order	KCVO
	Knight or Dame Commander of the Most Excellent Order of the British Empire	KBE/DBE
	Companion of the Most Honourable Order of the Bath	CB
	Companion of the Most Exalted Order of the Star of India	CSI
	Companion of the Most Distinguished Order of St. Michael & St. George	CMG
	Companion of the Most Eminent Order of the Indian Empire	CIE

From Army Council Instruction 1 of 1923 (cont)

Change Titles   Post-nominals

Commander of the Royal Victorian Order   CVO

Commander of the Most Excellent Order of the British Empire   CBE

Companion of the Distinguished Service Order   DSO

Member of the Fourth Class of the Royal Victorian Order   MVO

Officer of the Most Excellent Order of the British Empire   OBE

Companion of the Imperial Service Order   ISO

Member of the Fifth Class of the Royal Victorian Order   MVO

Member of the Most Excellent Order of the British Empire   MBE

Member of the Royal Red Cross   RRC

Distinguished Service Cross   DSC

Military Cross   MC

Distinguished Flying Cross   DFC

Air Force Cross   AFC

Associate of the Royal Red Cross   ARRC

Order of British India   OBI

Indian Order of Merit (Military)   IOM

Kaisar-i-Hind Medal (Classes I & II)

Order of St. John of Jerusalem in England (All Classes)

Albert Medal (Sea & Land; Classes I & II (Gold & Bronze))   AM

Medal for Distinguished Conduct in the Field   DCM

Conspicuous Gallantry Medal   CGM

Distinguished Service Medal   DSM

Military Medal   MM

Distinguished Flying Medal   DFM

Air Force Medal   AFM

Indian Distinguished Service Medal   IDSM

War Medals (in order of date)

Arctic Medal 1815-1855

Arctic Medal 1876

Antarctic Medal 1901-1903

1914-1923

From Army Council Instruction 1 of 1923 (cont)

Change	Titles	Post-nominals
	Constabulary Medal (Ireland)	
	Board of Trade Medal for Saving Life at Sea	
	Indian Order of Merit (Civil)	IOM
	Edward Medal (1st & 2nd Classes)(Silver and Bronze)	EM
	King's Police Medal	
	Queen Victoria's Jubilee Medal, 1887 (Gold, Silver & Bronze)	
	Queen Victoria's Jubilee Medal, 1897 (Gold, Silver & Bronze)	
	Queen Victoria's Police Jubilee Medal, 1897	
	Queen Victoria's Commemoration Medal, 1900 (Ireland)	
	King Edward's Coronation Medal, 1902	
	King Edward's Police Coronation Medal, 1902	
	King Edward's Durbar Medal, 1903 (Gold, Silver & Bronze)	
	King Edward's Police Medal, 1903 (Scotland)	
	King's Visit Commemoration Medal, 1903 (Ireland)	
	King George's Coronation Medal, 1911	
	King George's Police Coronation Medal, 1911	
	King's Visit Police Commemoration Medal, 1911 (Ireland)	
	King George's Durbar Medal, 1911 (Gold, Silver & Bronze)	
	Long Service and Good Conduct Medal	
	Naval Long Service and Good Conduct Medal	
	Medal for Meritorious Service	(MSM)
	Indian Long Service and Good Conduct Medal (for Europeans of Indian Army)	
	Indian Meritorious Service Medal (for Europeans of Indian Army)	
	Royal Marine Meritorious Service Medal	
*	Indian Long Service and Good Conduct Medal (for Indian Army)	
*	Indian Meritorious Service Medal (for Indian Army)	
	Volunteer Officers' Decoration	VD
	Volunteer Long Service Medal	

"Medals Will Be Worn"

From Army Council Instruction 1 of 1923 (cont)

Change	Titles	Post-nominals
	Volunteer Officers' Decoration (for India & the Colonies)	VD
	Volunteer Long Service Medal (for India & the Colonies)	
	Colonial Auxiliary Forces Officers' Decoration	
	Colonial Auxiliary Forces Long Service Medal	
	Medal for Good Shooting (Naval)	
	Militia Long Service Medal	
	Imperial Yeomanry Long Service Medal	
	Territorial Decoration	
	Territorial Efficiency Medal	
	Special Reserve Long Service and Good Conduct Medal	
	Decoration for Officers of the Royal Naval Reserve	RD
	Decoration for Officers of the Royal Naval Volunteer Reserve	VD
	Royal Naval Reserve Long Service and Good Conduct Medal	
	Royal Naval Volunteer Reserve Long Service and Good Conduct Medal	
+	Board of Trade Rocket Apparatus Volunteer Long Service Medal	
	Special Constabulary Medal	
	Union of South Africa Commemoration Medal	
	Royal Victorian Medal (Gold and Silver)	
	Imperial Service Medal	
	Medal of the Order of the British Empire	
	Medal of the Order of St. John of Jerusalem in England	
	Badge of the Order of the League of Mercy	
	Royal Victorian Medal (Bronze)	
	Foreign Orders (in order of date of award)	
	Foreign Decorations (in order of date of award)	
	Foreign Medals (in order of date of award)	

Key to "Change"
"+" = addition   "- (??)" = deleted from this list   "*" = change of position/title.

CHAPTER 5

1924 TO 1951

IT might have been expected that, once matters were tidied up after the War, the subject of medals would drop from the public interest. So it is rather surprising that a further *London Gazette* was published as early as 1929 and contained some more significant changes.

The less dramatic features were to add the limit of a maximum of four stars of Orders to be worn, and it placed a further limit of three on neck decorations. This actually applied only to a couple of forms of military dress, most forms of dress were actually limited to one neck badge. It also added notes regarding the position of wear for Baronet's Badges and Knight's Bachelor Badges and the order of wear of the 1914 War stars and medals.

In addition some new awards were inserted in fairly predictable places including the new RAF Long and Meritorious Service Medals and some naval reserves Long Service Medals. The Royal Victorian Medal in bronze moved up a couple of places and there was some alteration of names with the Order of St. John and its associated medals in that they dropped "of Jerusalem in England". The headings for medals of the Order of the British Empire also became more specific.

Unsurprising was the addition of the Medal of the Order of the British Empire for Gallantry (EGM) which was instituted in 1922 and so missed the earlier *London Gazette*. Not so predictable was that it came in directly to a position ahead of war medals. Other civilian bravery awards had struggled before achieving this. It appeared to bring with it some of these struggling awards. The Constabulary Medal (Ireland); Board of Trade Medal for Saving Life at Sea; Indian Order of Merit (Civil); Edward Medal; and King's Police Medal; all moved up from a position behind War and Polar medals to a place between the Indian Distinguished Service Medal and the EGM. The Life Saving Medal of St. John was added immediately after the EGM. It seems likely that the aftermath of the War plus events leading up to the General Strike might have influenced thinking on civilian bravery.

An Army Dress Regulation of 1934 did nothing to the existing list except to omit the Baronets and Knights Bachelor. Curiously neither this regulation, nor any list since then, has noted the change of the Long Service and Good Conduct Medal for the Army. In October it changed from "(Army)" to "(Military)". Not perhaps a great alteration but both medals could be earned and worn together, so their relative positions should have been specified.

The next list was in the *London Gazette* of 1936 and it would appear that African troops were at last achieving recognition. As there had been no major campaigns involving them since the War it must be assumed this was a belated reaction to their War effort and to the recognition already afforded to Indian troops. Whatever the reasons the Royal West African Frontier Force and King's African Rifles are singled out for the first time in these lists. The Distinguished Conduct Medals (DCM) and Long Service and Good Conduct Medals of both forces are recognised. The long service awards go in a predictable place after similar ones for Indian troops. The DCMs, which should equate to the British DCM, are put after the naval DSM, i.e. amongst awards one level lower than they themselves. Other newcomers included the Efficiency Decoration and Medal, African Police Medal for Meritorious Service,

Colonial Police and Fire Brigade Long Service Medal, Royal Naval Wireless Auxiliary Reserve Long Service and Good Conduct Medal, King George's Silver Jubilee Medal and Voluntary Medical Service Medal, all in predictable places. Finally the Arctic and Antarctic medals which had been specified individually, now took on a collective title "Polar Medals (in order of date)".

There were no further moves until 1941. Britain was again at war, and we find this influences the order of wear and enhances interest in the subject. The prime reasons for the re-publication were the additions of the George Cross and George Medal. Even so the George Medal, second in line for civilian bravery, was given a lowly place after the third level military group containing the Military Medal. The Edward Medal moved up to join it as did a number of other gallantry medals for the Indian Police, Burma Police and Colonial Police, many of these organisations now subjected directly to the effects of the war. In addition the Order of Burma, Burma Gallantry Medal and the Police Medals for Distinguished Service all made their debut. The Trans-Jordan Frontier Force Long Service and Good Conduct Medal also joined for its first appearance right at the bottom of the long service list. This was strange as numerous other variations on long service medals had never been included. The Medal for Saving Life at Sea dropped the cumbersome reference to the Board of Trade.

Notable amongst the significant changes is the recognition of Police and Fire Service bravery. Earlier the "King's Police Medal" had been placed before War medals and after the Edward Medals. The Fire Service had no medal of its own and did not appear in the Police Medal title. Now, with the "blitzkrieg" bombing bringing the war into our streets the Police Medal encompassed the Fire Service in the title and took two positions depending on whether it had been awarded for gallantry or merit.

One last change in the list for 1941 was the massive leap upwards of the British Empire Medal. It had, until now, languished almost at the end, just before foreign awards. Now it moved right up to a position just before war medals, this took it up over the long service medals, jubilee, etc., medals, polar medals, war medals and even the Life Saving Medal of the Order of St. John.

The next list was that immediately post war in 1947 and, no doubt, reflected feelings from the war particularly regarding "native" troops, as was the case in 1918. The Indian Order of Merit and Order of Burma for gallantry moved up to a position ahead of the Military Cross group while the Order of Burma for Good Service remained in the former position for the Order. The Union of South Africa King's Medals for Bravery (1939) in gold and silver took their places amongst the second and third level bravery awards, but rather surprisingly ahead of the existing awards. The Distinguished Conduct Medal adopted this title dropping the "in the field".

The military third level bravery medals all moved down to below the second level awards of various kinds including the African DCMs, Indian Distinguished Service Medal, Burma Gallantry Medal and the civilian bravery awards such as the George Medal, Edward Medal, and Police and Fire medals for gallantry. In addition the Canada Medal was added while the medals belonging to Orders (Victorian and Imperial Service) moved right up to behind Polar Medals and were immediately followed by the various Police medals for distinguished service. These last had moved up over the jubilee, etc., group. The Royal Household Long and Faithful Service medals appeared for the first time and there was a quiet upheaval in the long service order of wear as well as some new additions. The Trans-Jordan Long Service and Good Conduct Medal moved into a more appropriate place just after its Indian and African counterparts, only to disappear altogether from the next list in 1949. The South African Medal for War Services was added last of all, rather an odd place since it was in effect their civil defences, etc., "Defence Medal", admittedly without the dangers of bombing.

The order of wear for the 1939-45 War stars and medals was published with comments on some post-war campaign medals. Also the collective "War Medals (in order of date)" had "of the campaign for which awarded" added to the phrase in parenthesis. Finally the first notes on Mentions in Despatches and King's Commendations were included.

Unconnected with the listings another regulation was altered about this time having a bearing on wearing medal ribbons. At some time between the end of the war and the Korean War medal ribbons on army uniform were rearranged. Up to the end of the war they had been worn with any incomplete row at the bottom and this practice continued into the 1950s. Since then it has been the rule that the incomplete row is worn at the top.

The new list in 1949 was notable firstly for its deletions. All the Burma awards were deleted without exception. This may be due to the fact that all had been awarded only to Burmese personnel, now in an independent nation, but over the years since then the same argument could be used to delete medals relating to survivors entitled to a number of medals. Indian long service medals to the Indian Army; Victorian Jubilee medals; the Canada Medal; the African DCMs. All these have passed into history by now, yet they remain in the lists.

One other deletion without explanation was the Life Saving Medal of St. John. In fact this has been added to those worn on the right breast joining the Royal Humane Society Medals, Stanhope Gold Medal and Royal National Lifeboat Institution Medals and is mentioned in Queen's Regulations. Curious, actually, that these do not appear in the *London Gazette* lists and nowhere are recipients told how to wear these medals. Is the "senior" award placed towards the centre of the chest or does it follow the method on the left breast of senior to the right? Anyway, which is "senior", the first earned or the highest grade? Does a RNLI bronze medal take precedence over a silver one earned later? No guidance appears to have been considered necessary for these hard earned bravery awards.

Other changes in 1949 were quite minor. The Indian Independence Medal was the only addition. A note was added about the King's permission being needed before wearing foreign awards. Also, in the note about the order of wear for 1939-45 awards the Volunteer Service Medal of Canada moved ahead of the War Medal and the New Zealand and Southern Rhodesian equivalents were added after the Indian Service Medal and Africa Service Medal of the Union of South Africa.

The next list in 1951 added a few new awards including Ceylon Police medals, Police Long Service Medal, Cadet Forces Medal, Canadian Forces Decoration and Royal Observer Corps Medal. It also moved the King's Police and Fire Services Medal for Distinguished Service ahead of war medals. In the notes about the order of wear for war medals the Australian Service Medal was added after the Southern Rhodesian Service Medal. More surprising the African General Service Medal 1902 was added to the medals worn in the order of date of participation in the campaign concerned. This was surprising as the, then, most recent clasp to this medal was for "Somaliland 1920", thirty-one years previously. The next, and probably last clasp for this medal was to be for "Kenya", but that campaign did not begin until 21 October 1952 and the award was not published until 1955 so it could not have affected the list in 1951.

The other notable change to this footnote was the part about participation in the campaign. For the first time it is made clear that the order of wear for General Service Medals, etc., depended on the individual's dates of participation, not on the dates of the campaign. This was made necessary because the short sharp battles of the Victorian era, where all participants took part on the same day or days, were over. Protracted counter terrorist campaigns had taken their place and the dates of participation could be vastly different between individuals. Northern Ireland has lasted so long that fathers and sons wear the same medal.

Appendix 1 to Chapter 5

From *London Gazette* dated 22 November 1929

Change	Titles	Post-nominals
	Victoria Cross	VC
	Knight of the Most Noble Order of the Garter	KG
	Knight of the Most Ancient and Most Noble Order of the Thistle	KT
	Knight of the Most Illustrious Order of St. Patrick	KP
	Knight Grand Cross of the Most Honourable Order of the Bath	GCB
	Member of the Order of Merit	OM
+	Baronet's Badge	Bt or Bart
	Knight Grand Commander of the Most Exalted Order of the Star of India	GCSI
	Knight Grand Cross of the Most Distinguished Order of St. Michael & St. George	GCMG
	Knight Grand Commander of the Most Eminent Order of the Indian Empire	GCIE
	The Imperial Order of the Crown of India	CI
	Knight or Dame Grand Cross of the Royal Victorian Order	GCVO
	Knight or Dame Grand Cross of the Most Excellent Order of the British Empire	GBE
	Member of the Order of the Companions of Honour	CH
	Knight Commander of the Most Honourable Order of the Bath	KCB
	Knight Commander of the Most Exalted Order of the Star of India	KCSI
	Knight Commander of the Most Distinguished Order of St. Michael & St. George	KCMG
	Knight Commander of the Most Eminent Order of the Indian Empire	KCIE
	Knight Commander of the Royal Victorian Order	KCVO
	Knight or Dame Commander of the Most Excellent Order of the British Empire	KBE/DBE
+	Knight Bachelor's Badge	
	Companion of the Most Honourable Order of the Bath	CB
	Companion of the Most Exalted Order of the Star of India	CSI
	Companion of the Most Distinguished Order of St. Michael & St. George	CMG
	Companion of the Most Eminent Order of the Indian Empire	CIE

From *London Gazette* dated 22 November 1929 (cont)

Change	Titles	Post-nominals
	Commander of the Royal Victorian Order	CVO
	Commander of the Most Excellent Order of the British Empire	CBE
	Companion of the Distinguished Service Order	DSO
	Member of the Fourth Class of the Royal Victorian Order	MVO
	Officer of the Most Excellent Order of the British Empire	OBE
	Companion of the Imperial Service Order	ISO
	Member of the Fifth Class of the Royal Victorian Order	MVO
	Member of the Most Excellent Order of the British Empire	MBE
	Member of the Royal Red Cross	RRC
	Distinguished Service Cross	DSC
	Military Cross	MC
	Distinguished Flying Cross	DFC
	Air Force Cross	AFC
	Associate of the Royal Red Cross	ARRC
	Order of British India	OBI
	Indian Order of Merit (Military)	IOM
	Kaisar-i-Hind Medal (Classes I & II)	
*	Order of St. John (All Classes)	
	Albert Medals (Sea & Land; Classes I & II (Gold & Bronze))	AM
	Medal for Distinguished Conduct in the Field	DCM
	Conspicuous Gallantry Medal	CGM
	Distinguished Service Medal	DSM
	Military Medal	MM
	Distinguished Flying Medal	DFM
	Air Force Medal	AFM
	Indian Distinguished Service Medal	IDSM
	Constabulary Medal (Ireland)	
*	Board of Trade Medal for Saving Life at Sea	
*	Indian Order of Merit (Civil)	IOM

From *London Gazette* dated 22 November 1929 (cont)

Change	Titles	Post-nominals
*	Edward Medal (1st & 2nd Classes)(Silver and Bronze)	EM
*	King's Police Medal	
+	Medal of the Order of the British Empire for Gallantry	
*	Life Saving Medal of the Order of St. John	
	War Medals (in order of date)	
	Arctic Medal 1815-1855	
	Arctic Medal 1876	
	Antarctic Medal 1901-1903	
	Queen Victoria's Jubilee Medal, 1887 (Gold, Silver & Bronze)	
	Queen Victoria's Police Jubilee Medal, 1887	
	Queen Victoria's Jubilee Medal, 1897 (Gold, Silver & Bronze)	
	Queen Victoria's Police Jubilee Medal, 1897	
	Queen Victoria's Commemoration Medal, 1900 (Ireland)	
	King Edward's Coronation Medal, 1902	
	King Edward's Police Coronation Medal, 1902	
	King Edward's Durbar Medal, 1903 (Gold, Silver & Bronze)	
	King Edward's Police Medal, 1903 (Scotland)	
	King's Visit Commemoration Medal, 1903 (Ireland)	
	King George's Coronation Medal, 1911	
	King George's Police Coronation Medal, 1911	
	King's Visit Police Commemoration Medal, 1911 (Ireland)	
	King George's Durbar Medal, 1911 (Gold, Silver & Bronze)	
	Long Service and Good Conduct Medal	
	Naval Long Service and Good Conduct Medal	
	Medal for Meritorious Service	(MSM)
	Indian Long Service and Good Conduct Medal (for Europeans of Indian Army)	
	Indian Meritorious Service Medal (for Europeans of Indian Army)	
	Royal Marine Meritorious Service Medal	

1924-1951

From *London Gazette* dated 22 November 1929 (cont)

Change	Titles	Post-nominals
+	Royal Air Force Meritorious Service Medal	
+	Royal Air Force Long Service and Good Conduct Medal	
	Indian Long Service and Good Conduct Medal (for Indian Army)	
	Indian Meritorious Service Medal (for Indian Army)	
	Volunteer Officers' Decoration	VD
	Volunteer Long Service Medal	
	Volunteer Officers' Decoration (for India & the Colonies)	VD
	Volunteer Long Service Medal (for India & the Colonies)	
	Colonial Auxiliary Forces Officers' Decoration	VD
	Colonial Auxiliary Forces Long Service Medal	
	Medal for Good Shooting (Naval)	
	Militia Long Service Medal	
	Imperial Yeomanry Long Service Medal	
	Territorial Decoration	TD
	Territorial Efficiency Medal	
	Special Reserve Long Service and Good Conduct Medal	
	Decoration for Officers of the Royal Naval Reserve	RD
	Decoration for Officers of the Royal Naval Volunteer Reserve	VD
	Royal Naval Reserve Long Service and Good Conduct Medal	
	Royal Naval Volunteer Reserve Long Service and Good Conduct Medal	
	Board of Trade Rocket Apparatus Volunteer Long Service Medal	
	Special Constabulary Medal	
+	Royal Naval Auxiliary Sick Berth Reserve Long Service and Good Conduct Medal	
+	Royal Fleet Reserve Long Service and Good Conduct Medal	
+	King's Medal (for Champion Shots in the Military Forces)	
	Union of South Africa Commemoration Medal	
	Royal Victorian Medal (Gold and Silver)	
	Imperial Service Medal	

From *London Gazette* dated 22 November 1929 (cont)

Change Titles   Post-nominals

*   Medal of the Order of the British Empire
          (awarded prior to 29th December 1922)

*   Medal of the Order of the British Empire for Meritorious Service

*   Royal Victorian Medal (Bronze)

*   Service Medal of the Order of St. John

          Badge of the Order of the League of Mercy

          Foreign Orders (in order of date of award)

          Foreign Decorations (in order of date of award)

          Foreign Medals (in order of date of award)

Key to "Change"
"+" = addition   "- (??)" = deleted from this list   "" = change of position/title.*

Appendix 2 to Chapter 5

From *London Gazette* dated 4 April 1936

Change	Titles	Post-nominals
	Victoria Cross	VC
	Knight of the Most Noble Order of the Garter	KG
	Knight of the Most Ancient and Most Noble Order of the Thistle	KT
	Knight of the Most Illustrious Order of St. Patrick	KP
	Knight Grand Cross of the Most Honourable Order of the Bath	GCB
	Member of the Order of Merit	OM
	Baronet's Badge	Bt or Bart
	Knight Grand Commander of the Most Exalted Order of the Star of India	GCSI
	Knight Grand Cross of the Most Distinguished Order of St. Michael & St. George	GCMG
	Knight Grand Commander of the Most Eminent Order of the Indian Empire	GCIE
	The Imperial Order of the Crown of India	CI
	Knight or Dame Grand Cross of the Royal Victorian Order	GCVO
	Knight or Dame Grand Cross of the Most Excellent Order of the British Empire	GBE
	Member of the Order of the Companions of Honour	CH
	Knight Commander of the Most Honourable Order of the Bath	KCB
	Knight Commander of the Most Exalted Order of the Star of India	KCSI
	Companion of the Most Distinguished Order of St Michael and St George	CMG
	Knight Commander of the Most Eminent Order of the Indian Empire	KCIE
	Knight or Dame Commander of the Royal Victorian Order	KCVO/ DCVO
	Knight or Dame Commander of the Most Excellent Order of the British Empire	KBE/DBE
	Knight Bachelor's Badge	
	Companion of the Most Honourable Order of the Bath	CB
	Companion of the Most Exalted Order of the Star of India	CSI
	Companion of the Most Distinguished Order of St. Michael & St. George	CMG
	Companion of the Most Eminent Order of the Indian Empire	CIE

From *London Gazette* dated 4 April 1936 (cont)

Change	Titles	Post-nominals
	Commander of the Royal Victorian Order	CVO
	Commander of the Most Excellent Order of the British Empire	CBE
	Companion of the Distinguished Service Order	DSO
	Member of the Fourth Class of the Royal Victorian Order	MVO
	Officer of the Most Excellent Order of the British Empire	OBE
	Companion of the Imperial Service Order	ISO
	Member of the Fifth Class of the Royal Victorian Order	MVO
	Member of the Most Excellent Order of the British Empire	MBE
	Member of the Royal Red Cross	RRC
	Distinguished Service Cross	DSC
	Military Cross	MC
	Distinguished Flying Cross	DFC
	Air Force Cross	AFC
	Associate of the Royal Red Cross	ARRC
	Order of British India	OBI
	Indian Order of Merit (Military)	IOM
	Kaisar-i-Hind Medal (Gold, Silver & Bronze)	
	Order of St. John (All Classes)	
	Albert Medals (Sea & Land; Classes I & II (Gold & Bronze))	AM
	Medal for Distinguished Conduct in the Field	DCM
	Conspicuous Gallantry Medal	CGM
	Distinguished Service Medal	DSM
+	Royal West African Frontier Force Distinguished Conduct Medal	DCM
+	King's African Rifles Distinguished Conduct Medal	DCM
	Military Medal	MM
	Distinguished Flying Medal	DFM
	Air Force Medal	AFM
	Indian Distinguished Service Medal	IDSM
	Constabulary Medal (Ireland)	
	Board of Trade Medal for Saving Life at Sea	

From *London Gazette* dated 4 April 1936 (cont)

Change	Titles	Post-nominals
	Indian Order of Merit (Civil)	IOM
	Edward Medal (1st & 2nd Classes)(Silver and Bronze)	EM
	King's Police Medal	
	Medal of the Order of the British Empire for Gallantry	
	Indian Police Medal	
	Life Saving Medal of the Order of St. John	
	War Medals (in order of date)	
*	Polar Medals (in order of date)	
	Queen Victoria's Jubilee Medal, 1887 (Gold, Silver & Bronze)	
	Queen Victoria's Police Jubilee Medal, 1887	
	Queen Victoria's Jubilee Medal, 1897 (Gold, Silver & Bronze)	
	Queen Victoria's Police Jubilee Medal, 1897	
	Queen Victoria's Commemoration Medal, 1900 (Ireland)	
	King Edward's Coronation Medal, 1902	
	King Edward's Police Coronation Medal, 1902	
	King Edward's Durbar Medal, 1903 (Gold, Silver & Bronze)	
	King Edward's Police Medal, 1903 (Scotland)	
	King's Visit Commemoration Medal, 1903 (Ireland)	
	King George's Coronation Medal, 1911	
	King George's Police Coronation Medal, 1911	
	King's Visit Police Commemoration Medal, 1911 (Ireland)	
	King George's Durbar Medal, 1911 (Gold, Silver & Bronze)	
	King George's Silver Jubilee Medal	
	Long Service and Good Conduct Medal	
	Naval Long Service and Good Conduct Medal	
	Medal for Meritorious Service	(MSM)
	Indian Long Service and Good Conduct Medal (for Europeans of Indian Army)	
	Indian Meritorious Service Medal (for Europeans of Indian Army)	
	Royal Air Force Meritorious Service Medal	

From *London Gazette* dated 4 April 1936 (cont)

Change	Titles	Post-nominals
	Royal Air Force Long Service and Good Conduct Medal	
	Indian Long Service and Good Conduct Medal (for Indian Army)	
+	Royal West African Frontier Force Long Service and Good Conduct Medal	
+	King's African Rifles Long Service and Good Conduct Medal	
	Indian Meritorious Service Medal (for Indian Army)	
	Volunteer Officers' Decoration	VD
	Volunteer Long Service Medal	
	Volunteer Officers' Decoration (for India & the Colonies)	VD
	Volunteer Long Service Medal (for India & the Colonies)	
	Colonial Auxiliary Forces Officers' Decoration	VD
	Colonial Auxiliary Forces Long Service Medal	
	Medal for Good Shooting (Naval)	
	Militia Long Service Medal	
	Imperial Yeomanry Long Service Medal	
	Territorial Decoration	TD
+	Efficiency Decoration	TD/ED
	Territorial Efficiency Medal	
+	Efficiency Medal	
	Special Reserve Long Service and Good Conduct Medal	
	Decoration for Officers of the Royal Naval Reserve	RD
	Decoration for Officers of the Royal Naval Volunteer Reserve	VD
	Royal Naval Reserve Long Service and Good Conduct Medal	
	Royal Naval Volunteer Reserve Long Service and Good Conduct Medal	
	Board of Trade Rocket Apparatus Volunteer Long Service Medal	
+	African Police Medal for Meritorious Service	
	Special Constabulary Medal	
	Royal Naval Auxiliary Sick Berth Reserve Long Service and Good Conduct Medal	

From *London Gazette* dated 4 April 1936 (cont)

Change	Titles	Post-nominals
	Royal Fleet Reserve Long Service and Good Conduct Medal	
	King's Medal (for Champion Shots in the Military Forces)	
+	Colonial Police and Fire Brigades' Long Service Medal	
+	Royal Naval Wireless Auxiliary Reserve Long Service and Good Conduct Medal	
	Union of South Africa Commemoration Medal	
	Royal Victorian Medal (Gold and Silver)	
	Imperial Service Medal	
	Medal of the Order of the British Empire (awarded prior to 29th December 1922)	
	Medal of the Order of the British Empire for Meritorious Service	
	Royal Victorian Medal (Bronze)	
	Service Medal of the Order of St. John	
	Badge of the Order of the League of Mercy	
+	Voluntary Medical Service Medal	
	Foreign Orders (in order of date of award)	
	Foreign Decorations (in order of date of award)	
	Foreign Medals (in order of date of award)	

Key to "Change"
"+" = addition   "- (??)" = deleted from this list   "" = change of position/title.*

Appendix 3 to Chapter 5

From *London Gazette* dated 22 February 1941

Change	Titles	Post-nominals
	Victoria Cross	VC
+	George Cross	GC
	Knight of the Most Noble Order of the Garter	KG
	Knight of the Most Ancient and Most Noble Order of the Thistle	KT
	Knight of the Most Illustrious Order of St. Patrick	KP
	Knight Grand Cross of the Most Honourable Order of the Bath	GCB
	Member of the Order of Merit	OM
	Baronet's Badge	Bt or Bart
	Knight Grand Commander of the Most Exalted Order of the Star of India	GCSI
	Knight Grand Cross of the Most Distinguished Order of St. Michael & St. George	GCMG
	Knight Grand Commander of the Most Eminent Order of the Indian Empire	GCIE
	The Imperial Order of the Crown of India	CI
	Knight or Dame Grand Cross of the Royal Victorian Order	GCVO
	Knight or Dame Grand Cross of the Most Excellent Order of the British Empire	GBE
	Member of the Order of the Companions of Honour	CH
	Knight Commander of the Most Honourable Order of the Bath	KCB
	Knight Commander of the Most Exalted Order of the Star of India	KCSI
	Knight Commander of the Most Distinguished Order of St. Michael & St. George	KCMG
	Knight Commander of the Most Eminent Order of the Indian Empire	KCIE
	Knight or Dame Commander of the Royal Victorian Order	KCVO/DCVO
	Knight or Dame Commander of the Most Excellent Order of the British Empire	KBE/DBE
	Knight Bachelor's Badge	
	Companion of the Most Honourable Order of the Bath	CB
	Companion of the Most Exalted Order of the Star of India	CSI
	Companion of the Most Distinguished Order of St. Michael & St. George	CMG

From *London Gazette* dated 22 February 1941 (cont)

Change	Titles	Post-nominals
	Companion of the Most Eminent Order of the Indian Empire	CIE
	Commander of the Royal Victorian Order	CVO
	Commander of the Most Excellent Order of the British Empire	CBE
	Companion of the Distinguished Service Order	DSO
	Member of the Fourth Class of the Royal Victorian Order	MVO
	Officer of the Most Excellent Order of the British Empire	OBE
	Companion of the Imperial Service Order	ISO
	Member of the Fifth Class of the Royal Victorian Order	MVO
	Member of the Most Excellent Order of the British Empire	MBE
	Member of the Royal Red Cross	RRC
	Distinguished Service Cross	DSC
	Military Cross	MC
	Distinguished Flying Cross	DFC
	Air Force Cross	AFC
	Associate of the Royal Red Cross	ARRC
	Order of British India	OBI
	Indian Order of Merit (Military)	IOM
	Kaisar-i-Hind Medal (Gold, Silver & Bronze)	
+	Order of Burma	
	Order of St. John (All Classes)	
	Albert Medals (Sea & Land; Classes I & II (Gold & Bronze))	AM
	Medal for Distinguished Conduct in the Field	DCM
	Conspicuous Gallantry Medal	CGM
	Distinguished Service Medal	DSM
	Royal West African Frontier Force Distinguished Conduct Medal	DCM
	King's African Rifles Distinguished Conduct Medal	DCM
	Military Medal	MM
	Distinguished Flying Medal	DFM
	Air Force Medal	AFM

From *London Gazette* dated 22 February 1941 (cont)

Change	Titles	Post-nominals
*	King's Police and Fire Services Medal for Gallantry	
+	George Medal	GM
*	Edward Medal (1st & 2nd Classes)(Silver and Bronze)	EM
	Indian Distinguished Service Medal	
	Constabulary Medal (Ireland)	
*	Medal for Saving Life at Sea	SGM
	Indian Order of Merit (Civil)	IOM
*	Indian Police Medal for Gallantry	
+	Burma Police Medal for Gallantry	
+	Colonial Police Medal for Gallantry	
+	Burma Gallantry Medal	
	British Empire Medal	
	Life Saving Medal of the Order of St. John	
	War Medals (in order of date of campaign for which awarded)	
	Polar Medals (in order of date)	
	Queen Victoria's Jubilee Medal, 1887 (Gold, Silver & Bronze)	
	Queen Victoria's Police Jubilee Medal, 1887	
	Queen Victoria's Jubilee Medal, 1897 (Gold, Silver & Bronze)	
	Queen Victoria's Police Jubilee Medal, 1897	
	Queen Victoria's Commemoration Medal, 1900 (Ireland)	
	King Edward VII's Coronation Medal, 1902	
	King Edward VII's Police Coronation Medal, 1902	
	King Edward VII's Durbar Medal, 1903 (Gold, Silver & Bronze)	
	King Edward VII's Police Medal, 1903 (Scotland)	
	King's Visit Commemoration Medal, 1903 (Ireland)	
	King George V's Coronation Medal, 1911	
	King George V's Police Coronation Medal, 1911	
	King's Visit Police Commemoration Medal, 1911 (Ireland)	
	King George V's Durbar Medal, 1911 (Gold, Silver & Bronze)	

Corporal Levi Ashley displaying his array of recent medals which are for UNFICYP, Gulf, UNPROFOR with second tour numeral, UNAVEM III and NATO former Yugoslavia.
Courtesy the Ministry of Defence.

Prince Charles and General Sir Rupert Smith wearing their neck badges from miniature ribbons in Service Dress (see page 6).
Courtesy Richard Wyatt.

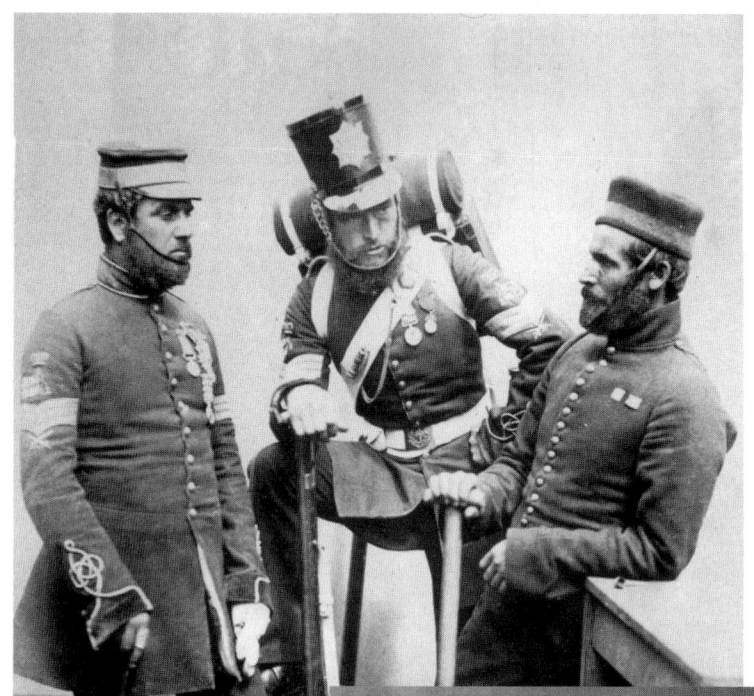

Photographed in about 1857 the Colour Serjeant on the left favours a "diamond" arrangement for his medals while the Private on the right is wearing ribbons alone. In all three cases the medals and ribbons are affixed separately with gaps between them (see page 35).

Courtesy of the Director, National Army Museum, London.

Serjeant Major Edwards, Scots Fusilier Guards, is wearing a tunic withdrawn from service in 1856 but he seems to have anticipated some of the rules in QR 1868 (see page 35).

Courtesy of the Director, National Army Museum, London.

Rifles Volunteers with two of them displaying shooting badges and regimental shooting medals (see page 36).

Courtesy of the Director, National Army Museum, London.

A photograph taken in 1910 of six VCs from the Indian Mutiny. From the left: Lieutenant General Sir James Hills-John, Major General Luke O'Connor, Field Marshal Sir Evelyn Wood, Field Marshal The Right Honourable Earl Roberts, Field Marshal Sir George White and Colonel Sir Edwards Thackeray. General O'Connor has a second row of medals beneath his first row. FM Sir Evelyn Wood has four stars in square arrangement while FMs Earl Roberts and Sir George White both wear five stars in differing patterns (see page 62).

Courtesy of the Director, National Army Museum, London.

"Medals Will Be Worn"

General Sir Charles Guthrie, GCB, LVO, OBE, ADC (see page 115).
Courtesy the Ministry of Defence.

Colonel L. Robson, CMG, DSO, VD, TD (see page 174).
Photo—OMRS Magazine.

Lieutenant E. W. K. Walton, AM, DSC, at a ceremony in 1972 (see page 176).
Photo—Major A. F. Flatow, TD.

1924–1951

From *London Gazette* dated 22 February 1941 (cont)

Change	Titles	Post-nominals
	King George V's Silver Jubilee Medal, 1935	
	King George VI's Coronation Medal, 1937	
	King's Police and Fire Services Medal for Distinguished Service	
*	Indian Police Medal for Meritorious Service	
+	Burma Police Medal for Meritorious Service	
+	Colonial Police Medal for Meritorious Service	
	Long Service and Good Conduct Medal	
	Naval Long Service and Good Conduct Medal	
	Medal for Meritorious Service	(MSM)
	Indian Long Service and Good Conduct Medal (for Europeans of Indian Army)	
	Indian Meritorious Service Medal (for Europeans of Indian Army)	
	Royal Marine Meritorious Service Medal	
	Royal Air Force Meritorious Service Medal	
	Royal Air Force Long Service and Good Conduct Medal	
	Indian Long Service and Good Conduct Medal (for Indian Army)	
	Royal West African Frontier Force Long Service and Good Conduct Medal	
	King's African Rifles Long Service and Good Conduct Medal	
	Indian Meritorious Service Medal (for Indian Army)	
	Volunteer Officers' Decoration	VD
	Volunteer Long Service Medal	
	Volunteer Officers' Decoration (for India & the Colonies)	VD
	Volunteer Long Service Medal (for India & the Colonies)	
	Colonial Auxiliary Forces Officers' Decoration	VD
	Colonial Auxiliary Forces Long Service Medal	
	Medal for Good Shooting (Naval)	
	Militia Long Service Medal	
	Imperial Yeomanry Long Service Medal	
	Territorial Decoration	TD

From *London Gazette* dated 22 February 1941 (cont)

Change	Titles	Post-nominals
	Efficiency Decoration	TD/ED
	Territorial Efficiency Medal	
	Efficiency Medal	
	Special Reserve Long Service and Good Conduct Medal	
	Decoration for Officers of the Royal Naval Reserve	RD
	Decoration for Officers of the Royal Naval Volunteer Reserve	VD
	Royal Naval Reserve Long Service and Good Conduct Medal	
	Royal Naval Volunteer Reserve Long Service and Good Conduct Medal	
	Board of Trade Rocket Apparatus Volunteer Long Service Medal	
	African Police Medal for Meritorious Service	
	Special Constabulary Medal	
	Royal Naval Auxiliary Sick Berth Reserve Long Service and Good Conduct Medal	
	Royal Fleet Reserve Long Service and Good Conduct Medal	
	King's Medal (for Champion Shots in the Military Forces)	
	Colonial Police and Fire Brigades' Long Service Medal	
	Royal Naval Wireless Auxiliary Reserve Long Service and Good Conduct Medal	
+	Trans-Jordan Frontier Force Long Service and Good Conduct Medal	
	Union of South Africa Commemoration Medal	
	Royal Victorian Medal (Gold and Silver)	
	Imperial Service Medal	
	Royal Victorian Medal (Bronze)	
	Service Medal of the Order of St. John	
	Badge of the Order of the League of Mercy	
	Voluntary Medical Service Medal	
	Foreign Orders (in order of date of award)	
	Foreign Decorations (in order of date of award)	
	Foreign Medals (in order of date of award)	

Key to "Change"
"+" = addition   "- (??)" = deleted from this list   "*" = change of position/title.

Appendix 4 to Chapter 5

From *London Gazette* dated 11 February 1947

Change	Titles	Post-nominals
	Victoria Cross	VC
	George Cross	GC
	Knight of the Most Noble Order of the Garter	KG
	Knight of the Most Ancient and Most Noble Order of the Thistle	KT
	Knight of the Most Illustrious Order of St. Patrick	KP
	Knight Grand Cross of the Most Honourable Order of the Bath	GCB
	Member of the Order of Merit	OM
	Baronet's Badge	Bt or Bart
	Knight Grand Commander of the Most Exalted Order of the Star of India	GCSI
	Knight Grand Cross of the Most Distinguished Order of St. Michael & St. George	GCMG
	Knight Grand Commander of the Most Eminent Order of the Indian Empire	GCIE
	The Imperial Order of the Crown of India	CI
	Knight or Dame Grand Cross of the Royal Victorian Order	GCVO
	Knight or Dame Grand Cross of the Most Excellent Order of the British Empire	GBE
	Member of the Order of the Companions of Honour	CH
	Knight Commander of the Most Honourable Order of the Bath	KCB
	Knight Commander of the Most Exalted Order of the Star of India	KCSI
	Knight Commander of the Most Distinguished Order of St. Michael & St. George	KCMG
	Knight Commander of the Most Eminent Order of the Indian Empire	KCIE
	Knight or Dame Commander of the Royal Victorian Order	KCVO/DCVO
	Knight or Dame Commander of the Most Excellent Order of the British Empire	KBE/DBE
	Knight Bachelor's Badge	
	Companion of the Most Honourable Order of the Bath	CB
	Companion of the Most Exalted Order of the Star of India	CSI
	Companion of the Most Distinguished Order of St. Michael & St. George	CMG

"Medals Will Be Worn"

From *London Gazette* dated 11 February 1947 (cont)

Change	Titles	Post-nominals
	Companion of the Most Eminent Order of the Indian Empire	CIE
	Commander of the Royal Victorian Order	CVO
	Commander of the Most Excellent Order of the British Empire	CBE
	Companion of the Distinguished Service Order	DSO
	Member of the Fourth Class of the Royal Victorian Order	MVO
	Officer of the Most Excellent Order of the British Empire	OBE
	Companion of the Imperial Service Order	ISO
	Member of the Fifth Class of the Royal Victorian Order	MVO
	Member of the Most Excellent Order of the British Empire	MBE
*	Indian Order of Merit (Military)	IOM
+	Order of Burma (for gallantry)	OB
	Member of the Royal Red Cross	RRC
	Distinguished Service Cross	DSC
	Military Cross	MC
	Distinguished Flying Cross	DFC
	Air Force Cross	AFC
	Associate of the Royal Red Cross	ARRC
	Order of British India	OBI
	Kaisar-i-Hind Medal (Gold, Silver & Bronze)	
*	Order of Burma (for good service)	OB
	Order of St. John (All Classes)	
	Albert Medals (Sea & Land; Classes I & II (Gold & Bronze))	AM
+	Union of South Africa King's Medal for Bravery (in Gold)	
*	Distinguished Conduct Medal	DCM
	Conspicuous Gallantry Medal	CGM
*	George Medal	GM
	King's Police and Fire Services Medal for Gallantry	
*	Edward Medal (1st & 2nd Classes)(Silver and Bronze)	EM
*	Royal West African Frontier Force Distinguished Conduct Medal	DCM

From *London Gazette* dated 11 February 1947 (cont)

Change	Titles	Post-nominals
*	King's African Rifles Distinguished Conduct Medal	DCM
*	Indian Distinguished Service Medal	IDSM
*	Burma Gallantry Medal	BGM
+	Union of South Africa King's Medal for Bravery (in Silver)	
	Distinguished Service Medal	DSM
	Military Medal	MM
	Distinguished Flying Medal	DFM
	Air Force Medal	AFM
	Constabulary Medal (Ireland)	
*	Medal for Saving Life at Sea	SGM
	Indian Order of Merit (Civil)	IOM
	Indian Police Medal for Gallantry	
*	Burma Police Medal for Gallantry	
	Colonial Police Medal for Gallantry	
	British Empire Medal	BEM
+	Canada Medal	CM/MduC
	Life Saving Medal of the Order of St. John	
	War Medals (in order of date of campaign for which awarded)	
	Polar Medals (in order of date)	
*	Royal Victorian Medal (Gold, Silver & Bronze)	
*	Imperial Service Medal	
*	King's Police and Fire Services Medal for Distinguished Service	
*	Indian Police Medal for Meritorious Service	
*	Burma Police Medal for Meritorious Service	
*	Colonial Police Medal for Meritorious Service	
	Queen Victoria's Jubilee Medal, 1887 (Gold, Silver & Bronze)	
	Queen Victoria's Police Jubilee Medal, 1887	
	Queen Victoria's Jubilee Medal, 1897 (Gold, Silver & Bronze)	
	Queen Victoria's Police Jubilee Medal, 1897	

From *London Gazette* dated 11 February 1947 (cont)

Change   Titles   Post-nominals

            Queen Victoria's Commemoration Medal, 1900 (Ireland)

            King Edward VII's Coronation Medal, 1902

            King Edward VII's Police Coronation Medal, 1902

            King Edward VII's Durbar Medal, 1903 (Gold, Silver & Bronze)

            King Edward VII's Police Medal, 1903 (Scotland)

            King's Visit Commemoration Medal, 1903 (Ireland)

            King George V's Coronation Medal, 1911

            King George V's Police Coronation Medal, 1911

            King's Visit Police Commemoration Medal, 1911 (Ireland)

            King George V's Durbar Medal, 1911 (Gold, Silver & Bronze)

            King George V's Silver Jubilee Medal, 1935

            King George VI's Coronation Medal, 1937

+   King George V's Long and Faithful Service Medal

+   King George VI's Long and Faithful Service Medal

            Long Service and Good Conduct Medal

            Naval Long Service and Good Conduct Medal

            Medal for Meritorious Service   (MSM)

            Indian Long Service and Good Conduct Medal
            (for Europeans of Indian Army)

            Indian Meritorious Service Medal
            (for Europeans of Indian Army)

            Royal Marine Meritorious Service Medal

            Royal Air Force Meritorious Service Medal

            Royal Air Force Long Service and Good Conduct Medal

            Indian Long Service and Good Conduct Medal
            (for Indian Army)

            Royal West African Frontier Force Long Service
            and Good Conduct Medal

            King's African Rifles Long Service
            and Good Conduct Medal

            Indian Meritorious Service Medal (for Indian Army)

1924-1951

From *London Gazette* dated 11 February 1947 (cont)

Change	Titles	Post-nominals
*	Trans-Jordan Frontier Force Long Service and Good Conduct Medal	
*	African Police Medal for Meritorious Service	
+	Royal Canadian Mounted Police Long Service Medal	
*	Colonial Police and Fire Brigades' Long Service Medal	
	Volunteer Officers' Decoration	VD
	Volunteer Long Service Medal	
	Volunteer Officers' Decoration (for India & the Colonies)	VD
	Volunteer Long Service Medal (for India & the Colonies)	
	Colonial Auxiliary Forces Officers' Decoration	VD
	Colonial Auxiliary Forces Long Service Medal	
	Medal for Good Shooting (Naval)	
	Militia Long Service Medal	
	Imperial Yeomanry Long Service Medal	
	Territorial Decoration	TD
	Efficiency Decoration	TD/ED
	Territorial Efficiency Medal	
	Efficiency Medal	
	Special Reserve Long Service and Good Conduct Medal	
	Decoration for Officers of the Royal Naval Reserve	RD
	Decoration for Officers of the Royal Naval Volunteer Reserve	VRD
	Royal Naval Reserve Long Service and Good Conduct Medal	
	Royal Naval Volunteer Reserve Long Service and Good Conduct Medal	
	Royal Naval Auxiliary Sick Berth Reserve Long Service and Good Conduct Medal	
	Royal Fleet Reserve Long Service and Good Conduct Medal	
	Royal Naval Wireless Auxiliary Reserve Long Service and Good Conduct Medal	
+	Air Efficiency Award	
*	King's Medal (for Champion Shots in the Military Forces)	
*	Rocket Apparatus Volunteer Long Service Medal	

From *London Gazette* dated 11 February 1947 (cont)

Change   Titles   Post-nominals

        Special Constabulary Medal

        Union of South Africa Commemoration Medal

        Service Medal of the Order of St. John

        Badge of the Order of the League of Mercy

        Voluntary Medical Service Medal

+   South African Medal for War Services

        Foreign Orders (in order of date of award)

        Foreign Decorations (in order of date of award)

        Foreign Medals (in order of date of award)

Key to "Change"
"+" = addition   *"- (??)" = deleted from this list*   *"*" = change of position/title.*

Appendix 5 to Chapter 5

From *London Gazette* dated 12 July 1949

Change	Titles	Post-nominals
	Victoria Cross	VC
	George Cross	GC
	Knight of the Most Noble Order of the Garter	KG
	Knight of the Most Ancient and Most Noble Order of the Thistle	KT
	Knight of the Most Illustrious Order of St. Patrick	KP
	Knight Grand Cross of the Most Honourable Order of the Bath	GCB
	Member of the Order of Merit	OM
	Baronet's Badge	Bt or Bart
	Knight Grand Commander of the Most Exalted Order of the Star of India	GCSI
	Knight Grand Cross of the Most Distinguished Order of St. Michael & St. George	GCMG
	Knight Grand Commander of the Most Eminent Order of the Indian Empire	GCIE
	The Imperial Order of the Crown of India	CI
	Knight or Dame Grand Cross of the Royal Victorian Order	GCVO
	Knight or Dame Grand Cross of the Most Excellent Order of the British Empire	GBE
	Member of the Order of the Companions of Honour	CH
	Knight Commander of the Most Honourable Order of the Bath	KCB
	Knight Commander of the Most Exalted Order of the Star of India	KCSI
	Knight Commander of the Most Distinguished Order of St. Michael & St. George	KCMG
	Knight Commander of the Most Eminent Order of the Indian Empire	KCIE
	Knight or Dame Commander of the Royal Victorian Order	KCVO/DCVO
	Knight or Dame Commander of the Most Excellent Order of the British Empire	KBE/DBE
	Knight Bachelor's Badge	
	Companion of the Most Honourable Order of the Bath	CB
	Companion of the Most Exalted Order of the Star of India	CSI

From *London Gazette* dated 12 July 1949 (cont)

Change	Titles	Post-nominals
	Companion of the Most Distinguished Order of St. Michael & St. George	CMG
	Companion of the Most Eminent Order of the Indian Empire	CIE
	Commander of the Royal Victorian Order	CVO
	Commander of the Most Excellent Order of the British Empire	CBE
	Companion of the Distinguished Service Order	DSO
	Member of the Fourth Class of the Royal Victorian Order	MVO
	Officer of the Most Excellent Order of the British Empire	OBE
	Companion of the Imperial Service Order	ISO
	Member of the Fifth Class of the Royal Victorian Order	MVO
	Member of the Most Excellent Order of the British Empire	MBE
	Indian Order of Merit (Military)	IOM
-	(Order of Burma (for gallantry))	
	Member of the Royal Red Cross	RRC
	Distinguished Service Cross	DSC
	Military Cross	MC
	Distinguished Flying Cross	DFC
	Air Force Cross	AFC
	Associate of the Royal Red Cross	ARRC
	Order of British India	OBI
	Kaisar-i-Hind Medal (Gold, Silver & Bronze)	
-	(Order of Burma (for good service))	
	Order of St. John (All Classes)	
	Albert Medals (Sea & Land; Classes I & II (Gold & Bronze)	AM
	Union of South Africa Queen's Medal for Bravery (in Gold)	
	Distinguished Conduct Medal	DCM
	Conspicuous Gallantry Medal	CGM
	George Medal	GM
	King's Police and Fire Services Medal for Gallantry	
	Edward Medal (1st & 2nd Classes)(Silver and Bronze)	EM

From *London Gazette* dated 12 July 1949 (cont)

Change	Titles	Post-nominals
	Royal West African Frontier Force Distinguished Conduct Medal	DCM
	King's African Rifles Distinguished Conduct Medal	DCM
	Indian Distinguished Service Medal	IDSM
-	(Burma Gallantry Medal)	
	Union of South Africa Queen's Medal for Bravery (in Silver)	
	Distinguished Service Medal	DSM
	Military Medal	MM
	Distinguished Flying Medal	DFM
	Air Force Medal	AFM
	Constabulary Medal (Ireland)	
	Medal for Saving Life at Sea	SGM
	Indian Order of Merit (Civil)	IOM
	Indian Police Medal for Gallantry	
-	(Burma Police Medal for Gallantry)	
	Colonial Police Medal for Gallantry	
	British Empire Medal	BEM
	Canada Medal	CM/MduC
-	(Life Saving Medal of the Order of St. John)	
	War Medals (in order of date of campaign for which awarded)	
	Polar Medals (in order of date)	
	Royal Victorian Medal (Gold, Silver & Bronze)	
	Imperial Service Medal	
	King's Police and Fire Services Medal for Distinguished Service	
	Indian Police Medal for Meritorious Service	
-	(Burma Police Medal for Meritorious Service)	
	Colonial Police Medal for Meritorious Service	
	Queen Victoria's Jubilee Medal, 1887 (Gold, Silver & Bronze)	
	Queen Victoria's Police Jubilee Medal, 1887	
	Queen Victoria's Jubilee Medal, 1897 (Gold, Silver & Bronze)	

From *London Gazette* dated 12 July 1949 (cont)

Change Titles   Post-nominals

    Queen Victoria's Police Jubilee Medal, 1897

    Queen Victoria's Commemoration Medal, 1900 (Ireland)

    King Edward VII's Coronation Medal, 1902

    King Edward VII's Police Coronation Medal, 1902

    King Edward VII's Durbar Medal, 1903 (Gold, Silver & Bronze)

    King Edward VII's Police Medal, 1903 (Scotland)

    King's Visit Commemoration Medal, 1903 (Ireland)

    King George V's Coronation Medal, 1911

    King George V's Police Coronation Medal, 1911

    King's Visit Police Commemoration Medal, 1911 (Ireland)

    King George V's Durbar Medal, 1911 (Gold, Silver & Bronze)

    King George V's Silver Jubilee Medal, 1935

    King George VI's Coronation Medal, 1937

    King George V's Long and Faithful Service Medal

    King George VI's Long and Faithful Service Medal

    Long Service and Good Conduct Medal

    Naval Long Service and Good Conduct Medal

    Medal for Meritorious Service   (MSM)

    Indian Long Service and Good Conduct Medal
    (for Europeans of Indian Army)

    Indian Meritorious Service Medal
    (for Europeans of Indian Army)

    Royal Marine Meritorious Service Medal

    Royal Air Force Meritorious Service Medal

    Royal Air Force Long Service and Good Conduct Medal

    Indian Long Service and Good Conduct Medal
    (for Indian Army)

    Royal West African Frontier Force Long Service and Good Conduct Medal

    King's African Rifles Long Service and Good Conduct Medal

    Indian Meritorious Service Medal (for Indian Army)

    African Police Medal for Meritorious Service

1924-1951

From *London Gazette* dated 12 July 1949 (cont)

Change	Titles	Post-nominals
	(Trans-Jordan Frontier Force Long Service and Good Conduct Medal)	
	Royal Canadian Mounted Police Long Service Medal	
	Colonial Police and Fire Brigades' Long Service Medal	
	Volunteer Officers' Decoration	VD
	Volunteer Long Service Medal	
	Volunteer Officers' Decoration (for India & the Colonies)	VD
	Volunteer Long Service Medal (for India & the Colonies)	
	Colonial Auxiliary Forces Officers' Decoration	VD
	Colonial Auxiliary Forces Long Service Medal	
	Medal for Good Shooting (Naval)	
	Militia Long Service Medal	
	Imperial Yeomanry Long Service Medal	
	Territorial Decoration	TD
	Efficiency Decoration	TD/ED
	Territorial Efficiency Medal	
	Efficiency Medal	
	Special Reserve Long Service and Good Conduct Medal	
	Decoration for Officers of the Royal Naval Reserve	RD
	Decoration for Officers of the Royal Naval Volunteer Reserve	VRD
	Royal Naval Reserve Long Service and Good Conduct Medal	
	Royal Naval Volunteer Reserve Long Service and Good Conduct Medal	
	Royal Naval Auxiliary Sick Berth Reserve Long Service and Good Conduct Medal	
	Royal Fleet Reserve Long Service and Good Conduct Medal	
	Royal Naval Wireless Auxiliary Reserve Long Service and Good Conduct Medal	
	Air Efficiency Award	
	King's Medal (for Champion Shots in the Military Forces)	
	Rocket Apparatus Volunteer Long Service Medal	
	Special Constabulary Medal	

From *London Gazette* dated 12 July 1949 (cont)

Change Titles   Post-nominals

	Title
	Union of South Africa Commemoration Medal
+	Indian Independence Medal
	Service Medal of the Order of St. John
	Badge of the Order of the League of Mercy
	Voluntary Medical Service Medal
	South African Medal for War Services
	Foreign Orders (in order of date of award)
	Foreign Decorations (in order of date of award)
	Foreign Medals (in order of date of award)

Key to "Change"
"+" = *addition*   "- (??)" = *deleted from this list*   "*" = *change of position/title.*

Appendix 6 to Chapter 5

From *London Gazette* dated 27 July 1951

Change	Titles	Post-nominals
	Victoria Cross	VC
	George Cross	GC
	Knight of the Most Noble Order of the Garter	KG
	Knight of the Most Ancient and Most Noble Order of the Thistle	KT
	Knight of the Most Illustrious Order of St. Patrick	KP
	Knight Grand Cross of the Most Honourable Order of the Bath	GCB
	Member of the Order of Merit	OM
	Baronet's Badge	Bt or Bart
	Knight Grand Commander of the Most Exalted Order of the Star of India	GCSI
	Knight Grand Cross of the Most Distinguished Order of St. Michael & St. George	GCMG
	Knight Grand Commander of the Most Eminent Order of the Indian Empire	GCIE
	The Imperial Order of the Crown of India	CI
	Knight or Dame Grand Cross of the Royal Victorian Order	GCVO
	Knight or Dame Grand Cross of the Most Excellent Order of the British Empire	GBE
	Member of the Order of the Companions of Honour	CH
	Knight Commander of the Most Honourable Order of the Bath	KCB
	Knight Commander of the Most Exalted Order of the Star of India	KCSI
	Knight Commander of the Most Distinguished Order of St. Michael & St. George	KCMG
	Knight Commander of the Most Eminent Order of the Indian Empire	KCIE
	Knight or Dame Commander of the Royal Victorian Order	KCVO/ DCVO
	Knight or Dame Commander of the Most Excellent Order of the British Empire	KBE/DBE
	Knight Bachelor's Badge	
	Companion of the Most Honourable Order of the Bath	CB
	Companion of the Most Exalted Order of the Star of India	CSI

From *London Gazette* dated 27 July 1951 (cont)

Change	Titles	Post-nominals
	Companion of the Most Distinguished Order of St. Michael & St. George	CMG
	Companion of the Most Eminent Order of the Indian Empire	CIE
	Commander of the Royal Victorian Order	CVO
	Commander of the Most Excellent Order of the British Empire	CBE
	Companion of the Distinguished Service Order	DSO
	Member of the Fourth Class of the Royal Victorian Order	MVO
	Officer of the Most Excellent Order of the British Empire	OBE
	Companion of the Imperial Service Order	ISO
	Member of the Fifth Class of the Royal Victorian Order	MVO
	Member of the Most Excellent Order of the British Empire	MBE
	Indian Order of Merit (Military)	IOM
	Member of the Royal Red Cross	RRC
	Distinguished Service Cross	DSC
	Military Cross	MC
	Distinguished Flying Cross	DFC
	Air Force Cross	AFC
	Associate of the Royal Red Cross	ARRC
	Order of British India	OBI
	Kaisar-i-Hind Medal (Gold, Silver & Bronze)	
	Order of St. John (All Classes)	
	Albert Medals (Sea & Land; Classes I & II (Gold & Bronze)	AM
	Union of South Africa Queen's Medal for Bravery (in Gold)	
	Distinguished Conduct Medal	DCM
	Conspicuous Gallantry Medal	CGM
	George Medal	GM
	King's Police and Fire Services Medal for Gallantry	
	Edward Medal (1st & 2nd Classes)(Silver and Bronze)	EM
	Royal West African Frontier Force Distinguished Conduct Medal	DCM
	King's African Rifles Distinguished Conduct Medal	DCM

From *London Gazette* dated 27 July 1951 (cont)

Change	Titles	Post-nominals
	Indian Distinguished Service Medal	IDSM
	Union of South Africa Queen's Medal for Bravery (in Silver)	
	Distinguished Service Medal	DSM
	Military Medal	MM
	Distinguished Flying Medal	DFM
	Air Force Medal	AFM
	Constabulary Medal (Ireland)	
	Medal for Saving Life at Sea	SGM
	Indian Order of Merit (Civil)	IOM
	Indian Police Medal for Gallantry	
+	Ceylon Police Medal for Gallantry	
	Colonial Police Medal for Gallantry	
	British Empire Medal	BEM
	Canada Medal	CM/MduC
*	King's Police and Fire Services Medal for Distinguished Service	
	War Medals (in order of date of campaign for which awarded)	
	Polar Medals (in order of date)	
	Royal Victorian Medal (Gold, Silver & Bronze)	
	Imperial Service Medal	
	Indian Police Medal for Meritorious Service	
+	Ceylon Police Medal for Merit	
	Colonial Police Medal for Meritorious Service	
	Queen Victoria's Jubilee Medal, 1887 (Gold, Silver & Bronze)	
	Queen Victoria's Police Jubilee Medal, 1887	
	Queen Victoria's Jubilee Medal, 1897 (Gold, Silver & Bronze)	
	Queen Victoria's Police Jubilee Medal, 1897	
	Queen Victoria's Commemoration Medal, 1900 (Ireland)	
	King Edward VII's Coronation Medal, 1902	
	King Edward VII's Police Coronation Medal, 1902	
	King Edward VII's Durbar Medal, 1903 (Gold, Silver & Bronze)	

From *London Gazette* dated 27 July 1951 (cont)

Change Titles   Post-nominals

- King Edward VII's Police Medal, 1903 (Scotland)
- King's Visit Commemoration Medal, 1903 (Ireland)
- King George V's Coronation Medal, 1911
- King George V's Police Coronation Medal, 1911
- King's Visit Police Commemoration Medal, 1911 (Ireland)
- King George V's Durbar Medal, 1911 (Gold, Silver & Bronze)
- King George V's Silver Jubilee Medal, 1935
- King George VI's Coronation Medal, 1937
- King George V's Long and Faithful Service Medal
- King George VI's Long and Faithful Service Medal
- Long Service and Good Conduct Medal
- Naval Long Service and Good Conduct Medal
- Medal for Meritorious Service   (MSM)
- Indian Long Service and Good Conduct Medal (for Europeans of Indian Army)
- Indian Meritorious Service Medal (for Europeans of Indian Army)
- Royal Marine Meritorious Service Medal
- Royal Air Force Meritorious Service Medal
- Royal Air Force Long Service and Good Conduct Medal
- Indian Long Service and Good Conduct Medal (for Indian Army)
- Royal West African Frontier Force Long Service and Good Conduct Medal
- King's African Rifles Long Service and Good Conduct Medal
- Indian Meritorious Service Medal (for Indian Army)
- \+ Police Long Service and Good Conduct Medal
- African Police Medal for Meritorious Service
- Royal Canadian Mounted Police Long Service Medal
- \+ Ceylon Police and Fire Services Long Service Medal
- Colonial Police and Fire Brigades Long Service Medal
- Volunteer Officers' Decoration   VD

From *London Gazette* dated 27 July 1951 (cont)

Change	Titles	Post-nominals
	Volunteer Long Service Medal	
	Volunteer Officers' Decoration (for India & the Colonies)	VD
	Volunteer Long Service Medal (for India & the Colonies)	
	Colonial Auxiliary Forces Officers' Decoration	VD
	Colonial Auxiliary Forces Long Service Medal	
	Medal for Good Shooting (Naval)	
	Militia Long Service Medal	
	Imperial Yeomanry Long Service Medal	
	Territorial Decoration	TD
	Efficiency Decoration	TD/ED
	Territorial Efficiency Medal	
	Efficiency Medal	
	Special Reserve Long Service and Good Conduct Medal	
	Decoration for Officers of the Royal Naval Reserve	RD
	Decoration for Officers of the Royal Naval Volunteer Reserve	VRD
	Royal Naval Reserve Long Service and Good Conduct Medal	
	Royal Naval Volunteer Reserve Long Service and Good Conduct Medal	
	Royal Naval Auxiliary Sick Berth Reserve Long Service and Good Conduct Medal	
	Royal Fleet Reserve Long Service and Good Conduct Medal	
	Royal Naval Wireless Auxiliary Reserve Long Service and Good Conduct Medal	
	Air Efficiency Award	
	King's Medal (for Champion Shots in the Military Forces)	
+	Cadet Forces Medal	
	Rocket Apparatus Volunteer Long Service Medal	
*	Special Constabulary Long Service Medal	
+	Canadian Forces Decoration	CD
+	Royal Observer Corps Medal	
	Union of South Africa Commemoration Medal	

From *London Gazette* dated 27 July 1951 (cont)

Change	Titles	Post-nominals
	Indian Independence Medal	
	Service Medal of the Order of St. John	
	Badge of the Order of the League of Mercy	
	Voluntary Medical Service Medal	
	South African Medal for War Services	
	Foreign Orders (in order of date of award)	
	Foreign Decorations (in order of date of award)	
	Foreign Medals (in order of date of award)	

Key to "Change"
"+" = *addition*   "- (??)" = *deleted from this list*   "*" = *change of position/title.*

Chapter 6

1952 TO 1995

IN 1954 the first list of the Queen's reign was published in which the various "King's" titles changed to "Queen's". The Queen's Medal for Chiefs was added immediately before War Medals and the Badge of Honour just before Jubilee, etc., medals. Interestingly the latter is worn by a recent Chief of the General Staff, General Sir Charles Guthrie, GCB, LVO, OBE, who wears on his medal bar the LVO, OBE, General Service Medal 1962 with two clasps, Badge of Honour and Jubilee Medal.

Other additions were the separation of the Fire Service from the Police medals; the Army Emergency Reserve Decoration; Ceylon Police and Fire Services medals, the Queen's Medal for Shooting for the RAF and the Pakistan Medal. In addition the notes on wearing campaign medals added the Pakistan General Service Medal 1951.

In the 1955 list there were no alterations except that those awards which carried the right to letters after the name were indicated for the first time. This did not, and never has, extended to showing what the actual letters to be used are as these details are included in the relevant warrants. The usual letters in use at the time are shown in all appendices to chapters of this book. These are based largely on those authorised in the warrants, and include the MSM in brackets as these were used, as a matter of custom, by recipients of the Royal Naval Meritorious Service Medal before 20 July 1928 and by no one else.

1958 saw only the addition of notes on the Order and Medal of the British Empire relating to the gallantry emblem plus the addition of several Colonial Police, Fire Service, Prisons and Special Constabulary Medals.

1961 added the Queen's Medal for Shooting in the New Zealand Navy, Civil Defence Long Service Medal and Women's Voluntary Service Medal as well as independence type medals for Ceylon, Nigeria and Sierra Leone. It also added a footnote to explain that the holder of a Colonial Police Medal for Merit who subsequently received a bar for gallantry would continue to wear the meritorious service ribbon with an added bar, but in the position for a gallantry award. Basically this is ahead of the BEM and campaign medals; the meritorious version is worn after the Polar Medals, Royal Victorian Medal and Imperial Service Medal. This exemplifies the lack of forethought often exhibited. This solution no doubt met the immediate problem of a second award of this nature. However, there was, and is, every possibility of someone receiving a meritorious bar to a gallantry award. A bar to the existing medal would appear to be for gallantry. The proper solution should have been to treat the two awards as two separate medals at a cost of the odd medal now and again. Instead here is a ruling which will not meet up to a very real possibility.

Finally in 1961 the listing included a totally new category, that of Commonwealth Members Orders, Decorations and Medals which had been instituted since 1949, but not by the Queen, to come between the detailed "British" list and foreign awards. This heading specifically included the awards of the States of the Federation of Malaya. Unlike foreign awards there was no rider to the effect that permission is required to accept these honours.

The next list in 1964 added certain Sierra Leone Military Forces, Police and Fire Brigades medals and three more independence medals to Jamaica, Uganda and Malawi. The notes on campaign medals included the new General Service Medal

1962 and the Sierra Leone General Service Medal 1961. To the note on the other "non-Queen's" Commonwealth awards post 1949 was added the State of Brunei.

The only deletion was that of the Nigerian Independence Medal which had ceased to be a "Queen's" medal in 1964 as explained in detail elsewhere.

In September 1966 the Queen agreed to vary an earlier regulation by allowing the wear of one neck decoration and one breast star with dinner jackets. The earlier regulation was in September 1948 when those not in possession of evening dress (tails) were allowed, *as a temporary measure*, to wear miniatures with dinner jacket. Such is the march of time that this later variation is now extended to lounge suits for neck decorations.

Army Dress Regulations for Officers 1969 are basically unchanged from the *London Gazette* lists. However, there are some curious features and amendments deserving comment. Several Ugandan awards are shown as being added in Appendix 6; in fact they were already included in Army Clothing Regulations for 1961 and brought into this document from there. They have never appeared in a *London Gazette* listing. Presumably they were dropped before they could get into the *Gazette* in 1964 but were known to the Ministry of Defence in 1961. If so, it is hard to understand how they can now be omitted; presumably the Ugandans under Idi Amin were even more unpopular than were the Burmese in 1949.

The Queen's Gallantry Medal was added by amendment in 1976 in the wrong place after the QFSM for gallantry. The Royal Warrant of 1974 placed it after the Colonial Police Medal for gallantry; also arguably the wrong place. Also added, or re-instated, by this amendment was the Burma Gallantry Medal in its old position. This is very curious, especially as the other Burma medals are not mentioned. Perhaps a holder of the BGM joined the British forces.

Also in the 1976 amendment a note added the provision that any grade of the Order of the British Empire for gallantry, on promotion to a higher grade, retained and wore the gallantry insignia (not the emblem only) as well as that of the higher grade.

Right up until amendments of 1978 the Sierra Leone medals added into the *London Gazette* lists continued to be ignored. They are not shown as deletions in Appendix 6 as they continue to appear in the later *London Gazettes*.

The most recent list in the *London Gazette* was published in 1983 with various changes and the introduction of new features. The Knight Bachelor's Badge is now to be worn round the neck suspended from a ribbon. Originally this badge had been worn in the manner of a star of an order below the medal bar on the left hand pocket. This was not universally favoured by recipients and in 1973 the Queen authorised a neck badge and a miniature. Recipients were given the option of wearing the badge at the neck, though they could continue to wear it on the left pocket if they wished. Now the *London Gazette* indicates that it is worn at the neck only and the breast badge has been discontinued.

Notable deletions include the Albert Medal and Edward Medal despite the fact that there may still be some survivors who declined to exchange their original awards for the George Cross in 1972. The Conspicuous Gallantry Medal (Flying) was added for the first time, as was the Queen's Gallantry Medal. Post-nominal letters were added for the Police and Fire Services Medals, the Colonial Police Medal and the Royal Victorian Medals. The latter also leapt from a position behind Polar Medals to immediately ahead of the BEM.

The Meritorious Service Medal, since December 1977 open to all of the Armed Forces, moved from behind to in front of the Long Service and Good Conduct Medal

(Military). The older MSMs for the RN, RM, RAF and former Empire retain their old positions. Other additions include some Mauritian Long Service medals, two Ulster Defence Regiment Long Service awards, a Ceylon Armed Forces Long Service Medal and a Queen's Medal for Shooting in the Royal Navy and Royal Marines. This latter was instituted in 1953 so achieved mention after a mere thirty years. The Royal Naval Auxiliary Service Medal also joins the list only eighteen years after being instituted in 1965.

In addition two awards which really fall into other categories are added before independence medals. They are the Rhodesia Medal and the Royal Ulster Constabulary Service Medal. Despite their position these are more allied to campaign medals than to commemorative or long service medals. Also three more independence medals for Fiji, Papua New Guinea and Solomon Islands are added plus the notes on honorary membership of Commonwealth awards dealt with in more detail elsewhere.

Post-nominal letters are indicated for the following in addition to those previously notified (the authorisation year is shown in brackets): CGM (Flying) (1943); QPM (1969); QFSM (1969); CPM (1973); QGM (1974); RVM (1980); AE (1975 officer recipients only); UD (1982 officer recipients only). There is also a note that "Bt." or "Bart." comes directly after the surname and before all other post-nominal letters. The same applies to "Esq." but this is not included in the note.

The notes on other Commonwealth awards (post 1949) now include the provisions that they are worn in order of date of award and that the Sovereign's permission is required for them to be worn.

Lastly the notes allow the retention and wear of the lower "gallantry" grade of the Order of the British Empire if the recipient is promoted in the Order.

Since 1983 the only guide to any changes are contained in regulations other than the *London Gazette*. Army Material Regulations 1995 include what seems to be the latest list and attempts have been made to cull it as well as amplifying the headings, though not very successfully.

The guiding principles are said to be that awards are worn in the overall order: VC; GC; British orders; British decorations and medals; Commonwealth and United Nations medals; foreign orders, decorations and medals in date order.

This is followed by further instructions that medals fall into five distinct groups:

- Medals for gallantry in action or saving life in peace.
- Medals for war service including campaigns and United Nations service.
- Commemorative medals.
- Medals for efficiency and long service.
- Commonwealth medals.

In the detailed list of the order of wear, called the "preference list", there are groupings as shown below:

- VC and GC.
- Orders down to MBE followed by Baronet and Knight Bachelor out of order and with no notes to correct this. Knight Bachelor is also shown to carry the right to post-nominal letters.
- Decorations.
- Medals for Gallantry and Distinguished Service.
- Medals attached to Orders.
- War Medals.
- Alliance Medals including United Nations and "Economic Community".

- Commemoration Medals.
- Efficiency and Long Service Decorations and Medals.
- Foreign Orders, Decorations and Medals.
- Mentions in Despatches and Queen's Commendations for Bravery.

The "headings" (in bold type) for the various Commonwealth Orders etc. are omitted; so these awards fall under the long service header.

It will be noted that the three overall lists do not tally and the order of wearing the "Alliance Medals" is apart from other campaign medals, contrary to the DCIs notifying their acceptance.

The notes are roughly as in previous instructions but the order of wearing campaign medals, after repeating the 1939-45 list, has the Indian General Service Medal 1936; General Service Medal 1962; the Sierra Leone General Service Medal and United Nations medals. The deficiencies in this list have been examined elsewhere, but the mind boggles at including a 1936 medal while omitting a number of post-war medals.

It is equally strange to prune the overall list, including deleting the major Indian Orders, yet continue to include the Order of British India and Kaisar-i-Hind Medals. This instruction is to the Army and it seems highly unlikely that any holders of these latter awards are still serving. It is equally odd to add the MSM for South African Permanent Forces while omitting the Rhodesia Medal. Other facets which show poor staff work, illogical thought or ignorance, or a combination of all three are:

- Inclusion of the Queen's Service Order (New Zealand) while omitting the equivalent medal and the Badge of Honour worn by a recent Chief of the General Staff.
- Inventing a new medal "Efficiency Medal (HAC)" (in fact just a different ribbon) to be worn before the actual Efficiency Medal yet omitting the many other long service medals which may be worn by some of the Territorials and officers/adults in the Cadet Forces who wear Army uniform.
- Including the Air Efficiency Award while omitting all naval reserve long service awards. The fact that TAVRAs administer Air Force Reserves, but not Naval Reserves does not alter the fact that individuals can, and do, leave one service and join another for a variety of reasons, regardless of administration responsibilities. Twelve years in the Royal Naval Reserve followed by another twelve in the Territorial Army is not unknown bringing with it the two long service awards.
- Inventing a new set of post-nominal letters (CGM (F)) for the Conspicuous Gallantry Medal (Flying).
- Including the "King's or Queen's Police Medal for Gallantry" awarded only posthumously since 1954, while omitting the Distinguished Service versions to the Police and Fire Service, which are still awarded today, including to Ministry of Defence Police and Fire Service personnel.
- Omitting the Police and Fire Services long service awards, and the Imperial Service Medal, all of which may be awarded to civilians in the employ of the Ministry of Defence who may also be in the reserves.
- Omitting the Sea Gallantry Medal which, presumably, might be awarded to members of a Royal Logistic Corps Maritime unit.

Except in certain respects, like placing some new awards like the Conspicuous Gallantry Cross and Accumulated Campaign Service Medal into the listing, this regulation is wanting in many respects and does not give the guidance it should. Perhaps it could be said to be in the best traditions of the lists from the *London Gazette*.

Appendix 1 to Chapter 6

From *London Gazette* dated 15 June 1954

Change	Titles	Post-nominals
	Victoria Cross	VC
	George Cross	GC
	Knight of the Most Noble Order of the Garter	KG
	Knight of the Most Ancient and Most Noble Order of the Thistle	KT
	Knight of the Most Illustrious Order of St. Patrick	KP
	Knight Grand Cross of the Most Honourable Order of the Bath	GCB
	Member of the Order of Merit	OM
	Baronet's Badge	Bt or Bart
	Knight Grand Commander of the Most Exalted Order of the Star of India	GCSI
	Knight Grand Cross of the Most Distinguished Order of St. Michael & St. George	GCMG
	Knight Grand Commander of the Most Eminent Order of the Indian Empire	GCIE
	The Imperial Order of the Crown of India	CI
	Knight or Dame Grand Cross of the Royal Victorian Order	GCVO
	Knight or Dame Grand Cross of the Most Excellent Order of the British Empire	GBE
	Member of the Order of the Companions of Honour	CH
	Knight Commander of the Most Honourable Order of the Bath	KCB
	Knight Commander of the Most Exalted Order of the Star of India	KCSI
	Knight Commander of the Most Distinguished Order of St. Michael & St. George	KCMG
	Knight Commander of the Most Eminent Order of the Indian Empire	KCIE
	Knight or Dame Commander of the Royal Victorian Order	KCVO/ DCVO
	Knight or Dame Commander of the Most Excellent Order of the British Empire	KBE/DBE
	Knight Bachelor's Badge	
	Companion of the Most Honourable Order of the Bath	CB
	Companion of the Most Exalted Order of the Star of India	CSI

From *London Gazette* dated 15 June 1954 (cont)

Change	Titles	Post-nominals
	Companion of the Most Distinguished Order of St. Michael & St. George	CMG
	Companion of the Most Eminent Order of the Indian Empire	CIE
	Commander of the Royal Victorian Order	CVO
	Commander of the Most Excellent Order of the British Empire	CBE
	Companion of the Distinguished Service Order	DSO
	Member of the Fourth Class of the Royal Victorian Order	MVO
	Officer of the Most Excellent Order of the British Empire	OBE
	Companion of the Imperial Service Order	ISO
	Member of the Fifth Class of the Royal Victorian Order	MVO
	Member of the Most Excellent Order of the British Empire	MBE
	Indian Order of Merit (Military)	IOM
	Member of the Royal Red Cross	RRC
	Distinguished Service Cross	DSC
	Military Cross	MC
	Distinguished Flying Cross	DFC
	Air Force Cross	AFC
	Associate of the Royal Red Cross	ARRC
	Order of British India	OBI
	Kaisar-i-Hind Medal (Gold, Silver & Bronze)	
	Order of St. John (All Classes)	
	Albert Medals (Sea & Land; Classes I & II (Gold & Bronze)	AM
	Union of South Africa Queen's Medal for Bravery (in Gold)	
	Distinguished Conduct Medal	DCM
	Conspicuous Gallantry Medal	CGM
	George Medal	GM
*	Queen's Police Medal for Gallantry	
+	Queen's Fire Service Medal for Gallantry	
	Edward Medal (1st & 2nd Classes)(Silver and Bronze)	EM
	Royal West African Frontier Force Distinguished Conduct Medal	DCM

From *London Gazette* dated 15 June 1954 (cont)

Change	Titles	Post-nominals
	King's African Rifles Distinguished Conduct Medal	DCM
	Indian Distinguished Service Medal	IDSM
	Union of South Africa Queen's Medal for Bravery (in Silver)	
	Distinguished Service Medal	DSM
	Military Medal	MM
	Distinguished Flying Medal	DFM
	Air Force Medal	AFM
	Constabulary Medal (Ireland)	
	Medal for Saving Life at Sea	SGM
	Indian Order of Merit (Civil)	IOM
	Indian Police Medal for Gallantry	
	Ceylon Police Medal for Gallantry	
	Colonial Police Medal for Gallantry	
	British Empire Medal	BEM
	Canada Medal	CM/MduC
*	Queen's Police Medal for Distinguished Service	
+	Queen's Fire Service Medal for Distinguished Service	
+	Queen's Medal for Chiefs	
	War Medals (in order of date of campaign for which awarded)	
	Polar Medals (in order of date)	
	Royal Victorian Medal (Gold, Silver & Bronze)	
	Imperial Service Medal	
	Indian Police Medal for Meritorious Service	
	Ceylon Police Medal for Merit	
	Colonial Police Medal for Meritorious Service	
+	Badge of Honour	
	Queen Victoria's Jubilee Medal, 1887 (Gold, Silver & Bronze)	
	Queen Victoria's Police Jubilee Medal, 1887	
	Queen Victoria's Jubilee Medal, 1897 (Gold, Silver & Bronze)	
	Queen Victoria's Police Jubilee Medal, 1897	

From *London Gazette* dated 15 June 1954 (cont)

Change Titles   Post-nominals

        Queen Victoria's Commemoration Medal, 1900 (Ireland)

        King Edward VII's Coronation Medal, 1902

        King Edward VII's Police Coronation Medal, 1902

        King Edward VII's Durbar Medal, 1903 (Gold, Silver & Bronze)

        King Edward VII's Police Medal, 1903 (Scotland)

        King's Visit Commemoration Medal, 1903 (Ireland)

        King George V's Coronation Medal, 1911

        King George V's Police Coronation Medal, 1911

        King's Visit Police Commemoration Medal, 1911 (Ireland)

        King George V's Durbar Medal, 1911 (Gold, Silver & Bronze)

        King George V's Silver Jubilee Medal, 1935

        King George VI's Coronation Medal, 1937

+   Queen Elizabeth II's Coronation Medal, 1953

        King George V's Long and Faithful Service Medal

        King George VI's Long and Faithful Service Medal

+   Queen Elizabeth II's Long and Faithful Service Medal

        Long Service and Good Conduct Medal

        Naval Long Service and Good Conduct Medal

        Medal for Meritorious Service   (MSM)

        Indian Long Service and Good Conduct Medal
        (for Europeans of Indian Army)

        Indian Meritorious Service Medal
        (for Europeans of Indian Army)

        Royal Marine Meritorious Service Medal

        Royal Air Force Meritorious Service Medal

        Royal Air Force Long Service and Good Conduct Medal

        Indian Long Service and Good Conduct Medal
        (for Indian Army)

        Royal West African Frontier Force Long Service and Good Conduct Medal

        King's African Rifles Long Service and Good Conduct Medal

        Indian Meritorious Service Medal (for Indian Army)

From *London Gazette* dated 15 June 1954 (cont)

Change	Titles	Post-nominals
	Police Long Service and Good Conduct Medal	
+	Fire Brigade Long Service and Good Conduct Medal	
	African Police Medal for Meritorious Service	
	Royal Canadian Mounted Police Long Service Medal	
+	Ceylon Police Long Service Medal	
+	Ceylon Fire Services Long Service Medal	
	Colonial Police and Fire Brigades Long Service Medal	
+	Army Emergency Reserve Decoration	ERD
	Volunteer Officers' Decoration	VD
	Volunteer Long Service Medal	
	Volunteer Officers' Decoration (for India & the Colonies)	VD
	Volunteer Long Service Medal (for India & the Colonies)	
	Colonial Auxiliary Forces Officers' Decoration	VD
	Colonial Auxiliary Forces Long Service Medal	
	Medal for Good Shooting (Naval)	
	Militia Long Service Medal	
	Imperial Yeomanry Long Service Medal	
	Territorial Decoration	TD
	Efficiency Decoration	TD/ED
	Territorial Efficiency Medal	
	Efficiency Medal	
	Special Reserve Long Service and Good Conduct Medal	
	Decoration for Officers of the Royal Naval Reserve	RD
	Decoration for Officers of the Royal Naval Volunteer Reserve	VRD
	Royal Naval Reserve Long Service and Good Conduct Medal	
	Royal Naval Volunteer Reserve Long Service and Good Conduct Medal	
	Royal Naval Auxiliary Sick Berth Reserve Long Service and Good Conduct Medal	
	Royal Fleet Reserve Long Service and Good Conduct Medal	
	Royal Naval Wireless Auxiliary Reserve Long Service and Good Conduct Medal	

"MEDALS WILL BE WORN"

From *London Gazette* dated 15 June 1954 (cont)

Change	Titles	Post-nominals
	Air Efficiency Award	
*	Queen's Medal (for Champion Shots in the Military Forces)	
+	Queen's Medal (for Champion Shots of the Air Forces)	
	Cadet Forces Medal	
*	Coast Life Saving Corps Long Service Medal (formerly Rocket Apparatus Volunteer Long Service Medal)	
	Special Constabulary Long Service Medal	
	Canadian Forces Decoration	CD
	Royal Observer Corps Medal	
	Union of South Africa Commemoration Medal	
	Indian Independence Medal	
+	Pakistan Medal	
	Service Medal of the Order of St. John	
	Badge of the Order of the League of Mercy	
	Voluntary Medical Service Medal	
	South African Medal for War Services	
	Foreign Orders (in order of date of award)	
	Foreign Decorations (in order of date of award)	
	Foreign Medals (in order of date of award)	

Key to "Change"
"+" = addition   "- (??)" = deleted from this list   "" = change of position/title.*

Appendix 2 to Chapter 6

From *London Gazette* dated 19 April 1955

Change	Titles	Post-nominals
| |	Victoria Cross	VC
| |	George Cross	GC
| |	Knight of the Most Noble Order of the Garter	KG
| |	Knight of the Most Ancient and Most Noble Order of the Thistle	KT
| |	Knight of the Most Illustrious Order of St. Patrick	KP
| |	Knight Grand Cross of the Most Honourable Order of the Bath	GCB
| |	Member of the Order of Merit	OM
| |	Baronet's Badge	Bt or Bart
| |	Knight Grand Commander of the Most Exalted Order of the Star of India	GCSI
| |	Knight Grand Cross of the Most Distinguished Order of St. Michael & St. George	GCMG
| |	Knight Grand Commander of the Most Eminent Order of the Indian Empire	GCIE
| |	The Imperial Order of the Crown of India	CI
| |	Knight or Dame Grand Cross of the Royal Victorian Order	GCVO
| |	Knight or Dame Grand Cross of the Most Excellent Order of the British Empire	GBE
| |	Member of the Order of the Companions of Honour	CH
| |	Knight Commander of the Most Honourable Order of the Bath	KCB
| |	Knight Commander of the Most Exalted Order of the Star of India	KCSI
| |	Knight Commander of the Most Distinguished Order of St. Michael & St. George	KCMG
| |	Knight Commander of the Most Eminent Order of the Indian Empire	KCIE
| |	Knight or Dame Commander of the Royal Victorian Order	KCVO/ DCVO
| |	Knight or Dame Commander of the Most Excellent Order of the British Empire	KBE/DBE
	Knight Bachelor's Badge	
| |	Companion of the Most Honourable Order of the Bath	CB
| |	Companion of the Most Exalted Order of the Star of India	CSI
| |	Companion of the Most Distinguished Order of St. Michael & St. George	CMG

From *London Gazette* dated 19 April 1955 (cont)

Change	Titles	Post-nominals
I I	Companion of the Most Eminent Order of the Indian Empire	CIE
I I	Commander of the Royal Victorian Order	CVO
I I	Commander of the Most Excellent Order of the British Empire	CBE
I I	Companion of the Distinguished Service Order	DSO
I I	Member of the Fourth Class of the Royal Victorian Order	MVO
I I	Officer of the Most Excellent Order of the British Empire	OBE
I I	Companion of the Imperial Service Order	ISO
I I	Member of the Fifth Class of the Royal Victorian Order	MVO
I I	Member of the Most Excellent Order of the British Empire	MBE
I I	Indian Order of Merit (Military)	IOM
I I	Member of the Royal Red Cross	RRC
I I	Distinguished Service Cross	DSC
I I	Military Cross	MC
I I	Distinguished Flying Cross	DFC
I I	Air Force Cross	AFC
I I	Associate of the Royal Red Cross	ARRC
I I	Order of British India	OBI
	Kaisar-i-Hind Medal (Gold, Silver & Bronze)	
	Order of St. John (All Classes)	
I I	Albert Medals (Sea & Land; Classes I & II (Gold & Bronze)	AM
	Union of South Africa Queen's Medal for Bravery (in Gold)	
I I	Distinguished Conduct Medal	DCM
I I	Conspicuous Gallantry Medal	CGM
I I	George Medal	GM
	Queen's Police Medal for Gallantry	
	Queen's Fire Service Medal for Gallantry	
I I	Edward Medal (1st & 2nd Classes)(Silver and Bronze)	EM
I I	Royal West African Frontier Force Distinguished Conduct Medal	DCM
I I	King's African Rifles Distinguished Conduct Medal	DCM
I I	Indian Distinguished Service Medal	IDSM

From *London Gazette* dated 19 April 1955 (cont)

Change	Titles	Post-nominals
	Union of South Africa Queen's Medal for Bravery (in Silver)	
||	Distinguished Service Medal	DSM
||	Military Medal	MM
||	Distinguished Flying Medal	DFM
||	Air Force Medal	AFM
	Constabulary Medal (Ireland)	
||	Medal for Saving Life at Sea	SGM
||	Indian Order of Merit (Civil)	IOM
	Indian Police Medal for Gallantry	
	Ceylon Police Medal for Gallantry	
	Colonial Police Medal for Gallantry	
||	British Empire Medal	BEM
||	Canada Medal	CM/MduC
	Queen's Police Medal for Distinguished Service	
	Queen's Fire Service Medal for Distinguished Service	
	Queen's Medal for Chiefs	
	War Medals (in order of date of campaign for which awarded)	
	Polar Medals (in order of date)	
	Royal Victorian Medal (Gold, Silver & Bronze)	
	Imperial Service Medal	
	Indian Police Medal for Meritorious Service	
	Ceylon Police Medal for Merit	
	Colonial Police Medal for Meritorious Service	
	Badge of Honour	
	Queen Victoria's Jubilee Medal, 1887 (Gold, Silver & Bronze)	
	Queen Victoria's Police Jubilee Medal, 1887	
	Queen Victoria's Jubilee Medal, 1897 (Gold, Silver & Bronze)	
	Queen Victoria's Police Jubilee Medal, 1897	
	Queen Victoria's Commemoration Medal, 1900 (Ireland)	
	King Edward VII's Coronation Medal, 1902	

From *London Gazette* dated 19 April 1955 (cont)

Change Titles   Post-nominals

       King Edward VII's Police Coronation Medal, 1902

       King Edward VII's Durbar Medal, 1903 (Gold, Silver & Bronze)

       King Edward VII's Police Medal, 1903 (Scotland)

       King's Visit Commemoration Medal, 1903 (Ireland)

       King George V's Coronation Medal, 1911

       King George V's Police Coronation Medal, 1911

       King's Visit Police Commemoration Medal, 1911 (Ireland)

       King George V's Durbar Medal, 1911 (Gold, Silver & Bronze)

       King George V's Silver Jubilee Medal, 1935

       King George VI's Coronation Medal, 1937

       Queen Elizabeth II's Coronation Medal, 1953

       King George V's Long and Faithful Service Medal

       King George VI's Long and Faithful Service Medal

       Queen Elizabeth II's Long and Faithful Service Medal

       Long Service and Good Conduct Medal

       Naval Long Service and Good Conduct Medal

| | Medal for Meritorious Service   (MSM)

       Indian Long Service and Good Conduct Medal
       (for Europeans of Indian Army)

       Indian Meritorious Service Medal
       (for Europeans of Indian Army)

       Royal Marine Meritorious Service Medal

       Royal Air Force Meritorious Service Medal

       Royal Air Force Long Service and Good Conduct Medal

       Indian Long Service and Good Conduct Medal
       (for Indian Army)

       Royal West African Frontier Force Long Service
       and Good Conduct Medal

       King's African Rifles Long Service and Good Conduct Medal

       Indian Meritorious Service Medal (for Indian Army)

       Police Long Service and Good Conduct Medal

       Fire Brigade Long Service and Good Conduct Medal

From *London Gazette* dated 19 April 1955 (cont)

Change	Titles	Post-nominals
	African Police Medal for Meritorious Service	
	Royal Canadian Mounted Police Long Service Medal	
	Ceylon Police Long Service Medal	
	Ceylon Fire Services Long Service Medal	
	Colonial Police and Fire Brigades' Long Service Medal	
| |	Army Emergency Reserve Decoration	ERD
| |	Volunteer Officers' Decoration	VD
	Volunteer Long Service Medal	
| |	Volunteer Officers' Decoration (for India & the Colonies)	VD
	Volunteer Long Service Medal (for India & the Colonies)	
| |	Colonial Auxiliary Forces Officers' Decoration	VD
	Colonial Auxiliary Forces Long Service Medal	
	Medal for Good Shooting (Naval)	
	Militia Long Service Medal	
	Imperial Yeomanry Long Service Medal	
| |	Territorial Decoration	TD
| |	Efficiency Decoration	TD/ED
	Territorial Efficiency Medal	
	Efficiency Medal	
	Special Reserve Long Service and Good Conduct Medal	
| |	Decoration for Officers of the Royal Naval Reserve	RD
| |	Decoration for Officers of the Royal Naval Volunteer Reserve	VRD
	Royal Naval Reserve Long Service and Good Conduct Medal	
	Royal Naval Volunteer Reserve Long Service and Good Conduct Medal	
	Royal Naval Auxiliary Sick Berth Reserve Long Service and Good Conduct Medal	
	Royal Fleet Reserve Long Service and Good Conduct Medal	
	Royal Naval Wireless Auxiliary Reserve Long Service and Good Conduct Medal	
	Air Efficiency Award	
	Queen's Medal (for Champion Shots in the Military Forces)	

From *London Gazette* dated 19 April 1955 (cont)

Change	Titles	Post-nominals
	Queen's Medal (for Champion Shots of the Air Forces)	
	Cadet Forces Medal	
	Coast Life Saving Corps Long Service Medal (formerly Rocket Apparatus Volunteer Long Service Medal)	
	Special Constabulary Long Service Medal	
l l	Canadian Forces Decoration	CD
	Royal Observer Corps Medal	
	Union of South Africa Commemoration Medal	
	Indian Independence Medal	
	Pakistan Medal	
	Service Medal of the Order of St. John	
	Badge of the Order of the League of Mercy	
	Voluntary Medical Service Medal	
	South African Medal for War Services	
	Foreign Orders (in order of date of award)	
	Foreign Decorations (in order of date of award)	
	Foreign Medals (in order of date of award)	

Key to "Change"
"l l" = post-nominal letters permitted.

Appendix 3 to Chapter 6

From *London Gazette* dated 14 January 1958

Change	Titles	Post-nominals
	Victoria Cross	VC
	George Cross	GC
	Knight of the Most Noble Order of the Garter	KG
	Knight of the Most Ancient and Most Noble Order of the Thistle	KT
	Knight of the Most Illustrious Order of St. Patrick	KP
	Knight Grand Cross of the Most Honourable Order of the Bath	GCB
	Member of the Order of Merit	OM
	Baronet's Badge	Bt or Bart
	Knight Grand Commander of the Most Exalted Order of the Star of India	GCSI
	Knight Grand Cross of the Most Distinguished Order of St. Michael & St. George	GCMG
	Knight Grand Commander of the Most Eminent Order of the Indian Empire	GCIE
	The Imperial Order of the Crown of India	CI
	Knight or Dame Grand Cross of the Royal Victorian Order	GCVO
	Knight or Dame Grand Cross of the Most Excellent Order of the British Empire	GBE
	Member of the Order of the Companions of Honour	CH
	Knight Commander of the Most Honourable Order of the Bath	KCB
	Knight Commander of the Most Exalted Order of the Star of India	KCSI
	Knight Commander of the Most Distinguished Order of St. Michael & St. George	KCMG
	Knight Commander of the Most Eminent Order of the Indian Empire	KCIE
	Knight or Dame Commander of the Royal Victorian Order	KCVO/DCVO
	Knight or Dame Commander of the Most Excellent Order of the British Empire	KBE/DBE
	Knight Bachelor's Badge	
	Companion of the Most Honourable Order of the Bath	CB
	Companion of the Most Exalted Order of the Star of India	CSI

"Medals Will Be Worn"

From *London Gazette* dated 14 January 1958 (cont)

Change	Titles	Post-nominals
	Companion of the Most Distinguished Order of St. Michael & St. George	CMG
	Companion of the Most Eminent Order of the Indian Empire	CIE
	Commander of the Royal Victorian Order	CVO
	Commander of the Most Excellent Order of the British Empire	CBE
	Companion of the Distinguished Service Order	DSO
	Member of the Fourth Class of the Royal Victorian Order	MVO
	Officer of the Most Excellent Order of the British Empire	OBE
	Companion of the Imperial Service Order	ISO
	Member of the Fifth Class of the Royal Victorian Order	MVO
	Member of the Most Excellent Order of the British Empire	MBE
	Indian Order of Merit (Military)	IOM
	Member of the Royal Red Cross	RRC
	Distinguished Service Cross	DSC
	Military Cross	MC
	Distinguished Flying Cross	DFC
	Air Force Cross	AFC
	Associate of the Royal Red Cross	ARRC
	Order of British India	OBI
	Kaisar-i-Hind Medal (Gold, Silver & Bronze)	
	Order of St. John (All Classes)	
	Albert Medals (Sea & Land; Classes I & II (Gold & Bronze)	AM
	Union of South Africa Queen's Medal for Bravery (in Gold)	
	Distinguished Conduct Medal	DCM
	Conspicuous Gallantry Medal	CGM
	George Medal	GM
	Queen's Police Medal for Gallantry	
	Queen's Fire Service Medal for Gallantry	
	Edward Medal (1st & 2nd Classes)(Silver and Bronze)	EM
	Royal West African Frontier Force Distinguished Conduct Medal	DCM
	King's African Rifles Distinguished Conduct Medal	DCM

From *London Gazette* dated 14 January 1958 (cont)

Change	Titles	Post-nominals
	Indian Distinguished Service Medal	IDSM
	Union of South Africa Queen's Medal for Bravery (in Silver)	
	Distinguished Service Medal	DSM
	Military Medal	MM
	Distinguished Flying Medal	DFM
	Air Force Medal	AFM
	Constabulary Medal (Ireland)	
	Medal for Saving Life at Sea	SGM
	Indian Order of Merit (Civil)	IOM
	Indian Police Medal for Gallantry	
	Ceylon Police Medal for Gallantry	
	Colonial Police Medal for Gallantry	
	British Empire Medal	BEM
	Canada Medal	CM/MduC
	Queen's Police Medal for Distinguished Service	
	Queen's Fire Service Medal for Distinguished Service	
	Queen's Medal for Chiefs	
	War Medals (in order of date of campaign for which awarded)	
	Polar Medals (in order of date)	
	Royal Victorian Medal (Gold, Silver & Bronze)	
	Imperial Service Medal	
	Indian Police Medal for Meritorious Service	
	Ceylon Police Medal for Merit	
	Colonial Police Medal for Meritorious Service	
	Badge of Honour	
	Queen Victoria's Jubilee Medal, 1887 (Gold, Silver & Bronze)	
	Queen Victoria's Police Jubilee Medal, 1887	
	Queen Victoria's Jubilee Medal, 1897 (Gold, Silver & Bronze)	
	Queen Victoria's Police Jubilee Medal, 1897	
	Queen Victoria's Commemoration Medal, 1900 (Ireland)	

"Medals Will Be Worn"

From *London Gazette* dated 14 January 1958 (cont)

Change Titles   Post-nominals

    King Edward VII's Coronation Medal, 1902

    King Edward VII's Police Coronation Medal, 1902

    King Edward VII's Durbar Medal, 1903 (Gold, Silver & Bronze)

    King Edward VII's Police Medal, 1903 (Scotland)

    King's Visit Commemoration Medal, 1903 (Ireland)

    King George V's Coronation Medal, 1911

    King George V's Police Coronation Medal, 1911

    King's Visit Police Commemoration Medal, 1911 (Ireland)

    King George V's Durbar Medal, 1911 (Gold, Silver & Bronze)

    King George V's Silver Jubilee Medal, 1935

    King George VI's Coronation Medal, 1937

    Queen Elizabeth II's Coronation Medal, 1953

    King George V's Long and Faithful Service Medal

    King George VI's Long and Faithful Service Medal

    Queen Elizabeth II's Long and Faithful Service Medal

    Long Service and Good Conduct Medal

    Naval Long Service and Good Conduct Medal

    Medal for Meritorious Service   (MSM)

    Indian Long Service and Good Conduct Medal
    (for Europeans of Indian Army)

    Indian Meritorious Service Medal
    (for Europeans of Indian Army)

    Royal Marine Meritorious Service Medal

    Royal Air Force Meritorious Service Medal

    Royal Air Force Long Service and Good Conduct Medal

    Indian Long Service and Good Conduct Medal
    (for Indian Army)

    Royal West African Frontier Force Long Service and Good Conduct Medal

    King's African Rifles Long Service and Good Conduct Medal

    Indian Meritorious Service Medal
    (for Indian Army)

    Police Long Service and Good Conduct Medal

From *London Gazette* dated 14 January 1958 (cont)

Change	Titles	Post-nominals
	Fire Brigade Long Service and Good Conduct Medal	
	African Police Medal for Meritorious Service	
	Royal Canadian Mounted Police Long Service Medal	
	Ceylon Police Long Service Medal	
	Ceylon Fire Services Long Service Medal	
*	Colonial Police Long Service Medal	
+	Colonial Fire Brigades' Long Service Medal	
+	Colonial Prison Service Medal	
	Army Emergency Reserve Decoration	ERD
	Volunteer Officers' Decoration	VD
	Volunteer Long Service Medal	
	Volunteer Officers' Decoration (for India & the Colonies)	VD
	Volunteer Long Service Medal (for India & the Colonies)	
	Colonial Auxiliary Forces Officers' Decoration	VD
	Colonial Auxiliary Forces Long Service Medal	
	Medal for Good Shooting (Naval)	
	Militia Long Service Medal	
	Imperial Yeomanry Long Service Medal	
	Territorial Decoration	TD
	Efficiency Decoration	TD/ED
	Territorial Efficiency Medal	
	Efficiency Medal	
	Special Reserve Long Service and Good Conduct Medal	
	Decoration for Officers of the Royal Naval Reserve	RD
	Decoration for Officers of the Royal Naval Volunteer Reserve	VRD
	Royal Naval Reserve Long Service and Good Conduct Medal	
	Royal Naval Volunteer Reserve Long Service and Good Conduct Medal	
	Royal Naval Auxiliary Sick Berth Reserve Long Service and Good Conduct Medal	
	Royal Fleet Reserve Long Service and Good Conduct Medal	

"Medals Will Be Worn"

From *London Gazette* dated 14 January 1958 (cont)

Change Titles   Post-nominals

        Royal Naval Wireless Auxiliary Reserve Long Service
        and Good Conduct Medal

        Air Efficiency Award

        Queen's Medal (for Champion Shots in the Military Forces)

        Queen's Medal (for Champion Shots of the Air Forces)

        Cadet Forces Medal

        Coast Life Saving Corps Long Service Medal
        (formerly Rocket Apparatus Volunteer Long Service Medal)

        Special Constabulary Long Service Medal

        Canadian Forces Decoration   CD

        Royal Observer Corps Medal

        Union of South Africa Commemoration Medal

        Indian Independence Medal

        Pakistan Medal

        Service Medal of the Order of St. John

        Badge of the Order of the League of Mercy

        Voluntary Medical Service Medal

        South African Medal for War Services

+   Colonial Special Constabulary Medal

        Foreign Orders (in order of date of award)

        Foreign Decorations (in order of date of award)

        Foreign Medals (in order of date of award)

Key to "Change":
"+" = *addition*   "- (??)" = *deleted from this list*   "*" = *change of position/title.*

Appendix 4 to Chapter 6

From *London Gazette* dated 28 April 1961

Change	Titles	Post-nominals
	Victoria Cross	VC
	George Cross	GC
	Knight of the Most Noble Order of the Garter	KG
	Knight of the Most Ancient and Most Noble Order of the Thistle	KT
	Knight of the Most Illustrious Order of St. Patrick	KP
	Knight Grand Cross of the Most Honourable Order of the Bath	GCB
	Member of the Order of Merit	
	Baronet's Badge	Bt or Bart
	Knight Grand Commander of the Most Exalted Order of the Star of India	GCSI
	Knight Grand Cross of the Most Distinguished Order of St. Michael & St. George	GCMG
	Knight Grand Commander of the Most Eminent Order of the Indian Empire	GCIE
	The Imperial Order of the Crown of India	CI
	Knight or Dame Grand Cross of the Royal Victorian Order	GCVO
	Knight or Dame Grand Cross of the Most Excellent Order of the British Empire	GBE
	Member of the Order of the Companions of Honour	CH
	Knight Commander of the Most Honourable Order of the Bath	KCB
	Knight Commander of the Most Exalted Order of the Star of India	KCSI
	Knight Commander of the Most Distinguished Order of St. Michael & St. George	KCMG
	Knight Commander of the Most Eminent Order of the Indian Empire	KCIE
	Knight or Dame Commander of the Royal Victorian Order	KCVO/ DCVO
	Knight or Dame Commander of the Most Excellent Order of the British Empire	KBE/DBE
	Knight Bachelor's Badge	
	Companion of the Most Honourable Order of the Bath	CB
	Companion of the Most Exalted Order of the Star of India	CSI
	Companion of the Most Distinguished Order of St. Michael & St. George	CMG

From *London Gazette* dated 28 April 1961 (cont)

Change Titles	Post-nominals
Companion of the Most Eminent Order of the Indian Empire	CIE
Commander of the Royal Victorian Order	CVO
Commander of the Most Excellent Order of the British Empire	CBE
Companion of the Distinguished Service Order	DSO
Member of the Fourth Class of the Royal Victorian Order	MVO
Officer of the Most Excellent Order of the British Empire	OBE
Companion of the Imperial Service Order	ISO
Member of the Fifth Class of the Royal Victorian Order	MVO
Member of the Most Excellent Order of the British Empire	MBE
Indian Order of Merit (Military)	IOM
Member of the Royal Red Cross	RRC
Distinguished Service Cross	DSC
Military Cross	MC
Distinguished Flying Cross	DFC
Air Force Cross	AFC
Associate of the Royal Red Cross	ARRC
Order of British India	OBI
Kaisar-i-Hind Medal (Gold, Silver & Bronze)	
Order of St. John (All Classes)	
Albert Medals (Sea & Land; Classes I & II (Gold & Bronze)	AM
Union of South Africa Queen's Medal for Bravery (in Gold)	
Distinguished Conduct Medal	DCM
Conspicuous Gallantry Medal	CGM
George Medal	GM
Queen's Police Medal for Gallantry	
Queen's Fire Service Medal for Gallantry	
Edward Medal (1st & 2nd Classes)(Silver and Bronze)	EM
Royal West African Frontier Force Distinguished Conduct Medal	DCM
King's African Rifles Distinguished Conduct Medal	DCM
Indian Distinguished Service Medal	IDSM

From *London Gazette* dated 28 April 1961 (cont)

Change	Titles	Post-nominals
	Union of South Africa Queen's Medal for Bravery (in Silver)	
	Distinguished Service Medal	DSM
	Military Medal	MM
	Distinguished Flying Medal	DFM
	Air Force Medal	AFM
	Constabulary Medal (Ireland)	
	Medal for Saving Life at Sea	SGM
	Indian Order of Merit (Civil)	IOM
	Indian Police Medal for Gallantry	
	Ceylon Police Medal for Gallantry	
	Colonial Police Medal for Gallantry	
	British Empire Medal	BEM
	Canada Medal	CM/MduC
	Queen's Police Medal for Distinguished Service	
	Queen's Fire Service Medal for Distinguished Service	
	Queen's Medal for Chiefs	
	War Medals (in order of date of campaign for which awarded)	
	Polar Medals (in order of date)	
	Royal Victorian Medal (Gold, Silver & Bronze)	
	Imperial Service Medal	
	Indian Police Medal for Meritorious Service	
	Ceylon Police Medal for Merit	
	Colonial Police Medal for Meritorious Service	
	Badge of Honour	
	Queen Victoria's Jubilee Medal, 1887 (Gold, Silver & Bronze)	
	Queen Victoria's Police Jubilee Medal, 1887	
	Queen Victoria's Jubilee Medal, 1897 (Gold, Silver & Bronze)	
	Queen Victoria's Police Jubilee Medal, 1897	
	Queen Victoria's Commemoration Medal, 1900 (Ireland)	
	King Edward VII's Coronation Medal, 1902	

From *London Gazette* dated 28 April 1961 (cont)

Change   Titles   Post-nominals

    King Edward VII's Police Coronation Medal, 1902

    King Edward VII's Durbar Medal, 1903 (Gold, Silver & Bronze)

    King Edward VII's Police Medal, 1903 (Scotland)

    King's Visit Commemoration Medal, 1903 (Ireland)

    King George V's Coronation Medal, 1911

    King George V's Police Coronation Medal, 1911

    King's Visit Police Commemoration Medal, 1911 (Ireland)

    King George V's Durbar Medal, 1911 (Gold, Silver & Bronze)

    King George V's Silver Jubilee Medal, 1935

    King George VI's Coronation Medal, 1937

    Queen Elizabeth II's Coronation Medal, 1953

    King George V's Long and Faithful Service Medal

    King George VI's Long and Faithful Service Medal

    Queen Elizabeth II's Long and Faithful Service Medal

    Long Service and Good Conduct Medal

    Naval Long Service and Good Conduct Medal

Medal for Meritorious Service   (MSM)

Indian Long Service and Good Conduct Medal
(for Europeans of Indian Army)

Indian Meritorious Service Medal
(for Europeans of Indian Army)

    Royal Marine Meritorious Service Medal

    Royal Air Force Meritorious Service Medal

    Royal Air Force Long Service and Good Conduct Medal

    Indian Long Service and Good Conduct Medal (for Indian Army)

Royal West African Frontier Force Long Service
  and Good Conduct Medal

    King's African Rifles Long Service and Good Conduct Medal

    Indian Meritorious Service Medal (for Indian Army)

    Police Long Service and Good Conduct Medal

    Fire Brigade Long Service and Good Conduct Medal

    African Police Medal for Meritorious Service

From *London Gazette* dated 28 April 1961 (cont)

Change	Titles	Post-nominals
	Royal Canadian Mounted Police Long Service Medal	
	Ceylon Police Long Service Medal	
	Ceylon Fire Services Long Service Medal	
	Colonial Police Long Service Medal	
	Colonial Fire Brigades' Long Service Medal	
	Colonial Prison Service Medal	
	Army Emergency Reserve Decoration	ERD
	Volunteer Officers' Decoration	VD
	Volunteer Long Service Medal	
	Volunteer Officers' Decoration (for India & the Colonies)	VD
	Volunteer Long Service Medal (for India & the Colonies)	
	Colonial Auxiliary Forces Officers' Decoration	VD
	Colonial Auxiliary Forces Long Service Medal	
	Medal for Good Shooting (Naval)	
	Militia Long Service Medal	
	Imperial Yeomanry Long Service Medal	
	Territorial Decoration	TD
	Efficiency Decoration	TD/ED
	Territorial Efficiency Medal	
	Efficiency Medal	
	Special Reserve Long Service and Good Conduct Medal	
	Decoration for Officers of the Royal Naval Reserve	RD
	Decoration for Officers of the Royal Naval Volunteer Reserve	VRD
	Royal Naval Reserve Long Service and Good Conduct Medal	
	Royal Naval Volunteer Reserve Long Service and Good Conduct Medal	
	Royal Naval Auxiliary Sick Berth Reserve Long Service and Good Conduct Medal	
	Royal Fleet Reserve Long Service and Good Conduct Medal	
	Royal Naval Wireless Auxiliary Reserve Long Service and Good Conduct Medal	
	Air Efficiency Award	

From *London Gazette* dated 28 April 1961 (cont)

Change	Titles	Post-nominals
+	Queen's Medal (for Champion Shots of the New Zealand Naval Forces)	
	Queen's Medal (for Champion Shots in the Military Forces)	
	Queen's Medal (for Champion Shots of the Air Forces)	
	Cadet Forces Medal	
	Coast Life Saving Corps Long Service Medal (formerly Rocket Apparatus Volunteer Long Service Medal)	
	Special Constabulary Long Service Medal	
	Canadian Forces Decoration	CD
	Royal Observer Corps Medal	
+	Civil Defence Long Service Medal	
	Union of South Africa Commemoration Medal	
	Indian Independence Medal	
	Pakistan Medal	
+	Ceylon Armed Forces Inauguration Medal	
+	Ceylon Police Independence Medal (1948)	
+	Nigerian Independence Medal	
+	Sierra Leone Independence Medal	
	Service Medal of the Order of St. John	
	Badge of the Order of the League of Mercy	
	Voluntary Medical Service Medal	
+	Women's Voluntary Service Medal	
	South African Medal for War Services	
	Colonial Special Constabulary Medal	
+	Other Commonwealth Members' Orders Decorations and Medals	
	Foreign Orders (in order of date of award)	
	Foreign Decorations (in order of date of award)	
	Foreign Medals (in order of date of award)	

Key to "Change":
"+" = addition   "- (??)" = deleted from this list   "*" = change of position/title.

Appendix 5 to Chapter 6

From *London Gazette* dated 27 October 1964

Change	Titles	Post-nominals
	Victoria Cross	VC
	George Cross	GC
	Knight of the Most Noble Order of the Garter	KG
	Knight of the Most Ancient and Most Noble Order of the Thistle	KT
	Knight of the Most Illustrious Order of St. Patrick	KP
	Knight Grand Cross of the Most Honourable Order of the Bath	GCB
	Member of the Order of Merit	OM
	Baronet's Badge	Bt or Bart
	Knight Grand Commander of the Most Exalted Order of the Star of India	GCSI
	Knight Grand Cross of the Most Distinguished Order of St. Michael & St. George	GCMG
	Knight Grand Commander of the Most Eminent Order of the Indian Empire	GCIE
	The Imperial Order of the Crown of India	CI
	Knight or Dame Grand Cross of the Royal Victorian Order	GCVO
	Knight or Dame Grand Cross of the Most Excellent Order of the British Empire	GBE
	Member of the Order of the Companions of Honour	CH
	Knight Commander of the Most Honourable Order of the Bath	KCB
	Knight Commander of the Most Exalted Order of the Star of India	KCSI
	Knight Commander of the Most Distinguished Order of St. Michael & St. George	KCMG
	Knight Commander of the Most Eminent Order of the Indian Empire	KCIE
	Knight or Dame Commander of the Royal Victorian Order	KCVO/ DCVO
	Knight or Dame Commander of the Most Excellent Order of the British Empire	KBE/DBE
	Knight Bachelor's Badge	
	Companion of the Most Honourable Order of the Bath	CB
	Companion of the Most Exalted Order of the Star of India	CSI

"Medals Will Be Worn"

From *London Gazette* dated 27 October 1964 (cont)

Change Titles	Post-nominals
Companion of the Most Distinguished Order of St. Michael & St. George	CMG
Companion of the Most Eminent Order of the Indian Empire	CIE
Commander of the Royal Victorian Order	CVO
Commander of the Most Excellent Order of the British Empire	CBE
Companion of the Distinguished Service Order	DSO
Member of the Fourth Class of the Royal Victorian Order	MVO
Officer of the Most Excellent Order of the British Empire	OBE
Companion of the Imperial Service Order	ISO
Member of the Fifth Class of the Royal Victorian Order	MVO
Member of the Most Excellent Order of the British Empire	MBE
Indian Order of Merit (Military)	IOM
Member of the Royal Red Cross	RRC
Distinguished Service Cross	DSC
Military Cross	MC
Distinguished Flying Cross	DFC
Air Force Cross	AFC
Associate of the Royal Red Cross	ARRC
Order of British India	OBI
Kaisar-i-Hind Medal (Gold, Silver & Bronze)	
Order of St. John (All Classes)	
Albert Medals (Sea & Land; Classes I & II (Gold & Bronze)	AM
Union of South Africa Queen's Medal for Bravery (in Gold)	
Distinguished Conduct Medal	DCM
Conspicuous Gallantry Medal	CGM
George Medal	GM
Queen's Police Medal for Gallantry	
Queen's Fire Service Medal for Gallantry	
Edward Medal (1st & 2nd Classes)(Silver and Bronze)	EM
Royal West African Frontier Force Distinguished Conduct Medal	DCM

From *London Gazette* dated 27 October 1964 (cont)

Change	Titles	Post-nominals
	King's African Rifles Distinguished Conduct Medal	DCM
	Indian Distinguished Service Medal	IDSM
	Union of South Africa Queen's Medal for Bravery (in Silver)	
	Distinguished Service Medal	DSM
	Military Medal	MM
	Distinguished Flying Medal	DFM
	Air Force Medal	AFM
	Constabulary Medal (Ireland)	
	Medal for Saving Life at Sea	SGM
	Indian Order of Merit (Civil)	IOM
	Indian Police Medal for Gallantry	
	Ceylon Police Medal for Gallantry	
+	Sierra Leone Police Medal for Gallantry	
+	Sierra Leone Fire Brigades' Medal for Gallantry	
	Colonial Police Medal for Gallantry	
	British Empire Medal	BEM
	Canada Medal	CM/MduC
	Queen's Police Medal for Distinguished Service	
	Queen's Fire Service Medal for Distinguished Service	
	Queen's Medal for Chiefs	
	War Medals (in order of date of campaign for which awarded)	
	Polar Medals (in order of date)	
	Royal Victorian Medal (Gold, Silver & Bronze)	
	Imperial Service Medal	
	Indian Police Medal for Meritorious Service	
	Ceylon Police Medal for Merit	
+	Sierra Leone Police Medal for Meritorious Service	
+	Sierra Leone Fire Brigades Medal for Meritorious Service	
	Colonial Police Medal for Meritorious Service	
	Badge of Honour	

"Medals Will Be Worn"

From *London Gazette* dated 27 October 1964 (cont)

Change Titles   Post-nominals

    Queen Victoria's Jubilee Medal, 1887 (Gold, Silver & Bronze)

    Queen Victoria's Police Jubilee Medal, 1887

    Queen Victoria's Jubilee Medal, 1897 (Gold, Silver & Bronze)

    Queen Victoria's Police Jubilee Medal, 1897

    Queen Victoria's Commemoration Medal, 1900 (Ireland)

    King Edward VII's Coronation Medal, 1902

    King Edward VII's Police Coronation Medal, 1902

    King Edward VII's Durbar Medal, 1903 (Gold, Silver & Bronze)

    King Edward VII's Police Medal, 1903 (Scotland)

    King's Visit Commemoration Medal, 1903 (Ireland)

    King George V's Coronation Medal, 1911

    King George V's Police Coronation Medal, 1911

    King's Visit Police Commemoration Medal, 1911 (Ireland)

    King George V's Durbar Medal, 1911 (Gold, Silver & Bronze)

    King George V's Silver Jubilee Medal, 1935

    King George VI's Coronation Medal, 1937

    Queen Elizabeth II's Coronation Medal, 1953

    King George V's Long and Faithful Service Medal

    King George VI's Long and Faithful Service Medal

    Queen Elizabeth II's Long and Faithful Service Medal

    Medal for Long Service and Good Conduct

    Naval Long Service and Good Conduct Medal

    Medal for Meritorious Service   (MSM)

    Indian Long Service and Good Conduct Medal
    (for Europeans of Indian Army)

    Indian Meritorious Service Medal (for Europeans of Indian Army)

    Royal Marine Meritorious Service Medal

    Royal Air Force Meritorious Service Medal

    Royal Air Force Long Service and Good Conduct Medal

    Indian Long Service and Good Conduct Medal (for Indian Army)

From *London Gazette* dated 27 October 1964 (cont)

Change	Titles	Post-nominals
	Royal West African Frontier Force Long Service and Good Conduct Medal	
+	Royal Sierra Leone Military Forces Long Service and Good Conduct Medal	
	King's African Rifles Long Service and Good Conduct Medal	
	Indian Meritorious Service Medal (for Indian Army)	
	Police Long Service and Good Conduct Medal	
	Fire Brigade Long Service and Good Conduct Medal	
	African Police Medal for Meritorious Service	
	Royal Canadian Mounted Police Long Service Medal	
	Ceylon Police Long Service Medal	
	Ceylon Fire Services Long Service Medal	
+	Sierra Leone Police Long Service Medal	
	Colonial Police Long Service Medal	
+	Sierra Leone Fire Brigades Long Service Medal	
	Colonial Fire Brigades Long Service Medal	
	Colonial Prison Service Medal	
	Army Emergency Reserve Decoration	ERD
	Volunteer Officers' Decoration	VD
	Volunteer Long Service Medal	
	Volunteer Officers' Decoration (for India & the Colonies)	VD
	Volunteer Long Service Medal (for India & the Colonies)	
	Colonial Auxiliary Forces Officers' Decoration	VD
	Colonial Auxiliary Forces Long Service Medal	
	Medal for Good Shooting (Naval)	
	Militia Long Service Medal	
	Imperial Yeomanry Long Service Medal	
	Territorial Decoration	TD
	Efficiency Decoration	TD/ED
	Territorial Efficiency Medal	
	Efficiency Medal	

"Medals Will Be Worn"

From *London Gazette* dated 27 October 1964 (cont)

Change	Titles	Post-nominals
	Special Reserve Long Service and Good Conduct Medal	
	Decoration for Officers of the Royal Naval Reserve	RD
	Decoration for Officers of the Royal Naval Volunteer Reserve	VRD
	Royal Naval Reserve Long Service and Good Conduct Medal	
	Royal Naval Volunteer Reserve Long Service and Good Conduct Medal	
	Royal Naval Auxiliary Sick Berth Reserve Long Service and Good Conduct Medal	
	Royal Fleet Reserve Long Service and Good Conduct Medal	
	Royal Naval Wireless Auxiliary Reserve Long Service and Good Conduct Medal	
	Air Efficiency Award	
	Queen's Medal (for Champion Shots of the New Zealand Naval Forces)	
	Queen's Medal (for Champion Shots in the Military Forces)	
	Queen's Medal (for Champion Shots of the Air Forces)	
	Cadet Forces Medal	
	Coast Life Saving Long Service Medal (formerly Rocket Apparatus Volunteer Long Service Medal)	
	Special Constabulary Long Service Medal	
	Canadian Forces Decoration	CD
	Royal Observer Corps Medal	
	Civil Defence Long Service Medal	
	Union of South Africa Commemoration Medal	
	Indian Independence Medal	
	Pakistan Medal	
	Ceylon Armed Forces Inauguration Medal	
	Ceylon Police Independence Medal (1948)	
-	(Nigeria Independence Medal)	
	Sierra Leone Independence Medal	
+	Jamaica Independence Medal	
+	Uganda Independence Medal	

From *London Gazette* dated 27 October 1964 (cont)

Change   Titles   Post-nominals

+   Malawi Independence Medal

         Service Medal of the Order of St. John

         Badge of the Order of the League of Mercy

         Voluntary Medical Service Medal

         Women's Voluntary Service Medal

         South African Medal for War Services

         Colonial Special Constabulary Medal

         Other Commonwealth Members' Orders Decorations and Medals

         Foreign Orders (in order of date of award)

         Foreign Decorations (in order of date of award)

         Foreign Medals (in order of date of award)

Key to "Change":
"+" = addition   "- (??)" = deleted from this list   "" = change of position/title.*

Appendix 6 to Chapter 6

From Army Dress Regulations 1969

Change	Titles	Post-nominals
	Victoria Cross	VC
	George Cross	GC
	Knight of the Most Noble Order of the Garter	KG
	Knight of the Most Ancient and Most Noble Order of the Thistle	KT
	Knight of the Most Illustrious Order of St. Patrick	KP
	Knight Grand Cross of the Most Honourable Order of the Bath	GCB
	Member of the Order of Merit	OM
	Baronet's Badge	Bt or Bart
	Knight Grand Commander of the Most Exalted Order of the Star of India	GCSI
	Knight or Dame Grand Cross of the Most Distinguished Order of St. Michael & St. George	GCMG
	Knight Grand Commander of the Most Eminent Order of the Indian Empire	GCIE
	The Imperial Order of the Crown of India	CI
	Knight or Dame Grand Cross of the Royal Victorian Order	GCVO
	Knight or Dame Grand Cross of the Most Excellent Order of the British Empire	GBE
	Member of the Order of the Companions of Honour	CH
	Knight Commander of the Most Honourable Order of the Bath	KCB
	Knight Commander of the Most Exalted Order of the Star of India	KCSI
	Knight or Dame Commander of the Most Distinguished Order of St. Michael & St. George	KCMG/ DCMG
	Knight Commander of the Most Eminent Order of the Indian Empire	KCIE
	Knight or Dame Commander of the Royal Victorian Order	KCVO/ DCVO
	Knight or Dame Commander of the Most Excellent Order of the British Empire	KBE/DBE
	Knight Bachelor's Badge	
	Companion of the Most Honourable Order of the Bath	CB
	Companion of the Most Exalted Order of the Star of India	CSI

From Army Dress Regulations 1969 (cont)

Change	Titles	Post-nominals
	Companion of the Most Distinguished Order of St. Michael & St. George	CMG
	Companion of the Most Eminent Order of the Indian Empire	CIE
	Commander of the Royal Victorian Order	CVO
	Commander of the Most Excellent Order of the British Empire	CBE
	Companion of the Distinguished Service Order	DSO
	Member of the Fourth Class of the Royal Victorian Order	MVO
	Officer of the Most Excellent Order of the British Empire	OBE
	Companion of the Imperial Service Order	ISO
	Member of the Fifth Class of the Royal Victorian Order	MVO
	Member of the Most Excellent Order of the British Empire	MBE
	Indian Order of Merit (Military)	IOM
	Member of the Royal Red Cross	RRC
	Distinguished Service Cross	DSC
	Military Cross	MC
	Distinguished Flying Cross	DFC
	Air Force Cross	AFC
	Associate of the Royal Red Cross	ARRC
	Order of British India	OBI
	Kaisar-i-Hind Medal (Gold, Silver & Bronze)	
	Order of St. John (All Classes)	
	Albert Medals (Sea & Land; Classes I & II (Gold & Bronze)	AM
	Union of South Africa Queen's Medal for Bravery (in Gold)	
	Distinguished Conduct Medal	DCM
	Conspicuous Gallantry Medal	CGM
	George Medal	GM
	Queen's Police Medal for Gallantry	QPM
	Queen's Fire Service Medal for Gallantry	QFSM
+	Queen's Gallantry Medal (added by amendment of 6 Sep 76)	QGM
	Edward Medal (1st & 2nd Classes)(Silver and Bronze)	EM

From Army Dress Regulations 1969 (cont)

Change	Titles	Post-nominals
	Royal West African Frontier Force Distinguished Conduct Medal	DCM
	King's African Rifles Distinguished Conduct Medal	DCM
	Indian Distinguished Service Medal	IDSM
+	Burma Gallantry Medal (added by amendment of 6 Sep 76)	BGM
	Union of South Africa Queen's Medal for Bravery (in Silver)	
	Distinguished Service Medal	DSM
	Military Medal	MM
	Distinguished Flying Medal	DFM
	Air Force Medal	AFM
	Constabulary Medal (Ireland)	
	Medal for Saving Life at Sea	SGM
	Indian Order of Merit (Civil)	IOM
	Indian Police Medal for Gallantry	
	Ceylon Police Medal for Gallantry	
	Colonial Police Medal for Gallantry	
+	Uganda Services Medal for Gallantry	
	British Empire Medal	BEM
	Canada Medal	CM/CduM
	Queen's Police Medal for Distinguished Service	
	Queen's Fire Service Medal for Distinguished Service	
	Queen's Medal for Chiefs	
	War Medals (in order of date of campaign for which awarded)	
	Polar Medals (in order of date)	
	Royal Victorian Medal (Gold, Silver & Bronze)	
	Imperial Service Medal	
	Indian Police Medal for Meritorious Service	
	Ceylon Police Medal for Merit	
	Sierra Leone Police Medal for Meritorious Service	
	Sierra Leone Fire Brigades Medal for Meritorious Service	
	Colonial Police Medal for Meritorious Service	

1952 to 1995

From Army Dress Regulations 1969 (cont)

Change	Titles	Post-nominals
+	Uganda Services Medal for Meritorious Service	
	Badge of Honour	
	Queen Victoria's Jubilee Medal, 1887 (Gold, Silver & Bronze)	
	Queen Victoria's Police Jubilee Medal, 1887	
	Queen Victoria's Jubilee Medal, 1897 (Gold, Silver & Bronze)	
	Queen Victoria's Police Jubilee Medal, 1897	
	Queen Victoria's Commemoration Medal, 1900 (Ireland)	
	King Edward VII's Coronation Medal, 1902	
	King Edward VII's Police Coronation Medal, 1902	
	King Edward VII's Durbar Medal, 1903 (Gold, Silver & Bronze)	
	King Edward VII's Police Medal, 1903 (Scotland)	
	King's Visit Commemoration Medal, 1903 (Ireland)	
	King George V's Coronation Medal, 1911	
	King George V's Police Coronation Medal, 1911	
	King's Visit Police Commemoration Medal, 1911 (Ireland)	
	King George V's Durbar Medal, 1911 (Gold, Silver & Bronze)	
	King George V's Silver Jubilee Medal, 1935	
	King George VI's Coronation Medal, 1937	
	Queen Elizabeth II's Coronation Medal, 1953	
	King George V's Long and Faithful Service Medal	
	King George VI's Long and Faithful Service Medal	
	Queen Elizabeth II's Long and Faithful Service Medal	
+	Queen Elizabeth II's Silver Jubilee Medal, 1977 (added 7 Jul 78, poorly worded in wrong place)	
	Long Service and Good Conduct Medal	
	Naval Long Service and Good Conduct Medal	
	Medal for Meritorious Service	(MSM)
	Indian Long Service and Good Conduct Medal (for Europeans of Indian Army)	
	Indian Meritorious Service Medal (for Europeans of Indian Army)	
	Royal Marine Meritorious Service Medal	

From Army Dress Regulations 1969 (cont)

Change	Titles	Post-nominals
	Royal Air Force Meritorious Service Medal	
	Royal Air Force Long Service and Good Conduct Medal	
	Indian Long Service and Good Conduct Medal (for Indian Army)	
	Royal West African Frontier Force Long Service and Good Conduct Medal	
	Royal Sierra Leone Military Forces Long Service and Good Conduct Medal	
	King's African Rifles Long Service and Good Conduct Medal	
	Indian Meritorious Service Medal (for Indian Army)	
	Police Long Service and Good Conduct Medal	
	Fire Brigade Long Service and Good Conduct Medal	
	African Police Medal for Meritorious Service	
	Royal Canadian Mounted Police Long Service Medal	
	Ceylon Police Long Service Medal	
	Ceylon Fire Services Long Service Medal	
	Sierra Leone Police Long Service Medal	
	Colonial Police Long Service Medal	
	Sierra Leone Fire Brigades Long Service Medal	
	Colonial Fire Brigades Long Service Medal	
	Colonial Prison Service Medal	
+	Uganda Long Service and Good Conduct Medal	
	Army Emergency Reserve Decoration	ERD
	Volunteer Officers' Decoration	VD
	Volunteer Long Service Medal	
	Volunteer Officers' Decoration (for India & the Colonies)	VD
	Volunteer Long Service Medal (for India & the Colonies)	
	Colonial Auxiliary Forces Officers' Decoration	VD
	Colonial Auxiliary Forces Long Service Medal	
	Medal for Good Shooting (Naval)	
	Militia Long Service Medal	

1952 to 1995

From Army Dress Regulations 1969 (cont)

Change	Titles	Post-nominals
	Imperial Yeomanry Long Service Medal	
	Territorial Decoration	TD
	Efficiency Decoration	TD/ED
	Territorial Efficiency Medal	
	Efficiency Medal	
	Special Reserve Long Service and Good Conduct Medal	
	Decoration for Officers of the Royal Naval Reserve	RD
	Decoration for Officers of the Royal Naval Volunteer Reserve	VRD
	Royal Naval Reserve Long Service and Good Conduct Medal	
	Royal Naval Volunteer Reserve Long Service and Good Conduct Medal	
	Royal Naval Auxiliary Sick Berth Reserve Long Service and Good Conduct Medal	
	Royal Fleet Reserve Long Service and Good Conduct Medal	
	Royal Naval Wireless Auxiliary Reserve Long Service and Good Conduct Medal	
	Air Efficiency Award	
	Queen's Medal (for Champion Shots of the New Zealand Naval Forces)	
	Queen's Medal (for Champion Shots in the Military Forces)	
	Queen's Medal (for Champion Shots of the Air Forces)	
	Cadet Forces Medal	
	Coast Life Saving Corps Long Service Medal (formerly Rocket Apparatus Volunteer Long Service Medal)	
	Special Constabulary Long Service Medal	
	Canadian Forces Decoration	CD
	Royal Observer Corps Medal	
	Civil Defence Long Service Medal	
	Union of South Africa Commemoration Medal	
	Indian Independence Medal	
	Pakistan Medal	
	Ceylon Armed Forces Inauguration Medal	

From Army Dress Regulations 1969 (cont)

Change Titles   Post-nominals

        Ceylon Police Independence Medal (1948)

        Sierra Leone Independence Medal

        Jamaica Independence Medal

        Uganda Independence Medal

        Malawi Independence Medal

        Service Medal of the Order of St. John

        Badge of the Order of the League of Mercy

        Voluntary Medical Service Medal

        Women's Voluntary Service Medal

        South African Medal for War Services

        Colonial Special Constabulary Medal

        Other Commonwealth Members' Orders Decorations and Medals

        Foreign Orders (in order of date of award)

        Foreign Decorations (in order of date of award)

        Foreign Medals (in order of date of award)

Key to "Change":
"+" = addition   "- (??)" = deleted from this list   "*" = change of position/title.

Appendix 7 to Chapter 6

From *London Gazette* dated 28 October 1983

Change	Titles	Post-nominals
	Victoria Cross	VC
	George Cross	GC
	Knight of the Most Noble Order of the Garter	KG
	Knight of the Most Ancient and Most Noble Order of the Thistle	KT
	Knight of the Most Illustrious Order of St. Patrick	KP
	Knight or Dame Grand Cross of the Most Honourable Order of the Bath	GCB
	Member of the Order of Merit	OM
	Baronet's Badge	Bt or Bart
	Knight Grand Commander of the Most Exalted Order of the Star of India	GCSI
	Knight or Dame Grand Cross of the Most Distinguished Order of St. Michael & St. George	GCMG
	Knight Grand Commander of the Most Eminent Order of the Indian Empire	GCIE
	The Imperial Order of the Crown of India	CI
	Knight or Dame Grand Cross of the Royal Victorian Order	GCVO
	Knight or Dame Grand Cross of the Most Excellent Order of the British Empire	GBE
	Member of the Order of the Companions of Honour	CH
	Knight or Dame Commander of the Most Honourable Order of the Bath	KCB/DCB
	Knight Commander of the Most Exalted Order of the Star of India	KCSI
	Knight or Dame Commander of the Most Distinguished Order of St. Michael & St. George	KCMG/ DCMG
	Knight Commander of the Most Eminent Order of the Indian Empire	KCIE
	Knight or Dame Commander of the Royal Victorian Order	KCVO/ DCVO
	Knight or Dame Commander of the Most Excellent Order of the British Empire	KBE/DBE
	Knight Bachelor's Badge	
	Companion of the Most Honourable Order of the Bath	CB

"Medals Will Be Worn"

From *London Gazette* dated 28 October 1983 (cont)

Change Titles   Post-nominals

Change	Titles	Post-nominals
	Companion of the Most Exalted Order of the Star of India	CSI
	Companion of the Most Distinguished Order of St. Michael & St. George	CMG
	Companion of the Most Eminent Order of the Indian Empire	CIE
	Commander of the Royal Victorian Order	CVO
	Commander of the Most Excellent Order of the British Empire	CBE
	Companion of the Distinguished Service Order	DSO
	Member of the Fourth Class of the Royal Victorian Order	MVO
	Officer of the Most Excellent Order of the British Empire	OBE
	Companion of the Imperial Service Order	ISO
	Member of the Fifth Class of the Royal Victorian Order	MVO
	Member of the Most Excellent Order of the British Empire	MBE
	Indian Order of Merit (Military)	IOM
	Member of the Royal Red Cross	RRC
	Distinguished Service Cross	DSC
	Military Cross	MC
	Distinguished Flying Cross	DFC
	Air Force Cross	AFC
	Associate of the Royal Red Cross	ARRC
	Order of British India	OBI
	Kaisar-i-Hind Medal (Gold, Silver & Bronze)	
	Order of St. John (All Classes)	
-	(Albert Medals (Sea & Land; Classes I & II (Gold & Bronze)))	
	Union of South Africa Queen's Medal for Bravery (in Gold)	
	Distinguished Conduct Medal	DCM
	Conspicuous Gallantry Medal	CGM
+	Conspicuous Gallantry Medal (Flying)	CGM
	George Medal	GM
	Queen's Police Medal for Gallantry	QPM
	Queen's Fire Service Medal for Gallantry	QFSM

From *London Gazette* dated 28 October 1983 (cont)

Change	Titles	Post-nominals
	(Edward Medal (1st & 2nd Classes)(Silver and Bronze))	
	Royal West African Frontier Force Distinguished Conduct Medal	DCM
	King's African Rifles Distinguished Conduct Medal	DCM
	Indian Distinguished Service Medal	IDSM
	Union of South Africa Queen's Medal for Bravery (in Silver)	
	Distinguished Service Medal	DSM
	Military Medal	MM
	Distinguished Flying Medal	DFM
	Air Force Medal	AFM
	Constabulary Medal (Ireland)	
	Medal for Saving Life at Sea	
	Indian Order of Merit (Civil)	IOM
	Indian Police Medal for Gallantry	
	Ceylon Police Medal for Gallantry	
	Sierra Leone Police Medal for Gallantry	
	Sierra Leone Fire Brigades Medal for Gallantry	
	Colonial Police Medal for Gallantry	CPM
·	Queen's Gallantry Medal	QGM
·	Royal Victorian Medal (Gold, Silver & Bronze)	RVM
	British Empire Medal	BEM
	Canada Medal	CM
	Queen's Police Medal for Distinguished Service	QPM
	Queen's Fire Service Medal for Distinguished Service	QFSM
	Queen's Medal for Chiefs	
	War Medals (in order of date of campaign for which awarded)	
	Polar Medals (in order of date)	
	Imperial Service Medal	
	Indian Police Medal for Meritorious Service	
	Ceylon Police Medal for Merit	

"Medals Will Be Worn"

From *London Gazette* dated 28 October 1983 (cont)

Change	Titles	Post-nominals
	Sierra Leone Police Medal for Meritorious Service	
	Sierra Leone Fire Brigades Medal for Meritorious Service	
	Colonial Police Medal for Meritorious Service	CPM
	Badge of Honour	
	Queen Victoria's Jubilee Medal, 1887 (Gold, Silver & Bronze)	
	Queen Victoria's Police Jubilee Medal, 1887	
	Queen Victoria's Jubilee Medal, 1897 (Gold, Silver & Bronze)	
	Queen Victoria's Police Jubilee Medal, 1897	
	Queen Victoria's Commemoration Medal, 1900 (Ireland)	
	King Edward VII's Coronation Medal, 1902	
	King Edward VII's Police Coronation Medal, 1902	
	King Edward VII's Durbar Medal, 1903 (Gold, Silver & Bronze)	
	King Edward VII's Police Medal, 1903 (Scotland)	
	King's Visit Commemoration Medal, 1903 (Ireland)	
	King George V's Coronation Medal, 1911	
	King George V's Police Coronation Medal, 1911	
	King's Visit Police Commemoration Medal, 1911 (Ireland)	
	King George V's Durbar Medal, 1911 (Gold, Silver & Bronze)	
	King George V's Silver Jubilee Medal, 1935	
	King George VI's Coronation Medal, 1937	
	Queen Elizabeth II's Coronation Medal, 1953	
+	Queen Elizabeth II's Silver Jubilee Medal, 1977	
	King George V's Long and Faithful Service Medal	
	King George VI's Long and Faithful Service Medal	
	Queen Elizabeth II's Long and Faithful Service Medal	
*	Medal for Meritorious Service (all Services since 1 December 1977)	
*	Medal for Long Service and Good Conduct (Military)	
	Naval Long Service and Good Conduct Medal	
+	Medal for Meritorious Service (Royal Navy 1918-1928)	MSM

1952 to 1995

From *London Gazette* dated 28 October 1983 (cont)

Change Titles   Post-nominals

	Title	Post-nominals
	Indian Long Service and Good Conduct Medal (for Europeans of Indian Army)	
	Indian Meritorious Service Medal (for Europeans of Indian Army)	
*	Royal Marines Meritorious Service Medal (1849-1947)	
*	Royal Air Force Meritorious Service Medal (1918-1928)	
	Royal Air Force Long Service and Good Conduct Medal	
+	Medal for Long Service and Good Conduct (Ulster Defence Regiment)	
	Indian Long Service and Good Conduct Medal (for Indian Army)	
	Royal West African Frontier Force Long Service and Good Conduct Medal	
	Royal Sierra Leone Military Forces Long Service and Good Conduct Medal	
	King's African Rifles Long Service and Good Conduct Medal	
	Indian Meritorious Service Medal (for Indian Army)	
	Police Long Service and Good Conduct Medal	
	Fire Brigade Long Service and Good Conduct Medal	
	African Police Medal for Meritorious Service	
	Royal Canadian Mounted Police Long Service Medal	
	Ceylon Police Long Service Medal	
	Ceylon Fire Services Long Service Medal	
	Sierra Leone Police Long Service Medal	
	Colonial Police Long Service Medal	
	Sierra Leone Fire Brigades Long Service Medal	
+	Mauritius Police Long Service and Good Conduct Medal	
+	Mauritius Fire Services Long Service and Good Conduct Medal	
+	Mauritius Prisons Service Long Service and Good Conduct Medal	
	Colonial Fire Brigades Long Service Medal	
	Colonial Prison Service Medal	
	Army Emergency Reserve Decoration	ERD
	Volunteer Officers' Decoration	VD

From *London Gazette* dated 28 October 1983 (cont)

Change	Titles	Post-nominals
	Volunteer Long Service Medal	
	Volunteer Officers' Decoration (for India & the Colonies)	VD
	Volunteer Long Service Medal (for India & the Colonies)	
	Colonial Auxiliary Forces Officers' Decoration	VD
	Colonial Auxiliary Forces Long Service Medal	
	Medal for Good Shooting (Naval)	
	Militia Long Service Medal	
	Imperial Yeomanry Long Service Medal	
	Territorial Decoration	TD
+	Ceylon Armed Forces Long Service Medal	
	Efficiency Decoration	TD/ED
	Territorial Efficiency Medal	
	Efficiency Medal	
	Special Reserve Long Service and Good Conduct Medal	
	Decoration for Officers of the Royal Naval Reserve	RD
	Decoration for Officers of the Royal Naval Volunteer Reserve	VRD
	Royal Naval Reserve Long Service and Good Conduct Medal	
	Royal Naval Volunteer Reserve Long Service and Good Conduct Medal	
	Royal Naval Auxiliary Sick Berth Reserve Long Service and Good Conduct Medal	
	Royal Fleet Reserve Long Service and Good Conduct Medal	
	Royal Naval Wireless Auxiliary Reserve Long Service and Good Conduct Medal	
+	Royal Naval Auxiliary Service Medal	
	Air Efficiency Award	AE
+	Ulster Defence Regiment Medal	UD
+	Queen's Medal (for Champion Shots in the Royal Navy and Royal Marines)	
	Queen's Medal (for Champion Shots of the New Zealand Naval Forces)	
	Queen's Medal (for Champion Shots in the Military Forces)	

From *London Gazette* dated 28 October 1983 (cont)

Change	Titles	Post-nominals
	Queen's Medal (for Champion Shots of the Air Forces)	
	Cadet Forces Medal	
*	Coast Guard Auxiliary Long Service Medal (formerly Rocket Apparatus Volunteer Long Service Medal, later Coast Life Saving Corps Long Service Medal)	
	Special Constabulary Long Service Medal	
	Canadian Forces Decoration	CD
	Royal Observer Corps Medal	
	Civil Defence Long Service Medal	
+	Rhodesia Medal	
+	Royal Ulster Constabulary Service Medal	
	Union of South Africa Commemoration Medal	
	Indian Independence Medal	
	Pakistan Medal	
	Ceylon Armed Forces Inauguration Medal	
	Ceylon Police Independence Medal (1948)	
	Sierra Leone Independence Medal	
	Jamaica Independence Medal	
	Uganda Independence Medal	
	Malawi Independence Medal	
+	Fiji Independence Medal	
+	Papua New Guinea Independence Medal	
+	Solomon Islands Independence Medal	
	Service Medal of the Order of St. John	
	Badge of the Order of the League of Mercy	
	Voluntary Medical Service Medal	
	Women's Voluntary Service Medal	
	South African Medal for War Services	
	Colonial Special Constabulary Medal	
+	Honorary Membership of Commonwealth Orders (instituted by The Sovereign)(by date of award)	

From *London Gazette* dated 28 October 1983 (cont)

Change Titles   Post-nominals

　　　　Other Commonwealth Members' Orders Decorations and Medals
　　　　(instituted since 1949, otherwise than by The Sovereign)
　　　　and awards by the States of Malaysia
　　　　and the State of Brunei (in order of date of award)

　　　　Foreign Orders (in order of date of award)

　　　　Foreign Decorations (in order of date of award)

　　　　Foreign Medals (in order of date of award)

Key to "Change":
"+" = addition　　　*"- (??)" = deleted from this list*　　　*"*" = change of position/title.*

Appendix 8 to Chapter 6

From Army Material Regulations 1995

Change	Titles	Post-nominals
	VICTORIA CROSS	VC
	GEORGE CROSS	GC
	BRITISH ORDERS OF KNIGHTHOOD AND OTHER ORDERS	
	Knight of the Most Noble Order of the Garter	KG
	Knight of the Most Ancient and Most Noble Order of the Thistle	KT
-	(Knight of the Most Illustrious Order of St. Patrick)	
	Knight or Dame Grand Cross of the Most Honourable Order of the Bath	GCB
	Member of the Order of Merit	OM
-	(Knight Grand Commander of the Most Exalted Order of the Star of India)	
	Knight or Dame Grand Cross of the Most Distinguished Order of St. Michael & St. George	GCMG
-	(Knight Grand Commander of the Most Eminent Order of the Indian Empire)	
-	(The Imperial Order of the Crown of India)	
	Knight or Dame Grand Cross of the Royal Victorian Order	GCVO
	Knight or Dame Grand Cross of the Most Excellent Order of the British Empire	GBE
	Member of the Order of the Companions of Honour	CH
	Knight or Dame Commander of the Most Honourable Order of the Bath	KCB/DCB
-	(Knight Commander of the Most Exalted Order of the Star of India)	
	Knight or Dame Commander of the Most Distinguished Order of St. Michael & St. George	KCMG/ DCMG
-	(Knight Commander of the Most Eminent Order of the Indian Empire)	
	Knight or Dame Commander of the Royal Victorian Order	KCVO/ DCVO
	Knight or Dame Commander of the Most Excellent Order of the British Empire	KBE/DBE
	Companion of the Most Honourable Order of the Bath	CB
-	(Companion of the Most Exalted Order of the Star of India)	
	Companion of the Most Distinguished Order of St. Michael & St. George	CMG

From Army Material Regulations 1995 (cont)

Change	Titles	Post-nominals
-	(Companion of the Most Eminent Order of the Indian Empire)	
	Commander of the Royal Victorian Order	CVO
	Commander of the Most Excellent Order of the British Empire	CBE
	Companion of the Distinguished Service Order	DSO
*	Member of the Fourth Class of the Royal Victorian Order	LVO/MVO
	Officer of the Most Excellent Order of the British Empire	OBE
+	Companion of the Queen's Service Order (of New Zealand)	QSO
	Companion of the Imperial Service Order	ISO
	Member of the Fifth Class of the Royal Victorian Order	MVO
	Member of the Most Excellent Order of the British Empire	MBE
-	(Indian Order of Merit (Military))	
*	Baronet's Badge	Bt or Bart
*	Knight Bachelor's Badge	Kt
	DECORATIONS	
+	Conspicuous Gallantry Cross	CGC
*	Royal Red Cross (Class 1)	RRC
	Distinguished Service Cross	DSC
	Military Cross	MC
	Distinguished Flying Cross	DFC
	Air Force Cross	AFC
*	Royal Red Cross (Class 2)	ARRC
	Order of British India	OBI
*	Kaisar-i-Hind Medal (Classes 1-3)	
	Order of St. John (All classes)	
	MEDALS FOR GALLANTRY AND DISTINGUISHED SERVICE	
-	(Union of South Africa Queen's Medal for Bravery (in Gold))	
	Distinguished Conduct Medal	DCM
	Conspicuous Gallantry Medal	CGM
*	Conspicuous Gallantry Medal (Flying)	CGM (F)
	George Medal	GM

1952 to 1995

From Army Material Regulations 1995 (cont)

Change	Titles	Post-nominals
*	King's or Queen's Police Medal for Gallantry	KPM/ KPFSM/QPM
-	(Queen's Fire Service Medal for Gallantry)	
-	(Royal West African Frontier Force Distinguished Conduct Medal)	
-	(King's African Rifles Distinguished Conduct Medal)	
-	(Indian Distinguished Service Medal)	
-	(Union of South Africa Queen's Medal for Bravery (in Silver))	
	Distinguished Service Medal	DSM
	Military Medal	MM
	Distinguished Flying Medal	DFM
	Air Force Medal	AFM
-	(Constabulary Medal (Ireland))	
-	(Medal for Saving Life at Sea)	
-	(Indian Order of Merit (Civil))	
-	(Indian Police Medal for Gallantry)	
-	(Ceylon Police Medal for Gallantry)	
-	(Sierra Leone Police Medal for Gallantry)	
-	(Sierra Leone Fire Brigades Medal for Gallantry)	
-	(Colonial Police Medal for Gallantry)	
	Queen's Gallantry Medal	QGM
	MEDALS ATTACHED TO ORDERS	
	Royal Victorian Medal (Gold, Silver & Bronze)	RVM
	British Empire Medal	BEM
-	(Canada Medal)	
-	(Queen's Police Medal for Distinguished Service)	
-	(Queen's Fire Service Medal for Distinguished Service)	
-	(Queen's Medal for Chiefs)	
	WAR MEDALS	
	worn in order of date of campaign	

From Army Material Regulations 1995 (cont)

Change Titles   Post-nominals

ALLIANCE MEDALS

\+ United Nations (UN)

\+ Economic Community (EC)

\- (Polar Medals)

\- (Imperial Service Medal)

\- (Indian Police Medal for Meritorious Service)

\- (Ceylon Police Medal for Merit)

\- (Sierra Leone Police Medal for Meritorious Service)

\- (Sierra Leone Fire Brigades Medal for Meritorious Service)

\- (Colonial Police Medal for Meritorious Service)

\- (Badge of Honour)

COMMEMORATION MEDALS

\- (All Commemorative medals awarded prior to the following)

   Queen Elizabeth II's Coronation Medal, 1953

   Queen Elizabeth II's Silver Jubilee Medal, 1977

EFFICIENCY AND LONG SERVICE DECORATIONS AND MEDALS

\- (All Royal Long and Faithful Service Medals)

   Medal for Meritorious Service

\+ Accumulated Campaign Service Medal

   Medal for Long Service and Good Conduct (Military)

   Naval Long Service and Good Conduct Medal

\- (Medal for Meritorious Service (Royal Navy 1918-1928))

\- (Indian Long Service and Good Conduct Medal (for Europeans of Indian Army))

\- (Indian Meritorious Service Medal (for Europeans of Indian Army))

\- (Royal Marines Meritorious Service Medal (1849-1947))

\- (Royal Air Force Meritorious Service Medal (1918-1928))

   Royal Air Force Long Service and Good Conduct Medal

\+ Meritorious Service Medal (South African Permanent Forces)

   Medal for Long Service and Good Conduct (UDR) (obsolescent)

From Army Material Regulations 1995 (cont)

Change	Titles	Post-nominals
-	(Indian Long Service and Good Conduct Medal (for Indian Army))	
-	(Royal West African Frontier Force Long Service and Good Conduct Medal)	
-	(Royal Sierra Leone Military Forces Long Service and Good Conduct Medal)	
-	(King's African Rifles Long Service and Good Conduct Medal)	
-	(Indian Meritorious Service Medal (for Indian Army))	
-	(Police Long Service and Good Conduct Medal)	
-	(Fire Brigade Long Service and Good Conduct Medal)	
-	(African Police Medal for Meritorious Service)	
-	(Royal Canadian Mounted Police Long Service Medal)	
-	(Ceylon Police Long Service Medal)	
-	(Ceylon Fire Services Long Service Medal)	
-	(Sierra Leone Police Long Service Medal)	
-	(Colonial Police Long Service Medal)	
-	(Sierra Leone Fire Brigades Long Service Medal)	
-	(Mauritius Police Long Service and Good Conduct Medal)	
-	(Mauritius Fire Services Long Service and Good Conduct Medal)	
-	(Colonial Fire Brigades Long Service Medal)	
-	(Colonial Prison Service Long Service Medal)	
-	(Army Emergency Reserve Decoration)	
-	(Volunteer Officers' Decoration)	
-	(Volunteer Long Service Medal)	
-	(Volunteer Officers' Decoration (for India & the Colonies))	
-	(Volunteer Long Service Medal (for India & the Colonies))	
-	(Colonial Auxiliary Forces Officers' Decoration)	
-	(Colonial Auxiliary Forces Long Service Medal)	
-	(Medal for Good Shooting (Naval))	
-	(Militia Long Service Medal)	
-	(Imperial Yeomanry Long Service Medal)	
-	(Territorial Decoration)	

From Army Material Regulations 1995 (cont)

Change	Titles	Post-nominals
-	(Ceylon Armed Forces Long Service Medal)	
*	Efficiency Decoration (Territorial)	TD
*	Efficiency Decoration	ED
-	(Territorial Efficiency Medal)	
+	Efficiency Medal (HAC)	
*	Efficiency Medal (Territorial)	
-	(Efficiency Medal)	
-	(Special Reserve Long Service and Good Conduct Medal)	
-	(Decoration for Officers of the Royal Naval Reserve)	
-	(Decoration for Officers of the Royal Naval Volunteer Reserve)	
-	(Royal Naval Reserve Long Service and Good Conduct Medal)	
-	(Royal Naval Volunteer Reserve Long Service and Good Conduct Medal)	
-	(Royal Naval Auxiliary Sick Berth Reserve Long Service and Good Conduct Medal)	
-	(Royal Fleet Reserve Long Service and Good Conduct Medal)	
-	(Royal Naval Wireless Auxiliary Reserve Long Service and Good Conduct Medal)	
-	(Royal Naval Auxiliary Service Medal)	
	Air Efficiency Award	AE
	Ulster Defence Regiment Medal (obsolescent)	UD
*	Queen's Medal (for Champion Shots in the Royal Navy and Royal Marines)	
-	(Queen's Medal (for Champion Shots of the New Zealand Naval Forces))	
	Queen's Medal (for Champion Shots in the Military Forces)	
	Queen's Medal (for Champion Shots of the Air Forces)	
	Cadet Forces Medal	
-	(Coast Guard Auxiliary Long Service Medal (formerly Rocket Apparatus Volunteer Long Service Medal, later Coast Life Saving Corps Long Service Medal))	
-	(Special Constabulary Long Service Medal)	

From Army Material Regulations 1995 (cont)

Change   Titles   Post-nominals

- (Canadian Forces Decoration)
- (Royal Observer Corps Medal)
- (Civil Defence Long Service Medal)
- (Rhodesia Medal)
- (Royal Ulster Constabulary Service Medal)
- (Union of South Africa Commemoration Medal)
- (Indian Independence Medal)
- (Pakistan Medal)
- (Ceylon Armed Forces Inauguration Medal)
- (Ceylon Police Independence Medal (1948))
- (Sierra Leone Independence Medal)
- (Jamaica Independence Medal)
- (Uganda Independence Medal)
- (Malawi Independence Medal)
- (Fiji Independence Medal)
- (Papua New Guinea Independence Medal)
- (Solomon Islands Independence Medal)
- (Service Medal of the Order of St. John)
- (Badge of the Order of the League of Mercy)
- (Voluntary Medical Service Medal)
- (Women's Voluntary Service Medal)
- (South African Medal for War Services)
- (Colonial Special Constabulary Medal)

Honorary Membership of Commonwealth Orders
(instituted by the Sovereign; worn in order of the date of award).
(Not highlighted as a title)

Other Commonwealth Member's Orders, decorations and medals
(instituted since 1949, otherwise than by the Sovereign)
and awards by the States of Malaysia and the State of Brunei
in order of date of award. (Not highlighted as a title)

From Army Material Regulations 1995 (cont)

Change	Titles	Post-nominals
	FOREIGN ORDERS	
	FOREIGN DECORATIONS	
	FOREIGN MEDALS	
+	**MENTIONS IN DESPATCHES**	
	QUEEN'S COMMENDATIONS FOR BRAVERY	
+	Queen's Commendation for Bravery (QCB)	
+	Queen's Commendation for Bravery in the Air (QCBA)	
+	Queen's Commendation for Valuable Service (QCVS)	

Key to "Change":
"+" = addition   "- (??) -" = omitted from this list   "" = change of position/title.*

Chapter 7

Mentioned in Despatches and Similar Subjects

EVER since commanders in the field have submitted despatches to their masters they have "mentioned" individuals who had been singled out by reason of bravery or particular excellence. Indeed some of the more tangible rewards, such as the DSO used to require a "mention" as a prerequisite to the award, the mention taking the place of a citation.

This situation continued right through and after the 1914-18 War and at first appeared to satisfy the need. In the 1914-18 War commanders were instructed to submit lists of not more than one per cent of their total strength half yearly with their honours list. Nothing was given to the person "mentioned" unless they got hold of a copy of the order showing the full list of recipients. As time progressed, and the numbers involved grew, it became impossible to produce lists up to the set limit so they were cut to a convenient size for publication. During the war some 141,000 people were "mentioned" which amounts to only about one quarter of one per cent each six months.

However, during the war many of our servicemen had seen allies who received their countries' "mentions" awarded in the form of a medal, indeed not a few of our troops had received them in the form of the French or Belgian Croix de Guerre and other countries' equivalent awards. This led to discontent which must have been on a grand scale. There were demands for something more than a few words in a despatch seen by very few. British troops wanted something giving visible evidence that they had been noticed for their acts. To some extent this need was met by Corps Commanders' and Divisional Commanders' certificates. These were issued to those recognised within these formations, but were, in fact, unofficial and anyway below the level of the official "mention". So they had the dual effect of meeting a need while underlining the inadequacy of the official system.

The recognition of this need, and action to meet it, was delayed until Army Order 166 of May 1919, nearly five years after the outbreak of war and seven months after it ended. Even this only took the form of a certificate, signed by the Secretary of State for War, to be issued to all those "mentioned" during the war. Notably it included all three services and the Indian, Dominion, Colonial and Egyptian Forces plus certain civilian organisations who had served with troops in the field, such as the YMCA, YWCA and included civilians of both sexes. This again did not meet the demand and eventually, in January 1920, the King approved an oak leaf emblem to be worn on the Victory Medal for those so mentioned. One emblem only could be worn regardless of the number of times a person was "mentioned" and it was in addition to the earlier certificate. The Military Secretary's Review of awards in 1920 refers to this as a "special concession", which sounds somewhat grudging.

After the war the subject appears to have been left dormant. The wound stripes and service chevrons adopted during the war were quickly discontinued and it would appear that the same fate was, by default, being hoped for in the case of oak leaves. No further instructions were issued between the wars and it was not until the Command Paper of August 1943, detailing the conditions for the 1939-43 Star and Africa Star that the subject arose again. This paper dealt with not only the new stars but also with mentions, wound stripes and service chevrons for the Second World War. The design of the oak leaf was different to the previous one and one new emblem was to be worn directly on the coat, not on any ribbon, for any number of "mentions" "during the present war". This was promulgated to the Army in Army Order 18 of 1944. After the war the wound stripes and service chevrons again quickly became defunct, but the oak leaf remained as part of the honours system. In the *London Gazette* list of the order of wear for 1947 Mentions in Despatches and the other innovations, King's Commendations for Brave Conduct and for Valuable Service in the Air, all received official and lasting recognition.

The original 1914-18 emblem of bronze oak leaves, worn on the Victory Medal, is said to have ceased on 10 August 1920. This ignores the fact that in the period 1914 to 1920 there had been a number of campaign medals awarded, other than the trio for the war, with a number of clasps. These could have been awarded to personnel who did not qualify for the wartime trio and, it must be presumed that their various Commanders issued despatches and so would "mention" people. The campaigns concerned include Indian General Service Medal 1908 with three clasps; the African General Service Medal 1902 with seven clasps; the Naval General Service Medal 1914 with two clasps; and the General Service Medal (Army and RAF) 1918 with three clasps. Although less clear-cut, but deserving note in view of the inclusion of Egyptian Forces in the original provision for "mentions", is the Khedive's Sudan Medal with nine clasps. Army Order 109 of 1947 did include provision for the oak leaves emblem to be worn on the General Service Medal 1918 but this has not been reflected in the *London Gazette*. The Army Order also permitted the use of the new oak leaf emblem and the King's Commendation emblem to be worn on campaign medals awarded between the wars.

In addition to these campaign medals in 1914-20 there were personnel who received the War Medal but not the Victory Medal. It has been said that, in these cases, the emblem was worn on the War Medal, but no authority for this has been found. In the Navy this lack of the Victory Medal applied to those "mobilised" for the war but not serving in an operational theatre. In the Army the rules appear to preclude it, but it was possible to receive the War Medal without the Victory Medal. Lieutenant Colonel L. Robson, VD, commanded the coastal artillery at Hartlepool in 1914 when a German naval squadron bombarded the coast. Colonel Robson was awarded the DSO and his gunners received three DCMs and two MMs. At that time a mention in despatches was an essential prerequisite for a DSO. However, as a photograph taken after 1919 clearly shows, he was not wearing the emblem and he had no Victory Medal. His awards are the CMG at the neck, and on the bar his DSO, Order of St. John of Jerusalem, War Medal, Coronation Medal 1911, VD and TD. In fact he was "mentioned" twice in 1917 and there were at least three other "mentions" connected with the Hartlepool bombardment. As Colonel Robson was awarded his TD in January 1920 this photograph must post-date that, and it is long enough afterwards for him to have received his oak leaves emblem.

After the 1939-45 War, in practical terms, the situation was that the old oak leaves emblem was worn on the Victory Medal, General Service Medal, and possibly others, for service up to 1920. After that the new oak leaf emblem was worn on the appropriate campaign medal for service between the wars and on the War Medal 1939-45 for the war. After the 1939-45 War it was worn on the appropriate campaign medal. Those entitled to the King's and Queen's Commendations in the armed forces, and in the Merchant Navy during the War, wore the same oak leaf emblem as for a mention. Other civilians wore a silver laurel leaf directly on the coat unless it was awarded for Civil Defence type activities qualifying for the Defence Medal during the war; in this case the emblem was worn on the Defence Medal. The Commendation for Valuable

Service in the Air, when worn by civilians was represented by an oval silver badge worn on the coat beneath any medals.

Until relatively recently the rule of wearing only one emblem on one ribbon regardless of the number of mentions begged the question of what to wear if an individual in the armed forces had both a commendation and a mention in the same campaign. This was addressed for civilians in the Army Orders instituting the Africa General Service Medal, 1902, for "Kenya" and that for the General Service Medal, 1918, for "Cyprus". In these cases a civilian with both wore the silver laurel leaves emblem on the medal ribbon and the oak leaf emblem on the coat after all ribbons. However, a recent Pamphlet on Military Honours and Awards states, with great ambiguity, "No more than one oak leaf emblem is to be worn on the ribbon of one medal. Two or more awards in service qualifying for one medal are to be denoted by only one emblem. However, if there are awards of a QCBC and of a MID two emblems are worn to denote the two different kinds of award." It refers to Material Regulations revised 1981 but there is no explanation of how these two emblems are to be worn.

Since these documents were produced there were more changes in this field when Defence Council Instruction 214 of 1994 announced that the old awards were to be replaced by four new ones. The last named award below really replaces the old mention in despatches for anything other than gallantry. All are represented by silver emblems, where possible of similar design to the old ones. Post-nominal letters are not used. These new awards are:

- A Mention in Despatches (MID) for gallantry in active operations against the enemy from 3 September 1993. The emblem is unchanged from the old except that it is silver instead of bronze.

- A Queen's Commendation for Bravery (QCB) replacing the Queen's Commendation for Brave Conduct from, and including, 26 April 1994. The emblem is virtually unchanged from the old civilian Queen's Commendation for Brave Conduct.

- A Queen's Commendation for Bravery in the Air (QCBA) replacing the Queen's Commendation for Valuable Service in the Air from, and including, 26 April 1994. The emblem is new.

- A Queen's Commendation for Valuable Service (QCVS) for services which, while in an operational theatre, are not in active operations against the enemy from 3 September 1993. The emblem is a silver representation similar to the 1914-20 Mention in Despatches emblem.

The instructions for wear, as originally issued, were virtually the same as the old ones except that the emblems were not allowed to be worn on United Nations medals. This has now been rescinded bringing the rules into line with those pertaining for the United Nations Service Medal (Korea) on which the emblem for a Queen's

Commendation for Bravery could be worn, whereas the emblem for a Mention in Despatches was worn on the Queen's Korea Medal. However, the old rules of wearing them on the ribbon of the appropriate medal or on the coat if no medal has been awarded remain. The problems of multiple awards for one theatre, now increased, were totally ignored until Material Regulations of 1995.

These regulations do attempt to meet the problem, though they remain vague in certain areas. Firstly they restrict the total number of each emblem on one medal to one. They also refer to "mentions in despatches" so it is not clear if someone who already has an old bronze mention and receives the new silver emblem may wear both, it seems not. Secondly they lay down the order of seniority for the awards, this is MID, QCB, QCBA and QCVS and state that emblems on the same ribbon, or directly on the coat, should be worn in that order from the top to bottom or right to left. What is not said is how to wear the two types of MID for one campaign. Also, although the method of wear on a ribbon carrying a medal is given, this is not explained for more than one emblem when ribbons alone are worn. Even overlapping it does not seem likely that more than two emblems would fit on a single ribbon about 30mm by 10mm. If they do not fit how can they be worn—directly on the coat? It is quite possible to imagine, in these days of multi-skills, that one individual will go to a long standing operational area on several tours in different roles and be awarded two or more of these emblems. If the overflow is worn on the coat and a similar set of emblems are awarded for another theatre; would more than one of any emblem be allowed to be worn directly on the coat? This is a possible scenario and should be addressed before it occurs. If the emblems worn on the coat are worn on a full-sized or miniature medal bar on a piece of material, what colour should that be? The 1981 Army rules mention that with miniatures they may be worn on a backing of the colour of the jacket. Even for miniatures this begs the problem of wearing them on different occasions on, say a scarlet or white mess jacket or on a black dinner jacket. For full-sized medals it could be a khaki jacket, blue or green Number 1 Dress, scarlet tunic or pin striped suit. The backing colour, regardless of the form of dress, needs to be laid down.

While meeting a need to distinguish between gallantry and merit in different types of situation these new emblems merely serve to increase the practical difficulties. They have been introduced at a time when the General Service Medal 1962 is still in issue and will sometimes carry the old mentioned emblem.

In addition these awards are supposed to be the fourth level of the Queen's gallantry awards or, presumably, the second level of merit after the MBE. Yet they are liable to be worn last—that is, not only after all British medals, but after Commonwealth and foreign ones too. The number of servicemen with Commonwealth or foreign awards is not inconsiderable.

Although this is possibly acceptable when ribbons alone are worn, the question of how to display these emblems has never properly been addressed when wearing full sized or miniature medals. One man's solution is shown in a photograph of Lieutenant E. W. K. Walton, AM, DSC, who declined to exchange his Albert Medal for the George Cross. He is shown with his Commendation for Brave Conduct emblem apparently soldered to the end of the bar. Imagine the same solution for the four new emblems. It would constitute a health hazard to passers-by. For interest his medals are the AM, DSC, 1939-45 Star, Atlantic Star with a rosette (it should be a bar), Africa Star, Burma Star, War Medal with oak leaf, Polar Medal in silver with clasp "Antarctic 1946-47".

The obvious solution to these problems is to produce a medal for each category instead of an emblem. This is probably deemed too expensive and to re-introduce, say, the MM, EGM, DFM and BEM, for all ranks to take the place of these awards would probably be both too expensive and too radical. It would also run into problems for holders of the same awards for their original purposes.

So we are probably stuck with the current emblems but they really should take a more appropriate significance. A simple and cheap method of doing this would be to elevate them to a suitable position in the order of wear and adopt the Australian idea of designating a particular ribbon for each. When worn with medals the first award would be worn on a ribbon, at a height level with the centre of the average medal. Second and subsequent awards of the same emblem could be added to the same ribbon, just as bars are added to other awards. Each of the four awards would have its own coloured ribbon—for example these might be red for MID, dark blue for QCB, light blue for QCVA and dark green for QCVS. This might look slightly odd in the middle of a row of "proper" medals, but it not any worse than a "scythe" of metal leaves soldered together and, perhaps, worn after one United Nations Medal. In addition there seems no reason to deny recipients the use of the post-nominal letters which are widely used in military publications already.

Whatever is decided the regulations must address every eventuality and produce a practical way of wearing these emblems either by themselves or on medal bars with or without full-sized and miniature awards.

Australian Commendation for Brave Conduct displayed on a full length ribbon.
Courtesy Michael Maton, Honours and Awards of Australia.

Chapter 8

Restricted Wear and the Two Medal Myth

THE Foreign Office, now the Foreign and Commonwealth Office, has always had a considerable voice in the acceptance of awards for overseas service. This is correct as they are the arbiters of our policy overseas and should be in the most advantageous position to defend Britain's best interests abroad.

Where an individual takes part in the activities of foreign armies, let us say as a member of some foreign legion, it is understandable that on returning to this country some awards might be objectionable and permission to wear withheld. On the other hand if such operations are undertaken with the blessing of the British Government, as in the case of loaned service personnel, it seems logical that any awards made should be accepted.

There is also a line to be drawn between justifiable comment on our interests and totally illogical and inconsistent decisions, possibly at the whim of an individual, just because the right to comment is there. If viewed from an overall global position the inconsistencies in past edicts are all too apparent. Unfortunately it must be suspected that the Foreign Office attitude is often backed by "blimpishness" and lack of awareness in the Ministry of Defence.

Wearing Commonwealth or Foreign awards may be granted with either "restricted" or "unrestricted" permission. This is perfectly understandable in relation to such events as State visits. Foreigners are frequently more liberal than we are with their distribution of honours. At the pinnacle of society, in the Royal and Government circles, honours are exchanged with other Nations. Those involved in numerous events of this nature can pick up a chest full of awards, virtually just for being there. It has been the custom that these are accepted with "restricted" permission to wear. "Restricted" permission is, in actual fact, no permission at all unless the individual is in, or at a function of, the country giving the honour. In practical terms the restriction can be made to work for an Order which is not worn on the medal bar, because that can be worn, or not, separate from other medals with no inconvenience to the owner. In the case of a "restricted" medal normally worn last it could be worn pinned to the tunic separate from other medals and so is just workable for, say, a function at the London High Commission or Embassy concerned.

However, if "restricted" permission is given for an award normally mounted amongst others some major practical difficulties arise. To do this for a single occasion becomes a costly endeavour for the wearer. To accommodate such "unrestricted" medals, the entire medal bar would have to be remounted for the occasion and returned to normal afterwards, and it must be remembered that failure to wear such an award could cause offence to the host nation.

A good example arose as a result of operations on behalf of the United Nations in the Congo in 1960 to 1964. British troops as such were not involved, but a number of individuals were, those who served on loan with Commonwealth Nations. These people served variously with Nigerian, Ghanaian and Royal Sierra Leone forces. In 1962 instructions were issued in Army Orders allowing these personnel to wear the United Nations Service Medal with Congo bar for the campaign. It was to be worn amongst British campaign medals as a British award. About the same time Army Council Instruction 289 of 1962 was issued giving restricted permission for wear of the Ghana Congo Medal.

Impressions from that time, based on no hard evidence, indicated that the reason for "restricted" permission being given was twofold.

- First it was against policy to give two medals for one operation and the United Nations medal was the official medal.
- Secondly Ghana was not too popular with Britain.

The first reason ignored the Korean campaign (usually called a War but that was not declared) from 1950 to 1953 when two medals were awarded—the Queen's and the United Nations. Further back in history two medals were awarded to many involved in the Boer War and in some of the campaigns in Egypt/Sudan earlier in the century. The North West Frontier during 1914-18 attracted three medals as against the single General Service Medal awarded before and after that period in the same area. Of course the First World War itself attracted two or three medals and it was impossible to receive the Victory Medal without also getting the British War Medal. That those servicemen deserved much more is not in issue, but it is a fact that the so-called two-medal rule was broken.

So much for the "policy" in 1953, yet even more recently we have a somewhat similar case. The General Service Medal (Army & RAF) 1918 with clasp "Malaya" ceased to be in issue on 31 July 1960. This was the first time since 1936, apart from much of the War period, when this medal had not been awarded somewhere in the world involving a total of nine different clasps (fifteen since its inception). It was an ideal time to switch medals to a new campaign medal. Instead, when the Brunei revolt broke out the old medal was re-issued with the clasp "Brunei" for the period 8 to 23 December 1962. The new General Service Medal 1962, with the clasp "Borneo" started on 24 December 1962. Most of our troops involved in the Brunei rebellion must have thought Father Christmas had come a day early. Once again the two-medal rule had been broken though in a slightly different way.

The second reason given above, if correct, seems a little hard on recipients because official sanction was present if our personnel were allowed to serve with Ghanaian forces at all, and they must have gone to the Congo with our Government's blessing.

The next problem arose from this decision. In 1965 DCIs notified the award of the Sierra Leone General Service Medal with bar "Congo". Presumably for the reasons already given above, it was also awarded with restricted permission, but if worn it was to be placed amongst British campaign medals since it was a "Queen's" award. In addition, this medal was instituted by the Queen, so it is very doubtful that it was proper to restrict its wear. On the other hand, having restricted wear for Ghana made it difficult to explain any reasons for not doing so for Sierra Leone.

An added complication arose in that the United Nations Medal was in fact the United Nations Truce Supervisory Organisation Medal for Palestine with an added bar for the Congo. In 1966 the ribbon was altered and the bar removed. So this became the first of the United Nations Medals series where the identical medal is used but with different ribbons for many operations world-wide. At least one man, who served with the Nigerians, wore the old United Nations Medal with bar as well as the new one. He claimed that the old one was the Nigerian Congo Medal. Even if this was the case and he received individual permission to wear, it should have been "restricted" to accord with the decisions on the other two.

The *London Gazette* lists ignore such minor matters and in 1964 the Sierra Leone

General Service Medal was added to the list in the footnote of those war medals "instituted by the Queen". No instructions are given as to wearing these except that the note refers to all "British" war medals so it must be presumed that the Commonwealth ones are worn amongst British awards. With the possible exception of the Pakistan General Service Medal instituted by the King in 1951, and for which no other instructions have been traced, all the other medals listed are certainly "unrestricted."

Lack of consistent decisions can be further illustrated by taking three examples of similar situations—the Jebel Akhdar Campaign in Muscat and Oman in 1959-61, the Malayan Emergency in the same period and the Dhofar War, in Oman, in 1969 to 1976.

Jebel Akhdar War included considerable British involvement at a time when the Government did not want publicity for this type of action East of Suez, even in support of friends. A medal for those involved was proposed and, eventually, with great reluctance it was agreed to award the General Service Medal, 1918-62 with the clasp "Arabian Peninsula". But the main reason for its issue was concealed as all troops in the Arabian Peninsula received it. This included many who were not involved in any operations e.g. those in Bahrein, many in the Gulf States and in Aden Colony. A few personnel were, during the Jebel Akhdar period, loaned to the Sultan of Muscat and Oman's forces and should have been eligible for his medal for the operation. Acceptance, not just wear, of this medal was turned down. The reason might have been "British interests" or the old chestnut of not receiving two medals for the same campaign. It was probably a mixture of the two. If so, it is worth considering the case of Malaya which follows, and wondering why decisions made "in British interests" cannot be reconsidered when our involvement has been made public in books and articles in later years.

The Malayan Emergency began in 1948 and continued until 1960. The General Service Medal 1918-62 with clasp "Malaya" was awarded to all the British and Commonwealth troops involved. Some personnel were loaned to the Malay Regiment and they received both the General Service Medal 1918 and the Malay Active Service Medal for their efforts. This not only breached the "two-medal" rule, it was very unfair to others in Commonwealth units, including British, Australian, New Zealand, West African and Fijian, who received only the one medal. There are plenty of cases where the "two medal" restriction has been ignored as already illustrated, but in all the others quoted it was on a similar basis for all involved. In this case it applied to just a few.

By contrast in another "secret war" in the Dhofar Province of the Sultanate of Oman British personnel, both those on loan and those on contract, to the Sultan's Armed Forces were allowed to receive and wear the Omani General Service Medal with clasp "Dhofar" for service in that province during the War from 1965 to 1976. For a long time troops in British units also serving in Dhofar received no medal, presumably on the grounds that it was not in our interests to acknowledge our presence there. Later the need for a medal was agreed and the General Service Medal 1964 with clasp "Dhofar" was approved for service in British units in Dhofar but only from 1969 to 1976. This medal was denied to British personnel who served in Dhofar only with the Sultan's forces on the grounds that their service had already been recognised by the Sultan's medal. Again the two-medal rule but in contrast to Malaya. Later still in 1977 unrestricted permission to wear the Sultan's "As Sumood" Medal was granted. This commemorated service in the Sultan's Armed Forces during the period of the War, but not necessarily in the operational area. Those who served in the operational area, Dhofar Province, got both the General Service and As Sumood

Medals both with unrestricted permission to wear. What happened to the two-medal rule there?

The above illustrates differences in policy around the world. Other decisions, some in connection with operations but, more especially, with commemorative awards seem even more inclined to the illogical.

First some operational awards. After the Malaya Emergency finished in 1960 the Malaysians had further trouble on their northern border. They deployed their own troops who received the Malaysian General Service Medal. Some Australians, New Zealanders and a few British personnel, including Army aircrew, also joined the operations. The Malaysians offered to award all of them the Malaysian medal, but this was rejected, on what grounds is not known. This was a friendly country, where we had fought for years to maintain their rulers and where we still had both bases and interests. It is difficult to see why we refused their medal. It is also interesting to note that, in their increasing detachment from our awards system, both Australia and New Zealand have recently made retrospective awards of their own campaign medals for the period 1960 to 1964 in Malaysia. These are the Australian Service Medal, 1945-1975 with clasp "Malaysia/Thailand Border" and the New Zealand General Service Medal in silver with clasp "Malaya". Of course, neither of these medals is available for British troops.

A contrasting example in 1954 is connected with serious floods in the Baghdad area when assistance was requested of RAF Habbaniya. An airlift of sandbags and relief supplies was organised and those taking part were awarded, and allowed to wear with unrestricted permission, the Iraq Flood Rescue Medal, 1954.

Moving to commemorative medals there is even greater confusion. Many are probably covered by individual permission issued by the Foreign Office. As they do not keep records allowing access by individual names, or even by countries of origin of the award, there is no realistic way to compile lists of recipients even if the files were to be accessible. However, some awards are covered in "blanket" Defence Council Instructions and the reasons behind "restricted" and "unrestricted" acceptance of awards is beyond comprehension. When added to one known "unrestricted" individual award it becomes even less understandable. This one was to a RAF officer in Iran during the Shah's reign, who received in 1970 unrestricted permission to wear the Shah's Coronation Medal. He was probably not alone in this as, of course, it was at a time when we were engaged in selling large quantities of military hardware to Iran.

Independence Medals, unless instituted by the Sovereign and paid for by the new country, are not normally allowed to be worn. Nigeria inadvertently circumvented this by agreeing to the terms for a "Queen's Medal" in 1961 and then changing its mind by 1964. The result was that the Nigerian Independence Medal originally got included in the order of wear amongst others and was treated as British. It was later deleted, as it became a Commonwealth award, and worn after all British medals. However, the unrestricted permission to wear was continued despite the changed status of the award. Others, such as the Ghana Republic Day Commemorative Medal and Vanuatu Independence Medal received only restricted permission for wear. Another, which presumably also falls foul of the "two-medal" rule, is the Zimbabwe Independence Medal. The Rhodesia Medal is a Queen's award for the same period, so the Zimbabwe medal is restricted, but if worn it takes precedence before the Rhodesia Medal.

The Ceylon Armed Forces Inauguration Medal, 1955, although listed in the order of wear as a Queen's award, was originally "restricted". This has never been rescinded but at least one recipient has been seen wearing it in British uniform. The same thinking probably affected acceptance of the Royal Brunei Malay Regiment Inauguration Medal and the Uniformed Services Malaysia Medal. The latter is a Singapore award, not Malaysian despite the title. Both these medals are Commonwealth awards but are granted only restricted permission for wear.

In contrast the Brunei Service Medal received unrestricted permission for wear. Although this was initially a campaign medal it was awarded for the duration of the "Emergency" and remains in issue in 1998 after about thirty years of pretty peaceful "Emergency".

Other awards, more understandably, awarded with unrestricted permission to wear include the Kenya Campaign Medal (North Eastern Kenya), and the Malaysian General Service Medal.

On the other hand there seems little difference between an Inauguration Medal for local forces and anniversary medals for a ruler. The Accession Medal, Tenth, Fifteenth, Twentieth and Twenty-Fifth Anniversary Medals commemorating the Sultan of Oman's reign are all given unrestricted permission for wear. The reasons for these contrasting decisions are difficult to determine. For one of these, the fifteenth, all officers also received the Order of the Special Royal Emblem and, on the two-medal theory, permission was given to wear only the Order. No one yet encountered has followed this, and both the Order and medal are commonly worn together both in British uniform and by former contract officers.

Some of the foregoing awards have been permitted with unrestricted permission to wear. It seems logical to allow all awards given by Commonwealth or Foreign Governments for services approved by the British Government to be worn with unrestricted permission. If there is some reason, such as concealing our involvement, demanding a curb on publicity, then denial of wearing those awards should be reviewed periodically and rescinded at an appropriate time.

Where British units or individuals work with foreign forces in relief, or military, operations and the foreign Government awards a medal there can be no valid reason to deny these awards to those involved, unless a British medal was also awarded. Even in these circumstances there was a strong feeling for those involved in the Gulf War that they should have been able to wear their Saudi and Kuwaiti medals; but the two-medal rule stepped in. This is all the harder to understand in the light of the introduction of the Accumulated Campaign Service Medal in 1994. This is a blatant breach of the two-medal rule by the Ministry of Defence itself, though thinly disguised as an award of "excellence" signified by the gold stripe in the centre of the ribbon. It is, in fact, nothing more than a campaign medal and the qualification is that the recipient has done three years, since 14 August 1969, in places earning the General Service Medal 1964 with one or more clasps. So anyone getting it must, by definition, have already earned a medal for the same service.

If there is to be a "two-medal" rule, and that is understandable in that it tends to make our medals more valued as they are harder won than some, it must be adhered to. Exceptions for no valid reason, such as Korea and Malaya illustrated in this chapter, must be avoided, but the Accumulated Campaign Service Medal seems to have broken the "rule" for all time.

Some further examples of inconsistencies can be found in the medals commemorating the anniversary of the end of the Second World War.

The Russians produced a medal, commonly thought to be for Arctic Convoys, but distributed on a wider basis, for the 40th anniversary of the end of the war in 1985. This, to some extent, met the discontent held by those in the Arctic Convoys that their efforts had been ignored. They had received the Atlantic Star but this was given to all those in the Atlantic and had a requirement of a total of a full year at sea; qualifying for the 1939-45 Star for six months and the Atlantic Star by a further six months. So it was difficult to qualify for and it did nothing to indicate participation in the Arctic Convoys.

However, permission to wear this Russian medal was denied so initially it joined the ranks of the unofficial medals so often outnumbering and detracting from the official row. After much campaigning permission was grudgingly given for the medal to be worn officially in 1994 nine years after its award, "in view of the changed position of and progress made by the Russians". What nonsense and only a Whitehall Mandarin could think up such a reason to affect wearing a medal?

In 1994 also the Maltese Government produced a medal commemorating the 50th anniversary of the War. It was for award to all, including British servicemen, involved in the defence or re-supply of the island and applications had to be in by 15 April 1994. This medal was accepted for unrestricted wear except for those in Crown Service. The Queen happened to be paying a visit to Malta at about this time. Could this have been a significant factor in the thinking behind the decision?

The Greek Government has also awarded commemorative medals (1940–41 and 1941–45) for those participating in the campaigns in Greece and Crete from 28 October 1940 to 8 May 1945. These were first offered in the early 1990s and require a Ministry of Defence certificate of service in the relevant areas. Applicants to the Greece Embassy for these medals are told by the Greeks that our Foreign and Commonwealth Office (Protocol Department, Honours Section) have asked them to emphasise that "in bestowing these Medals, the Greek Government is aware that under the long established regulations governing the acceptance and wearing of foreign orders, decorations and medals by United Kingdom citizens, permission may not be granted for the acceptance and wearing of medals which are proposed more than five years after the performance of the service they are intended to recognise. Accordingly the Greek commemorative medals for campaigns 1940-41 and 1941-45 will be presented on the understanding that they will be "in the nature of a keepsake and will not be worn." Long established regulations? Where are these to be found and why did they not apply to Russia and Malta?

What is the difference between these three Governments' awards? It looks suspiciously like the Queen's visit to Malta in 1994. This is no way to run a system which touches on ordinary people, even if only a very few of them. What harm can there be in accepting and wearing these medals which would be worn with pride? Where is the sense in refusing these "official" medals while "unofficial" medals, purchased from commercial companies are being worn, sometimes on the official medal bar, and no one takes one jot of notice?

There is every reason to regularise matters, accept official foreign awards and even consider accepting some of the unofficial commercial ones to reduce the harm done by being unable to prevent discontented people wearing something to represent service which they consider deserved recognition.

The most deserving of the latter might be said to be recognition of National Service and of service in the Canal Zone. There is a case for many others—Prisoners of War; Arctic Convoys; Bomber Command; Dunkirk; uncomfortable "peacetime" service overseas and many others. To some extent the Arctic Convoy issue is addressed by the Russian Medal. It is a pity that this was not eliminated early on by a bar to the Atlantic Star. Similar bars would have been a cheap and effective way to deal with the others—"Dunkirk" on the 1939-45 Star; "Bomber Command" on the Air Crew Europe Star; and "Prisoners of War" on the War Medal.

To recognise all these now would probably be wrong, but National Service touched so many, disrupting their lives, though many would say for the better, that it does deserve consideration. The medal sold for this purpose is widely worn in the unofficial row and permitting it to be moved to the official row, but still at the expense of the wearer, would cost nothing and achieve a lot of acclaim from those who did their stint.

The Canal Zone, despite all the arguments dreamed up by various Government Departments, deserves a General Service Medal. This is the one suggestion in this book involving significant costs, but in terms of the Defence budget even that would be peanuts. Life in the Canal Zone was uncomfortable and for many dangerous. Military action was taken on occasion on a scale surpassing some of that in Palestine for which a medal was given. Forty odd years may have passed, but surely that makes is easier to override any arguments, which were said to be an obstacle earlier, of upsetting the Egyptian Government which, anyway, gave its own people a medal.

Chapter 9

Ideas for the Future

THE recommendations repeated in the summary at the beginning of the book are discussed below. It is quite obvious that any changes made to the system must be justified in their own right but must also be affordable. This has been born in mind throughout and only one recommendation has any cost implications.

There are many ways to regard national awards systems. We tend to be sparing with ours, arguing that it is better to give a few awards which are treasured, rather than a lot which are not so well valued. Other nations favour the opposite view and give a relatively large numbers of awards. Much of continental Europe is inclined towards this concept and our position as a member of the European Community, together with our increasing involvement in United Nations and NATO operations, is bringing our troops into closer contact with their counterparts of other nations. This, in turn, rather like the events of 1914-18 that led to the institution of the "mentions" emblem, gives rise to discontent. Why should they wear a medal and we can't? The fighting in the Gulf War was short for most soldiers and with few casualties. Yet the decision to deny our troops permission to wear the foreign campaign medals awarded was very poorly received. It was entirely in accordance with our traditions, but possibly these need a review for our new role in the world.

Even if the current practices are maintained there is no reason to fail to rectify some of the deficiencies of the past which are noted in this volume. Poor staff work and illogical solutions that have not been thought through do our excellent armed forces no favours.

It must be said that popular opinion today demands recognition for individuals as never before. Everyone wants a say in how things are run and modern life, with such things as television interviews with passers-by, has made people much more ready to express their thoughts in public, as well as being more fluent in doing so.

Honours do not often come to the minds of the public, but there is interest when ordinary people perform brave acts. The number of awards available seems totally adequate, though the fact that a George Cross has not been awarded to a civilian since 1976 does excite comment. There seems little point in an award demanding near certain death to qualify that is, therefore, almost never given. That aside there are the other levels for bravery in the form of the GM, QGM and Queen's Commendation for Brave Conduct. This is perfectly adequate but does not bear comparison with the only other award most recipients might possibly receive, though for merit, the MBE. Should a brave person currently receive both these, they wear the MBE before either the GM or QGM just because it is part of an Order. Most people would unhesitatingly put bravery before merit. That there would be universal approval for the order of wear to be GM, OBE, QGM, MBE is certain. The accident of history that makes these two awards for merit part of an Order carries no weight in the twentieth century, let alone in the twenty-first. We already have a precedent of sorts in the position afforded to the VC and GC. They may be crosses and given for outstanding heroism, but they are not "Orders". The above is reflected in the suggested future order of wear.

Mr Major said he wanted a classless society and Mr Blair is of the same mind. The honours system tried to move in that direction though the net result seems to be to give fewer awards to the lower levels of our society while maintaining all those to the elite. Many Generals and top executives in civilian life become "Sir", whereas "ordinary" people can only become MBEs. In fact, the honours lists seem little different now from what they were in the past, except by deletion of the BEM and most of its potential recipients. This social advance has taken on the appearance of an accountant's cost cutting exercise. Also there is no structured award system for merit for the common man and woman. The man who is able to climb the ladder to his own particular stardom may get an MBE then CBE followed by a becoming a Knight Bachelor. A lady could get an MBE or OBE then a DBE and be called "Dame". Joe Soap might get an MBE for years of voluntary toil. Few can aspire to anything above this level even if they continue to do their good work for a further and equal period. If we need a structured system for the mighty then we should have one for lesser mortals.

The suggestion here is that there should be a three level structure for merit. This equates to the gallantry structure if the virtually unattainable VC/GC level is left out. The levels would be, in descending order, OBE, MBE and Queen's Commendation for Valuable Service (QCVS). This last is currently given only for operational service. It is difficult to see why there is an argument for a reward of this level for merit in an operational theatre, but none in ordinary life. Even in the military it is often the case that, without very hard work and long hours by those in depots and home establishments, operations would not succeed. "Praise the Lord and pass the ammunition" and that starts at the manufacturers, through the depots, the ports, the shipping, and the rear areas before it finally arrives at the sharp end.

Turning to other walks of life a policeman can be given various types of bravery commendation but no national reward for hours of diligent work indexing data on a serial rapist case, unless it is so good as to merit a Queen's Police Medal. But these, more often than not, go to the very senior ranks. So why not open up the QCVS to all, including civilians and servicemen at home?

If this system were adopted the OBE, MBE and QCVS would become steps in a ladder of merit, unrelated to rank. Again why not allow recipients to wear all the insignia, rather in the same concept as "bars". No doubt the traditionalist would protest that you cannot do this for "Orders". Really? We already do. As mentioned earlier, it was allowed, with both sets of post-nominal letters, for the 1914-18 holders of the Order of the British Empire later rewarded a second time. It still applies to the insignia, but not the post-nominal letters, for those who were appointed for gallantry and later for merit in the Order of the British Empire. It has always applied for promotions from one division to the other both for the Order of the Bath and the British Empire. What better "precedent"? As mentioned earlier it would be difficult to fail to find a precedent for anything at all in the medal world; but three for the same argument must carry weight!

Another region that could benefit from a close look is that of post-nominal letters. Most awards for bravery or merit do have these letters. The area that needs consideration is in the long service region. There is no valid argument for allowing officers to use certain letters while denying this right to others. There is every argument for having the same for all, either with or without post-nominal letters. It is suggested that, in these days when it is increasingly difficult to get people to give "service" it would be a good idea to allow the use of these letters for all and encourage such sacrifice. This could be done on the Canadian lines where they scrapped a number of long service awards and instituted the Canada Decoration for all servicemen. But why should this apply only to the armed forces? The civilian services on which we all rely also need encouragement in this respect. Also, why should we abandon the wealth of history, pageantry and identification with the organisation concerned by ditching all our current long service awards. Why not just group long service awards and give the groups post-nominal letters.

The suggestion here is that the wealth of current long service awards is maintained but that they are grouped under two collective headings. Those doing their service on a full time basis would fall into the "Queen's Service Decoration" category. Those who are voluntary part-timers would be in the "Voluntary Service Decoration" class. The post nominal letters would then be either "QSD" or "VSD" for use by anyone awarded one of the long service awards in the official *London Gazette* listing. Long service awards for all ranks of the regular and reserve armed forces are understood to be in hand and these would be included in both categories. One minor difficulty might lie in the Fire Service since with them both full time and retained (part time) fire fighters receive the same medal. However, there seems no reason why this medal cannot fall into the one or other of the two categories dependent on the service given. We have a precedent of sorts in the Air Efficiency Award and Ulster Defence Regiment Medal where officers may use post-nominal letters but other ranks may not. Anyone qualifying from a mix of service would go into the category for which they had the most service. Anyone qualifying for two or more medals in the same category would use the appropriate post-nominal letters once only. In addition the order of wear of long service awards seems to bear no relation to any logical order. Seniority of service, officers before other ranks, regulars before part-timers, date of institution of the award —none of these is consistently used. Also very few people get more than one long service award so why not use the date the award was earned to determine the individual order of wear?

So, in the light of the foregoing the recommendations, in order of priority, are:

Afford the fourth level bravery/merit awards, mentions and commendations, an appropriate place in the order of wear and display them on their own ribbons.

This has been discussed at length in Chapter 7. There are considerable practical difficulties in wearing little metal emblems in conjunction with medals. They purport to be the Queen's fourth level of award yet can be hidden by, or worn after, an award for a foreign event which is, in Britain, insignificant.

The suggestion is that the emblems are worn on their own ribbons, with the emblem level with the centre of other medals in a position appropriate to their status. Subsequent awards can be marked by additional emblems on the full sized ribbon though this is impractical when ribbons alone are worn.

Readjust the order of wear to reflect the relative merits of awards for gallantry and for merit regardless of the title of the insignia.

Appendix 1 to this Chapter gives a suggested order of wear for the future dealing with most current awards, one which recognises the man-in-the-street's concept of the relative importance of gallantry, meritorious and other awards, disregarding the mystique currently afforded to "Orders". The higher level of orders is unchanged, except to suggest a two-tier system, for reasons already mentioned in the Preface. Some awards which are no longer given are omitted, but these could easily be placed in the same position as their old relative places; that is relative to their "equals".

In particular the suggested order tries to intermingle comparable levels of gallantry and merit regardless of what type of award is given.

By way of comparison Appendices 2 to 4 to this Chapter show the current orders of wear used by Canada, Australia and New Zealand. In addition to the new awards peculiar to all three Nations they have also instituted medals to fill perceived deficiencies in the British system of campaign medals. All three have instituted post-war medals for which no British equivalent exists and the Australians have altered some of the qualifications for British Wartime awards. For example the Africa Star now goes to Australians for some Middle East service where British troops still have to be content with the 1939-45 Star alone.

Make use of the OBE, MBE and QCVS to reflect three levels of achievement so that the "ordinary" citizen may share in the structured honours system.

This is dealt with in this Chapter. The suggestion being that, not only are the above linked as steps in a reward system, but that all may be worn by anyone receiving them.

Permit a much wider use of post-nominal letters to recognise "Service", especially, voluntary work.

Dealt with in this Chapter, the suggestion is that full time personnel should receive the existing awards under the collective title "Queen's Service Decoration (QSD)" and part time or voluntary workers their existing awards under the collective title "Voluntary Service Decoration (VSD)".

Revise and re-issue the *London Gazette* lists on wearing awards on a regular basis to give accurate and up-to-date information.

Discussed in Chapter 2, the present situation allowing more than a decade between lists is totally unacceptable, as are the illogical omissions and inclusions. This listing should be a clerical exercise since all the arguments of where a new medal is worn have been completed in work leading up to the new medal. The only work involved should be to keep a record of changes and collate them into the *London Gazette* entry. Yet this is said to be several year's worth of work. More like a concentrated afternoon's work!

Allow holders of multiple neck decorations to wear one at the neck and the rest on the medal bar on the left breast. Also use the ribbon appropriate to their later wear at the investiture.

Discussed in Chapter 1 this is a means, for those with two high awards, of displaying awards that are currently rarely seen. It also eliminates the untidy way that neck decorations are presently supposed to be worn on a ribbon that is not up to the task.

Come to an equitable, and better explained, method of displaying "Queen's Commonwealth Awards"; one which applies equally to Royalty and commoner.

No specific suggestions are made here, but the reasons behind the need for this are explained in Chapter 1. History makes the subject awkward for all the Monarchies concerned but a set of rules, which actually addresses all the problems, is required. It is suggested that, if the difficulty of subjugating, where necessary, "Orders" to "Medals" were overcome in our own lists the possibility of slotting in other Commonwealth Monarchies' awards would present no problems. We could all then have a common list acceptable to all, though each might choose to publish only their own portion of it.

Permit the acceptance and wear of awards from Foreign Governments on a relaxed and logical basis and one that is the same for different areas across the world.

This is dealt with in Chapter 8. A firm and fair system should be devised and adhered to. The current arguments regarding two-medal and five-year rules are transparently deficient and designed to support the denial of medals rather than the facts.

Award a General Service Medal for the Canal Zone.

Considered in Chapter 8 this is the only "campaign" in which British troops have taken part, with significant casualties, since 1945 which has not been recognised by a medal. Although the cost would be significant it is high time that this campaign was given the recognition it deserved at the time, and still deserves.

Try to limit the number of unofficial medals by allowing certain selected ones to be purchased and worn on the official bar behind all other awards including foreign medals.

This suggestion, dealt with in this Chapter, will probably stick in the craw more than most. However, the proliferation of unofficial medals does nothing for the official row. It has come about entirely because the ex-servicemen from all walks of life feel deprived of visible recognition of their services in certain areas. It may be abhorrent to "recognise" these medals, but it is far better to do this than to see multiple rows on Remembrance Day, where the "proper" one is also the most insignificant.

Appendix 1 to Chapter 9

Suggested Order of Wear Using a Logical Sequence

Cat	Title	Post-nominals
Awards of the First Level of Bravery		
	Victoria Cross	VC
	George Cross	GC
Awards of Extreme Excellence for Merit		
	Knight of the Most Noble Order of the Garter	KG
	Knight of the Most Ancient and Most Noble Order of the Thistle	KT
	Knight of the Most Illustrious Order of St. Patrick	KP
	Knight or Dame Grand Cross of the Most Honourable Order of the Bath	GCB
	Member of the Order of Merit	OM
	Baronet's Badge	Bt or Bart
	Knight Grand Commander of the Most Exalted Order of the Star of India	GCSI
	Knight or Dame Grand Cross of the Most Distinguished Order of St. Michael & St. George	GCMG
	Knight Grand Commander of the Most Eminent Order of Indian Empire	GCIE
	The Imperial Order of the Crown of India	CI
	Knight or Dame Grand Cross of the Royal Victorian Order	GCVO
	Knight or Dame Grand Cross of the Most Excellent Order of the British Empire	GBE
Awards of Outstanding Merit		
	Member of the Order of the Companions of Honour	CH
	Knight or Dame Commander of the Most Honourable Order of the Bath	KCB/DCB
	Knight Commander of the Most Exalted Order of the Star of India	KCSI
	Knight or Dame Commander of the Most Distinguished Order of St. Michael & St. George	KCMG/ DCMG
	Knight Commander of the Most Eminent Order of Indian Empire	KCIE

Suggested Order of Wear Using a Logical Sequence (cont)

Cat	Title	Post-nominals
Awards of Outstanding Merit (cont)		
	Knight or Dame Commander of the Royal Victorian Order	KCVO/DCVO
	Knight or Dame Commander of the Most Excellent Order of the British Empire	KBE/DBE
	Knight Bachelor	
Awards of First Level of Achievement		
	Companion of the Most Honourable Order of the Bath	CB
	Companion of the Most Exalted Order of the Star of India	CSI
	Companion of the Most Distinguished Order of St. Michael & St. George	CMG
	Companion of the Most Eminent Order of Indian Empire	CIE
	Commander of the Royal Victorian Order	CVO
	Commander of the Most Excellent Order of the British Empire	CBE
Awards of the Second Level of Bravery and Gallant Leadership		
	Companion of the Distinguished Service Order	DSO
	Conspicuous Gallantry Cross	CGC
	Distinguished Conduct Medal	DCM
	Conspicuous Gallantry Medal	CGM
	Conspicuous Gallantry Medal (Flying)	CGM
	George Medal	GM
	Medal for Saving Life at Sea (Gold)	GSGM
Awards of the Second Level of Achievement		
	Lieutenant of the Royal Victorian Order	LVO
	Officer of the Most Excellent Order of the British Empire	OBE
	Companion of the Imperial Service Order	ISO
	Member of the Royal Red Cross	RRC
	Royal Victorian Medal (Gold)	GRVM
Awards of the Third Level of Bravery and Gallant Leadership		
	Distinguished Service Cross	DSC
	Military Cross	MC

Suggested Order of Wear Using a Logical Sequence (cont)

Cat	Title	Post-nominals
Awards of the Third Level of Bravery and Gallant Leadership (cont)		
	Distinguished Flying Cross	DFC
	Air Force Cross	AFC
	Distinguished Service Medal	DSM
	Military Medal	MM
	Distinguished Flying Medal	DFM
	Air Force Medal	AFM
	Queen's Gallantry Medal	QGM
	Medal for Saving Life at Sea (Silver)	SSGM
	Colonial Police Medal for Gallantry	CPMG
Awards of the Third Level of Achievement		
	Member of the Royal Victorian Order	MVO
	Member of the Most Excellent Order of the British Empire	MBE
	Associate of the Royal Red Cross	ARRC
	Order of St. John (All classes)	OStJ etc
	Royal Victorian Medal (Silver)	SRVM
	Queen's Medal for Chiefs	
Awards of the Fourth Level of Bravery, Leadership and Achievement		
	Medal for Saving Life at Sea (Bronze)	BSGM
	Queen's Police Medal for Distinguished Service	QPM
	Queen's Fire Service Medal for Distinguished Service	QFSM
	Colonial Police Medal for Meritorious Service	CPMM
	Royal Victorian Medal (Bronze)	BRVM
	Badge of Honour	
	Meritorious Service Medals (in order of date of award)	MSM
	Mentioned in Despatches (Silver) (post 1993)	MID
	Mentioned in Despatches (Bronze) (pre-1994)	MID
	Queen's Commendation for Brave Conduct (pre 1994)	QCBC
	Queen's Commendation for Bravery (post 1993)	QCB

Ideas for the Future

Suggested Order of Wear Using a Logical Sequence (cont)

Cat	Title	Post-nominals

Awards of the Fourth Level of Bravery, Leadership and Achievement (cont)

    Queen's Commendation for Brave Conduct in the Air (post 1993) — QCBA

    Queen's Commendation for Valuable Service in the Air (pre 1994) — QCVSA

    Queen's Commendation for Valuable Service (post 1993) — QCVA

Campaign Medals

    War Medals in date of participation in a campaign or as specified for Wars

    Accumulated Campaign Service Medal

    Rhodesia Medal

    Royal Ulster Constabulary Service Medal

Polar Medals

    Polar Medals in order of date of expedition

Medals for Shooting Prowess

    Queen's Medal (for Champion Shots in the Royal Navy and Royal Marines)

    Queen's Medal (for Champion Shots in the Military Forces)

    Queen's Medal (for Champion Shots of the Air Forces)

Long Service Awards

    Sovereign's Long and Faithful Service Medals (in order of date of award)

    Long Service Awards in order of date of award (including the Imperial Service Medal)†
    †NB. All *"regular"* awards (*Queen's Service Decorations*) — QSD
    All *"part-time"* awards (*Voluntary Service Decorations*) — VSD

Commemorative Medals

    Coronation, Jubilee and Commemorative Medals (in order of date of event)

    Independence Medals (in order of date of independence)

Honorary Membership of Commonwealth Awards (instituted by The Sovereign)*

    Orders (in order of date of award)

    Decorations (in order of date of award)

    Medals (in order of date of award)

Suggested Order of Wear Using a Logical Sequence (cont)

Cat   Title   Post-nominals

Other Commonwealth Awards

    Orders (in order of date of award)

    Decorations (in order of date of award)

    Medals (in order of date of award)

Foreign Awards

    Orders (in order of date of award)

    Decorations (in order of date of award)

    Medals (in order of date of award)

* If the above order of wear were to be adopted there would be no great impediment to including Queen's Commonwealth awards in the "British" listing since the position of "stars" and "medals" before "Orders" would have been established in the United Kingdom. Awards of similar "rank" could be equal; those of the parent country coming first and others, if any, in order of date of award. This would place all four VCs in prime position.

Appendix 2 to Chapter 9

Canadian Order of Wear for Their Own Awards

(Those inset are basically British awards but the Victorian Order/Medal, Order of St. John and Jubilee, etc., Medals are accepted as Canadian through the Crown)

Title	Post-nominals
Highest Valour	
Victoria Cross (Canadian)	VC
Cross of Valour (special status)	CV
Orders	
Companion of the Order of Canada	CC
Commander of the Order of Military Merit	CMM
Commander of the Royal Victorian Order	CVO
Officer of the Order of Canada	OC
Officer of the Order of Military Merit	OMM
Lieutenant of the Royal Victorian Order	LVO
Member of the Order of Canada	CM
Member of the Order of Military Merit	MMM
Member of the Royal Victorian Order	MVO
The Most Venerable Order of St. John of Jerusalem (All grades)	
Provincial Orders	
Ordre National du Quebec	GOQ/ OQ/CQ
Saskatchewan Order of Merit	SOM
Order of Ontario	OOn
Order of British Columbia	OBC
Decorations	
Star of Military Valour	SMV/EVM
Star of Courage	SC/EC
Meritorious Service Cross	MSC/CSM
Medal of Military Valour	MMV/ MVM
Medal of Bravery	MB

Canadian Order of Wear for Their Own Awards (cont)

Title	Post-nominals

Decorations (cont)

Meritorious Service Medal (Civil or Military) — MSM

    Royal Victorian Medal (Gold, Silver & Bronze) — RVM

War Medals

    World War I in the usual sequence.

    World War II in the usual sequence.

Service Medals

Canadian Korean War Medal

Canadian Volunteer Service Medal for Korea

Gulf and Kuwait Medal

Special Service Medal

United Nations' Medals

Service Medal (Korea)

Emergency Force (UNEF)

Truce Supervision Organisation in Palestine (UNTSO)

Observer Group in Lebanon (UNOGIL)

Military Observer Group in India and Pakistan (UNMOGIP)

Organisation in the Congo (ONUC)

Temporary Executive Authority in New Guinea (UNTEA)

Yemen Observer Group (UNYOM)

Force in Cyprus (UNFICYP)

India Pakistan Observation Mission (UNIPOM)

Emergency Force Middle East (UNEFME)

Disengagement Force (Golan Heights) (UNDOF)

Interim Force in Lebanon (UNIFIL)

Angola Verification Mission (UNAVEM)

Military Observation Group in Iran/Iraq (UNIIMOG)

Transition Assistance Group in Namibia (UNTAG)

Observer Group in Central America (ONUCA)

Canadian Order of Wear for Their Own Awards (cont)

Title   Post-nominals

United Nations' Medals (cont)

Iraq/Kuwait Observer Mission (UNIKOM)

Observer Mission in El Salvador (ONUSAL)

Protection Force in Yugoslavia (UNPROFOR)

Transitional Authority in Cambodia (UNTAC)

Advanced Mission in Cambodia (UNAMIC)

Mission for the Referendum in Western Sahara (MINURSO)

Operations in Somalia (UNOSOM)

Operations in Mozambique (UNIMOZ)

Good Offices Mission in Afghanistan and Pakistan (UNGOMAP)

Assistance Mission in Rwanda (UNAMIR)

Observer Mission in Liberia (UNOMIL)

Mission in Haiti (UNMIH)

Verification Mission in Guatemala (MINUGUA)

Military Observer Mission in Prevlaka (UNMOP)

Preventive Deployment Force (Macedonia) (UNPREDEP)

Mission in Bosnia and Herzegovina/International Police Task Force (UNMIBH/IPTF)

Special Services (UNSS)

International Commission Medals

International Commission for Supervision and Control (Indo-China) (ICSC)

International Commission for Control and Supervision (Vietnam/Cambodia) (ICCS)

Multinational Force and Observers (Sinai) (MFO)

Coalition force in Somalia (ECMMY)

Commemorative Medals

Canadian Centennial Medal, 1967

Queen Elizabeth II Silver Jubilee Medal, 1977

Canada 125th Anniversary Medal, 1992

Canadian Order of Wear for Their Own Awards (cont)

Title   Post-nominals

Long Service and Good Conduct Medals

Royal Canadian Mounted Police Long Service Medal

Canadian Forces Decoration   CD

Police Exemplary Service Medal

Corrections Exemplary Service Medal

Fire Service Exemplary Service Medal

Coast Guard Exemplary Service Medal

Other Medals

Queen's Medal for Champion Shots

      Service Medal of the Order of St. John

Commonwealth Decorations and Medals

Foreign Decorations and Medals

Ideas for the Future

Appendix 3 to Chapter 9

Canadian Order of Wear for Their Own Awards with British Orders Awarded pre-1 June 1972

(Those inset are basically British awards)

Title	Post-nominals
Awards for Gallant/Meritorious Service	
Victoria Cross	VC
George Cross	GC
Cross of Valour	CV
Order of Merit	OM
Companion of Honour	CH
Companion of the Order of Canada	CC
Commander of the Order of Military Merit	CMM
Officer of the Order of Canada	OC
Companion of the Order of the Bath	CB
Companion of the Order of St. Michael & St. George	CMG
Commander of the Royal Victorian Order	CVO
Commander of the Order of the British Empire	CBE
Distinguished Service Order	DSO
Officer of the Order of Military Merit	OMM
Lieutenant of the Royal Victorian Order	LVO
Officer of the Order of the British Empire	OBE
Imperial Service Order	ISO
Member of the Order of Canada	CM
Member of the Order of Military Merit	MMM
Member of the Royal Victorian Order	MVO
Member of the Order of the British Empire	MBE
Member of the Royal Red Cross	RRC
Distinguished Service Cross	DSC

Canadian Order of Wear for Their Own Awards with British Orders Awarded pre-1 June 1972 (cont)

Title	Post-nominals
Military Cross	MC
Distinguished Flying Cross	DFC
Air Force Cross	AFC
Star of Courage	SC/EC
Medal of Bravery	MB
Associate of the Royal Red Cross	ARRC
The Most Venerable Order of St. John of Jerusalem (All grades)	
Distinguished Conduct Medal	DCM
Conspicuous Gallantry Medal	CGM
George Medal	GM
Distinguished Service Medal	DSM
Military Medal	MM
Distinguished Flying Medal	DFM
Air Force Medal	AFM
King's Police and Fire Service Medal	KPFSM
Royal Victorian Medal	RVM
British Empire Medal	BEM

War Medals

World War I in the usual sequence/World War II in the usual sequence.

Canadian Korean War Medal and other post war campaign medals in order of date of award.

United Nations Medals

Polar Medals

Commemorative Medals

King George V Jubilee, 1935

King George VI Coronation, 1937

Queen Elizabeth II Coronation, 1953

Canadian Centennial Medal, 1967

Queen Elizabeth II Silver Jubilee Medal, 1977

Ideas for the Future

Canadian Order of Wear for Their Own Awards with British Orders Awarded pre-1 June 1972 (cont)

Title	Post-nominals
Canadian 125th Anniversary Medal, 1993	
Long Service and Good Conduct Medals	
Army Long Service and Good Conduct Medal	
Naval Long Service and Good Conduct Medal	
Air Force Long Service and Good Conduct Medal	
Royal Canadian Mounted Police Long Service and Good Conduct Medal	
Volunteer Officer's Decoration	VD
Volunteer Long Service Medal	
Colonial Auxiliary Forces Officer's Decoration	VD
Colonial Auxiliary Forces Long Service Medal	
Efficiency Decoration	ED
Naval Volunteer Reserve Decoration	VRD
Naval Volunteer Reserve Long Service and Good Conduct Medal	
Air Efficiency Award	
Queen's Medal for Champion Shots	
Canadian Forces Decoration	CD
Service Medal of the Order of St. John of Jerusalem	

Appendix 4 to Chapter 9

Australian Order of Wear for Their Own Awards with British Awards

(Those inset are basically British awards but the Garter, Thistle, Order of Merit, Victorian Order/Medal, Order of St. John and Jubilee, etc., Medals are accepted as Australian through the Crown)

Title	Post-nominals
Victoria Cross (Australian)	VC
George Cross	GC
Cross of Valour	CV
Knight/Lady of the Garter	KG/LG
Knight/Lady of the Thistle	KT/LT
Knight or Dame Grand Cross of the Order of the Bath	GCB
Order of Merit	OM
Knight or Dame of the Order of Australia (discontinued 1986)	AK/AD
Knight or Dame Grand Cross of the Order of St. Michael & St. George	GCMG
Knight or Dame Grand Cross of the Royal Victorian Order	GCVO
Knight or Dame Grand Cross of the Order of the British Empire	GBE
Companion of the Order of Australia	AC
Companion of Honour	CH
Knight or Dame Commander of the Order of the Bath	KCB/DCB
Knight or Dame Commander of the Order of St. Michael & St. George	KCMG/DCMG
Knight or Dame Commander of the Royal Victorian Order	KCVO/DCVO
Knight or Dame Commander of the Order of the British Empire	KBE/DBE
Knight Bachelor	
Officer of the Order of Australia	AO
Companion of the Order of the Bath	CB
Companion of the Order of St. Michael & St. George	CMG
Commander of the Royal Victorian Order	CVO
Commander of the Order of the British Empire	CBE

Ideas for the Future

Australian Order of Wear for Their Own Awards with British Awards (cont)

Title	Post-nominals
Star of Gallantry	SG
Star of Courage	SC
Companion of the Distinguished Service Order	DSO
Distinguished Service Cross (Australian)	DSC
Member of the Order of Australia	AM
Lieutenant of the Royal Victorian Order	LVO
Officer of the Order of the British Empire	OBE
Companion of the Imperial Service Order	ISO
Member of the Royal Victorian Order	MVO
Member of the Order of the British Empire	MBE
Conspicuous Service Cross	CSC
Nursing Service Cross	NSC
Royal Red Cross (1st Class)	RRC
Distinguished Service Cross	DSC
Military Cross	MC
Distinguished Flying Cross	DFC
Air Force Cross	AFC
Royal Red Cross (2nd Class)	ARRC
Medal for Gallantry	MG
Bravery Medal	BM
Distinguished Service Medal (Australian)	DSM
Public Service Medal	PSM
Australian Police Medal	APM
Australian Fire Service Medal	AFSM
Medal of the Order of Australia	OAM
Order of St. John of Jerusalem (All grades)	
Distinguished Conduct Medal	DCM
Conspicuous Gallantry Medal	CGM
George Medal	GM

Australian Order of Wear for Their Own Awards with British Awards (cont)

Title	Post-nominals
Conspicuous Service Medal	CSM
Australian Antarctic Medal	AAM
Queen's Police Medal for Gallantry	QPM
Queen's Fire Service Medal for Gallantry	QFSM
Distinguished Service Medal	DSM
Military Medal	MM
Distinguished Flying Medal	DFM
Air Force Medal	AFM
Queen's Gallantry Medal	QGM
Royal Victorian Medal	RVM
British Empire Medal	BEM
Queen's Police Medal for Distinguished Service	QPM
Queen's Fire Service Medal for Distinguished Service	QFSM
Commendation for Gallantry	
Commendation for Brave Conduct	
Queen's Commendation for Brave Conduct	
Commendation for Distinguished Service	
War Medals - in the usual order	
Australian Active Service Medal	
Australian Service Medal (not the one for 1939-45, presumably includes both 1945-75 and post-1975)	
Police Overseas Service Medal	
Polar Medal	
Imperial Service Medal	
Coronation and Jubilee Medals (in order of date of receipt)	
Defence Force Service Medal	
Reserve Force Decoration	RFD
Reserve Force Medal	
National Medal	

Australian Order of Wear for Their Own Awards with British Awards (cont)

Title   Post-nominals

Champion Shots Medal

    Long Service Medals (not specified but must be old British awards)

    Independence and Anniversary Medals (in order of date of receipt)

Foreign Awards (in order of date of authorisation of acceptance and wearing)

"Medals Will Be Worn"

Appendix 5 to Chapter 9

New Zealand Order of Wear

(Note a new order of wear is imminent)

Title	Post-nominals
Victoria Cross	VC
George Cross	GC
Knight or Lady of the Order of the Garter	KG/LG
Knight or Lady of the Order of the Thistle	KT/LT
Knight or Dame Grand Cross of the Order of the Bath	GCB
Order of Merit	OM
Member of the Order of New Zealand	ONZ
Baronet's Badge	Bt or Bart
Knight or Dame Grand Companion of the New Zealand Order of Merit	GNZM
Knight or Dame Grand Cross of the Order of St. Michael & St. George	GCMG
Knight or Dame Grand Cross of the Royal Victorian Order	GCVO
Knight or Dame Grand Cross of the Order of the British Empire	GBE
Companion of Honour	CH
Knight or Dame Companion of the New Zealand Order of Merit	KNZM/DNZM
Knight or Dame Commander of the Order of the Bath	KCB/DCB
Knight or Dame Commander of the Order of St. Michael & St. George	KCMG/DCMG
Knight or Dame Commander of the Royal Victorian Order	KCVO/DCVO
Knight or Dame Commander of the Order of the British Empire	KBE/DBE
Knight Bachelor	
Companion of the New Zealand Order of Merit	CNZM
Companion of the Order of the Bath	CB
Companion of the Order of St. Michael & St. George	CMG
Commander of the Royal Victorian Order	CVO
Commander of the Order of the British Empire	CBE
Companion of the Distinguished Service Order	DSO

Ideas for the Future

New Zealand Order of Wear (cont)
(Note a new order of wear is imminent)

Title	Post-nominals
Lieutenant of the Royal Victorian Order	LVO
Companion of the Queen's Service Order	QSO
Officer of the New Zealand Order of Merit	ONZM
Officer of the Order of the British Empire	OBE
Companion of the Imperial Service Order	ISO
Member of the Royal Victorian Order	MVO
Member of the New Zealand Order of Merit	MNZM
Member of the Order of the British Empire	MBE
Member of the Royal Red Cross	RRC
Distinguished Service Cross	DSC
Military Cross	MC
Distinguished Flying Cross	DFC
Air Force Cross	AFC
Associate of the Royal Red Cross	ARRC
Order of St. John of Jerusalem (Six Grades)	
I Baliff or Dame Grand Cross	GCStJ
II Knight or Dame of Justice or Grace	KStJ
III Chaplain	ChStJ
III Commander (Brother or Sister)	CStJ
IV Officer (Brother or Sister)	OStJ
V Serving Brother or Serving Sister	SBStJ / SSStJ
VI Esquire	EsqStJ
Distinguished Conduct Medal	DCM
Conspicuous Gallantry Medal	CGM
George Medal	GM
Queen's Police Medal for Gallantry	QPM
Queen's Fire Service Medal for Gallantry	QFSM
Distinguished Service Medal	DSM
Military Medal	MM

New Zealand Order of Wear (cont)
(Note a new order of wear is imminent)

Title	Post-nominals
Distinguished Flying Medal	DFM
Air Force Medal	AFM
Queen's Gallantry Medal	QGM
Royal Victorian Medal (Gold, Silver & Bronze)	RVM
Queen's Service Medal	QSM
British Empire Medal	BEM
Queen's Police Medal for Distinguished Service	QPM
Queen's Fire Service Medal for Distinguished Service	QFSM

War Medals (in order of date of campaign for which awarded with the normal notes but with the New Zealand Service Medal, 1946-49 added after the New Zealand War Service Medal 1939-45 and the New Zealand General Service Medal, 1992 taking its place by order of date of award)

Polar Medals (in order of date of award)

Imperial Service Medal

Coronation and Jubilee Medals (in order of date awarded)

King George V's Silver Jubilee Medal, 1935

King George VI's Coronation Medal, 1937

Queen Elizabeth II's Coronation Medal, 1953

Queen Elizabeth II's Silver Jubilee Medal, 1977

New Zealand 1990 Commemoration Medal

New Zealand Suffrage Centennial Medal

New Zealand Meritorious Service Medal

New Zealand Armed Forces Award

New Zealand Army Long Service and Good Conduct Medal

Royal New Zealand Navy Long Service and Good Conduct Medal

Royal New Zealand Air Force Long Service and Good Conduct Medal

New Zealand Police Long Service and Good Conduct Medal

New Zealand Fire Brigades Long Service and Good Conduct Medal

New Zealand Prison Service Medal

New Zealand Traffic Service Medal

Ideas for the Future

New Zealand Order of Wear (cont)
(Note a new order of wear is imminent)

Title	Post-nominals
New Zealand Efficiency Decoration	ED
New Zealand Efficiency Medal	
Royal New Zealand Naval Reserve Decoration	RD
Royal New Zealand Naval Volunteer Reserve Decoration	VRD
Royal New Zealand Naval Volunteer Reserve Long Service and Good Conduct Medal	
Royal Naval Reserve Long Service and Good Conduct Medal	
Air Efficiency Award	AE
Queen's Medal for Champion Shots of the New Zealand Naval Forces	
Queen's Medal for Champion Shots in the Military Forces	
Queen's Medal for Champion Shots of the Air Naval Forces	
Cadet Forces Medal	
Rhodesia Medal, 1980	
Commonwealth Independence Medals (Instituted by The Sovereign. Worn in order of the date of award)	
Service Medal of the Order of St. John	

Commonwealth Members Orders
Commonwealth Members Decorations
Commonwealth Members Medals
} Instituted by The Sovereign in Right of a particular Member State, other than in Right of the United Kingdom. Worn in order of date of award.

Other Commonwealth Members Orders
Other Commonwealth Members Decorations
Other Commonwealth Members Medals
} Instituted since 1949, otherwise than by The Sovereign, and awards by the States of Malaysia and the State of Brunei. Worn in order of date of award. These awards may be worn only when The Sovereign's permission has been given.

Foreign Orders
Foreign Decorations
Foreign Medals
} Worn in order of date of award.

see over

New Awards for combat situations	Replacing British awards
Victoria Cross for New Zealand (VC)	VC
New Zealand Gallantry Star (NZGS)	DSO, DCM, CGM
New Zealand Gallantry Decoration (NZGD)	DSC, MC, DFC, AFC, DSM, MM, DFM, AFM.
New Zealand Gallantry Medal (NZGM)	Mention in Despatches

New Awards for non-combat or civilians	Replacing British awards
New Zealand Cross (NZC)	GC
New Zealand Bravery Star (NZBS)	GM
New Zealand Bravery Decoration (NZBD)	QGM, QPM, QFSM, AFC, AFM
New Zealand Bravery Medal (NZBM)	Queen's Commendations for Brave Conduct and Valuable Service in the Air

Some changes in long service and Polar awards may also be instituted.

Bibliography

This lists sources from which details have been researched. Although by no means exhaustive it also includes some useful references which may not impinge directly on the text.

King's or Queen's Regulations (KR or QR) with the relevant year. Those checked are from the years:

    1868, 1873, 1881, 1883, 1888, 1889, 1892, 1893, 1894, 1895, 1898, 1881, 1923, 1935, 1940, amendment to 1940 (probably 1945), 1955, 1961,

Dress Regulations (DR) including reference to medals, etc, in the years:

    1891, 1894, 1900, 1902, 1904, 1911, 1934, amendment of June 1937 to DR 1934, and DR for Officers 1969. Pamphlet 1 and 1983.

Clothing Regulations Pamphlet Number 10 (CR) dated 9 March 1961 with amendments dated:

    10 October 1962, 26 February 1964, 4 June 64, 8 November 1965.

Material Regulations Pamphlet Number 10 (MR) of 1995.

    Latest detailed order and method of wear.

London Gazettes (LG) giving orders of wear:
    22 April 1921
    22 November 1929
    24 April 1936
    18 April 1941—Supplement of 22 April 1941.
    7 February 1947—Second Supplement of 11 February 1947.
    8 July 1949—Third Supplement of 12 July 1949.
    24 July 1951—Supplement of 27 July 1951.
    11 June 1954—Third Supplement of 15 June 1954.
    15 Apr 1955—Supplement of 19 April 1955.
    14 January 1958—Supplement of 14 January 1958.
    25 April 1961—Supplement of 28 April 1961.
    23 October 1964—Fourth Supplement of 27 October 1964.
    27 October 1983—Supplement of 28 October 1983.

Admiralty Fleet Orders
    458/1947—Sea Cadet Corps officers not eligible for War Medal 1939–º45.
        —Silver cross approved for wear on ribbon of Order of St. John.
    720/1947—MID emblem approved for wear on Naval GSM 1914.
    721/1947—Naval GSM 1914 for South East Asia, Minesweeping, Bomb & Mine Clearance.
    2722/1947—Short title for RNVR Decoration changed from "VD" to "VRD".
    2817/1947—Clarifies conditions for Atlantic Star.
    2991/1947—Further details regarding Naval GSM 1914—AFO 721/1947.
    3523/1947—Terminal dates for Minesweeping for Naval GSM 1914.
    4085/1947—Naval GSM 1914 for Palestine.

Army Orders (AO)
    241/1890 and 181/1902—relating to wearing medals.
    196/1905 of 1 October 1905—amending DR 1904.

Army Orders (AO) (cont)
- 17/1912—added RNLI medals to right breast.
- 246/1912—promulgating amendment of 1 August 1912 to DR 1911.
- Army Order of 1 August 1913—amending DR 1911
- 249/1916—on wound stripes.
- 290/1916—giving emblems to be worn to denote bars to VC, DSO, MC, DCM and MM.
- 202 and 236/1917—on wound stripes.
- 13/1918—permitting the use of post-nominal letters for all gallantry awards.
- 357/1918—added RRC to AO 290/1916.
- 114/1917—added cross on ribbon at all times for VC and second cross for bar.
- 9/1918—allowing wound stripes on civilian clothes.
- 13/1918—permitted use of DCM and MM after the name for officers and soldiers.
- 53/1918—added Military Nursing Service to AO 13/1918 for MM.
- 389/1919—relating to wearing medals.
- 27/1931—listing non-military awards permitted for wear in uniform.
- 31/1947 (amended by 109/48, 30/50 & 40/57)—GSM 1918 for Bomb & Mine Clearance 1945-49 and 1945-56; South East Asia 1945-46.
- 146/1947 (amended by 15/48, 76/48 & 143/51)—GSM 1918 for Palestine 1945-48.
- 58/1950 (amended by 144/51, 80/52, 111/55, 135/56, 56/57, 14/59. 46/60 & 77/60)—GSM 1918 for Malaya.
- 149/1951 (amended by 167/53, 137/56 & 90/57)—UN Medal (Korea).
- 103/1951 (amended by 145/51, 40/52, 41/53, 109/53, 122/53, 166/53 & 136/56)—Queen's Korea Medal
- 15/1955 (amended by 74/55, 4/56, 27/56, 134/56 & 7/57) Africa GSM 1902 for Kenya.
- 80/1957 (amended by 60/58, 31/59, 82/59 & 57/60)—GSM 1918 for Cyprus.
- 81/1957—GSM 1918 for Near East.
- 9/1961—GSM 1918 for Arabian Peninsula.
- 50/1962 (amended by 15/66)—UN Congo Medal.
- 44/1962 (amended by 19/64 & 52/65)—GSM 1918 for Brunei.
- 61/1964—GSM 1964 inaugurated.
- 62/1964 (amended by 53/65, 30/66, 54/66 8/67 & 29/67)—GSM 1964 for Borneo.
- 37/1965—GSM 1964 for Radfan.
- 56/1964 (amended by 18/65)—UNFICYP Medal.
- 30/1966 (amended by 52/67 & 22/68)—GSM 1964 for South Arabia.
- 44 & 45/1967—short term changes to Reserve awards on TAVR transition.
- 79/1967 (amended by 68/68 & 68/70)—GSM 1964 for Malay Peninsula.
- 43 & 44/1969 (amended by 71 & 72/69)—changes to awards to Army Reserves.
- 65/1971 (amended by DCI (Army) 4/78)—GSM 1964 for Northern Ireland.

Army Council Instructions (ACI)
- 754/1918—(5 July 1918) giving order of wear.
- 1230/1918—(6 Nov 18 but list dated 6 Aug 18) amending order of wear.
- 522/1919—order of wear for 1914-1919 stars and medals.
- 751/1920—revised order of wear for 1914-1919 stars and medals (1914 OR 1914-15 Star and added Indian General Service Medal 1908 for Afghanistan 1919).—It also published the list from LG 22 April 1921.
- 396/1922—first reference to mounting medals to be level at lower edges.
- 1/23—amending order of wear.
- 337/1949—Indian Independence Medal.
- 641/1952—Pakistan Medal.
- 241/1961—Ghana Republic Commemoration Medal.
- 67/1961 (amended by DCI 69/64)—Nigeria Independence Medal.
- 193/1961—Sierra Leone Independence Medal.
- 289/1962—Ghana Congo Medal.
- 296/1962—Jamaica Independence Medal.
- 43/1963—Uganda Independence Medal.
- 139/1964—Malawi Independence Medal.

Bibliography

Defence Council Instructions
    240/1964—Malaya Active Service Medal.
    (Royal Navy) 1531/1965—RN Auxiliary Service Medal inaugurated.
    (Army) 256/1965—Sierra Leone General Service Medal.
    (Army) 263/1966—Royal Brunei Malay Regiment Inauguration Medal.
    (Army) 4/1967—Uniformed Services Malaysian Medal (Singapore).
    (Army) 110/1968 (amended by 228/68)—Dhofar Campaign Medal (Oman).
    (Army) 87/1968 (amended by 181/68)—Brunei Service Medal.
    (Army) 276/1968 (amended by 146/6 & 59/70)—Kenya Campaign Medal
    J 1053/1969—specified operational and non-operational awards.
    J 1075/1969—civil awards and those from Societies.
    (Army) 198/1970—Malaysian General Service Medal.
    (General) S48/1975—GSM 1964 for Dhofar.
    (Army) 258/1977 (amended by 3312/77 & 79/78)—The As Sumood Medal (Oman).
    (Army) 4/1978—reduces LS&GCM to 15 years service from 1 Dec 1977.
    122/1979 (amended by 158/79)—placed MSM before LS&GCM.
    (Army) J330/1979—numerals for second, etc, tours with UN Forces.
    (Army) J160/1980—Vanuatu Independence Medal.
    (Army) J 244/1980—Approval for use of "RVM".
    (Army) J 103/1981—Rhodesia Medal.
    (Army) J 135/1981—Zimbabwe Independence Medal.
    (General) 259/1993—Omani 20th National Day Medal.
    (General) 118/1994—Accumulated Campaign Service Medal.
    (General) 214/1994—Changes to MID and Commendations.
    (General) 38/1995—UNAMIR Medal.
    (General) 267/1995—NATO Medal for former Yugoslavia.
    (General) 324/1995—UNAVEM III Medal.
    (General) 15/1997—UN Special Service Medal.
    With (Army) 28-39/1997—Northern Ireland Home Service Medal.
    119/1997—UN Special Service Medal.
    200/1997—Numerals on UN/NATO/WEU Medals.
    201/1997—MIDs/QCBs etc. worn on UN Medals.

Commonwealth of Australia Gazette 60 of 4 July 1968—GSM 1964 for South Vietnam and the Queen's Vietnam Medal.

War Office letter 0137/9638(QMG 7) of 2 June 1921 restricted the maximum number of breast stars to four.

A review of new Orders, Decorations and gallantry Medals instituted by His Majesty during the War 1914-1920, of changes made in existing Orders, Decorations and gallantry Medals, and of certain privileges accorded to recipients of the same and to recipients of a "Mention in Despatches," together with notes on procedure in respect of "posthumous" and "immediate" rewards, and a record of the total number of "Mentions in Despatches" and specific rewards for Military Services conferred during the War.—Department of the Military Secretary, the War Office, 31st May, 1920 (Revised November 1920).

Pamphlet on Military Honours and Awards 1960 and an undated issue probably post 1983.

Pamphlet on Campaign Stars and Commemorative Medals Instituted for the 1939-45 War by Command of the Army Council, The War Office 11 June 1948.

Air Ministry Order A532/1945—Campaign Stars and clasps and the Defence Medal.

Ministry of Transport/Board of Trade Notice to Mariners Number 279
    —Merchant Navy rules for Campaign Stars and War Medal 1939-45.

Journal of the Orders and Medals Research Society:
    Winter 1977—Hartlepool bombardment, 1914.
    Spring 1978—Iraq Flood Medal, 1954.
    Autumn 1984—Lieutenant E. W. K. Walton, AM, DSC, King's Commendation.

British Gallantry Awards by P. E. Abbott and J. M. A. Tamplin.

Ribbons and Medals by Captain H. Taprell Dorling, DSO, RN.

British Battles and Medals by Major L. L. Gordon.

The Victorian and Edwardian Army from old photographs by John Fabb and W. Y. Carman.

The National Honours and Awards of Australia by Michael Maton.

World War I by Susan Everett.

The Territorial Battalions, A Pictorial History 1859-1985 by Ray Westlake.

The Queen's Orders of Chivalry by Brigadier Sir Ivan de la Bere, KCVO, CB, OBE.

Canadian Orders, Decorations, and Medals (4th Edition) by Surgeon Commander F. J. Blatherwick, CD.

Orders, Decorations and Medals awarded to New Zealanders by Geoffrey P. Oldham and Brett Delahunt.

Supplement to the *New Zealand Gazette* of Thursday, 23 July 1987. This, with amendments up to 2 May 1996 provided by Mr P. P. O'Shea, LVO, New Zealand Herald at Arms, is the basis of the New Zealand listing.

The Island Becomes You

The Island Becomes You

Jennifer Barstow

Copyright © 2023 Jennifer Barstow

ISBN-13: 9798767209835

All rights reserved

No part of this publication may be reproduced, stored in a retrieval system, or transmitted, in any form or by any means, without the prior permission in writing of the author, nor be otherwise circulated in any form of binding or cover other than that in which it is published and without a similar condition including this condition being imposed on the subsequent purchaser.

Cover design by Will Barstow

Dedication

Thank you, Mum, for encouraging my love of writing when I was a child. To my family and friends, especially my husband and three sons, thank you for supporting me to keep going and finish this story.

Prologue

Looking out across the horizon we saw our first glimpse of the island. Finally, it was there, within our reach, it beckoned to us.

Dan held me tightly as we watched the last rays of the sunset slip below the horizon. The boat rocked gently and the breeze was cool on my skin. I pulled the blanket higher above my shoulder, holding the half-full champagne glass in my other hand. For ages we just sat, entranced by the island's presence. I tried to imagine what secrets were hidden within the outline of the island.

Suddenly, a high-pitched squawk awoke us from our trance. Out of the corner of my eye, I saw winged movement. There was a fast blur as something swooped down low, knocking the empty champagne bottle over that was perched on an upturned barrel. The bottle bounced onto the wooden deck before shattering into pieces. We both watched as the bird dived again towards us. This time I could clearly see its sharp talons were holding something shiny and round. Quickly, Dan grabbed the blanket and held it up to protect us from the imminent attack but it did not come. The bird squawked again and started to climb higher into the night sky, it circled the boat once more before it disappeared in the direction of the island.

We both stood on the deck, not quite believing what had just happened. Something glinted on the far side of the deck. The boat lurched slightly and the object started rolling towards us, resting at my feet. I looked down and gasped. Staring back at me were the hollow eyes of a human skull.

Chapter 1

Sitting up in bed, the sunlight was streaming in through the crack in the curtain. I glanced over at the clock; it was 9:00 a.m. My head ached slightly. I remembered the champagne from the previous night. Dan's side of the bed was empty. Where was he? Quickly, I got out of bed and grabbed my faithful pair of jeans, a nondescript blue t-shirt and white trainers. Looking in the mirror, a very pale, washed-out face stared back. Hurriedly, I ran my fingers through my long brown hair and gave my cheeks a pinch for a bit of colour - I always remember my grandmother Alice sharing that tip with me.

Making my way to the cabin door, I shouted for Dan as I climbed up the steps to the deck. Briefly, I was blinded by the bright sunlight. Taking a few steps forward I realised that the deck was completely deserted. I ran back down the steps and turned into the gulley expecting to see Dan but this too was empty. I felt the kettle but it was cold. Our champagne glasses from the previous night were left on the drainer. Looking across at the table his great-grandfather's diary was missing.

An uneasy feeling began to grow in my stomach. There was one more thing to check. I raced back onto the deck and peered over the port side. The white, motorised dinghy was gone. Staring out towards the island I muttered, "Why couldn't you have waited for me, Dan?"

Emptying all the cupboards above the cooker, I finally found the emergency inflatable dinghy. I picked up my rucksack, filling it with a few provisions, drinks, a torch, a penknife, spare clothes and a notebook – all the usual. I smiled to myself as I remembered the Girl Guide motto 'Be Prepared.' That was me to a tee – always thinking of every eventuality. My girlfriends always despaired at the sight of my bulging suitcase whenever we arranged a long weekend away.

Carefully, I climbed down the ladder on the side of the boat. I held on tightly as I pulled the rip cord of the inflatable dinghy. There was a loud whoosh and the dinghy expanded. I made a jump for the centre and ended up half in and half out. Hauling my wet trainers and jeans into the dinghy was not my idea of fun. I started to manipulate the one oar I had into a rhythm and felt pleased as I began to gain some distance from our boat, 'The Adventurer.' However, the current was quite strong and I began veering in the opposite direction to where I needed to go. Perhaps the dinghy knew something I did not and wisely tried to steer away from the island. I vaguely recalled Dan had told me about paddling the opposite side to the direction you needed to go. Thanks, Dan it worked, I began a steady course towards the island.

Just as I reached the ring of stones surrounding the island, the dinghy suddenly lurched violently to the left. I went to put my oar in the water but it met with hard resistance. I panicked not wanting to look beneath the water's surface. I dropped the oar and held on tightly to the rope around the dinghy – the shoreline was about thirty metres away. My breath was coming out in short bursts, my stomach was doing somersaults. What was it? I then remembered the film 'Jaws.' A bright yellow inflatable dinghy and a huge shark did not bode well. I held my breath and tried to keep absolutely, still. I could hear the waves breaking on the beach. I was so close to safety. I could see the lines of coconut trees swaying gently and beyond them a huge mountain with what looked like a huge golden temple on top. There was a steeple of a ruined church to the left and more objects dotted around.

Perhaps it had gone, the water looked calm like a watery mirror, reflecting back at me. I was not ready for the second jolt, it hit me from underneath. The dinghy travelled by itself for ten metres before being tossed out of the water. I landed head first into the sea. Struggling to find my bearings I tried to aim for the beach – my life depended on it. Something grabbed my foot. I kicked out as hard as I could. Reaching in my rucksack I searched for the first heavy object I could find. Gripping my torch, I banged it hard against whatever was holding me, in the blind hope that it would release me. I closed my eyes and lashed out in the water. I did not know what I was fighting. I thought of Dan and his smiling face looking at

THE ISLAND BECOMES YOU

me. I so badly wanted to see him again. I made another desperate lunge at my unknown assailant and suddenly I was free. Spluttering and choking I half ran, half crawled through the breaking surf. At last, the sand was beneath my feet. I thought I heard a loud thud as something smacked the surface but as I slowly turned to look, the sea was a picture of calmness. Gasping with relief, I fell backwards onto the sand and lay there trying to comprehend what had just happened to me.

Eventually, I sat up and noticed the upturned dinghy bobbing on the incoming waves. I stared at it for ages, wondering if I dared to enter the water again. But how would I get back to our boat? I looked around me for something to extend my reach. My eyes fell upon a long metal pole, it looked rather rusty but it would do. Bravely, I fought back my nerves and entered the water again. After only a few more steps, the water was now up to my thighs. I looked around for any sign of the creature but nothing. Just then I realised how quiet the island was – there seemed to be no sign of life. No birds bobbing on the sea or hovering around the rocks or trees. There was absolute silence except for my beating heart.

I held the pole tightly, ready to use as a weapon for defence. With my arm fully outstretched I tried to catch the ropes that looped around the outside of the dinghy. I nearly managed to hook it but a wave carried it out slightly further away from my reach. I took another step closer. The sandy bottom fell away sharply and I fell forward into the surf. Realising I was out of my depth, panic filled my lungs as I tried to twist and kick back to the safety of the sandy shore. I heard a familiar sound; a loud thud and splash came from behind me. This time, I dared myself to turn around and look. Rising out of the water was a monstrous fish head the size of an elephant. Its scales glistened in the sun and there seemed to be huge tentacles coming from its body.

Meanwhile, its huge tail wrapped itself around the yellow dinghy. There was no emotion in its cold, black eyes as it looked at me. The creature's mouth began to open revealing several pairs of razor-sharp teeth. I was transfixed by those lifeless eyes unable to move. The monster came towards me, spreading out its huge tentacles. A large bang followed by a whooshing sound broke the spell as the yellow dinghy burst and flew straight at the monster's face. A screeching wail came from its mouth as it plunged back into the water. I had escaped for the second time.

Slowly, my breathing steadied as I took my time to survey the beach and my surroundings. There appeared to be no sign of life. Calmer now, my mind started to focus on what to do next. I needed to find Dan. His white, motorised dinghy must be moored on the beach somewhere. Do I go left or right? There was a huge pile of rocks to my right. Maybe if I climbed on top, I could have a better view of the island.

I started to climb. Every so often I grabbed a handful of moss to steady myself. I seemed to find good footholds as I clambered up the rock. It was almost as if the rock moulded itself to the shape of my feet. I felt surprisingly secure. Before I knew it, I was standing on the top. Looking around, the rocks extended further inland than I first thought. Also, the water was lapping at the outer edges of the rocks. I was sure the sandy beach stretched further around them when I first began climbing. Brushing those thoughts to one side, I concentrated on the amazing view of the island. The beach continued to curve around the island and behind me was quite a dense forest waiting to be explored. As I looked towards the sea, I could just make out our boat the Adventurer, anchored in the distance. I wished I had bought a pair of binoculars with me – so much for being prepared! Shielding my eyes from the sun, I screwed them up in a vain attempt to see further. A faint, shiny glint caught my eye, just where the beach ahead arched out of sight. Perhaps it was the motor on Dan's dinghy. If I was right, then it would take two or three hours to walk there. Tears started to trickle down my face. I sat down and held my face in my hands. I had experienced so many emotions in the last twenty-four hours but the worse was the fear of being left alone on this island and never seeing Dan again.

I was crying so much and feeling sorry for myself that I did not notice the rocks shifting slightly and a low rumble emerging beneath them. Gradually, I became aware of this movement and abruptly stopped crying. Looking back towards the forest the rocks appeared higher, almost blocking out the foliage. Likewise, at the beach end, they had raised up considerably. What was going on? Was I imagining all this? Did I have heat stroke? I reached for my bottled water. This time the rumbling spread along the entire line of rocks, ending at the bottom where I sat. I watched as they began to part in the middle and a gap appeared in front of me. My mouth opened to form a scream but no voice came out. It was all happening too quickly. The rocks to the right of me seemed to lift off the ground. Before I could even attempt to move, they had encircled me. It was at this point that I passed out. I welcomed the embrace of darkness – it wiped away all my fears.

I awoke very disorientated. Was I dreaming? I appeared to be flying through the air; my feet had no contact with the ground. I was aware of hard grey rock surrounding me ... had I slipped into a crevice? I tried to focus my eyes harder to help my brain make sense of what was happening. To my horror, I remembered the rock I was sitting on had started to move and that same rock seemed to be carrying me through the air. I looked upwards and saw two boulder-shaped eyes staring back at me. They were part of a rock-shaped face with a neck and shoulders. Oh no, some sort of rock giant had me in his grasp. It was then that I looked down and realised how high up I was. Panic set in, what if this thing let go of me?

My life hung in the balance for what seemed like forever. I tried to make sense of what was happening, I tried to calm down and think logically. If it had wanted to kill me it could have crushed my body in a second. Maybe it had some other purpose for me in mind. The way it had looked down at me showed some curiosity and intelligence. Perhaps it wanted to try to communicate. Different thoughts and scenarios flashed through my mind, but the foremost was, where was it taking me?

We were heading further into the jungle. The tops of the trees brushed against my feet. Ahead of me, I could see a huge mountain. Suddenly, we veered to the right. The rock giant seemed distracted, his grip on me relaxed slightly and I felt myself slipping. Desperately, I tried to latch onto one of his rough-edged fingers but they were too large. I gradually began slipping further down its palm. I made one more lunge for a groove in his hand. I was falling and I could not stop myself. I could see the canopy of trees below me; they might break my fall but at the expense of several broken limbs. I did not stand a chance. I closed my eyes and imagined the worst. Slowly, I became aware of my feet touching a solid platform. I dropped to my knees; yes, it felt like the rock that had been encircling me. The rock giant had caught me with his other hand. Looking up I could see the giant peering down at me. He brought his head closer and with one of his fingers, he gently touched me as if he was checking that I was okay. His eyes looked full of concern. I felt slightly reassured. I attempted to smile back, followed by a weak sounding, "Thank you." The giant made a low rumble in response then turned his head away again. He appeared preoccupied with something else. It was then that I heard an agonised howl. It seemed to be coming from the other side of the mountain.

Carefully, the rock giant lowered me to the ground. I began to think this might be my chance to escape. However, I was completely wrong. Instead of freedom, I had been placed in the bottom of a deep crevice with sloping vertical sides. One prison had been substituted for another. A shadow was cast over me as the rock giant stood up again, blocking out the sun. Then the ground began to shake as the rock giant moved away, presumably towards the location where that eerie howling originated.

A shaft of sunlight covered one-half of my prison. I cowered in the shaded part, trying to come to terms with what had happened. Would I be left to rot here? Looking up, the sides of my prison were smooth; there were no footholds, ledges, or anything significant to hold on to. I opened my rucksack and tipped out the contents onto the ground for inspiration. There was a bottle of water, a first aid kit, a jumper, a t-shirt, shorts, a penknife, a compass, a lighter, a waterproof coat, a whistle, a mars bar, an apple and a notebook and pen. Nothing there could be transformed into a rope with a hook to make my escape. Perhaps I could burn my jumper and send smoke signals to Dan. Being realistic though, the rock giant had covered so much ground and placed me so deep in the forest, that there was no possibility he would be able to see me let alone reach me without walking for at least three days!

I was starting to feel very defeated; the mars bar looked incredibly inviting. What time was it anyway? My watch had stopped at 9:45 am, probably the time I was jolted into the water by that sea serpent monster. I looked up to the sky to gauge the position of the sun. It looked quite high up, making it early afternoon perhaps. At that point, I paused to consider the revelation that I was simply just dreaming of all that had happened. This made more sense than the reality of the existence of rock giants and sea monsters. Finally, I reached for the mars bar, after all, it was getting hotter and the chocolate would melt.

I was about to take a second bite of the mars bar when some rocks were dislodged from the top of the crevice. Something, sticky and stretchy landed on my shoe. Glancing upwards I could make out a shape leaning over the top. It did not look familiar. Shading the sun from my eyes I looked up again. It seemed to momentarily disappear before a huge hairy claw reached down towards me at the bottom. I screamed in fright and edged backwards until I touched the furthest wall of the crevice. The claw extended out towards me. I held my breath trying to make myself as small as possible as I pressed my body against the rock. The huge, sharp, jagged claw was trying to touch my face. Swiftly, I sank to my feet and tried to curl up into a ball. More saliva from the beast dripped around me. I could smell the stench of rotted teeth in its breath. Oh Dan, why weren't you here defending me? Why did you leave me on the boat and why did I stupidly try to follow you?

I thought back, to the safety of our cabin, on the Adventurer. Our journey had started as so much fun. Dan had seduced me with tales of his great-grandfather's adventures, especially his search for a mysterious hidden island. Dan loved exploring the unknown and the chance to find an island, still undiscovered on this planet was too irresistible. His great-grandfather's journal held the key to the location of the island. We just had to crack the clues, hidden in the stories handed down by an old Indonesian tribe of Indians. Dan's research had helped him locate the area where his great-grandfather had disappeared, near the Solomon Islands in the Pacific Ocean. However, the territory was well explored and mapped out, there were no mysterious islands undiscovered in this area.

The stories told by the Indians spoke of a giant god who was cast out by the other gods for mischievously causing the death of the much-loved son of the leader. They were so enraged by his deed and the fact that he showed no remorse for his part, that he was banished to a life of exile. He was cast out to the human realm where he landed in the middle of a huge sea. There was a gigantic volcanic eruption and as a result, a new island was formed. The gods created an invisible magical barrier around the island to protect the humans from finding the island and keeping the god a prisoner there. But, unbeknown to the other gods, over the years a minute opening had formed at the seal. Just big enough for humans to view the island but only when the sun and stars were in a certain position. During the spring and autumn equinox, it became visible. On sight of the island, the magic was overcome and humans were able to access it. However, the magic remained strong from inside the island so there was no escape for the god. Whether that applied to any human visitors was still a mystery as no one had ever returned from the island. The Indians believed that the island was cursed. Although it housed amazing treasures and could fulfil unlimited dreams, they believed the island possessed a will of its own and had become like the god imprisoned there. Very bitter, twisted and out to enact revenge on all who dared to seek its existence. After all, its intention was to fulfil your utmost dreams but with a twist to the outcome in a mischievous way. This final warning had been ignored by Dan; its only purpose he believed was to deter the weak-willed. He needed answers to his great-grandfather's disappearance plus he enjoyed the thrill of succeeding where others had failed by finally discovering the whereabouts of this island.

A high-pitched yelp brought me back to reality. Something rough stroked my head, then gently scooped me upwards. I blinked several times in the bright sunlight before I recognised the rock giant's concerned face, peering down at me. I looked down at the mouth of the crevice where he had placed me. On the edge were tuffs of bloodstained fur, obviously belonging to the thing with the huge claw that had tried to grab me. Worried about the creature's whereabouts, I did a 360-degree check of my surroundings. Thankfully, I could not see or hear any trace of it. My eyes were drawn back to the face of the rock giant. It seemed like it understood my fear and tried to reassure me by gently but firmly holding me and cupping his other hand underneath. He then almost smiled as he began striding towards the mountain that lay ahead of us.

Chapter 2

Dan could not sleep; his mind was full of questions about the island. He remembered the stories his dad told him at bedtime about the adventures his great-grandfather had exploring unknown places. But most of all he remembered the hidden island which had fascinated him as a child and driven his imagination. A tribe of Indonesian Indians had told his great-grandfather about this mystical, forbidden place, hidden from mortal view. You had to find the key to unlock the portal to its domain or occasionally the island would choose to reveal itself to unsuspecting travellers. It needed their life force to continue its existence. Many stories were passed down about small groups of fishermen disappearing without a trace.

His great-grandfather disappeared while seeking out the island. The fishing boat was found but there was no trace of him or the Indians who accompanied him. Only his diary was left behind. Dan had planned to search for this mysterious location with his dad but unfortunately, he never had the opportunity to do so. His dad was killed during the Falklands War in 1982, when Dan was only thirteen years old, just becoming a man. He remembered his mum gave him a wooden leather box after the funeral. He knew instantly what it contained and tears formed in his eyes as he had opened it. Inside was the diary and notes his great-grandfather had kept about the hidden island which his dad had shared with him.

Once he had possession of the journal, he wasted no time re-reading every, last detail. He wanted to memorise every fact, every conversation with the elders about stories handed down through the generations for clues to help him pinpoint possible locations for the island. Over the years, thorough research into other mysterious disappearances helped him narrow the search area to the Pacific Ocean, somewhere near the Solomon Islands. He was determined to retrace his great-grandfather's footsteps and after college he seized the opportunity during his gap year to do so.

The incident with the bird last night had only fuelled his curiosity more about the island. Maybe it was an omen or warning but he had spent so much time researching and travelling to get to this point – it was far too late to go back. To deny him the chance to find out if his dreams and imagination all matched the true reality of this island. That is why he found his impatience got the better of him. The urge was too strong; he had to leave NOW ... he could not wait any longer. Glancing over at the sleeping Helena, she looked so beautiful; it was a shame to disturb her. He loved her so much. A quick peek at the island was all he wanted. He could return before she had missed him – none the wiser.

Dawn was just starting to break through; there was a faint glow on the horizon. The sun was waiting to reclaim its rule of the day. Climbing into the motorised dinghy, he gently eased it away from the side of the Adventurer. The island stood waiting for him in all its glory. He manoeuvred the boat carefully between the exposed rocks that seemed to guard the entrance of the island. Before he knew it, the beach was upon him. Golden sand stretched out in front of him, coconut trees lined the shore a gateway to the jungle behind them. He could make out a huge mountain beyond this with a golden temple on top.

Dan stepped onto the sand and quickly glanced at his watch. Surprisingly, it was 6:30 am; it had taken him longer than he thought to get to the island. That meant he only had about an hour to explore then he needed to return to the boat before Helena would awaken.

The beach extended around the left-hand side of the island for as far as he could see. White, soft, powdery sand dotted with occasional shells. There was no sound except for the waves breaking against the rocks nearby. No insects buzzing around and certainly no birds; perhaps they could be found further inside the island. Then, as if on cue, he heard a loud buzzing noise coming from behind him. Turning around he came face to face with a huge bumble bee the size of a tennis ball. It almost seemed to grin at him before diving at his head. Dan instinctively raised his bag to shield his face. The insect continued with its attack so Dan started to swing his bag in order to swat the bee. Luckily, his second attempt scored a direct hit and he managed to stun it.

Dan took a closer look as it lay unconscious on the sand. He wished that he had his camera with him; he had never seen or heard of such huge bees existing. Perhaps that was part of the ethos of the island – certain creatures known to us on Earth had the chance to evolve differently on this island. They were undisturbed for years with no predators or environmental changes. Bending over the insect, Dan examined its features. If he was not mistaken the bee's face looked uncannily human. Dan remembered back to when he was four years old. His mum had warned him not to look too closely at the bee in case it flew up and stung him – but curiosity got the better of him and his mum's warning came true. The thought of history repeating itself made Dan quickly take a step back.

A low humming sound distracted him from his thoughts. It came from within the island, beyond the rows of coconut trees. The sound grew louder, it did not seem very welcoming. Looking down, the bee showed signs that it was waking up, its antenna twitched and a huge stinger began to curl and twist. Dan decided that he was not going to wait around to find out. He started to run back towards his boat. Meanwhile, the humming sound was becoming quite deafening, he did not dare look behind but he could tell the sound was gaining on him. Panicking, he desperately looked about for some cover – he knew he would not make it to the boat in time. Ahead of him was a group of rocks. They looked promising. A slight gap appeared – maybe he could squeeze in between it and fend off whatever was almost breathing down his neck. He charged for the gap and quickly slid between the welcoming clammy rocks.

The gap that he found began to widen as he forced his body further in. He had to duck suddenly and he seemed to be going downwards. As his eyes became accustomed to the darkness, he started to realise that the gap had transformed into a huge cave. Catching his breath, he crouched down and began rummaging through his rucksack for a torch. Turning it on, he took out his great-grandfather's diary. Scanning through the pages he found the passage he was looking for. His great-grandfather had attempted to decipher some tribal hieroglyphics he had found in their temple about the island. 'It was as if the island was alive as it was able to change its environment at will and in time, all living things that dwelt on it.'

At the mention of time, Dan was drawn to his watch. Puzzled he looked again as his watch still showed 6:30 am – the moment he had stepped onto the island. Helena popped into his mind. He really must get out of here. He did not have a clue how long he had been on the island and the last thing he wanted was for her to wake up worried and try to follow him. He was beginning to realise that this island had a mind of its own and anything could happen.

Standing up he tried to feel his way back to the gap. He remembered having to duck to avoid an overhanging rock. But the walls of the cave seemed to be closing in on him. The torchlight rebounded off the wet, glistening walls and there was no other light source. Dan dropped to the ground in desperation and started crawling, checking each inch with his fingers for the gap. He was trapped; there was no other route than to continue forward into the depths of the cave.

A clicking sound caught his attention. He stumbled forward, grazing his hand on the jagged rock edge as he tried to steady himself. The clicking noise stopped briefly then began again more intensely. It seemed to be following him. Dan froze, the noise was very close ... too close. He pressed his body hard against the rock behind him and tried to become part of its structure. To his horror, he could now make out the dim outline of the source of the clicking sound. Two huge antennas, a shiny armour-plated body and six legs. He stared in disbelief; it was a gigantic beetle. Turning its head towards him, its antenna twitched. It was so close he was sure it could smell the sweat running down his face. His hand instinctively tried to grab for some sort of weapon to defend himself. All he found was a loose rock. Holding it tightly in his clammy hand he threw it further into the inky blackness of the cave. The rock bounced against the wall of the cave and tumbled further along the floor. Luckily, the giant beetle cocked its head towards the sound then changed direction and moved away. Dan prised himself away from the damp rock and carefully edged himself around the corner. He waited for the beetle to move further away and then started to move slowly and quietly in the opposite direction. Using his torch, he tried to make out a safe path to follow, looking out for loose rocks and stones. Suddenly, a hand grabbed his arm and a voice whispered, "You don't want to go that way son – it leads to their nest." His torch shone directly onto the weathered face of a man, probably in his fifties. Dan crouched down beside him and shone his torch at the chamber he was heading towards. He could just about make out another twitching antenna and other low-clicking noises.

Relieved, he turned back to the man and said, "Thank you. I didn't think there was anyone else on the island and this is the last place I would expect to find someone. I'm so glad you were here but what are you doing in this cave?"

Grinning the older man looked straight at him, "If I had a choice, I wouldn't be here too but there is an underground stream nearby where I stock up on my water supplies. It's one of the safest places on the island. The beetles won't harm you, they are as blind as a bat, but their sense of hearing is very acute down here." Looking over at the nest, there were signs of movement which prompted the old man to say, "Let's move somewhere safer. I am sure you have many questions to ask and so do I!" With that, the older man got up and seemed to disappear between piles of rocks. Dan followed behind and realised as he drew nearer that there was a small, well-hidden hole, just big enough to climb through. On the other side, it was quite wet and slippery and he could hear running water. Also, shafts of sunlight hit various points on the surface of the cave. It was great to see the sun again; he had begun to think that he would be trapped forever in the confines of the cave.

Dan watched as the older man leaned over and filled up three canteen bottles with clear sparkling water. Realising he was thirsty; Dan bent down as well and scooped up some of the water in his hands. Refreshingly, it flowed down his throat and face. The older man laughed as he collected the full canteens and placed them in his bag.

"My name is Dan; I have only just arrived on the island. How long have you been here?"

The old man's face became very serious, "I was known as George Layton, many years ago. As for how long I have been here, I have no idea. Except that, once you are on this island, time seems to stand still. I have not aged since arriving here in a boat."

George watched Dan's face as it froze in shock and disbelief. He stammered, "Y-Y-You are George Lay-Layton, you can't be him. He was my great-grandfather. He disappeared in 1932. That would make you over 100 years old!!!"

"Whoa, calm down lad, my name may be George Layton but that doesn't make me your great-grandfather!" Staring at Dan's shoes he added, "I don't recognise your fashion sense, white lace-up shoes and gadgets which may come from a different era. But what proof do you have that you are related to me?"

Still in shock, Dan reached for the object that had always remained solid in his life, a crutch after losing his dad, his great-grandfather's diary. "Does this diary belong to you? It was found hidden in the rafts of an empty wooden boat. Along with an empty spectacle case and a leather pouch containing a strange metallic-looking crystal."

George looked at the diary and then at the hope etched on Dan's face. "May I have a look at the diary Dan?" George asked firmly. Dan was convinced the older man was his great-grandfather as he handed over the book. He looked closer at his features; especially his nose and ears. It was a family tradition that one ear was slightly higher than the other and the noses were always very long and prominent.

George felt the aged leather beneath his fingers, recognising the familiar smell. He turned the book over noting the small tear in the bottom left-hand corner, the slight tea stain on the front and finally looked at the spidery handwriting and doodles that filled the inside pages. Yes, it was his, just as he remembered it. A tear slowly ran down his face. At the back page, he carefully slid a finger under a gap in the cover and pulled out a very old black and white photo of a man and a woman holding a child. Dan had not known about the photo's existence until now. At that moment, his gut feelings were confirmed – this man must be his great-grandfather.

Chapter 3

Dan watched silently as George stared at the photograph. Eventually, he turned to Dan and asked, "What happened to my son and wife? It was the summer of 1932 when I arrived at the island so Edward would have been about 11 years old. I still have the last letter he wrote me. He was so excited about meeting me in Italy at the end of the year. It was to be his first trip abroad."

Dan collected his thoughts; he was not sure where to begin. From the letters he received from his dad, Edward was able to recall George's adventures and retell them to Dan's dad. That is how Dan found out about George by listening to his dad telling him the same adventures, such as when his great-grandfather was attacked by huge snakes in the Amazon, befriending remote tribes in the jungles and nearly being killed by a poisonous arrow. Luckily, the Indian tribe he befriended had an antidote for the poison.

He remembered that his great-grandmother died several years after her husband's disappearance but she had never stopped believing that one day he would come back to her. She continued corresponding with other explorers and missionaries, who were based in the vicinity of her husband's disappearance, asking for any further information relating to him or the missing Indians in his party. As for their son Edward, he grew up to be a fine pilot and fought the Luftwaffe during the Second World War.

George nodded his approval about his son's career, particularly when Dan mentioned that he had been awarded several medals for bravery during the Second World War. Once Dan had finished, George stood up. Slowly, he wiped away a stray tear on his face before saying, "Thank you, Dan, for finding me on this island, but unknowingly you have put your own life in danger. Originally, I arrived on this island with my best friend and fellow explorer, Arthur, along with five other Indians from the Solomon Islands. I am the only person left now. The island enjoys playing games with those unfortunate people who manage to make it here. It likes to set traps, appeals to your weaknesses and takes advantage of you. I have learnt the hard way about keeping one step ahead but I feel my time on this island is nearing the end. Soon it will be my turn to find out the true reason for the island's existence and why I was persuaded by incredible stories to seek its location out at all costs. You have heard of the saying 'Be careful what you wish for.' Well, I eventually found the island but at the cost of losing my loving family forever."

Dan did not know how to respond to this outburst. He began to see a similar pattern forming. He too had been mesmerised by his father's stories about his great-grandfather and these had sown the seeds for him to begin his journey to discover the island for himself and continue in his great-grandfather's footsteps. But what would the cost be for him? His thoughts immediately turned to Helena who he had left on the boat. Dan hoped and prayed that she was still there, safe on the boat and had not tried to follow him. He knew he had to quickly return to the beach and find his motorised dinghy. However, in his heart of hearts, he knew the answer would be no. Helena was always very impulsive, she would act before thinking and knowing her she would start to panic and immediately try to follow him to the island.

"Dan, are you okay? Sorry if I went on too much. I don't mean to frighten you but this island can be quite hostile to its inhabitants," George looked down rather sheepishly as he spoke.

"No George I was silently agreeing with every word you said, based on my first encounter with the island's creatures. However, I now realise how important it is to find my girlfriend Helena. There is a good chance that she tried to follow me onto the island. I need to get back to the beach straight away. Can you help me?"

"Of course, Dan," George replied. "We need to continue along this passage for a bit and it will eventually bring us back to the beach."

Purposely, George followed by Dan, strode off towards the entrance. Dan hesitated as he stepped onto the sand; he was listening for the loud buzzing noise that had scared him earlier. Luckily, everything was quiet except for the waves lapping against the shore. Once outside Dan checked his bearings, the beach seemed to stretch endlessly in both directions. Something caught his attention near the shoreline, something shiny and yellow. He dropped his rucksack and waded out into the water, then grabbed the yellow, raggedy material. It glistened in his hands as he turned it over. Immediately, he recognised it as part of the emergency inflatable dinghy that was stored in the top gulley cupboard on the Adventurer.

George watched Dan pace up and down the beach. He, like Dan, feared the worst for Helena. That inflatable dinghy would not have stood a chance if she had encountered the sea serpent that patrolled the waters surrounding the island. He still could vividly recall seeing his best friend, fellow explorer Arthur, being killed by the sea serpent as he tried to swim to safety. He decided it would be best to let Dan think that she had drowned after the dinghy hit the rocks.

Dan was inconsolable as he looked out across the sea. Yesterday, they had both been celebrating their arrival on the island. From a distance, it had looked so intriguing and exciting. What secrets did it hide? If only, they had paid more attention to their close encounter with the bird. Now it was obvious, it had tried to warn them both not to venture any closer.

George walked up to Dan and carefully placed an arm around his shoulders. "Dan, I'm so sorry but it's time to go. The light is fading and we need to find a safe place to sleep tonight."

Slowly, Dan nodded, he was not in the mood to question why this was necessary. He suddenly felt extremely tired and hungry and just wanted to collapse on the floor somewhere. He hoped that he would not need to walk too far. George turned back towards the cave they had ventured out from. Dan started to follow but he could not resist one last glimpse of the sea with the sun's dying rays reflecting on its surface. Lovely orange and pink hues formed a brilliant backdrop as the sun began to sink lower in the sky. Somewhere out there his beloved Helena was hopefully at peace. If only he had the chance to hold her in his arms once more and tenderly kiss her rosebud mouth. Run his fingers through her long brown hair and feel her heart beating against his chest. Reluctantly, he finally turned his back towards the past and slowly followed George's footprints in the sand. This journey had become a living nightmare, one that he could not wake up from.

Gradually, Dan opened his eyes after a pitiful sleep. He had been dreaming of Helena and he did not want it to end. The cold reality of day reminded him that he would only ever see her now in his dreams.

Sitting up, he looked around the cave for George. He was nowhere to be seen. His belongings and a crumpled blanket were left near the front of the cave. A little concerned, Dan got up and started to collect his things together. He was just about to head off towards the beach when he heard someone humming a sea shanty. A familiar face appeared around the corner of the cave, carrying some passion fruit and some unusual berries. George grinned and said, "Here's breakfast," as he handed Dan the fruit. Dan looked down at the assortment of fruit and gingerly tried a green berry. The texture was slimy in his mouth but it tasted surprisingly sweet and very refreshing. He looked at George and gave him a 'thumbs up' sign.

George continued, "The Indian tribe I stayed with, loved these berries. It was considered a great delicacy. When I found these growing profusely on the island, I instantly recognised them. The berries give you a real energy boost so I always carry extra to snack on during the day."

Dan felt better after eating his breakfast. It helped knowing he was not alone but every time he closed his eyes, he could still see Helena and it hurt so much. The need to leave the island was very strong now. He desperately wanted to escape the painful memories that the island held and take his great-grandfather with him. Turning to George he suggested, "Could we try to find my motorised dinghy and return to my cabin cruiser the Adventurer? We can escape the island together. It should be moored along the coast somewhere but I am not certain which direction to go."

Shaking his head, George replied, "It sounds like a good plan but I am afraid that you cannot escape the island the same way that you arrived here. I remember the Indian tribe said that once you are on the island the only way to return home is to make your way to the heart of the island."

Dan interrupted, "I presume the heart of the island must be in the centre. Perhaps within the golden temple on top of the mountain."

"Yes Dan," George continued. "Unfortunately, no one has ever made it back from this island to tell their story and explain further about what happens next once you manage to find the heart of the island!"

"Have you tried to climb up the mountain?" Dan asked intrigued. He wanted to know everything George had learned about the island.

THE ISLAND BECOMES YOU

"I made the journey once to the mountain but I lost two good friends on the way there. The island is extremely dangerous and unpredictable, especially at night time. The mountain itself is impossible to climb and there is virtually no protective cover during the night."

Dan interrupted again, "George, why do you keep on mentioning the need to keep safe during the night? What happens on the island?"

George paused and took a mouthful of the passion fruit before continuing. "I learnt my lesson the hard way. You do not venture outside during the night. When we first arrived on the island the light started to fade so the Indians and I made a campfire on the beach. Exhausted, we soon fell asleep around it. Later, I was abruptly woken by an ear-piercing screech. It was pitch black, the fire had died out and it took a while for my eyes to focus. I became aware of a loud beating sound above me and a nauseous stench in the air. The sand was getting churned upwards and around me. Everyone at my party was scared and running in different directions but had no clue what from.

Suddenly, something tugged at my left shoulder. I felt a sharp stabbing pain. Quickly, I dived to the ground and rolled over. Something brushed my face before I heard a scream. This time I could vaguely see one of the Indians called Dimitri being hoisted into the air. Instinctively, I tried to grab his leg. I felt a strong whoosh of air above me accompanied by a loud beating sound. I realised now that it belonged to a huge pair of wings. I looked around me; these screeching, winged creatures were everywhere. They were trying to grab us with their huge talons and then fly away with us in the direction of the mountain. I called out to the Indians who were left, to take cover and head for the rocks. I reached out again for Dimitri's leg and this time I succeeded and held on for dear life. But the creature was too strong and I found that I too, had started to lift off the ground. Reluctantly, I had no choice but to let go and landed on some rocks below where I was knocked unconscious. In the morning, the two remaining Indians found me. We were all in a state of shock and disbelief. The sharp talons had left several large gashes on my shoulder and my face was covered in lots of cuts and bruises from the fall. But at least I was alive!

The next night we made a makeshift campfire again on the beach but this time sought cover in the nearby cave. We waited for the creatures to return. Sure, enough they did not disappoint us. Their high-pitched screeching was the first thing we heard, followed by the loud beating of their wings. Three of the creatures landed by our campfire and we could clearly see the outline of their huge wings and bird-like bodies. They had a terrible long claw at the top of their wings and three huge talons on their feet. However, the most frightening feature was when they turned and looked towards our cave. They each possessed the face of a beautiful woman which suddenly transformed and contorted into a hideous, wizened shape. Smiling grotesquely at us, they revealed their sharp, crooked fangs before a horrendous ear-splitting screech transcended from their once rosebud lips. Luckily for us, the entrance to our cave was far too narrow for them to pursue us. They just let out another ear-piercing screech before taking flight again.

Relieved they had gone, we all looked knowingly at each other, trying not to imagine what terrible fate had befallen Dimitri and the others. Those, who remained, now knew how dangerous the island was at night."

Dan found himself both fascinated and scared of George's story. He remembered reading tales about creatures called 'Harpies' in his myths and legends books. George's description was almost identical except for their beautiful faces. The island seemed to mix reality with fiction. It enjoyed surprising and scaring its inhabitants. How did these creatures evolve on the island? Hopefully, the answer could be found on top of the mountain.

For a while, both men were lost in their own thoughts. At last, Dan broke the silence, "George, we need to get off this island. We need to warn people of its existence."

"I know, I know, Dan. I felt the same way after my first encounter with those creatures but it's not easy to leave the island. I've tried and failed and I'm afraid to say that finally I came to terms with the hopeless, unavoidable situation, I was in. There is no escape from this island, you can try your best to stay one step ahead but eventually, your fate is sealed. The island always wins in the end – I will never leave this island alive!"

Dan watched as a tear slowly rolled down George's cheek. Quickly, he wiped it away. He stood up and looked straight at Dan and said, "However, since you've arrived on this island, I have gained a glimmer of hope. I will try one last time to get off this island. It is too late for me, everyone I loved or cared about is dead. There is no reason for me to leave, but you Dan, have your whole life ahead of you. I will try one last time for you."

THE ISLAND BECOMES YOU

Dan gave George a huge hug and replied, "I know it must be extremely difficult for you to keep positive, you have witnessed the cruelty of this place. Also, I realise I have still much to learn about the island's secrets but hopefully, together we will succeed where others have failed. You are wrong George; you do still have a purpose, a reason to live for. I need you and there is still life to be experienced beyond this island. I won't stop trying until we both have escaped this island … together!"

Chapter 4

The sunlight was starting to wane and there was a chill in the air. The rock giant had been circling the mountain for ages. Finally, he slowed down and gently lowered me onto a small rocky ledge which opened out into a small cave, just big enough for me to move around in. There were several flattish rocks I could sit on and plenty of floor space for me to sleep. The ground vibrated as the rock giant carefully sat down near the entrance and rested his head against the side of the mountain. I watched as he relaxed his body and then with a deep sigh, he closed his eyes.

The light was fading fast now and I felt tired and exhausted. I decided to lie down too in the mouth of the cave using my rucksack as a pillow and my coat as a makeshift blanket. Tomorrow I would try to think of a solution to my predicament but tonight I desperately needed to sleep.

I awoke with a jolt in the morning, the left side of my body felt numb from lying on the solid, stone floor. I shivered; the heat from the sunlight had not reached the entrance of the cave yet. I blinked several times and tried to focus on the shadows within the cave. Had it all, just been a bad dream? Unfortunately, I still remember vividly how close I came to being eaten by the sea serpent and its cold lifeless eyes staring at me. It was then that I had an overwhelming feeling that I was not alone. Part of me wanted to turn my head and prove myself right but I felt too scared to move. Maybe if I pretended to sleep it would leave me alone. I just wanted more time to collect my thoughts and try to make sense of what had happened. After all, there had to be a viable explanation for everything I had witnessed yesterday on the island. Also, what had happened to Dan? My mind was in turmoil. Was he hurt or trapped somewhere on the island or had he made it back to our boat safely? If only I had stayed on the boat and not foolishly ventured off after him – we might be reunited by now.

My thoughts returned to the option, do I stay still or turn my head? Eventually, curiosity got the better of me and I lifted my head up slightly, pausing before turning to look behind me. I was greeted with a crooked smile from the rock giant as it sat peering into my new home. Immediately, I thought of myself a bit like a goldfish, I had become some sort of pet for the rock giant. How long had he been watching me? It felt rather intruding and unnerving.

Patiently, the rock giant waited for me to sit up and stretch my aching limbs. Then it gestured towards the right edge of the ledge where my eyes spotted a coconut broken in half on a bed of leaves. At this point my stomach rumbled, letting me know how appealing this looked. I remembered Dan showing me how to eat a coconut. First, make a hole and drink the moist liquid. Next, crack the husk open to reveal the soft flesh to scoop out. Using my penknife, I gratefully attacked the white flesh inside. It almost seemed like the rock giant chuckled to himself as he watched me devouring the coconut.

Once I had finished my breakfast, the rock giant held out the palm of his hand near the ledge. Presumably, he wanted me to step onto it. Hesitating, I gingerly placed one foot on his hand followed by the other. I knew, I had a choice. I could have squeezed myself into a tight corner at the back of the cave making it hard for his thick, rugged fingers to reach me. But I felt a powerful surge of curiosity, accompanied by an unbelievable sense of feeling safer whilst in his care rather than being on my own.

Gently, he curled his fingers protectively around me and I was flying through the air again. Looking down, I could make out the tops of the trees and in the distance, I could see the beach. Very quickly, the rock giant stopped in his tracks at a clearing in the trees. I could see a circle of protruding rocks as he lowered me down beside them. In between, was a mini waterfall flowing into a clear, sparkling pool. The water shimmered invitingly. Pointing to the pool the rock giant then touched his lips. I knelt on the rock and twirled my fingers in the water. Catching the water in both hands I held them up to my mouth. Glancing up, I saw the rock giant looking expectantly at me as I tasted the refreshing cool water. It was amazing, like an energising elixir. Just what I needed! Leaning further over, I splashed the water over my face; it trickled slowly down my neck. My body suddenly felt tired and aching. I longed to dive head-first into the pool and cover my whole body in it. Almost, sensing my need to do this, the rock giant gradually began to move away, then sat down with his back towards me.

Without hesitating I saw my opportunity and quickly removed my jeans and top, leaving just my underwear on. Sitting on the small rocks lining the water's edge, I dipped my toes into the water. Then I eagerly slipped my whole-body in. For several brief minutes, I was lost in the joy of submerging myself in the water. I felt so much better and my limbs did not seem to hurt anymore. I forgot about where I was and just enjoyed the experience.

A loud splash brought me back to reality as a loose rock hit the water. My eyes quickly shot over to where the rock giant had been sitting. Unknown to me, he had moved and was sheepishly grinning, while leaning on a pile of rocks near the pool. He had obviously, been watching my antics in the pool and probably dislodged one of the rocks. Immediately, I felt very self-conscious and started to turn red. Instinctively, I folded my arms in front of my chest. The rock giant slowly slid behind a wall of rocks until he had disappeared from sight. I stood in the pool, waiting for him to peep from behind the rocks but everything was quiet.

Carefully, as I watched the pile of rocks in front of me for any movement, I made my way to the pool edge. Pulling myself out of the water, I quickly grabbed my clothes and then sat down with my back towards the rocks. Using my old top, I tried to dry my body as best I could before I put on my spare pink t-shirt and blue shorts that were in my rucksack. Returning to the pool, I rinsed my blue top and jeans, squeezed out the excess water and tied them to the outside of my rucksack in the hope that they would dry. Then I refilled my nearly empty water bottle.

What should I do next? Could I run for it? The forest lay ahead of me; perhaps I could attempt to make my way back to the beach. My thoughts were interrupted by a hissing sound. Slowly, I turned around to face a huge cobra snake. It was monstrous, at least two metres high! Two sharp fangs protruded from its jaw. Its stripy body and flared hood reared up, ready to strike me. I did not stand a chance! Keeping perfectly still, my eyes searched frantically for the rock giant, I assumed he was still crouched behind the pile of rocks. He was my only hope! Unfortunately, there was no sign anywhere of him. My eyes begrudgingly returned to focus on the snake. My hands felt clammy and my mouth was dry. Perspiration was collecting on my forehead. I tried to think logically. How far was the snake's, striking distance? Perhaps if I edged slowly backwards it would increase my chances of it missing me. Alternatively, should I just make a run for it, or quickly dive back into the pool? Do snakes swim?

Suddenly, a picture of a snake charmer flashed in my mind. I remembered the snake being mesmerised by the swaying motion of the charmer rather than the musical instrument. I made my choice and began to sway from side to side. Maybe I was imagining it but the cobra seemed to relax slightly and its eyes started to follow my every movement. As I got a little braver, I started to edge backwards very slightly as I continued to move from side to side. I kept my eyes transfixed on the cobra. I was looking for any warning that it was about to strike me. This charade seemed to continue for ages. I began noticing the sun beaming down on me. My shoulders felt extremely heavy and my legs felt quite limp. My head ached from concentrating so much. I was beginning to feel light-headed. Who would eventually be the victor of this dance?

Gradually, I took another tiny step backwards. This time the ground was uneven under my foot. Too late, I realised I could not keep my balance. My ankle twisted slightly and with the additional weight from my swaying, I could not stop myself from falling backwards. Everything seemed to happen next in slow motion. The snake abruptly stopped its swaying motion. I screamed as it slithered towards me. It stopped a metre in front of me, then towering over me it started to arch its body ready to strike. I closed my eyes waiting for the inevitable to happen. But nothing did. Slowly, I opened my eyes, just in time to see the rock giant's hand as it squeezed the neck of the cobra. Its body hung limp in his grasp. I watched with disbelief as the rock giant tossed the cobra's body high in the air. It landed with a crunch against the rocky edge of the waterfall beside us.

My whole body was shaking; tears were streaming down my face. I thought I was going to die. The rock giant's face appeared from behind the group of rocks it had been sitting behind. His face looked angry, like thunder but once he saw how upset I was, it transformed into concern. Gently, he rested his finger on my shoulder. Although it felt rough and cold in a strange way it also felt comforting. I looked up at his sympathetic face and tried to smile, blinking away my tears. We remained in this position for a while. He waited until my shaking and tears had subsided. Then I allowed him to carefully scoop me up in his hand. This time I held on tightly to his smallest finger. I felt comforted in doing so. It was like we had started to become friends, there was a strong bond forming between us. Even though we could not communicate through words – I had started to understand him better through his facial expressions, unspoken reactions and kindness. But above all, I now felt completely safe in his hands.

Chapter 5

The rock giant gently placed me back on the cave ledge where I had spent my first night. He disappeared briefly, only to return with a selection of fruit still on their vines for me to eat. After my mini-feast, I sat and watched the rock giant. He was lying down outside my ledge looking at the sunset. Nearby, a flashing light caught my eye. To my astonishment, several fireflies each the size of my fist, were putting on a show. They danced around, producing intricate patterns. As I continued to watch, one of the fireflies veered off and started to fly towards me. It lit up the whole cave and started to explore every crack and corner before coming to an abrupt halt in front of my face. Mesmerised, I stared back at the hovering creature. Blinking several times, I could not quite believe what I was seeing; its face looked almost human in miniature. Two, pale blue eyes stared back at me. Its mouth began to open and a tiny voice whispered, "Nothing is what it seems. Beware!"

Confused, I looked around me but there was nowhere else that the voice could have come from. Returning my gaze towards the firefly, I noticed that its face now looked scared. Taking evasive action, it quickly darted upwards, just in time, as the rock giant's hand appeared from nowhere. I watched, still slightly in shock but mixed with relief, as the firefly turned sharply left and then shot out of the cave to rejoin its friends. Together the group of fireflies formed a circle and then disappeared into the forest.

Returning my attention back to the rock giant he appeared to be quite disgruntled about what had just happened. The ground shook as he got up and he seemed to stamp his foot in anger. I continued to watch him, puzzled as he turned slightly towards me, revealing his face which appeared very twisted and contorted. He stomped off in the same direction that the fireflies had gone. Although I was completely baffled about what I had just heard and seen, I felt overwhelmed with tiredness so I decided to snuggle down in the cave and try to get some sleep. Maybe tomorrow I would get some answers to my questions but most of all I hoped to be reunited with Dan.

The next morning, I woke up blissfully refreshed after dreaming about Dan being with me in the cave, holding me close and murmuring that we would never be parted again. At one point the dream seemed almost real as I felt his body next to mine and his lips brushing my cheek. Sitting up I glanced down at my watch, still stopped at 9:45 am. Taking it off my wrist, I smiled as I read the inscription on the back 'Dearest Helena with Love Always Dan'. I remember Dan took me out for a meal to celebrate my birthday and gave me the watch. I missed him so much. Placing the watch near my rucksack, I could feel tears starting to form in my eyes. Sighing deeply, I stood up and walked outside to the ledge.

The rock giant was nowhere to be seen. Was he still in a strop – still trying to find the fireflies? Poking, my head out of the cave, I looked for any sign of him. Unfortunately, the ledge I was on was too high for me to climb down safely. I started to feel a bit concerned, would I remain trapped here, waiting for the rock giant to return? What if something had happened to him? Sitting down at the edge of the cave I clasped my arms around my bent legs, placed my head on top of my knees and I closed my eyes and began to sob. I wished it was all a bad dream but reality was too terrifying to be just a dream.

The heat of the midday sun was beating down on the back of my neck. Looking up, my eyes were blurry from all my crying. An odd thought popped into my head, perhaps I should have tried to collect my tears and then drink them to rehydrate myself. I shuffled my body, slowly back into the cave and welcomed the coolness against my skin as I entered the shadows deeper inside. My body ached and I felt sleepy so I decided to lie on my side and curl up tightly into a ball.

Suddenly, I was awake, had I heard a high-pitched screech or was I just dreaming? The cave was black, I could not see a thing. There it was again; I was not imagining it after all. The screeching sound travelled straight through me, sending a shiver down my spine. Curiosity mixed with fear got the better of me. What on earth was making that sound?

Carefully, I crawled towards the mouth of the cave and my eyes gradually became accustomed to the darkness. Peering out from behind the entrance, I could not believe what I was seeing. Large winged creatures were majestically swooping and soaring in the night sky. Every so often a piercing screech would accompany their manoeuvres. I was mesmerised by the sheer beauty of their movements. I had no idea what these creatures were; they looked extremely powerful as they flapped their huge wings but at the same time were able to elegantly control their twists and turns. In some ways, it was like watching a synchronised acrobatic display.

Feeling a bit braver, I decided to edge nearer to get a better view. In the shadows, I leant against some rocks near the end of the ledge. I was so entranced by the show, I realised too late, what I had done. Several loose smaller rocks were dislodged and tumbled noisily down the side of the mountain. Immediately, the performance I was watching came to an abrupt halt. Six pairs of eyes now stared straight at me. I tried but failed to blend into the shadows of the cave. My heart was racing as I saw the creature with the fiery red hair throw its head backwards and let out an almighty scream. Desperately, I tried to shuffle my body backwards into the confines of the cave. At the same time, my eyes were fixed on the creatures now hovering in the sky. It was as if they were hesitating, unsure what to do next. Finally, the creature with the fiery red hair broke away from the group and headed straight for me. Oh, where was my rock giant – why wasn't he here to protect me?

It landed gracefully at the mouth of the cave. I could now clearly see how magnificent she was. The creature looked at me, she was so beautiful, her complexion milky white, fine cheekbones and vivid green eyes all surrounded by masses of red hair falling to her shoulders in endless ringlets. She had the body of a bird with huge, feathered wings and terrible, long talons on her feet.

She looked at me and smiled as she said, "My name is Serena. I was once beautiful like you but now look at me!" I watched in horror as her beautiful features transformed into a leathery, wizened face with sharp, pointed ears. She threw back her head, let out a high-pitched shriek and revealed a set of razor-sharp teeth. Then laughing through her gritted teeth, she hissed, "One day you will look like this when he grows tired of you."

Before I had a chance to say anything we were interrupted by another winged creature. "Quick my sister, it is time to go. We do not want to make him angry. Leave her to her fate."

Serena turned towards her sister and nodded. In a split second, her features resumed that of a beautiful woman. I thought I saw a glint of a tear in her eyes as she looked back at me and said, "He used to love me," before she stretched out her wings and flew off.

I continued to watch the creatures until they had completely disappeared into the darkness of the night. Serena left a huge impact on me. My mind was awash with thoughts and questions after what she had told me. The biggest question of all was who this person was or thing they were so scared of and when would I meet him. Maybe I had already, after all, the firefly had warned me that nothing was as it seemed on this island.

I spent the rest of the night sitting and hoping for their return. Who was this beautiful, yet monstrous-looking creature called Serena? Could she have been human once, along with her sister? Admittedly, all the strange creatures I had met so far on the island appeared to have traces of human facial features, especially their eyes.

The night sky was fading and a new day was waiting to begin. Eventually, I succumbed to my tiredness and drifted off to sleep. I dreamt that I was trying in vain to reach Dan. I was running in all directions but each time my path was blocked by the rock giant. To make matters worse Serena and her sisters were watching and each time I was forced to stop and change direction they cruelly laughed out loud.

The midday sun greeted me, as I opened my eyes, I hoped my surroundings may have changed from the bleak greyness of the cave I was imprisoned in. Looking around, my eyes fell upon some very welcoming colour. At the entrance, there was an assortment of different fruits, berries and nuts. My heart lifted; the rock giant must have returned while I was sleeping. If only he could talk, maybe he could answer all my questions. For now, my stomach took over ... its need to be full was much greater.

I dived over to the food and gorged myself until I felt much better. Afterwards, I felt rather foolish as I should have saved more of the food for later. After all, the rock giant might decide to leave again for hours or days. Taking a coconut leaf, I gathered up the nuts and fruit that remained, folded them up in it and placed them in my rucksack.

Next, I sat at the entrance of the cave so that my feet dangled over the edge. I looked closely to see if there were any possible foot holes or ledges I could use to escape from my prison. I was beginning to think that I was just a glorified pet for the rock giant plus I hated him for having so much control over my movements. I longed to try and escape so that I could be reunited with Dan but at the same time I knew how dangerous the island could be and the rock giant was able to protect me.

However, I was never one to take the easy option. Upon closer inspection of the rock face below me, I began to see possible areas that I could utilise to make my descent. An idea was starting to form in my head. Perhaps I could make some kind of rope from the coconut leaves that I used as my bed. Grabbing my penknife and the coconut leaves I set to work cutting the leaves into strips and then tying the ends together.

I tested various knots that Dan had spent many painstaking hours showing me. I struggled to remember all their names and I got confused about when to use each knot. Finally, we had mutually agreed I would master five knots only and try to remember when best to use them. Therefore, for this task, I decided to use a chain splice knot to join the three strips of coconut leaves together to make the rope. Next, I used a sheet bend knot to join the ends of the rope together. Once finished, I was very impressed with the rope I had made. I proceeded to test its strength by tying it around a boulder at the entrance of the cave and I pulled it with all my might. Pleased with myself that the knots held, I threw the rope over the edge of the cave and watched how far down it reached. To my dismay, it was just short of the ledge I was hoping to aim for. Thinking on my feet, I reached for my jeans that I had left drying out on a rock. Securely tying the end of the rope to one trouser leg would give me the extra length that I needed. Now all that was left was to take a final leap of faith and lower myself down the rope.

Just then my thoughts were interrupted by a familiar thud and shaking sensation. The rock giant had returned. Quickly, I retrieved the rope hanging over the edge, bundled it up into a dark corner of the cave and waited for the rock giant to appear.

Chapter 6

It was almost midday and Dan had been helping George collect together some provisions for their long journey to the mountain and construct weapons to fend off any unexpected monsters along the way.

As Dan was sharpening the point of a spear, he had made, he was interrupted by an awful, high-pitched howl that seemed to echo around the island. He stopped and looked over at George and said, "Have you got any idea what made that ear-piercing sound?"

George shook his head, "No, I have only heard it a handful of times but the screechy howling does seem much closer than before. If I let my imagination run wild, I'm sure I could concoct some amazing creature, part wolf, part peacock with razor-sharp teeth and claws."

Dan smiled at the thought of a half-feathered, half-furry animal and replied, "At the moment, to stay on the beach does seem the safer option but it is in my nature to always be a risk taker."

Dan's thoughts returned to Helena. Forlornly, his eyes glanced across the beach towards the oncoming waves. He remembered, too painfully how much he wanted to see Helena's face and hold her in his arms – one more time. Wiping away a tear he turned back to the task in hand.

In front of him was a pile of makeshift spears made from driftwood. Dan was quite pleased with his morning's work so far. The longer spear he was working on was nearly completed too. He looked across at George, who was busy trying to finish a rope he had plaited from tearing coconut leaves into strips. George smiled back, holding up his rope, proud of what he had accomplished so far. After a break for lunch, they both spent the rest of the afternoon deep in their own thoughts.

THE ISLAND BECOMES YOU

The evening light was starting to fade as the sun set lower in the sky. It looked so beautiful, all the different shades of orange, pink and red. Dan remembered how he felt when he first saw the island. He was filled with so many hopes and dreams of exploring this magical island and finding out its secrets with Helena. Nothing he imagined had come to pass only a never-ending nightmare. He had found his long-lost great-grandfather but at a cruel price ... he had lost his beloved Helena. He would carry this guilt with him for the rest of his life. The only thing which kept him going was his determination to escape the prison this island had become and set free his great-grandfather from his eternal life sentence. If he managed this feat then he vowed to himself, that he would personally destroy all evidence of the island's existence so no other poor soul would be seduced to find the island and suffer the same fate as him.

Dan's thoughts turned back to George and how strong and resourceful he needed to be to survive alone on this island. He had endured watching his friends die or experience a worse fate at the hands of the harpies. Dan felt a great deal of respect and love for George; he also recognised qualities in his character such as honesty, hope and bravery that were like his dad.

George was preoccupied with his own thoughts as he prodded the embers of the dying fire to keep them from going out. Dan joined him and stared into the flickering, smouldering flames. At last, George broke the silence and asked, "Please tell me about Helena. Where did you first meet each other?"

Slightly surprised by the question, Dan felt a bit choked as he recalled an image of Helena's smiling face. Then he too began to smile as he remembered that fateful house party, he went to at the end of his second year at college. It was the end of a crazy few weeks of exams and Dan was enjoying the chance to hang out and chill with his mates. He had just resat his AS exams and felt they had gone so much better than the previous year. He was so glad he had persevered and not given up college.

It was a very humid night; the party was in full swing and Dan decided to take a break and sat outside in the garden with a can of beer. Suddenly, he heard a rustling sound from one of the bushes. He watched somewhat bewildered as a beautiful girl wearing an itsy, weenie, yellow, polka dot bikini emerged from the bush. She cursed a few times and rubbed her legs and arms after catching them on the prickly branches. She did not notice

Dan sitting quietly on the step and jumped when he asked, "Do you often frequent bushes?"

She pulled a face and bit her bottom lip before replying, "Given the choice, no, but in dire circumstances I need them to escape detection. Have you seen a large guy wearing a hula skirt and coconuts around his neck by any chance?"

Dan was perplexed; he was at a gothic party not a beach party? "I can't say that I have?" he replied.

"Thank goodness, I've lost count of how long I have been hiding there. I think the mosquitoes have had a feast on my behalf." She held out her hand. "Hi, I'm Helena and honestly, I don't make a habit of hiding in bushes. It's just that Luke, the guy I described, has been stalking me all week and I made a big mistake wearing this outfit tonight. He cornered me in the kitchen and I had to make an evasive move to escape him. Fearing the repercussions, I fled the party and ended up here."

Dan smirked, "Dare I ask what the evasive manoeuvre was?"

Sheepishly Helena replied, "Let's just say he won't forget it in a hurry. I trapped his hand in the refrigerator door."

"Helena, would you mind if I offered you, my jacket? I could escort you safely back to your house. I have a black belt in karate if that helps to reassure you."

Laughing, Helena replied, "The guy I assaulted was a junior boxing champion for three years in a row. He is built like a tank!"

Not perturbed, Dan replied, "Ah... but from what you tell me, I have an advantage his hand was trapped in the refrigerator door."

"Yes ... but it was his left hand that was trapped and he is right-handed."

Not giving up, Dan replied, "I see, well I still have use of both hands and feet. I could still delay him long enough so that you could make a run for it!"

Helena sighed, "Okay you win Dan. It's getting cold and you might be useful at fending off any other unwanted attention I might encounter on my journey home. I've learnt my lesson for now; I will be fully dressed from head to toe in the future."

Dan shot a quick glance at her outfit again and said, "That would be a great shame!" Helena went a bright shade of red and looked away. Quickly, Dan added, "Sorry if I embarrassed you, but you are a very attractive young lady plus you are wearing a very daring fancy dress outfit. I expect there is never a dull moment in your life."

Helena pulled a face, grabbed his jacket, and marched off in the direction of her house with Dan trailing behind.

After that night, we found that we kept bumping into each other throughout the college. She was a keen swimmer and we often arranged to meet up at the pool on-site. Helena always took the lead at the beginning of our friendship, I always felt rather shy around her. She was full of life and had lots of friends but seemed scared to show her true feelings. I was gradually, falling in love with her. She eventually, confided in me about a previous boyfriend who had hurt her terribly and now she was reluctant to form another close relationship. So, I tried to play it cool and make the most of our friendship without overstepping the line.

This all changed at the Christmas Ball. Helena looked amazing in a blue velvet dress with a sweetheart neckline. I had bought her some diamante earrings that were burning a hole in my pocket as I did not have the courage to present them to her. I watched her dance with her friends and noticed all the guys staring at her and I was feeling incredibly jealous. I did not realise how intently I was staring at her too until she came over and asked me what was wrong. I stammered out, "Nothing". Then the music changed to a slow dance and she playfully grabbed my hand and led me onto the dance floor. Her body felt electric pressed against mine and the smell of her perfume was intoxicating. I found it hard not to pull her even closer towards me.

Halfway through the dance I felt her body stiffen slightly and she lifted her head, looking at me she said, "Don't you think it's time we admitted our true feelings for each other? Dan, I've fallen in love with you and I hope with all my heart that you feel the same way."

With that, I nodded; I was too choked to say anything back. I had waited so long, secretly hoping that she felt the same way as I did. Now the moment to reveal my true feelings had arrived, I did not have a clue what to say. I had acted out this moment in my head, many times but I found myself frozen to the spot staring deep into her eyes. Gently, she pressed her lips against mine and my whole body was awakened by our first kiss. We stayed holding each other on the dance floor – long after the slow dance had stopped. Eventually, one of her friends came over and broke the spell temporarily by saying she was going home. Helena nodded and returned her gaze to my face. Somehow, I managed to lead us off the dance floor and we went back to her house. There was no more need for words, we both knew what the other was feeling and there was no going back to being just good friends.

Dan was aware of someone calling his name. "Dan, Dan are you alright? Sorry, you looked so upset; I thought it might help to talk about Helena." Dan could now make out the flickering fire in front of him. His face felt wet from crying. "Dan, take it easy, you don't need to say anything. Helena was an amazing person no matter what happens in life no one can take away those precious memories that you both shared. In time, they will become less painful for you. I am sure she would want you to remember her but at the same time she would want you to be strong and find a way off this island."

Dan nodded in agreement and closed his eyes briefly so he could clearly recall her smiling face staring up at him. She was such a determined woman, he loved her for it, always trying to follow her dreams. In fact, his dreams had become hers. He had ignited in her the drive and burning desire to piece together the clues and find this hidden island together.

They had decided to devote their gap year to finding the island. Helena's parents were dead, they died in a car accident when she was six. Her parents had invested wisely so she inherited a huge fortune. She willingly withdrew some of her trust funds, against her aunt's wishes to finance this exploration. It purchased the 'Adventurer' boat. Meanwhile, I had been spending the previous two years perfecting the art of sailing on my uncle's boat and by the time I left college, I had completed the skipper's exam and was a very confident sailor.

We flew to Australia and picked up our boat, the Adventurer. From my research and George's clues in his diary, we knew the approximate location of the island. We waited for the September equinox and all our hopes were answered when we first set eyes on the island. But now, too late, he wished he could go back in time and somehow miss the window of opportunity to view the island. Perhaps a sudden change in weather could have blown them off course or maybe if they had both heeded the warning from their visitor, the night before venturing onto the island. Closing his eyes, he knew how pointless these 'What if' tormented thoughts were. They would not bring back his Helena!

Chapter 7

Next morning, Dan and George woke up early, both realising the need to get started and make the best use of the daylight. Over breakfast, they discussed their final plans for their journey. George used a stick to draw the outline of the island in the sand around a huge stone that represented the mountain they were aiming for.

"Dan this 'X' marks where we are on the beach. In two days, we should be able to make it to a group of caves near a waterfall. After that, it will take a further day or so to reach the mountain. But we must be careful and constantly be on our guard for any unexpected dangers from the forest floors to the skies above. However, our greatest danger is at night time. We must find suitable shelter from prying eyes who could locate our whereabouts, especially on our first night."

"I suppose you are referring to the dreaded harpies whom I have yet to meet," replied Dan.

"Yes, you must never underestimate their abilities. They tend to attack when you least expect it."

George knew only too well from personal experience how ferocious and determined they were to catch their prey. He so badly wanted Dan and him to succeed on their journey. Finding Dan on the island had given him a new sense of purpose, something to hope for and fight for. He did not want the same fate to befall his great-grandson as he had endured all these years. Endless solitude, being alone with your thoughts, fears and memories was the cruellest life sentence to suffer.

Dan picked up his rucksack filled with water bottles and provisions. He was feeling slightly apprehensive about the journey ahead of them. It was going to be a hazardous adventure, fraught with unknown challenges and encounters with unimaginable creatures. Then, in the end, they would have to conquer their biggest obstacle, the mountain. Still, deep down, he did not care that much about his own safety now Helena was lost to him. His only concern now was to succeed in helping his great-grandfather escape this terrible island. They both just needed to focus on one goal at a time, the first being to reach the waterfall before darkness fell.

The sandy beach quickly gave way to lush, green vegetation as they entered the forest. Strangely, they were met with an eerie silence as they walked further within. Perhaps all the creatures inhabiting the forest were waiting with bated breath, to see what their first challenge would be.

They made steady progress through the morning as they pushed on nearer to their first objective. The midday sun consumed all their energy. Sweat ran profusely down the back of Dan's neck. His t-shirt clung to his body and his legs ached from all the twists and turns they had to make. The path ahead of them was not clear. Strange plants bearing brightly coloured fruits and sharp thorny leaves often blocked their route, forcing them to go around them and add time to their journey. Dan resorted to using one of his large spears to hack away at the bushes as best he could. Poor George was struggling to keep up and used one of his spears as a walking stick.

At one point, Dan and George became separated after George lingered too long in one spot while he drank some water. The opening Dan had made in the bushes, mysteriously seemed to close around George, making him completely invisible. Luckily, Dan sensed something was wrong and backtracked. He heard George cry out and managed to quickly clear a path for him. After this incident, they made sure they always kept close together.

Eventually, Dan found a small clearing which looked safe to stop and eat. Relieved to be resting, George leaned against one of the boulders in the clearing, placing his improvised walking stick on the ground nearby.

Taking his hat off to fan his face, George said, "I had forgotten how tough the terrain is further into the island. It's as if the island knows what you are planning and tries its best to deter you."

"I agree George, especially when those bushes seemed to surround you. I could have easily lost sight of you if I hadn't stopped and retraced my steps."

Slowly, Dan sank to the ground, his back was against a huge boulder and

THE ISLAND BECOMES YOU

his feet stretched out before him. He grabbed his bag and gulped down a few mouthfuls of water.

George shouted, "Hey, slow down lad, we need to make the water last, remember."

"Sorry George, I momentarily forgot where we were. I used to love going on hiking trips with my dad. The best bit was always stopping to have a snack and a drink. Dad would always try and find a picturesque spot."

"Your dad sounds like he was lots of fun while you were growing up. Tell me about him?"

Grinning Dan replied, "Yes, he was lots of fun, George. I think he tried to make up for all the months he was away from home during his army service. Often, he would arrive back after several months abroad and announce that we were all going on an impromptu camping trip. Mum always hated those spur-of-the-moment trips – she would rather have kept him safely at home for a few days before venturing off into the unknown. Secretly, although she often protested, I think she thoroughly enjoyed the outdoors. That's why they got on so well."

Dan closed his eyes, trying to picture one of their various outings, this time to Loch Lomond in Scotland. It had been raining heavily and the ground was saturated. There was no way they were going to pitch their tent securely. While his mum, sought shelter under a tree, Dan and his dad vainly tried to keep their tent up. In the end, his mum overruled them both and they had to concede failure and head for the nearest B&B. Dan thought he probably got some of his stubborn streak from his dad as his mum was the more practical one with the common sense to know when to give up.

Something tickled his foot, his eyes opened, squinting he tried to make out the clearing in front of him. To his horror, all he could see was a wall of green prickly bushes. Quickly, glancing across at George, he could see him half sitting, half leaning against another boulder with his hat perched over his eyes, shading them from the sun. Panic and fear rapidly rose in Dan's throat, eventually, he managed to shout out, "George, open your eyes. We are surrounded by bushes!"

George jolted himself awake and his face took on a picture of utter alarm as he surveyed the area that was once a clearing. They were now surrounded by a wall of advancing bushes. He could not believe what was happening. He had never witnessed any plants being a threat to him during his time on the island. Why on earth were they attacking them now?

George was concerned about Dan. Why was he so quiet? He looked back over to where Dan had been lying; terrifyingly he was now cocooned in a network of roots that were wrapped around his limbs and face so he was unable to move. The only part visible was Dan's eyes which looked helplessly back at him. George watched as the roots slowly tried to drag Dan towards the wall of bushes. He knew he had to act quickly if he was going to save him – but what could he do?

Paralysed with shock, he looked back at Dan for inspiration and noticed that his eyes kept darting back towards his rucksack. Suddenly, it came to him what he had to do. Opening the back pocket of the rucksack, he grabbed the box of matches. He then set about lighting the spear he had been using as a walking stick. Thankfully, he managed to light it quickly, the coconut leaves securing the knife end burnt instantly. George then pointed the flaming end towards the bushes. Immediately, they started to recoil away from him. He waved it over the roots and runners that were wrapped tightly around Dan and they began to loosen their grip on him. Swiftly, Dan managed to kick one of his legs loose, followed by an arm. Putting his free hand in his pocket he was able to extract his penknife and began to cut into one of the roots secured around his other arm. Dan could not believe what he was hearing; a piercing screech seemed to escape from the bush nearest him as he continued to cut through the root. Pausing in disbelief Dan looked down at the root and then back at the bush.

"Dan," George yelled, "Look out, to the left of you!"

Out of the corner of his eye, Dan could see another long root about to strike out and try to grab his hand that was holding the penknife. In a flash, George jumped over the roots still attached to Dan's body and he waved the spear torch at the rogue root. It quickly slithered back to the bush where it had originated from. The other roots attached to Dan also loosened their grip and retreated to the wall of green.

Dan and George both tried to catch their breath during the slight reprieve from the bushes' onslaught. They looked at each other in shock. Next, Dan jumped up and reached for another spear and lit it too. All the time though, he kept one eye on the George and one eye on the bushes in case they regrouped for another attack.

"George, I'm not sure how long these lighted torches will keep them all away from us. Have you ever encountered hostile reactions from any other plants on this island?"

"No Dan, this is a first. It's only ever been attacks from creatures living on the island, not vegetation!"

Dan closely watched the reaction of the bushes as they were talking, it was almost like they shuddered or seemed to take offence at the word 'vegetation.' His attention was drawn to a bush slightly larger than the rest. Its roots seemed to run like tentacles along the entire circle of bushes that were enclosing them. Perhaps this was how it communicated its orders. Taking a step backwards, his suspicions were confirmed, the larger bush was the first to edge forward slightly, closely followed by the others. He decided to keep this information to himself rather than share it with George; it might come in useful later.

Dan realised this standoff would not last forever; the bushes would bide their time and then attack again at a moment of weakness. Besides, they would eventually, run out of matches and spears or grow tired from concentrating on the bushes every movement. Remembering the huge boulder behind them, Dan wondered if perhaps a height advantage could help them plan an escape.

"George, I think some extra height on the situation may help us." Dan motioned towards the boulder behind him. George nodded not daring to avert his eyes from the surrounding bushes. Surveying, the solid wall of bushes in front of him, there did not seem to be any means of escape in that direction.

Dan edged back slowly towards the boulder as George moved across to cover him. Once his legs felt the hard-cold surface he reached down and grabbed his rucksack. Quickly, he chucked his bag high in the air, aiming for the top of the boulder. He handed his burning spear to George and then rapidly turned and started to climb the boulder. In his hurry to climb, he grazed his knees and was halfway up when he heard George shout and charge forward. In that split second, he realised the bushes were one step ahead of them. He screamed out, "NO," but it was too late.

Unbeknown to them, at the back of the boulder, the bushes had been silently, closing in, sending root runners around the bottom edge. Immediately, after George surged forward the runners joined together behind where George was standing, now making it impossible to climb down or up the boulder. They were trapped! Dan watched powerless from the top of the boulder as the bushes closed in from both sides around George, who was desperately twisting and turning in the middle of the circle, trying to fend them off.

The bushes now formed a complete circle around the bottom of the boulder and a separate one around George. It looked like a figure of eight from above. Briefly, Dan caught sight of George's face – he knew George would never give up and would valiantly keep fighting until the very end.

Frantically, Dan looked around him for inspiration to help them escape. To his horror, the green throne of bushes were now tightly packed together around the base of the boulder. Their roots were now stealthily entwining themselves around the surface. Gradually, they were creeping upwards ... towards him. Dan sighed; it seemed pointless now – there was no escape. The boulder was too high for him to try and jump over the surrounding bushes without doing himself some harm. If only they had not stopped to rest and had just kept going, they could have avoided being trapped like a rabbit in the headlights of an oncoming car.

Glancing back down at George, he watched him courageously try to fight off the bushes. George was nearly three times older than him and at this precise moment seemed three times braver and more determined than Dan to survive. Dan knew he could not just give up and admit defeat. They had to fight to overcome the cruelty of this island and win their escape.

Immediately, his hands began searching for the other box of matches in his rucksack. Upon finding them he quickly lit some of the smaller wooden spears. Taking aim, he launched them at the leader bush and waited to see what happened. The bush set alight instantly and an ear-splitting scream echoed around the clearing. All the other bushes seemed to turn towards their ailing leader. The leader bush staggered backwards onto the ground then Dan watched gobsmacked as the other bushes turned away from George and started to pile on top of the burning bush, trying desperately to smother the flames that had taken hold.

George was completely stunned by what he was witnessing and the screeching sound was deafening now. Looking down at the two lit torches he still held, he now threw one of them on top of the pile that was forming around the first bush. He watched bewildered as more and more bushes threw themselves on top of the others.

THE ISLAND BECOMES YOU

Meanwhile, Dan saw his chance to escape. Moving quickly down the boulder, there was now plenty of room for him to descend. The roots that had held him at bay had now completely dispersed. Once at the bottom he hurriedly gathered up all his belongings and left-over spears. George was now by his side and together they left the burning heap of bushes behind as they made their escape. Not daring to look back or stop they continued their way to the waterfall.

They had only walked for a few minutes when suddenly there was an angry clap of thunder above their heads. Looking up, the sky had turned completely black, full of dark grey rain clouds, completely blocking out the sun. The rain started to pelt down on their heads. Dan felt there was enough space between him and the bushes to now look back. In the distance, he could see the huge pile of burning bushes; the flames were now being rapidly dampened by the ferocity of the rain. All that was left was a smouldering swirl of smoke billowing up into the sky. He watched disbelievingly as the bushes started to gingerly roll off the pile and regroup around their stricken leader bush. Dan decided he was not going to stay and watch any longer – it was important they continued moving and found shelter from the rain. Amazingly, at that very moment, the sky brightened and the storm clouds completely disappeared as quickly as they had arrived, leaving no trace of them in the sky.

Dan turned to George and said, "I still have no idea what has just happened to us. All I know for certain is that you must be always on your guard. This island seems to destroy with one hand and protect with another. I am certain all those bushes would have gone up in flames if the rain clouds hadn't just happened to appear and save the day!"

"I know Dan, I have long suspected that all the living things on this island are controlled or linked to something quite powerful. I expect that one day soon, I will get the answers to all my questions."

"George, let's hope the island soon reveals all its secrets so we can both escape its clutches and return home. But until then shall we stop at the group of large boulders ahead of us, they appear closely stacked together with some hidden hollows we could sleep in. We both need to rest up after today's adventure and be prepared for what tomorrow might bring!"

Feeling very tired after their prior adrenalin rush, George nodded and wearily restarted walking towards the boulders and a very much welcomed rest. He hoped they both might have a breathing space from any more living things attacking them. He was far too old for all this physical action and any more surprises.

Chapter 8

My reaction to the rock giant's grinning face surprised me. I thought I would feel angry that he had left me so long on my own but instead, I felt an overwhelming desire to give him a big hug. My biggest fear was being left alone and feeling scared. Having the rock giant around made me feel safe. If only he could communicate – perhaps he could help me find Dan.

The rock giant rested his fingers on the edge of the cave. Instinctively, I felt the need to sit next to his hand and rest my head on his smallest finger. Although the surface felt cold and hard against my face it also felt strangely calming and safe being next to him. I closed my eyes, savouring the moment. Unfortunately, this feeling of contentment ended abruptly. Suddenly, I found myself pushed to one side as the rock giant stood up quickly and stared in the direction of smoke billowing upwards into the sky. Far away, a faint orange glow simmered underneath the smoke. I watched the rock giant's face as it changed from surprise to anger. Before, I could say anything he strode off in the direction of the smoke. Then unexpectedly, he stopped, looked up at the sky and bellowed. I covered my ears; the sound like thunder was deafening as it rebounded around my little cave.

A strange thing happened immediately afterwards, the sky seemed to respond to the loud wail by turning black and huge rain clouds appeared from nowhere. A bolt of lightning streaked across the sky and it almost looked like the giant reached up to grab it as it took the shape of a spear. Next, the heavens opened, unleashing a thunderous downpour of rain.

I welcomed the rain and held out both my arms to catch it as I balanced precariously on the mouth of the cave. I bathed my face and hair in the refreshing liquid and took large gulps of it down my throat. Taking my pink t-shirt off, I soaked it in the rain and then used it to clean the rest of my body. Once I had finished, I laid it out to dry on a large rock inside the cave. As I did so the weather instantly changed to bright sunshine. Searching up at the sky, there was no evidence left of the dark, grey rain clouds from earlier. Putting on my spare top, I sat down again at the entrance of the cave with my feet dangling over the edge. The heat of the sun quickly dried all the moisture left on my body. It felt great. Looking out across the forest, the smoke was now a faint wisp.

The rock giant was nowhere to be seen. Which I thought rather strange. After all, he was so huge you could not miss him! A slight hint of panic coursed through my body. What if something had happened to him? My eyes began searching frantically for any sign of him in the forest and the surrounding area.

I was so intent on looking for the rock giant that at first, I did not notice the warm wet breeze against my bare legs. However, the proximity of an almighty howl, certainly made me react. I leapt up quickly to my feet, narrowly missing a huge furry paw that lashed out just where my legs had been dangling a few seconds earlier. Petrified, I slowly backed away from the entrance of the cave. To my horror, two piercing emerald eyes, belonging to a snarling grey snout peered through the entrance of the cave. I watched as the creature licked its mouth and opened it wide to reveal a set of jagged, pointed teeth. Saliva was starting to drip from its mouth in anticipation of me becoming its next meal. I continued to back away slowly. Perspiration was running down my face, it was an effort to move my legs as I was shaking with fear. Holding my hand up to my mouth I tried desperately to stifle a scream that was about to explode from my lips. My other hand had now reached the cold clammy rock at the back of the cave. I could go no further.

Sensing my fear and desperation the huge wolf seemed to smile knowingly and rested a paw on the edge of the cave. It then proceeded to flex its claws and sharpen them against the ceiling of the cave. The ear-splitting scratching sound was the last straw, my legs buckled from underneath me and I sank to the floor. Quickly, followed by my high-pitched scream as the wolf swiped his claw into the back of the cave – it narrowly missed me by inches. I felt overcome by the nauseous stink of his fowl breath as it filled the cave. I tried to focus on my surroundings; there was no other means of escape for me. The cave narrowed at the rear – too small for me to move back any further. I had explored it countless times looking for a passageway or other means of escape. It was so dark and gloomy; that I had even resorted to using my hands to feel for gaps or hollows – but there had been nothing significant.

My eyes returned to the wolf, he seemed to be savouring the situation, toying with me. I was certain that his paw could easily reach me at the furthest part of the cave. This time as he grinned mercilessly at me, his paw scratched the surface of the rock just above my head. I knew then, it was just a matter of time before he got fed up with this game. His eyes narrowed with intent as he raised his paw to strike at me again. Expecting the worst to happen, I quickly looked away and tried to picture Dan's smiling face. I did not want it to end this way, I so badly wanted to see him again. Suddenly, I felt a familiar shake vibrate around the cave, followed by a loud squeal. To my immense relief the wolf had gone; in its place was the rock giant's face.

He looked terribly concerned. Keeping my eyes fixed on him, I willed my legs to move towards the entrance of the cave. Peering down I could see that the rock giant was standing on the wolf's tail. The sound of the wailing wolf interrupted us. Looking apologetic the rock giant turned his attention back to the wolf. I watched mesmerised as the rock giant stomped backwards a couple of steps to face the gigantic wolf. I could clearly see the whole outline of the beast from nose to tail. The silvery fur body was taunt, poised, and ready for action. Its eyes were completely transfixed on the rock giant, watching his every move. The rock giant looked angry, raising his fists high in the air. I could not believe that I was about to become a spectator of a fight between two mammoth opponents. Of course, I would be rooting for the rock giant to win.

The wolf arched his back and threw his head back, letting out a deafening howl. He then momentarily, broke his gaze from the rock giant to look at me. He opened his mouth wide then snapped it shut menacingly. The wolf was trying to scare me – he obviously was not prepared to give up his tasty snack! I took a few steps backwards; the wolf was too close for comfort.

I calculated that although the rock giant was bigger, stronger, and more impenetrable the wolf had an advantage over him with its speed and agility, not forgetting cunningness. Never underestimate your opponent though. While the wolf was distracted by me, the rock giant seized his opportunity and brought one of his fists crashing down against the side of the wolf's right ear. Caught by surprise, the wolf yelped loudly. Quickly, gathering his composure he took a step backwards, growling under his breath. Pleased with himself the rock giant brought his fist down towards the other ear but this time the wolf deftly darted out of his way. Annoyed with the wolf's defensive action the rock giant's fists lashed out at the nearby pile of rocks, sending splinters of rock, tumbling down the valley. Wasting no time, the wolf leapt onto a nearby ledge and then proceeded to jump onto the rock giant's back.

I watched helplessly as the rock giant twisted and turned his body in order to release the wolf's grip. The wolf was using its teeth to dislodge the stones that held the rock giant's head and shoulders together. In desperation, the rock giant attempted to crush the wolf, clinging onto his back, against the steep mountain sides, but the wolf used its powerful hind legs to push himself out of danger. The rock giant's face transformed from a concentrating grimace to a strange look of surprise as he had underestimated the strength and force of the wolf. His shocked gaze met mine as his whole body wobbled, then succumbed to the momentum and force of gravity. There was a huge thud and the ground shook violently as the giant toppled forward.

I could not watch anymore; I was a sitting target if I stayed in this cave. My survival instinct kicked in – I had to escape. Glancing to the back of the cave, my eyes fell upon the makeshift rope I had made earlier. Without wasting another second, I grabbed it and secured it to the rock at the entrance of the cave, flinging the rest over the edge. Hastily, I picked up my rucksack, gave the rope a quick safety tug and carefully began to lower myself over the edge. Feeling scared and overdosing on adrenalin, I finally dared to look over to where the rock giant had fallen. Luckily, the wolf was too occupied with his initial victory to pay much attention to me. It was almost like the wolf was having a conversation with the rock giant while he pinned his face to the ground with his furry paw.

Halfway down the rope, I panicked, losing my grip as my palms were so sweaty. Fortunately, as I slipped further down the rope, the knot tying my jeans to it slowed my descent enough for me to regain control. Gradually, I lowered myself down holding on tightly to the hem of my jeans. Swinging slightly, I looked down at the ledge below me. It seemed further away than I had calculated. Taking a few more seconds, I tried to compose myself. Suddenly, my jeans began to slip down the end of my makeshift rope as the knot began to uncoil. I did not have the strength to climb back up so the only choice left was to jump. Closing my eyes, I took a leap of faith. To my relief, I landed safely on both feet, still holding onto my jeans.

Cautiously, I peered around the corner of the ledge. I could just make out the outstretched body of the rock giant who appeared to be making a low grumbling sound. Catching a glimpse of the wolf's tail spurred me on to keep moving. The greater the distance between the wolf and me, the better chance I had of surviving. Focusing my attention on what suitable footholds I could see below me; I carefully lowered my body over the side of the ledge. Holding on tightly, I guided my foot into the first secure hollow. I continued to pick my way slowly down the side of the mountain.

Nearing the bottom, I could hear the wolf howling a victory cry. Fearful, he might decide to return his attention to me and realise that I had escaped. I began to speed up my descent. Reaching down with my right foot, I misjudged the width of the foothold below me. Momentarily, I lost my balance as my right foot dangled precariously. I tried to grapple with the rock above me to regain a secure hold with both my hands. Eventually, I heaved a sigh of relief when I managed to find an alternative hollow for my right foot to rest on. Pausing for a moment, I listened. It seemed to me; that the sound of my heart pounding was nearly loud enough to drown out the sound of the wolf's howls. Thankfully, the wolf appeared not to have moved from his victory stance – his head was raised up as he stood on the back of the flailing rock giant.

Taking a few more deep breaths I continued climbing down. The ground was nearly reaching up to greet me, only a couple of feet to go. Stretching down, I grabbed the next protruding rock to hold onto. Unfortunately, to my utter dismay, it broke away from my hand and tumbled noisily to the ground, disturbing other loose stones in its path. Abruptly, the wolf's howling stopped. Instantly, my body froze and tried to embed itself into the mountain's surface in a weak attempt at camouflage. I heard the wolf jump off the giant's back. Slowly, I turned my head towards the wolf. I watched petrified as it raised its giant head in the air and took a few deep sniffs. Then the wolf turned its head towards me – its eyes firmly locked onto mine. Teasingly, the wolf's mouth curved into the shape of a smile.

Holding my breath, I steadied myself as the wolf leaned back on his hind legs ready to strike. Almost in slow motion, I watched as the wolf leapt high off the ground but seemed to freeze mid-jump. A blur of rock appeared from nowhere and grabbed the wolf's tail. Amazingly, the rock giant had managed to manoeuvre himself forward and make a lunge for its outstretched tail. He had saved me again! The wolf let out a frustrated whimper as the rock giant slowly got up while tightly gripping the wolf's tail. He attempted to wriggle out of the rock giant's hold but to no avail. Once the rock giant was standing, he gripped the tail with both hands and proceeded to swing the wolf around above his head several times before finally letting go. There was an awful smacking sound as the wolf's body hit the side of the mountain.

Wasting no more time, I half jumped and half clambered down the remainder of the mountain. Eventually, once I reached the bottom, I glanced up at the rock giant. His pleading eyes were fixed straight on me – his hand outstretched as he started to walk towards me. For a moment, I just stood there, thinking what to do next. The open forest and hopefully my way back to Dan was beckoning me in that direction or should I return to the safety of the rock giant? Seeming to sense my indecision the rock giant took another step forward. Would the rock giant chase me if I took the opposite path to him? However, if he let me go how long would I survive without his protection?

Focusing all my attention on the rock giant, I slowly smiled. He took another step forward and grinned back. As he took the next step forward a furry paw reached out and grabbed his ankle. Unfortunately, the rock giant was already committed to taking the next step. His eyes remained fixed on mine as he desperately tried to keep his balance. But too late, his body came crashing down in front of me. His outstretched hand almost reached me. The wolf let out a howl of delight. Shocked, I turned and ran as fast as I could towards the forest.

I lost count of how long I had been running, jumping over endless small bushes and tree roots. I kept on imagining I could feel the warm, ravenous breath of the wolf on the back of my neck. I dared not look around or stop in case my worst fears were realised and the wolf was right behind me in hot pursuit. I was running on pure adrenalin but eventually, I just ran out of steam, my legs felt like jelly and no longer belonged to me. I fell in a crumpled heap onto the forest floor. I covered my eyes with my hands and waited. The forest was eerily silent, except for my beating heart. There was no bird song, no ground shaking and most of all no howling.

Gingerly, I uncovered my eyes and looked around, there was nothing but shrubs and trees. In front of me, my eyes were drawn to a huge hollowed-out tree trunk. Feeling so exhausted, I crawled towards it. Using my rucksack as a pillow I curled up into a ball within the hollow and closed my eyes. Sleep swiftly overcame me – my body had had enough close encounters with death today. I welcomed Dan's smiling face into my dreams.

Chapter 9

Considering what they had been through, Dan and George both managed to sleep soundly, hidden from sight, inside the horizontal crevices of the boulders. The next morning, they felt refreshed and able to confront whatever challenges this new day might bring them.

George split open a coconut and gave one half to Dan. Hungrily, he immediately attacked it with his penknife. George smirked as he watched him and said, "I will never look at another bush the same way again after yesterday!"

Quickly swallowing a slice of coconut, Dan replied, "I know. I will always be on my guard now and expect the unexpected or unimaginable to happen."

George nodded, "Yes, I quite agree. Unfortunately, from now on our journey becomes even more perilous. We must find adequate cover from the harpies at night time or we risk them attacking us."

Dan looked ahead of him – the thick canopy of the forest greeted them. Through the trees, he could just glimpse the steep slope of the mountain. For a brief, fleeting moment he pictured the face of his beloved Helena, smiling and beckoning him onward. If only she was by his side now, she would help fuel his determination to keep going and overcome whatever obstacles presented themselves along the way. After yesterday's escapades, Dan was beginning to doubt, whether they would even manage to reach the mountain at all. But whatever his thoughts and reservations about this journey he had decided to keep up a positive front for George. After all, he had survived such a long time on this island it was only fair that he had one more chance to go home.

"Dan let's go soon. We need to make the best use of the daylight left."

"Sorry George, I was miles away, already imagining myself at the top of the mountain."

George laughed, "Wouldn't that be great if we could just imagine a place and then be transported there."

"Ah, but that would take away all the fun of trying to get there in the first place," replied Dan.

George added, "I'm not sure we will have a fun time getting to the top of this mountain – but the sooner we get there the better."

Smiling, Dan replied, "Well then, what are we waiting for?" Hauling their rucksacks over their shoulders, they strode off further into the forest.

They walked in silence for an hour or so, trying to conserve their energy. Periodically, George would stop to check his compass to make sure they were still bearing in a north direction. Once deep inside the forest, it was easy to lose your sense of direction. Everywhere, you had been and all around you looked the same, from the giant tree roots, the different shades of green foliage and the patches of moss on the tree trunks.

At last, they cautiously sat down to have a snack of berries and a drink of water. Dan found himself constantly looking at each tree and plant for any sign of movement. He did not plan to let his guard drop again for the rest of the journey. The forest was surprisingly silent. No bird's song or insects humming. Dan found this very strange. He would have expected such a vast island to be a thriving community of different species of creatures.

Dan broke the silence. "Tell me, George, have you seen many different insects, birds or animals on this island while you have been imprisoned here?"

"Dan, you have noticed it too, the lack of variety of creatures, during your brief time on the island. I have only found small groups of one creature. For instance, like the underground giant beetles and a small nest of oversized bees. They tend to stick together on a particular part of the island. It is only the harpies that seem to venture everywhere – almost like it is their job to police the whole island."

"Ah yes, I had an encounter with a huge bee on the first day. It was the size of a tennis ball and I remember upon closer inspection its face seemed almost human!"

"Dan, I think you may have hit the nail on the head. There does seem to be a human link between how the creatures on this island behave and their facial features. Perhaps the answer to this mystery lies at the top of the mountain."

"I really hope you are right," Dan answered encouragingly. "But more importantly, there must be a way to get off this island safely."

Gathering their things together, they resumed the long trek towards the mountain. Both, secretly hoped they would reach their goal with no further mishaps or hostile creature encounters.

The light was beginning to fade. George and Dan both sensed the urgency to find somewhere safe to make camp that night. The shadowy outlines of the bushes and trees were all starting to blur into one shape. The forest floor started to slope upwards on the right. Dan increased his pace, hoping the elevation would give him a better view of his surroundings. His gaze fell upon a small clearing within the trees, surrounded by rocks and a cascading waterfall.

Exhausted Dan and George both collapsed on the soft mossy ground. However, seeing the sparkling waterfall and relaxing pool was too good an invitation to miss. Discarding most of their clothes, both men ran and jumped into the cooling water. Pleasantly, the soothing water revitalised them, washing away the smoke, soot, sweat and fear of the last few hours. As Dan lay back and floated, he closed his eyes and immediately he saw Helena's face looking back at him. Oh, how he wished things could be different. If only he could turn back time, had not been so impatient and he had waited for them both to explore the island together. Or maybe it would have been better if they had never found the island in the first place but then he would never have met George.

Sighing he opened his eyes and was drawn to the top of the waterfall. Blinking several times, he tried to focus on that spot but there was nothing there. Unexpectedly, a slight shiver went down his spine. He felt he was being watched. Scanning his surroundings, his eyes darted in different directions. He noted George had his back to him, floating a few metres away. Out of the corner of his eye, he saw something move at the top of the waterfall. Blinking again he tried to focus more clearly on the object or thing. Slowly he made out a woman's silhouette and what he thought was the outline of two wings. No ... it could not be a harpy. Fear began to gradually take root in his stomach, steadily moving up to his throat. In desperation, he looked over to George who was still facing the other way. He was about to shout out to get his attention when his gaze was drawn back to the top of the waterfall. This time, there was no one there except for the remains of a tree trunk with two huge branches stretched outwards and upwards. Perhaps it was a trick of the light, combined with his imagination. Swimming over to George he wondered if he should mention his imaginary harpy sighting but George looked so relaxed and serene, he decided not to spoil the moment.

Opening his eyes George peered over at Dan and said, "I wish all our troubles could float away. Just for a few moments while I closed my eyes everything seemed much simpler, I forgot our predicament entirely until I opened them again."

Dan sighed, "Sorry to remind you but dusk is fast approaching and we need to set up camp inside the cave."

"I know son, ignore the inevitable at your peril." Reluctantly, they both made their way to the edge of the pool and hauled themselves out. Sitting down on some flat rocks they tried to dry off using the last remnants of the sun's heat.

Gathering up their belongings they made their way over to the cave ledge. Dan went ahead, clambering over a couple of boulders to reach the entrance. George was close behind and handed his rucksack over to Dan. After placing it in the cave entrance Dan returned to help George climb up. Gripping his hand tightly, he was about to pull him up onto the outer edge of the cave entrance when they heard a cry for help. Immediately, Dan loosened his grip and jumped back down. Standing alongside George both pairs of eyes were focused on the waterfall where the cry for help had come from.

"Help... Help me!" the voice cried out again followed by the sound of loose rocks scattering to the bottom.

George slowly walked towards the rocky boundary on the right side of the waterfall. Stepping forward Dan grabbed his arm, "Wait, it could be a trap."

"I know, but that voice sounds so familiar," George replied. "Okay, we'll go together." Bending down Dan picked up several large rocks. Keeping one in his right hand he put the others in his pocket. Together, they walked nearer. Constantly, they searched their surroundings, checking for any other sounds or movements.

More loose stones were dislodged and tumbled to the ground. Halfway up the waterfall, an outstretched hand was just visible. Immediately, both men ran towards the helpless figure. Dan dropped his rock as he scrambled up the right side of the waterfall. Above him was a rough ledge in the middle and he could clearly see a man desperately trying to hold onto an overhanging shrub while his legs dangled over the edge unable to find a foothold. Pausing, Dan considered his predicament allowing George time to catch up. Turning back to look at him Dan was shocked to see how much George's face had drained of colour as he pointed up at the distressed man. Eventually, George managed to utter, "Oh my God, it can't be. I don't believe it. It's Dimitri."

Hearing his name, the man swivelled his body slightly, turned his head and pleaded, "George, please help me...I can't hold on for much longer."

Quickly, Dan gestured to the right. "I'm going to make my way around and upwards to get to the ledge. It's too sheer, a drop from this angle; we won't be able to get much closer. Just keep talking to him. I will try to get to Dimitri as soon as I can."

"Be quick Dan, his life depends on it. He's losing his grip with each minute that passes. I lost him once. I don't want to lose him again."

George watched as Dan began his accent up the side of the waterfall. Each step brought him closer to Dimitri, his friend. Turning his attention back to Dimitri he shouted, "Dimitri, help is coming. Try and find a footing with your left foot, there is a slight indent further to your left. Edge your foot along a bit and you will find it." Watching helplessly, he willed Dimitri to find the foothold so that Dan would have more time to reach him. To his relief, Dimitri's left foot managed to find the slight ridge. George breathed in deeply.

Thankfully, Dan had now picked his way upwards and across the rocky ascent and found a way to the ledge. Lying down on the ledge he extended his right hand towards Dimitri who hesitated briefly before letting go with his right hand to grab it. Dan pulled Dimitri up and over the lip of the ledge to safely. For a few minutes, both men lay there exhausted before Dan sat up, looked down at George and smiled. Dimitri now also joined him and waved enthusiastically at his old friend.

THE ISLAND BECOMES YOU

Carefully, Dan led the way back down the side of the waterfall. The light was nearly gone and they both had to edge their way slowly down. George was waiting, elated at the bottom. He hugged Dan and thanked him before looking at Dimitri and said, "I never, ever thought we would meet again. How are you, my long-lost friend?"

Looking battered and bruised, Dimitri grinned and shook George's hand before both men clasped each other in a huge bear hug. "George it's so good to see you again. Is there anyone else left?"

Shaking his head George replied, "I'm sorry it's only me left. The others didn't make it. However, this is my great-grandson Dan who found me on this forsaken island."

Dimitri turned to Dan and asked, "How did you manage to do that? It's virtually impossible to come here unless the island wants it to happen."

"But Dimitri," George interrupted, "You forget, we managed to do it!"

Looking back at his dear friend, Dimitri smiled sheepishly, before adding, "I suppose so."

"George, I hate to break up this reunion but we must go back to the cave now. I can barely see a few inches in front of me," said Dan.

"Yes, yes...so many questions, so many unexpected answers but they can all wait. Dimitri before we go to the cave you may wish to quickly bathe your face and hands in the pool. But hurry, we must take cover from ...."

"It's okay George, you don't have to remind me. I've escaped their talons once before. I don't wish to encourage a reunion too soon!"

Chapter 10

The sound of a twig snapping woke me up with a jolt. I banged my head against the inside of the trunk – thus abruptly reminding me where I had been sleeping. My legs and joints ached; my hands were sore and covered with grazes due to yesterday's descent down the mountain slopes.

Shuffling my legs around I tried to sit up in the highest part of the tree trunk. My eyes were attracted to a shimmering, glistening substance just outside the hollow. I reached my hand out, it felt sticky and stretchy. The familiarity of the lucid smell reached my nostrils. I froze with horror as I recalled my previous encounter with this threatening substance. Another drop hit the ground with a smacking sound. The tree branch above me gave out a creaking groan and several leaves fluttered to the ground. I now knew what had been waiting patiently for me to wake up. Out of the corner of my eye, I could make out the tip of a grey furry tail. I clenched my teeth together and placed a hand over my mouth in a vain attempt to stifle a scream. But out it came anyway. Four familiar claws curled around the top edge of the hollowed-out trunk. I realised the wolf was toying with me again – dragging out the inevitable. Could my rock giant save me again? I held onto that faint hope with all my might.

Suddenly, the ground shook quite violently. I assumed that the wolf had jumped off its branch to get a closer look at me – but thankfully I was wrong. The whole tree trunk began to shake and groan. I heard a deafening cracking sound followed by a loud yelp. I held on tightly as I was lifted clean into the air. Looking below I could see a huge gaping hole where the tree's roots had been. Lying beside it was the wolf whose hind leg was pinned to the ground with the enormous, severed branches of the tree. The rock giant's hand appeared beneath me and carefully cupped the bottom of the trunk. Peering upwards I could see the relieved face of the rock giant staring down at me. I smiled and collapsed back into the safety of the hollow.

Disappointingly, the rock giant was carrying me back towards the mountain and my cave. Watching the rock giant closely, his face was a mixture of fierce determination and concern. He briefly paused at the entrance to my cave then turned his gaze to the top of the mountain. A solemn howl came from the forest. It seemed to help him make up his mind.

Slowly, he began to climb up the mountain slope, holding me and the tree trunk securely in his right hand. Near the top he stopped, the edges of the mountain were as smooth as glass so there was nothing to grip onto. The rock giant grimaced at me and instinctively I held on tighter. With great care, he began to hoist the tree trunk high in the air like a baton. From inside the trunk, I could feel myself starting to sway from side to side as he fully extended his arm above his head. I held on tighter. Feeling quite alarmed now, I felt the tree trunk start to flatten out horizontally. I was now lying on my back, all my limbs wedged against the inside of the tree trunk trying to brace myself for impact. Thankfully, I did not have to wait too long. I felt a thud above me that vibrated through the entire length of the tree trunk. The blue sky was visible through the hollow of the trunk.

My heart was racing now, dare I peep out of the hole? A reassuring grey finger appeared, blotting out the blue sky. Relaxing my grip, I sat up carefully, expecting the tree trunk to rock but to my surprise, it remained solid. More confident now, I edged my head nearer to the outer hollow and peered outside. To my relief, most of the tree trunk was now lying on the mountain top, just leaving the hollow I was sitting in and a couple of metres in front of it protruding over the edge. In addition, my end was carefully supported by the rock giant's hand. Gradually, I swivelled around so that I could peer across and down at the rock giant's face. My eyes met his encouraging gaze. I followed his eyes as they motioned towards the mountain edge. I knew what he wanted me to do but my legs did not want to respond.

For ages, I just sat there trying to muster up the courage to stand up and begin my climb along the remainder of the tree trunk to safety. Eventually, a chilling howl from the wolf below prompted me into action. I had completely forgotten about the wolf. His howls seemed far too close for comfort. The rock giant had been very patient with me but even he was starting to show alarm as he kept glancing down at the rocks below him and then back up at me. I forced myself up onto my feet and then made a big mistake looking down the mountain slope. As I suspected the wolf had started to climb up the mountain towards us. Time was running out for me.

The rock giant's eyes were now pleading with me to start moving and finally, I responded. Leaning out of the hollow I hauled myself up onto the tree trunk. Focusing my eyes solely on the edge of the mountain I started to shuffle along the trunk. My hands and knees began to feel sore as they scraped against the rough, uneven surface. Blocking out the pain I kept on going. I was about a metre from the edge of the mountain when the tree trunk shifted violently to the left. Clinging on tightly, I waited for the tree trunk to steady itself. Concentrating on my breathing I managed to calm myself down enough to look behind me. The rock giant's hand that had been supporting the tree trunk was no longer visible. The approaching wolf must have been dangerously close for him to take such evasive action and force the tree trunk further onto the mountain. Although more of the tree trunk was secure on top of the mountain, the angle was more acute making it precariously close to the edge of the mountain. The last thing I wanted was for my weight to dislodge it further and for it to roll off the edge. However, the distance was now shorter and I could easily make a jump for the mountain top.

I could now hear boulders stumbling down the mountain; I assumed the rock giant was trying to aim at the wolf. A new sense of urgency filled my lungs as I cautiously brought both knees up and attempted to stand up. Slowly, I spaced my feet further apart and steadied myself ready to jump. The gap between the tree trunk and the mountain edge was only about 30cm, the size of a ruler but I was more concerned about getting a good grip when I landed. If I accidentally slipped the sides of the mountain were so unusually smooth, there were no obvious footholds or anything to hold onto. Taking a deep breath, I took another leap of faith and aimed for a small grassy area in front of me.

At last, I felt solid ground beneath my feet and I let out a deep sigh, thankful I had made it to safety. This was confirmed when I stood up and peered over the edge. There was no way that the wolf could reach me at the top of the mountain. The length of the smooth, sheer sides made it impossible for the wolf to even try to leap up and join me. Realising, that it was pointless to continue, I watched the wolf begin to back down the mountain. He let out a howl of disappointment before turning and taking a giant leap off the mountain slope, then without stopping, he disappeared into the forest.

The rock giant leaned backwards against the side of the mountain and grinned, he looked very pleased with himself. I felt rather sad as it looked like we would have to part company; there was no way the rock giant could clamber up to the top either. Tears started to roll down my cheek. I watched him give me a final wave before he too started to make his way back down the mountain. I was left with one burning question on my mind. What was I supposed to do now? There was absolutely no way down the mountain. The only choice I had left was to head towards the temple I could see in the distance. Perhaps there, I would find answers to my questions and be reunited with my beloved Dan.

Looking down at my hands and arms, they were streaked with a mixture of blood and dirt. The inside of my thighs and lower calves had several deep scratches from gripping the rough tree trunk as I clambered across to reach the safety of the mountaintop. My body felt stiff and sore but most of all exhausted. I so desperately needed time to lick my wounds and recharge my energy levels. But most of all I needed to find somewhere which felt safe to shelter and rest. In the distance, the temple looked inviting and could offer me all those things but it would take several days to walk there. I noticed the warmth of the sun beating down on me and the dry thirst rising at the back of my throat. I needed to find some water. Picturing Maslow's pyramid hierarchy of needs in my mind, how aptly that fits my present situation.

Blocking out the penetrating sunlight with my arm I tried to scan the immediate area for anything of interest. My gaze was drawn to a circle of upright stones around some sort of monument in the centre and to the left the ruins of a church. Thinking it would offer some sort of shelter I decided to move towards it. The ground was uneven and harsh beneath my feet and I stumbled a few times. Wincing, I looked down at my battered and bleeding hands. I was very near the verge of giving up entirely. It would be so easy to just lie down and wait for the inescapable darkness to engulf me. Sighing to myself, I agreed it would be the easy option to give up. However, after briefly shutting my eyes, I recalled Dan's face spurring me on. The thought of seeing him again was just what I needed. Opening my eyes again, my view lingered over the sea. Faraway, I could just make out our boat. Dan must be on the island somewhere. He would not give up trying to find me. Unless he encountered the terrible sea monster on his return journey to the boat. I felt tears begin to well up in my eyes; quickly I dismissed this thought, pushing it to the back of my mind. Dan was safe and looking for me on the island. I had to believe in this. At all costs I had to keep this glimmer of hope alive – it was my only salvation.

Taking another step forward, I misjudged my footing completely and I found myself falling forward in slow motion. I tried to put my hands out to brace myself but too late, I felt a wince of pain as my knee made first contact with a loose rock followed quickly by another sharp pain to the head and then nothing.

Unknown in the shadows of the ruined church a pair of green eyes watched intently. Their harsh features had softened; relieved Helena had not awakened while she had carefully carried her nearer to the circle of stones. Just then a high-pitched screech echoed in the distance, a reminder of what she had become.

Chapter 11

I awoke disorientated; the hot sun was no longer beating down on me. It had been replaced by the soft, orange hues of dusk. I found myself sprawled out on the ground; my head throbbed. Reaching up to feel my forehead it seemed very sore and tender. Wiping the grit from my lips, I tried to swallow but my throat was too parched. Grimacing, I tried to get up. Forgetting I had landed heavily on my right knee, I tried to use it as leverage and it gave way. Trying again, I put my weight on my left leg and managed to stand and hobble forward.

Feeling very alone and scared, I thought again how easy it would be to just give up, to curl up in a ball and sob until my tears ran dry. Thankfully, I quickly dismissed these negative thoughts and carried on. Gradually, my eyes became accustomed to the fading light. A high-pitched screech in the distance reminded me I needed to find shelter urgently. To my surprise, the circle of stones appeared to be so much closer than I remembered. More hopeful of finding shelter, I stumbled forward until my hand rested on the first upright stone. Immediately, I recoiled my hand as the stone seemed to give me an electric shock. My body ached and longed for sleep; dismissing the stone I manoeuvred my tired body towards the ruined church. Picking up speed I forced my feet to walk towards the grey stone tower which was still intact. Dotted around haphazardly were various stones, weathered with age and covered in moss. A passing thought entered my mind – people must have lived on this island long ago.

Reaching the tower, I could make out the entrance where a huge door must have been. Climbing over a pile of wood and rubble, I entered the church. The ground levelled beneath my feet. Upturned, broken pews were scattered on either side of me. A metal cross lay silently to the left of me. As I moved towards it, I picked it up, hoping it could offer me some protection for the night. Broken glass littered the sides of the church. The crunching noise, under my feet strangely calmed me. Closing in on the remains of the altar I spied a door to the right which was still intact. I forced the handle slightly and to my surprise, it opened to reveal a small enclosed room, complete with a wooden table and bookcase. More invitingly I spied a pile of cushions. Wasting no time, I placed them in a row on the cold tiled floor, closed the door and lay down. Still clutching the metal cross, I welcomed sleep.

Slowly, I opened my eyes. Grey stone walls greeted me. I grimaced as my body reminded me how broken and bruised it was. Although, my cuts and grazes stung me and my body ached, my survival instinct was still strong. I had found shelter but I desperately needed water. Stretching my battered limbs out slowly I attempted to sit up gradually. I noticed the metal cross by my side and smiled – I had made it through the night. Sunlight was bursting in through a small hole at the top of the room. I had obviously slept well into the next day.

Surveying my poor hands, smeared with blood and dirt, I desperately needed to bathe them. Shuffling on my bottom, painfully towards the wooden table I used it for support as I tried to stand up. Concentrating my weight on my left good leg, I took a deep breath and managed to manoeuvre my body into a standing position. Pleased with myself I stood there for a while, gripping the table while I peered around the room for anything useful. Quickly, my eyes fell upon what looked like a sturdy walking stick. Continuing to use the table for support I moved around the edge to get closer. Stretching my left arm out my fingertips just missed the protruding bulbous wooden top. Summoning up all my remaining strength I took one step forward keeping my right arm hovering over the table. I reached out for the walking stick again. This time my left hand closed securely around the top and I carefully lifted it out from the pile of broken wood surrounding it. Taking a step back, I steadied myself against the table before supporting myself with the stick. Uncannily, it was just the right height for me. It felt solid, comforting and strangely like it was meant to be mine. Holding onto the table again I lifted it up to get a better look. The wood was a deep, chestnut colour and it was filled with intricate carvings of mythical creatures along the entire length. One carving stood out in particular – the sea serpent. It immediately sent a shiver down my spine as I recoiled at the memory of its cold, dead eyes fixated on me. Curious, I studied the other markings more closely. I picked out one that looked like harpies, there were others depicting other unusual beasts and possibly a dwarf. I paused and shuddered when I saw the carving of a wolf but sadly there was nothing resembling the rock giant. However, the walking stick proved I was not alone in witnessing these creatures, others before me obviously had to.

My tummy rumbled and interrupted my thoughts. Purposely, I moved the walking stick to my right hand. I practised using it to take some of the strain off my weakened knee. Just as I was about to leave the room my eyes were drawn to the bookcase, empty apart from one solitary leather journal lying face down on the shelf. Steadily, I made my way towards the bookcase and gently picked up the faded brown journal. It reminded me of Dan's grandfather's journal. Propping the walking stick carefully against the wall I examined the book cover. It looked extremely old. Slowly, I opened the book and read the inscription on the front cover. 'Dear Lord, protect us from this island's secrets. Keep my sisters and me safe and please help us find a way back home. Amen.' On the following page was 'This journal belongs to Rebecca Taylor 1872'. I turned the page eager to read more but I was disappointed to find the ink very faded in parts, almost illegible. My grumbling stomach reminded me how much I needed to find food. Tucking the journal into the waistband of my shorts, I turned back towards the way out. Picking up the walking stick I very soon found myself back outside the ruined church.

The afternoon sun greeted me. Shielding my eyes, I looked around. In front of me, proudly stood the large circle of stones I had spotted from a distance when I first reached the top of the mountain. In the centre, I could now clearly see the monument was once a beautiful sculptured marble statue of a mermaid perched on a rock looking down at a circular stone pool which at some point must have contained water. Large stone fishes adorned the circumference of the rock at the bottom with open mouths, poised to project water. I closed my eyes and imagined cool thirst-quenching water cascading from them into the round pool below. Opening my eyes, I stared disappointedly at the drab, grey stone and parched dry bottom of the pool.

There was no hint of water anywhere. Sighing and shaking my head slowly, my eyes searched desperately for anything to eat or drink.

My gaze focused on a small group of thorny bushes a few feet to my left. Upon closer inspection, they had a yellow plum-sized berry growing amongst the jagged leaves. Trying my best to avoid cutting myself, I tried to use a pincer movement using my thumb and finger to remove the fruit. I managed to manoeuvre my fingers carefully around one of the oval-shaped berries and removed it.

Surveying the yellow berry in my hand I recalled not seeing anything similar within the forest below me. The rock giant had never left any fruits like this for me to try. Hesitating, I picked it up and twisted it around slowly between my fingers before bringing it closer to my nose. I detected a faint whiff of aniseed. Was it safe to eat I wondered? A low rumble from my tummy reminded me how hungry I was. This time I purposely brought the berry towards my mouth and opened my lips. I imagined my teeth breaking the berry's skin so I could devour the rich refreshing nectar inside.

Within an inch of my expectant lips, a loud voice boomed, "Stop Helena! Stop!" Completely startled I dropped the fruit from my fingers and watched with regret as it landed on the dry hard ground. Turning around I looked in the direction of where the voice had come. My eyes were drawn back to the marble, weathered face of the mermaid perched on a rock. It seemed to have straightened its head. Mesmerised, I remained transfixed by the statue. Then slowly I became convinced it had blinked an eye. Thoroughly bewildered, I continued to watch as the mouth of the beautiful marble creature twitched. Was I imagining it? Suddenly the head swivelled round to the right to face me. Immediately, my feet gave way beneath me and I fell backwards to the ground but my eyes remained locked on the moving statue. The mermaid's lips pursed together to form a faint smile and the same voice uttered the words, "Helena thank goodness you heeded my warning! Those inviting berries are poisonous." Unable to move I sat speechless as the whole statue began to twist and move, ending with the tail flapping up and down.

Totally transfixed, I watched as the smiling lips opened again to speak. "Helena please do not be afraid, allow me to introduce myself. I am the goddess Freya. I have closely been watching your plight on this ruthless island, biding my time, waiting for the opportunity to help you. In return, you can help me seek my revenge against your cruel tormentor. But first," her voice softened as she looked down at me, "I would very much like to heal your wounds to your legs and arms. You will need all your strength to complete this undertaking." With this, I rose to my knees accompanied by an overwhelming desire to close my eyes. I felt a warm sensation start at my head, increasing with intensity as it slowly progressed down my body. It seemed to pause over my right knee, the warm sensation became almost burning in nature before gradually easing off again as it continued its journey through my body. I pictured a white beam of light flowing from my head and spreading throughout my body. Once it finally reached my toes it suddenly disappeared and my eyes fluttered open again. The statue was still smiling at me as I looked down at my limbs; amazingly all my cuts and grazes had disappeared. My knee no longer throbbed and my head felt fully alert.

Thankful but puzzled, I stared up at the statue unable to put into words what I had just experienced. "Helena, I hope you feel much better," the goddess Freya pointed a stone hand towards the foot of the statue before continuing, "Now for some sustenance." My gaze moved down to the stone fishes, their open mouths started to gurgle and splutter like an old tap. I watched astonished as water started to flow from their marble mouths into the parched dry pool below. Wasting no time, I went to stand up, half expecting my knee to give way, I paused but was pleasantly surprised when it took my weight easily. Five steps later my hands were submerged in the crystal-clear water as I splashed it over my face and tired body. Cupping my hands, I channelled the exquisite elixir into my welcoming mouth. Fully refreshed I sat on the edge of the stone circular pool and waited for the voice of Freya to continue.

"Sorry to scare you Helena but I had to react quickly if I was to stop you from eating those dreadful berries. For future reference, behind the back of the church, you will find some red cherry-like berries which should satisfy your hunger. I know you must have lots of questions for me but unfortunately, my time is precious. Channelling all my power this way, so I can communicate with you can leave me temporarily vulnerable. At all costs, I must avoid Loki finding out who I am."

Finding my voice at last, I managed to ask, "Who is Loki?"
The face of the mermaid grimaced slightly, then Freya replied, "Loki, he is a God who was imprisoned on this island many years ago as punishment by

Odin for tricking his son Hodur into killing his other son Baldur. My own grievance against Loki involved an enchanted Brisling necklace which bewitched me into betraying my beloved husband Odur. Ashamed, I used magic to keep the necklace secret but Loki is a shapeshifter. He turned himself into a fly and was able to find a way into my chamber and take the necklace. Armed with this evidence, he told my husband who was heartbroken and left me. I have spent many years searching for my husband to win his forgiveness. During my wandering, I heard whispers about the island and although Loki couldn't leave, his magic power was growing stronger. Over time Loki had become able to influence unsuspecting travellers to the island, where he would feed off their fear and become more powerful, hoping to one day free himself from his island prison. Worried that these whisperings could have some truth I was able to eventually locate the island and find a way to overcome the protective field around it so I could monitor what Loki was getting up to. However, I am unable to appear in my true form but I can possess and take control of non-living objects on the island."

Freya paused briefly; the mermaid's head moved forward so its eyes were fully fixed on mine. Lowering her voice slightly Freya continued, "I know Loki has a soft spot for you. He is acting out of character and has saved you numerous times. He is, taking his time with you, playing games then seeing how you react. I..."

Quickly I interrupted her, "I remember, Serena said the exact same thing to me. I don't understand..."

"Oh yes, poor Serena, I know her sad story. She has been on this forsaken island for many years. When she first arrived on this island, she was human. She has witnessed with her own eyes what games Loki likes to play to amuse himself and while away the time."

Panic mixed with realisation bubbled up in my throat. Suddenly, I felt everything was becoming clearer. I now had great sympathy for Serena and what she must have endured. My next question came tumbling out... "Will I become a harpy too?"

"Not if I can help it!" Freya replied. "Besides, Loki likes to take his time, he enjoys chasing or tormenting his victim rather than revealing his true intent straight away. However, with you, he has demonstrated quite a degree of concern and compassion. Without a doubt, he has a soft spot for you so I need you to use it to get closer to him in order to enact my revenge."

Letting out a deep sigh, I asked, "What do you need me to do?"

"You must continue to the golden temple on the other side of the island. Your task will be perilous however you can ask for my help three times. Deep inside the walls, you must find a hidden room. There you will find..."

The same pair of eyes from the previous day watched, out of sight. Curious to learn who was making the mermaid statue move, she yearned to get closer. However, her sisters' high-pitched screams in the distance brought the meeting below to an abrupt end before she had time to find out more. Quickly, she took off to intercept her sisters and slow them down.

"I'm sorry Helena but my time has run out. Please remember don't trust anyone on this island or tell anyone about me. It is our secret."

I stood up. My arms reached out pleadingly towards the statue. "Please don't go, I have so many questions. What do you want me to find? Where is Dan? Please tell me he is still alive and searching for me on the island." Tears started to trickle down my face at the mention of his name.

"Helena it's too late! They are here!" Freya shouted. I heard a familiar shrill screech from above. I did not need to look up. I froze. Freya screamed, "Helena please stand absolutely, still. Close your eyes tightly, count to 10 slowly...open them and walk away carefully. Trust me Helena..." her voice faded away.

I stood frozen to the spot; eyes welded together. I felt the air rush past my face and I sensed the vibration on the ground of their feet as they landed next to me. I thought I felt a feather brush against my nose. I continued to count slowly, 2, 3 ... then I heard them speak. "Serena, you were near the church did you see someone standing by this statue? I was certain it was her."

4, 5 ... "I heard your cry Patricia but didn't see anyone. Besides, I was looking out towards the sea in the wrong direction," replied Serena.

6, 7 ... I heard one of the harpies move towards the fountain. "That's odd; I often stop and look at the mermaid statue. I'm sure her face was always turned more to the left. It's now facing straight at me with her mouth open. Look Serena there is water at the bottom too!"

8... "I agree Patricia, this statue has changed slightly. Perhaps, Loki has been playing one of his games with us?"

"Maybe you are right Serena, but why would he do this?"

9, 10...Was it safe to open my eyes? Would I give way my location? The temptation was too great. Somehow, I was invisible to the harpies. It was too good an opportunity to miss, to see them up close. Slowly, I opened one eye followed by the other. My focus was slightly fuzzy. I stared at the statue; yes, Serena's sister was correct. The face was different.

My heart beat faster as Serena took a step backwards; we were barely separated by a hand's width. All the hairs on my body stood on end. My heart was beating so fast I was certain Serena would have heard it. At the same time being so close to her, I marvelled at the creature which was both human and beast. I could not take my eyes off her long glowing auburn locks. Her feathered wings reflected the golden hues of the sunset. The colours seemed to bounce off them in all directions. Returning to her face, her profile seemed softened giving me the chance to glimpse her true beauty. My gaze moved down to the sharp talons on her feet, reminding me of the beast she had become. A single tear slowly ran down my cheek but I was uncertain why. Did I pity her or was this to be my fate too?

Suddenly, Freya's words came back to me. I had stayed too long; I was supposed to move away after the count of 10. Taking a deep breath, I carefully took a step backwards followed by another. Becoming more confident, I increased my stride, but in my haste, I forgot to check where my next step would be placed. Caught off guard, my foot wobbled against a loose rock. I tried to steady myself but let out a slight whimper before I could bring my hand up against my mouth. Immediately, both harpies turned in my direction and their faces transformed into the hideous beasts they had become. Petrified, I tried not to scream, placing both hands over my mouth. Serena hesitated then took two steps forward. I could do nothing as her outstretched wing brushed against my shoulder. I watched as her eyes widened in realisation and seemed to look straight at mine. Then her face relaxed slightly and she turned to her sister and said, "Patricia there is no one here. Let's leave this place and rejoin our sisters."

Her sister nodded and together they took off, upwards. I felt the whoosh of air against my face. I saw Serena hover above me and look down at the place where I stood. She looked intently at me and seemed to wave knowingly before rejoining her sister higher in the sky. Why didn't she give me away? Pondering this, I made my way quickly to the safety of the church as I did not know how long my invisibility would last. Also, although Freya had healed my wounds, I still felt incredibly weak and tired. I longed to rest my head on the comfy cushions in the church.

Chapter 12

Meanwhile, Dan had already climbed up to the cave entrance. Just inside he noticed a pile of very old leaves. Turning back, he saw George and Dimitri lingering by the pool. He wished they would both hurry up and join him. Glancing up at the top of the waterfall, he desperately hoped what he thought he had seen had been a trick of the light.

George looked over at Dan staring down at them from the cave ledge and sensed his concern. Hurrying Dimitri up, they both made their way towards him.

Feeling happier, Dan explored a little deeper into the cave. On the left, it started to narrow considerably. He squeezed through a bit further. Remembering the matches in his pocket, he lit one and thrust his arm through the gap. To his surprise, it lit up a hidden chamber more than adequate for the three of them. Beckoning to George and Dimitri to follow him, they picked up their rucksacks and squeezed through into the inner chamber.

Exhausted, they all sat down on the hard, murky floor. Darkness surrounded them now except for a whisper of moonlight penetrating through the narrow gap. Dimitri let out a deep sigh and turned to Dan, "Thank you so very much for saving me. It was getting dark and I was in such a hurry to make my way down the waterfall, that I misjudged my footing and slipped several feet. I tried to cling onto a ledge but I found myself slipping further. Somehow, I managed to grab some sort of plant root but by then I had no strength left to haul myself back up. Looking down, I spotted both of you and cried out for help. In my panic, I didn't realise it was you, George, until you got closer. I'm so grateful to you both."

THE ISLAND BECOMES YOU

Dan replied, "It was very lucky we hadn't already entered the cave as your cries would have been muffled and we may not have reached you in time." He had really wanted to say the words 'very convenient' instead of lucky. Something did not seem quite right about this meeting. It appeared a little too staged.

Using another match, Dan lit up the cave chamber briefly so he could look through his rucksack for a snack and drink to share with everyone. Passing a handful of fruit to George and Dimitri his eyes noticed something drawn above their heads on the wall. Standing up he moved nearer and exclaimed, "Look at these drawings. These winged creatures must be the harpies you talk about and what is this huge fish-like creature in the water?"

Dan was about to light another match when George stopped him in his tracks. "Dan, it can wait until morning. Please don't waste any more matches. It's obvious, someone else has sought shelter here before us and decided to leave a reminder of their experiences on this island to act as a warning perhaps."

Dan put the matches back in his pocket, wondering why George had stopped him so abruptly from lighting another match. He took a handful of berries from his rucksack. Trying to get comfortable, he leaned back against the cool cave wall and thought about the last picture. Thinking of water, he immediately recalled the image of the remains of the battered yellow dinghy. Did Helena encounter this creature as she made her way to the island? Closing his eyes, he tried to dismiss this painful thought from his head.

Dimitri interrupted the uncomfortable silence. "I wish someone had shown us these pictures before we came to this island." Both George and Dan turned towards him in the darkness and quietly agreed. "We must be thankful that fate has brought us back together so we can face whatever battles lie ahead until we finally escape from this cruel island."

George sighed, "Yes fate has played her part but I too am responsible for bringing you both to the island. I feel guilty for leaving a trail for you to follow Dan and ..." pausing he looked towards Dimitri and said, "I'm sorry my friend that I was unable to hold on longer when the harpies took you. Please tell me what happened after I let go?"

"George please don't feel too bad about what happened. You tried your best to save me. I remember seeing you fall heavily to the ground. I watched helplessly as you didn't get up. Gradually, you became smaller and smaller; a mere dot as I rose higher and higher into the sky. I was absolutely petrified the harpies would let go of me at any time and tried to prepare myself. They took me towards the mountain. I caught a glimpse of a golden building in the distance before I blacked out – I was so scared.

I woke up with a start, I expected to be still flying up in the sky but I felt rough gravel on my face and under my hands. I was lying on the ground inside a huge, white-walled arena. In front of me was a golden stand with a raised seating area. A tall man with long dark hair, wearing a white robe, trimmed with gold sat on some sort of throne. He had a golden staff in one hand and raised it in the air. A chorus of cheers transcended around the arena. Disorientated, I struggled to get up. Then I realised my hands were chained. The cheers were quickly replaced by silence, I realised the dark-haired man had stood up.

He began to speak; I was not sure I completely understood what he was saying. I heard the words "Two will die and one will live – you will decide their fate…" Gradually, it dawned on me what he meant. Standing next to me were my two chained companions. Both looked utterly scared, their eyes darting frantically around the arena, trying desperately to make some sense of what was happening. We didn't have long to wait! A low rumbling sound came from the direction of two massive, golden gates. The ground began to shake. I tried to stand again, my comrades drew closer and we supported each other. All eyes including ours were now focused on the gates which were at least twenty feet tall by twelve feet wide. I could not have foretold what happened next. I could not believe what I saw. Suddenly, an enormous hairy fist holding a giant wooden mallet protruded from the gap in the golden gates. I was mesmerised and could not look away. A tremendous roar echoed around the arena. Everyone started clapping and cheering. The leader on the throne looked down at us and said, "Wits not brawn will overcome your mighty assailant if you have a chance to use them!" Smiling he turned back to the crowd in the arena and shouted, "Let the game of cat and mouse begin." A deafening din of cheers and clapping erupted in response.

I watched in total disbelief as the golden gates swung open and I could now see our assailant standing there. I had imagined the creature to be a giant but I wasn't prepared for how ugly and gruesome it was. I think the best description would be a hideous ogre. It had one large bulbous eye and a smaller beady one. Its face was leathery with huge creases and its sloping mouth opened in a grimace revealing crooked, jagged teeth. The smell of rotting flesh still trapped between its teeth added to the vile stench from its breath as it bellowed in our direction. I nearly passed out from shock. As it took another step forward, I could see it was dragging a length of rusty chain dotted with skulls belonging to its previous unfortunate victims.

    I desperately wanted to run and hide but my feet were frozen to the spot. All I could do was meekly watch as it waved an angry fist at the spectators before fixing its bulbous eye on us. One of my comrades let go of my arm and quickly ran towards the wall below the spectators. He attempted to climb the wall using any footholds he could find. I willed him on to succeed but he kept slipping down. The ogre let out another roar and changed direction, bearing down on him. I watched powerless but somehow, he managed to hoist himself up to the top of the wall and clung on for dear life. He pleaded with a spectator who looked like a dwarf to help him but the creature just laughed and tried to prize his hands off the wall. Meanwhile, the ogre was closing in fast. My comrade twisted around to check how far away he was. In slow motion, I watched as the ogre plucked him off the wall as if he was a ripe fruit. As the ogre played with him, dangling him by one leg, he seemed bemused by his endless screams and held him nearer to his cauliflower-shaped ear. Then abruptly, he lowered him into his lopsided mouth and chomped him in half. Grinning the ogre spat out the poor man's legs which came to rest just in front of us – still twitching. A thunderous cheer erupted from the arena, everyone was standing and clapping. Horrified and bewildered by what I had just witnessed I turned towards my other comrade who was shaking his head and pointing at what was left of his friend. He looked at me and muttered, "I'm not waiting to be next," and started to run towards the back of the arena. I shouted after him to keep still but to no avail. The ogre roared past me towards his next victim.

    Realising the ogre's sight must be poor, I took advantage of the situation and slowly backed towards the open golden gates. Terrified I witnessed the ogre catch up with my comrade as he cowered in the far corner of the arena. As the ogre towered in front of him, he fell to his knees and pleaded for his life. Showing no mercy, the ogre bent down to pick up his rusty skull chain and encircled it twice around his torso. Then the ogre dragged my comrade, still pleading for his life, towards him. Grabbing each of his limbs, one at a time, the ogre proceeded to rip them from his body and crunched them in his mouth. Unwrapping the chain from the lifeless torso he picked it up and roared as he held it aloft. The crowd roared back their approval as he tossed the torso to one side and stamped on it.

By now I was a few feet away from the gates. I stopped and sank slowly to the ground. The ogre turned to face me – sniffing the air. A spectator threw a rock in my direction. Immediately, the ogre started pounding towards me. Picking up the rock I threw it as hard as I could towards the other side of the arena. The ogre stopped in his tracks, turned, and changed direction towards where the rock fell while I slipped quietly through the gates.

A burly guard who looked like a bear was waiting for me in the shadows. He grabbed me and pinned me to the floor. "You've escaped one hell for another" he jeered. With that, he yanked me up by the scruff of the neck and dragged me back into the arena. The man on the throne stood up, pointed his golden staff at the ogre who meekly hung his head and walked back towards the gates. Just before he reached them, he glanced back in my direction before disappearing through the gates.

My attention returned to the leader who held my life in his hand. Addressing his audience, he said, "We have a winner. Here is your prize." He then held up his golden staff and pointed it in my direction. At that moment, the whole arena fell silent and I could clearly hear my heart beating. I waited for him to continue but he was interrupted by a dwarf who whispered something in his ear. Afterwards, his whole stance changed. He seemed very preoccupied with his thoughts. Finally, turning his attention back to me he commanded, "Take him to the cells below. I will deal with him later." Then he abruptly left the arena.

The guard turned to me and said, "It appears your fate is yet to be sealed." Roughly, he frogmarched me back towards the golden gates and down some well-worn steps. I was extremely scared and prayed I didn't come face-to-face with the vile ogre again. En route to my new home, we passed a chamber scattered with the remains of human and animal bones. The ogre sat with his back to me and appeared very subdued. I was very relieved once we had gone past. I wondered why the ogre obediently remained in his chamber when he could so easily overpower any of the guards.

THE ISLAND BECOMES YOU

I stayed in my cell for many months, perhaps years, the ruler had obviously forgotten about me. Every day a young boy would bring me bread, water and sometimes fruit. I don't know how I survived for so long, except that I never gave up hope of escaping one day. The opportunity came in the form of another poor soul's encounter with the ogre. I heard cheering and rumblings above me. When it was over the guard brought down food and wine from the celebrations. Afterwards, he quickly fell asleep and his snoring vibrated around my cell. Sometime later he lost his balance and rolled off his stone seat onto the floor but continued snoring. However, his keys had become dislodged in the process and conveniently rolled within arm's reach of my cell. I managed to creep past the guard plus another slumped near the gate in an alcoholic stupor too. Being so thin, I easily crawled under the gap at the bottom of the gates. Although it was dark, I was able to see my way using the moonlight and managed to scale the walls of the arena. Once at the top I paused and looked back down at the arena and remembered the two poor souls who lost their lives that day enabling me to survive. I found some steps out of the arena and climbed over several other walls and buildings until I reached an ornate courtyard with golden statues. Beyond this was one final wall then freedom.

I spent several days hiding during the night inside rocky mounds and an old abandoned church. I travelled through the day as much as possible. Sometimes overhead, I heard the screech of the harpies but managed to lay low. However, upon reaching the edge of the mountain I realised I was stuck - there was no way I could climb down such a sheer drop. In the end, I sat down and cried, everything seemed so hopeless. I remember picking up a rock and throwing it down in despair but to my surprise, it hit the ground and disappeared. Intrigued, I got up and investigated further. Suddenly, the ground gave way and I fell about five feet onto a platform. Bewildered I got up and looked around. I was in some sort of underground cave, there were steps leading further down into a huge cavern filled with walls of glittering gems. Carefully, I made my way to another ledge lower down using rope from a broken lift. Once safely on this ledge, there were several steps leading down to another platform, followed by more steps and another platform and so on until I finally reached the bottom. A door led me back outside and I journeyed for a couple of days until I found the waterfall and the rest you know."

George sighed deeply, "My word what a story. I'm so sorry about your two companions but I'm so thankful you managed to survive so we could be reunited again. I just wish our story could have a happy ending once and for all." Looking sadly across at Dan's sorrowful face, lit up slightly by the moonlight, he did not have to explain what he meant by those words.

Choosing to ignore the melancholy look that passed between them Dimitri decided to probe further. Turning to Dan he asked, "Tell me, how did you come to this island and did you come alone?" The word 'alone' seemed to splinter deep inside Dan's heart. He tried to shield his thoughts from Dimitri but his face was an open book. No words came, all he could do was shake his head slowly and turn away to hide the tears forming in his eyes.

George spoke for him. "Dimitri, they found my old journal which was left in a fishing boat and returned it to my wife and son. It was passed to Dan after his father died and he managed to piece together the clues like a jigsaw puzzle until eventually they led him here." Pausing he looked back at Dan before continuing, "Dan didn't come to the island alone. He brought his girlfriend Helena. Being too eager he decided to explore the island alone while she slept. Unfortunately, she awoke before he returned and used a dinghy to make her way from their boat to the island." Taking a deep breath, he hesitated then said, "We found the remains of the washed-up, yellow dinghy on the beach but there was no sign of Helena so we were left fearing the worse."

Understanding his pain now, Dimitri focused on Dan as he spoke, "There is still hope. You never found her body. She may still be somewhere else on the island searching for you. Just remember, I made it back from an impossible situation."

Dan's heart leapt slightly, then he felt extremely guilty. He had never allowed himself to contemplate she was still alive. He had assumed she had drowned. Wiping a tear away, Dan forced a smile, at that moment a change occurred inside him. A very faint slither of hope had embedded itself in his heart. After all, he thought to himself, this island was full of surprises both good and bad. George witnessed the change in Dan too. However, he was annoyed with Dimitri for giving him this new hope. He could not have forgotten their terrible encounter with the sea serpent when they first arrived on the island. Surely Helena's fate must have become entwined with this evil, unmerciful creature. Seeking to change the subject George said, "At least we now know there is a way up the mountain and hopefully off this island"

"Yes, Dimitri, you will have to show us the entrance to the cave," Dan added with renewed interest.

Dimitri grabbed George's arm, "Didn't you listen to my story? Your plan is too risky. You mustn't venture up the mountain, a worse fate will befall you if you try."

Dan replied, "We have no other choice if we are to get the answers we strive for."

Still holding George's arm, Dimitri begged, "Please George, rethink what you are planning. I don't want to witness any more of my friends dying in front of me."

"It's alright Dimitri, it has been such a long day and everyone is exhausted. Let's all get some much-needed sleep and talk about it more in the morning," George calmly replied.

Releasing his grip, Dimitri nodded. Looking at Dan he said, "I am so very happy to have found you both." After hugging everyone he settled down to sleep.

Completely drained, Dan laid down too, resting his head on his rucksack. So many thoughts and questions whirled around his head. Perhaps he had been a bit too hasty to be wary of Dimitri and not completely believe his story. Maybe Helena was still alive. He hoped and prayed this was true and allowed himself to imagine kissing her soft lips again. Eventually, he succumbed to the desire to sleep and allowed it to penetrate his thoughts.

In the midst of a dream about Helena, Dan became aware of shouting. Opening his eyes, all he could see was the inky blackness of the cave chamber. Gradually, he made out the silhouette of the rocky walls and felt around for George and Dimitri who should have been lying next to him. Immediately, he realised he was alone. Hearing the shouts for help again he quickly got up, squeezed through the gap out of the chamber and made his way to the cave entrance. The shouts were much louder now, the pale moonlight lit up the pool and waterfall. He could clearly make out two figures shouting. It must be George and Dimitri. Why were they taking such a risk? They knew they should not be outside at night.

He started to make his way down, towards them when too late, he heard a high-pitched shriek. That could only mean one thing! Both figures looked upwards towards the sky, they both turned and tried to run towards Dan. He watched powerless as a huge bird-like creature swooped down and picked up Dimitri. As he was lifted off the ground, he screamed as the talons ripped into his shoulders. It was like history repeating itself as George leapt up to grab Dimitri's leg. Hovering a few feet above George, the harpy seemed to enjoy teasing him. A tug of war developed between them neither gaining any ground. Finding his legs, Dan started to run towards them. Willing himself to get there in time to save Dimitri. His eyes were fixed on George, who was now gradually being lifted off the ground. With a pounding heart, he made a lunge for George's leg but missed. Conveniently, the harpy lurched higher in the sky.

Dan yelled, "George let go before it's too late!" Before he could answer another harpy swooped down and wrestled with George until he was forced to let go of Dimitri's leg. Looking down at Dan, a pained expression on his face mouthed the word "Sorry" before he was hoisted high into the sky. Dan shouted "No" as he watched helplessly until both men disappeared over the top of the mountain then he sank to his knees and cried. Curling up in a ball he waited for a harpy to come back for him but no one came. He was all alone, Helena and now George too had been taken from him. It was only a matter of time before he succumbed to the same fate.

A pair of piercing, green eyes from the top of the waterfall watched Dan's dejected figure slowly get up and then make its way back to the safety of the cave. She wondered why he had ignored her warning earlier when she appeared to him while he was swimming. Still, it was his choice not to warn the others. Alas too late now, she sighed, extending her wings she took off after her sisters.

Chapter 13

With a heavy heart Dan returned to the cave where hours earlier all three men had been together. Why had they left the safety of the cave and what had they been arguing about? Laying down, he closed his eyes and tried to formulate a plan of action. After a while of fretful thinking, he realised he had no choice but to carry on towards the mountain and try to rescue them. Sadly, he was also aware, he was powerless to do anything until first light. In fact, the whole situation was a mess and realistically what could he achieve on his own? Any hope he had was fading fast; he was desperately trying to hold onto the last glimmer of it. Eventually, he gave into a restless sleep where he found himself replaying the scene of George and Dimitri being taken by the harpies over and over again. Each version always ended the same – he was always left alone. Finally, he watched helplessly in his dream as Helena was carried away by them too. This was the last straw. Crying out Helena's name he awoke, drenched in sweat with the awful realisation that it was not just a bad dream but a living nightmare.

Sitting up he looked around the chamber, there was just enough light from the gap to see all the drawings painted on the walls. He could now clearly see the creatures he had spotted from the previous evening. Now, one drawing of a man, in the centre with arrows fanning out from his head pointing to different animal heads and human heads caught his attention. He was holding a golden staff in his hand. It must be the leader Dimitri had described in the arena. Nearby was another drawing of a golden temple. Standing at the top of the temple was a beautiful woman with gold braided hair dressed in a white robe. She wore a brilliant, emerald necklace; a gold, heart-shaped ring adorned the middle finger of her right hand and her left hand held a golden key. His gaze continued downwards until it reached the picture of the huge sea serpent whose long tentacles appeared to encircle the island. As his eyes lingered on this creature a vivid picture of the remains of his yellow dinghy flashed into his mind. Perhaps Helena's fate was connected with this sea creature – tears started to well up in his eyes. The thought of her encountering this sea serpent all alone was unbearable to think of. He remembered George's reaction to the drawings, in particular the sea creature. Maybe he had been trying to protect Dan by not mentioning the existence of the creature when they were on the beach searching for Helena. Just then a small voice in his head reminded him what Dimitri had said about not finding her body, therefore he should not give up hope. Helena might still be alive. Deciding to hold on to that tiny seed of hope, planted last night, Dan looked across at his rucksack.

Spurred on, he got up and checked the contents and added extra provisions and water from George's rucksack. Remembering George's journal, he retrieved it from the front pocket. It was like being reunited with a lost friend as his fingers traced the familiar cracks on the aged, brown leather cover. He was tempted to sit down, open the journal and get completely absorbed in reading the spidery handwriting that filled its pages. However, sighing, he knew time was of the essence so he placed it gently in the inner pocket of his rucksack. Standing at the entrance of the chamber, he took one last look around. Only a few hours ago it had been filled with total amazement as Dimitri recounted his incredible story of survival. He could remember the group hug they all shared. It left him feeling determined to be reunited with them both at any cost. He had to believe he would succeed and eventually escape this island.

Making his way outside the cave it all looked so different in the morning light. His eyes searched out the top of the waterfall, looking for the outstretched limbs of the tree he had mistaken for a harpy. Hiding his eyes from the glare of the rising sun, he looked again. There was no sign of the tree there. His heart crumbled and he fell to his knees when he realised too late, he could have prevented what happened. If only he had warned George about what he thought he had seen.

Some time passed before he was able to collect his thoughts enough to focus on the task ahead of him. Returning his gaze to the spot where George had struggled to keep hold of Dimitri's leg, he noticed something glinting in the sunlight. Climbing down the rocks he half ran, half walked towards it. Picking up George's spectacles he examined them closely, although slightly scratched, luckily, they were still intact. Carefully, folding them up, he placed them next to George's old journal. Positioning his rucksack back over his shoulders he set off with grim determination towards the mountain.

Picking his way gingerly up the side of the waterfall – he decided to retrace Dimitri's path as close as possible. The only problem he foresaw was the lack of detail he had regarding the entrance inside the mountain. It was bound to be hidden and could take him hours or days to find it. He was now at the ridge where Dimitri had dangled precariously over the edge. Hauling one leg up followed by the other, he managed to clamber up onto it. Pausing for a moment while he sat down on the ridge, he looked down over the edge at the pool and back across to the safety of the cave. Blinking away a single tear, he got up and he quickly spotted the next foothold to aim for. The top of the waterfall was almost within his reach. He had to be careful as Dimitri had dislodged some loose rocks when he slipped, making it much harder for him to find a secure foothold. Several times, he placed his foot down only for sections of it to crumble away leaving him hanging by his arms while his feet scrambled to regain stability beneath him. Also, as he got nearer to the top, he had to contend with water splashing against him as the summit narrowed, causing the surface of the rocks to become much more slippery each time he stretched upwards to grip them. Breathing heavily, sweat pouring down his face, Dan was extremely thankful when he finally reached the top.

His eyes could not help but stare at the spot where the imaginary tree stood with open arms. Sighing deeply, he wished again, that he had acted on what he thought he had seen and not dismissed it so easily. Turning away, he knew he had to go on, there was no point going over what had or had not happened. It was in the past – too late to change it now. Sipping some water his attention now centred on the impressive mountain standing in front of him. Looking at the sun, high in the sky, he realised it had taken much longer to reach the top of the waterfall. He would have to quicken his pace if he was to reach the mountain before darkness.

Chapter 14

George winced as the claw of the talon pierced his skin. The harpy strengthened her grip on his shoulders as she carried him higher into the night sky. Looking below, he could just make out the solitary figure of Dan reduced to a mere speck on the landscape. Closing his eyes, he could clearly picture Dan's shocked face, pleading with him to let go of Dimitri's leg. He would be by Dan's side now, looking up at Dimitri if he had listened to his pleas. But in his heart of hearts, he knew he could never have let go. The guilt would have eaten away at him just like last time but much worse. Opening his melancholy eyes, he looked above at the huge, powerful feathered wings beating in unison. A chilly breeze began to penetrate his body with each flap as they brought him closer to the golden temple. Ahead of him, he could see Dimitri, his body hanging limply below the harpy's feet. George sighed, he felt so sorry for his friend. After all, Dimitri had managed to escape his prison and had tasted freedom only for it to be cruelly taken from him again. He was right back where he started but this time, he knew what lay in wait for him.

With each beat of the wings above him George realised he had no choice but to surrender to his fate too. For so long now, he had managed to evade the clutches of the harpies but his luck had run out. Finally, it was time for all his questions about the island to be answered – at a price though! With a heavy heart, he wondered if he would ever see Dan again. Making the most of the precious minutes he had left he absorbed the beauty of the stars twinkling above him and tried to hold onto that memory.

Eventually, the temple loomed ahead of him and the moonlight reflected off the golden tones. Surrounding it was an almost impenetrable, stone wall which the harpies effortlessly carried him over. He caught quick glimpses of ornate statues framing a courtyard just like Dimitri had described. Further on were several buildings and in the centre, the huge golden temple dominated his view. Beside it was the walled arena with the foreboding golden gates. At this point, the harpies hovered and then began to descend quickly. The ground rushed up to meet him. George was not prepared for the abrupt moment his feet contacted the ground. At the same time, the harpy released her grip on his shoulder and his legs buckled underneath him. On all fours, he looked over at Dimitri who seemed equally dazed and bewildered. George began to crawl over to him; the ground was rough and uneven beneath his hands and knees. Dimitri also began to make his way slowly towards him but seemed to be dragging his left leg behind him.

A loud creaking noise behind them stopped them in their tracks. Dimitri's face froze with shock as he looked towards the gates. George's heart pounded as he watched the golden gates gradually open. Fear swamped his body as his eyes frantically searched the arena for signs of life. He expected groups of spectators to appear and start cheering but the arena was eerily silent. At last, two burly figures appeared at the gates followed closely by a peel of high-pitched laughter which echoed around the arena. The laughter subsided and the harpies moved forward and beckoned the two figures to come closer. Looming over Dimitri and George, the biggest harpy screeched, "Stand up!" Obediently, without thinking George stood up and walked slowly towards Dimitri. Supporting his friend, he helped him stand.

The other harpy with raven hair, now cruelly spoke, "Enjoy your last night for tomorrow you will face the master." Dimitri looked up at him and George could see tears were silently forming in his eyes. Holding him tighter, George tried to reassure him.

The two burly, bear-like guards had now reached them. George could see their hairy heads, narrow eyes and wrinkly noses in the moonlight. They towered over them, wearing a black body uniform and each held chains with wrist and ankle cuffs. Stepping forward the first guard motioned Dimitri towards him, saying as he jangled the chain, "You won't be escaping this time!" Dimitri shared a final apologetic look at George, lowered his head and took a step forward but stumbled. George reached out to help him but Dimitri shook his head. Pausing to regain his balance, he hesitated before he moved towards the guard but again his bad leg buckled underneath him.

George shouted in desperation, "Please, let me help him to his cell." Looking back at the harpies he added, "There is no chance of either of us escaping." The guard moved his paw to his chin and contemplated an answer.

Interrupting the silence, the raven-haired harpy shrieked, "Hurry up guard, we haven't got all night!" With that she callously took off, grabbed Dimitri roughly by the shoulder and deposited him outside the golden gates. Fearing the other harpy would grab him too, a shocked George began to walk briskly towards his friend, closely followed by the guards who continued to swing their chains threateningly. Reaching his friend, George again helped him to his feet and they both staggered through the gap in the gates. Once on the other side, George heard the raven-haired harpy say to her sister, "There are still two humans remaining on the island. Our master has plans for them. We must not interfere at our peril!"

Nodding the other harpy answered, "I agree with what you are saying but your warning is better aimed at our youngest sister. You know how defiant she can be. Come, let us go and find her." Together they stretched out their wings and leapt up into the sky. George caught the cooling breeze on his face as they circled once above the gates before disappearing into the night. He smiled inwardly, there was still hope for Dan. Helena must be the second human the harpy was referring to. Somewhere on this cursive island, she was still alive!

One of the guards moved ahead of them, blocking their way. Grinning, revealing two sets of sharp crooked teeth, he said, "Dimitri, it's time you became reacquainted with your cell. I hope you have warned your friend what the facilities are like here." Stepping forward the guard beckoned to him to stretch his arms out so he could fit the wrist chains he was carrying.

George immediately raised his free arm to protest, "Surely, the chains can wait until he reaches his cell. He can barely walk and the chains will only hinder his descent further."

Wavering, the guard looked down at Dimitri's swollen ankle and then across at the other guard behind them. The second guard joined his colleague, bending down he roughly prodded Dimitri's ankle making him cry out in pain. George cried in disbelief, "Was that really necessary?"

The guard looked up at him, let out a low growl then straightened up and laughed out loud. "Dimitri, your friend has a lot to learn." Then the guard roughly placed the iron cuffs around Dimitri's wrists, adding "You only have yourself to blame. Besides you can't delay your fate forever, it eventually catches up with you."

Dimitri half smiled at George and barely managed to whisper, "I'm okay," before the same guard quickly knelt down and locked the other iron chain around George's ankles.

Trying not to wince as the coarse iron grazed his skin, George kept both eyes fixed on the guard who was finding the whole situation very amusing. Eventually, he stopped laughing and added, "I hope you approve of my compromise. Now, enough time has been wasted, follow me to your cells."

Resigning themselves to their fate, both men shuffled forward. Leaning heavily on George's shoulder, Dimitri made his way slowly down the worn marble steps. Shadows from the lit torches danced abruptly across their path moving in unison with the jangle of their chains. Approaching a tight bend, Dimitri hesitated for a moment before adjusting the angle of his good foot to fit the narrowing step. George steadied himself too, expecting Dimitri to lose his footing but he did not. His left hand which was pressed firmly against the clammy wall for balance now picked up a slight vibration. Rounding the tight corner, he noticed the vibration seemed to get stronger as he felt along the passageway. Gradually, he became aware of a faint rumbling noise. His ears strained to decipher the sound. Suddenly, a memory clicked into place and George realised what it must be. Further on the marble steps widened, leading to a platform. Dimitri paused here, glanced back at George, then pointed with a shaky finger to where the heavy snoring obviously originated from. George could not resist snatching a look further into the open chamber and he was not disappointed. In the pale moonlight, several piles of bones glinted back at him along with several human skulls attached to a rusty, spiky chain.

Eventually, they reached the bottom of the steps where another burly guard greeted them. "Welcome back Dimitri. I've missed your company. I see you've brought a friend with you this time." Pointing to the cell in front of him, he added, "See your cell is just as you left it!"

The guard following behind, now stepped forward and gruffly said, "It's time to say your goodbyes." Before they had a chance to say anything, the guard roughly grabbed George's shoulder and forced him to let go of

Dimitri. Helplessly, he watched as Dimitri shuffled into his cell and gratefully sat down on the raised hard wooden bed. He attempted an awkward smile at his friend as the guard removed his wrist chains and then closed the door of his cell. George returned the smile with tearful eyes. He wished with all his heart, that this was all just a bad dream and he would wake up back with his wife and young son.

    The same guard now gestured to the empty cell next to Dimitri. George wiped a tear away and entered his cell. The guard bent down and removed his ankle irons. George automatically rubbed his sore ankles and looked around. He noted the damp, grey walls on three sides, a grim metal bucket sat in the corner and opposite a raised wooden slatted bed, barely wide enough to accommodate him. He listened as the bars of his cell greeted the lock on the wall. Strangely, he now felt slightly relieved, knowing this would probably be the last night he would be a prisoner on this island. At last, he would finally understand the purpose of the island's existence and his suffering would end. Lying down on the hard bed confirmed this, he realised how really tired he was. He had no fight left in him. At least he was not alone, his very dear friend Dimitri would be there with him at the end. As if on cue, he heard Dimitri give him a reassuring knock on the wall, which he replied to before sleep beckoned. His whole body welcomed the chance to escape, albeit temporarily, from this hideous nightmare.

Chapter 15

Slowly, George opened his eyes. The sad, grey walls stared back at him. Sitting up he watched as a guard approached his cell and shoved a metal plate with a piece of dry bread and a cup of water through the small gap below the bars. To his surprise, George's stomach grumbled at the sight of it. Thanking the guard, who growled and nodded at him, George returned to his hard bed. Sitting down, he slowly ate the bread and contemplated how long he had left before being summoned to the arena.

After a while, he knocked on the wall to try to get Dimitri's attention. There was no reply, maybe he was still sleeping. Resting his head back down he closed his eyes again and allowed himself to dream of his beloved wife and son.

Abruptly, George was awoken and dragged away from the arms of his wife. The cell door was open and the guard stood by the entrance holding out leg and wrist chains. Without saying anything, the guard clasped the iron bands around George's ankles. Meekly, George held his arms out to allow them to be chained together too. Slowly, he stood up and shuffled out of his cell. Immediately, he glanced to his left but Dimitri's cell was completely empty. How could he have not heard Dimitri being removed from his cell? Shaking his head in despair, he asked the guard, "Where is my friend Dimitri?"

The guard laughed before replying, "He is no friend of yours. Today is all about you. It is time you finally meet your master and accept your fate. There is no escape from this island. Only death, but only if the master commands it."

In complete shock, George stammered, "B...b...but, I don't understand.

What has happened to Dimitri? Please tell me, who is this master?"

"Be patient, you will meet the master very soon." Grabbing his right arm, the guard led him slowly up the worn marble steps, past the ogre's chamber and towards the golden gates. This time he was not greeted by silence but a roaring crowd of spectators deafened his ears. Cheering and clapping accompanied George as he was led out into the arena. It must have been midday as the sun blinded his eyes. He tried to focus on the crowd and pinpoint where the man with the golden staff was standing. He was desperately trying to remember Dimitri's account of what happened to him in the arena. Sure enough, the glint and reflection of the sun betrayed the position of the golden staff and the man it belonged to.

The guard pushed George forward and he stumbled falling onto his knees. The crowd stopped cheering and started to laugh. Casting his eyes around the arena George could see many strange faces staring back at him. Refocusing his attention back at the top of the arena. He zoomed in on the six towering harpies standing behind the white-robed, dark-haired man who sat on his throne holding his magnificent, golden staff. In the centre, stood a flame-haired harpy whose eyes seemed to follow his every move. He remembered, that she stood out on the beach when he first encountered them on the island. Today though, she looked almost beautiful. Her features were no longer wizened and pointed. She was in human form. Only her body exposed the creature she now was. As he scanned the crowd in more detail, he spotted dwarfs, huge brightly coloured insects and strange human-like animals. He even thought that he saw a few green bushes sitting at the end of the rows!

The sound of a loud gong abruptly pulled his attention back to the dark-haired man in the white robe edged with gold. Absolute silence radiated around the arena as he watched the man stand up, ready to address his audience. George felt his breaths become shorter as he tried to gulp in more oxygen to match his heart pumping more rapidly in anticipation of what the man was about to say. Also, a grim foreboding descended over him as he tried to prepare himself for the inevitability of what was going to happen next. At last, the deadly silence was broken.

"Welcome everyone. It has been a while since we have all gathered here again. Let me introduce you all to George Layton, a well-known adventurer in his time. I allowed him to live amongst us for years until recently when to my dismay, he and another began to disrupt the harmony of this island." Pausing briefly, he pointed over to the end of the row on his left-hand side where unmistakably two evergreen bushes were sat. "I hope you have recovered from the horrendous experience of seeing your fellow bushes subjected to such cruelty. I believe your chief is gradually growing back some of his limbs that were destroyed in the fire?"

In utter disbelief, George watched as both bushes appeared to nod in reply. Continuing the man said, "It hurts me deeply when guests to our island disrespect our hospitality and they have no regard for other creatures' feelings. Therefore, I feel it's my duty to make sure George is punished for his actions."

Still in shock, George kept his gaze on him as he commandingly made his way down the steep steps and entered the arena. He was closely followed by two of the raven-haired harpies. Standing before the crowd, he raised his golden staff in defiance and brought it crashing down onto the dry gravel ground. George felt the tremor radiate from the staff towards him. Even so, he was not prepared for the full force which hit him. Immediately, it knocked him off balance and he fell to the ground. Using his right hand to steady himself he remained on both knees as he listened to the whole arena erupt with cheers.

George was trying desperately to take it all in, the atmosphere was electric. He realised the golden staff must be the key to the man's power over everything on the island. However, his instinct to survive was still prevalent as he frantically scanned the arena looking at every exit but to his dismay, all were blocked by guards. Sensing he was being scrutinised he returned his gaze to the man holding all the power in his hand. Sure enough, his gaze was fixed only on George. A slim smile appeared on the man's lips and George realised in that instant the man knew what he was thinking and that it was futile.

So many questions revolved around inside George's head. Who was this powerful man? What else could the staff do? How come everyone was under his spell? What was the purpose of this island? What had happened to his friend Dimitri? The questions were endless, his head was starting to hurt. He felt the burden of time lost on this forsaken island weighing down on him, squishing any remaining hope he had of seeing Dan again or finally getting off this island. He wished so much that he had never pursued the urge to find this island so vigorously. If only, he had allowed himself to give up all thoughts of finding it. He could have lived out his final days being close to his family, his darling wife and son. Closing his eyes, he could almost feel them nearby – perhaps giving in to his fate would finally allow him to be with them again.

Suddenly, the deafening cheers and jeers were silent. "Stand George Layton," commanded the man. Tears blinded George's eyes as he tried to open them and focus on the man who stood before him in his golden-edged robe. A slight breeze in the arena gently moved the long, dark curly hair that hid most of the man's face revealing a chiselled stern expression. George could clearly see his dark blue eyes staring back at him. His statue was over six feet. Raising the golden staff above him he bellowed, "George Layton, I command you to stand before me now and accept your fate!"

Instantly, the arena responded by taking a sharp intake of breath. George found himself swallowing hard. Clinging onto his last morsel of dignity, he chose to make a last stand on his own terms. With all his willpower remaining he rose to face the man who would decide his future. Softening his voice slightly, the man continued, "George Layton, do you have anything to say?"

Taking a deep breath, George replied, "All my actions were in self-defence or to protect my great-grandson. Do what punishment you deem fit for me but please spare my friend, Dimitri, my great-grandson and if she is still alive, Helena."

Stunned, George watched as the man stared blankly at him and then roared with laughter. Turning to the crowd he blurted out, "He dares to tell me what to do!" The crowd answered with more laughter. Moments passed then the man waved his staff and silence returned to the stadium.

Shaking his head, he carried on, "You still don't know who I am?" Pausing for effect, his eyes narrowed and looked straight at George. "I am a God. I am the master of this island. My name is Loki."

The crowd started to cheer again but Loki waved his staff and cut them off. He moved closer to George and smiled cruelly as he spoke. "Your friend Dimitri pleaded for me to spare you too before he realised there was no escaping his fate. But I decided to show mercy and agreed not to harm you until you made a move against me. Therefore, your fate was sealed when you harmed one of our own." Again, he gestured towards the bushes to the left of him, now standing defiantly at the end of the row.

George looked down at the ground. So many questions in his head were clamouring together in a rush to get out. Who was this Loki God? He was certain it sounded familiar. Something triggered a memory regarding Norse legends. What power did Loki have over the island? What role did the golden staff play? Also, he did not remember Dimitri saying he had pleaded for George's life to be spared. Where was Dimitri now? Turning to look back at the golden gates he had come from, he squinted for any sign of Dimitri. Perhaps he had already been dealt with by Loki. But why hadn't he heard anything from his cell?

One single word, "Dimitri," uttered from Loki's lips instantly captured George's attention. Fully focused, he now concentrated on every word Loki was about to say next.

"Dimitri, step forward. I feel it is only fitting that you are the one who should prepare George for what is about to happen to him." The crowd was eerily silent as George looked for any movement in the arena. But there was none. His eyes returned to Loki who had been watching him intently with a huge smirk on his lips. Suddenly, this smirk was replaced with an eruption of mocking laughter which echoed around the arena before it seemed to stall in front of George.

"Oh George, I'm sorry Dimitri can't be with us today. I forgot ... he had a little run-in with an angry ogre and ended up becoming a lovely adornment to his fetching chain of skulls." George's mouth hung open in disbelief as he tried to comprehend what he was hearing.

Pretending to shake his head sadly, Loki added, "So sorry to disappoint you, but I didn't have the heart to tell you his true fate when we had our lovely reunion inside the cave with Dan and yourself. I couldn't bear to see the disappointment on your faces so I decided to be a bit resourceful with the truth and give you a happier outcome." Pausing, he then said thoughtfully, "The problem with humans is that you find hope so very hard to resist. Well, guess what, I'm about to obliterate yours completely today."

George found himself unable to react to what Loki was saying, apart from a shocked frozen expression on his face. "I'm getting the feeling George that you are still finding it hard to understand the reality of what I'm trying to tell you. Let me make it clearer for you."

At last, George finally understood as Loki changed himself into his dear friend Dimitri. "It was so lovely, catching up with you and meeting your great-grandson Dan. He smacks of foolhardiness and I daresay it won't be long before he is enlightened too. Shame he is broken-hearted about Helena though; she is far too good for him … so resourceful. Ahh, that is one encounter I'm very much looking forward to."

Finally, George managed to blurt out, "Helena is alive!"

"Oh yes, the beautiful Helena is very much alive and very well and before long will be joining us."

"Thank goodness she is safe. She survived the sea monster."

"George, George … always thinking of others. Don't you get it? I have the power to decide who survives or dies." Lowering his voice, Loki asked, "Aren't you a bit concerned about your own fate George? Perhaps you will be joining your friend Dimitri …"

Pausing Loki raised the golden staff high in the air and looked around the arena. The crowd responded with clapping and cheering. Bringing his staff down abruptly the arena instantly fell silent. "It is time George Layton. Your fate is in my hands. Now kneel before me and I might show some leniency," he ordered.

George remained standing, trying to blink back the tears forming in his eyes. His dear friend Dimitri was dead. He wished he had never left his journal on the boat. Now he could be responsible for his great-grandson's death too. It was only a matter of time. Closing his eyes, he tried to seek comfort from picturing his wife and son again.

"George, I said kneel," shouted Loki. Before George could react, he felt a rough push from behind his legs which forced him to his knees. He winced as a fiery pain shot down his lower right leg. Trying to stand up again as a show of defiance only made the pain worse so he reluctantly remained where he was, peering up at Loki. Momentarily, his eyes were drawn back to the harpy with the fiery red hair. Her eyes were transfixed on him like everyone else but he thought he saw a fleeting glimpse of concern.

"That's much better. Thank you, Kenzie, my loyal guard for helping George make the right decision." Looking up at the crowd again, Loki raised both arms and shouted, "Are you ready for the punishment?" A loud cheer transcended down towards them in the arena. The noise was quite deafening, reaching a peak before slowly ebbing away as Loki lowered his arms.

George noticed Loki had tightened his grip on the staff and it almost seemed to glow. Both harpies moved closer to Loki covering his left and right flank. Slowly he raised the golden staff and pointed it at George.

JENNIFER BARSTOW

Chapter 16

Serena was watching intently as events played out in the arena. She remembered how she felt when she and her sisters stood before their master. She too had no idea what would happen to her until she watched in horror as one by one her sisters were transformed into the hideous, wizened winged creatures they were today. Cruelly, Loki left her to last and asked her again, "Why did you betray our love for each other?" But there was no going back, her heart was broken into too many pieces. She knew the truth when she looked into her ex-lover's eyes – all she saw was the blackness of his soul staring back. After all, he was responsible for her father's brutal death and many others. How could she pick up the pieces and continue loving this monster?

Looking at what had become of her beloved sisters all she could say in return was, "Our love didn't stand a chance once I discovered your trickery. It was all based on lies. Please I beg of you, spare my sisters this cruel fate. Direct your anger only at me. Turn me into one of these vile creatures. Spare them, they didn't betray you like I did."

Smiling, apologetically he said, "It's too late my love. Once changed I can't undo the transformation. So, you have a choice my love – join them or die. There is no mercy for them or you."

Tears began to stream down her face as she looked at each of her sisters' helpless expressions before fixing her gaze on Loki. Finding her inner strength, she chokingly replied, "I choose to be with my sisters."

Shrugging his shoulders Loki answered, "So be it," and pointed the glowing staff at her. Immediately, she felt her body twist and stretch. Looking down at her feet she watched in horror as three huge talons protruded from the front of her shoes and another at the back. Her arms began to feel very heavy as they transformed into two mighty feathered wings. Her clothes were ripped from her body as she grew in stature and width. Only her face felt unchanged. Looking down, her shredded clothes lay beside her a cruel reminder that she was once human. Her five sisters gathered around her, the pain and disbelief etched on their faces mirrored her own. Serena stared at her feet and feathered legs. She kept hoping it was all a dream and she would awake and everything would be as it was.

Her sister Rebecca tried to comfort her but from her lips came a deafening high-pitched screech. Serena was experiencing a roller-coaster of emotions before turning her attention back to Loki and settling for anger. As she moved towards Loki, she felt her face harden and stretch. Her ears tingled as they sprouted into a point. She wanted desperately to avenge her sisters with all her might. Moving closer to Loki, almost within striking distance, she screeched and raised her right wing in the air. She was about to swipe him off the ground but halfway through the movement she was left frozen, rooted to the spot. The staff began to glow again. She felt a tightening around her throat and tried to cough. Her breath became laboured and slow. Pressure was building up in her lungs – she felt like she was going to explode. Her eyes were the only part of her body which could move. Using them she pleaded with Loki for mercy. In response, he just laughed, "Only now, far too late, do you realise just how powerful I am."

Serena sensed her sisters moving closer, either side of her. She watched them fall to the ground. Kneeling in front of Loki, Rebecca pleaded with him, "Please, please, release Serena from your deathly grip. In return, we will do whatever you ask."

Loki glared back in defiance at them all before lowering his staff. Serena dropped to the ground, coughing and spluttering as the air rushed back to her lungs. Her chest throbbed and her neck still burned from his grip. Softening his voice, Loki looked down at Serena and said, "Do you swear allegiance to me too, my love?" She felt his words choke her again. All she could manage to do was mouth the word "Yes" as a single tear trickled down her wrinkled cheek.

Suddenly, a dwarf stepped forward with a long, grey beard, pointy ears and beady eyes. He took out a long, black book and a silver pen. He began to read out their names in a hoarse gravelly voice, "Patricia, Diana, Rebecca,

Annette, Sophie and last of all Serena. Please stand before the master."

Still feeling extremely weak, Serena tried to stand but her new body felt strange and cumbersome. She could not find her balance so she fell to the floor again. Shaking his head, the dwarf paused and started shifting his small feet impatiently as he looked down at Serena. Quickly, her sisters Diana and Rebecca came to her aid and managed to use their wings to hoist her up. Serena found herself leaning heavily against them but she felt a little stronger having them so close.

Sighing the dwarf continued, "Now repeat this oath after me. I swear, I will honour and obey my master's every command without question. I will protect him with my life and obey the master's three rules." Pausing, he waited for the sisters to repeat these words. Afterwards, he added, "The three rules are: Never disobey the master's wishes they are the law. Never reveal the secrets of the island to any newcomers. Never try to leave the island." Trying to look sternly at the sisters the dwarf asked them, "Do you solemnly swear to abide by these rules?"

The sisters looked at each other for support before they answered together, "I do."

Serena smiled to herself as she remembered listening to the three rules. She had already broken two of them. It was only a matter of time before she broke all three.

A single scream of terror brought her back to reality. Her gaze focused on George in the arena. Loki was callously laughing as he pointed the glowing staff at him. George's face was contorted with pain and utter disbelief as he watched his limbs enlarge and thick coarse black hair sprouted from his skin. Sharp talons grew from his fingertips. His body doubled in length. A furry mane of hair cascaded down his chest and back as his shirt ripped apart. He felt his nose harden and stretch as it transformed into a long snout. Another scream passed from his lips as he reached up and felt two giant horns growing out of his head. Briefly, his tear-stained gaze met hers. She could feel his pain. Surprised, she realised a single tear had started to trickle down her cheek. Quickly, she nudged it away with her wing. She had not cried since she was changed, all emotion had been stripped from her until now. She realised the newcomers to the island had managed to penetrate her hardened shell. It was too late for George but maybe there was still time for her to help the others.

THE ISLAND BECOMES YOU

Every fibre of George's body ached, the searing pain during the transformation had nearly killed him. Now his body was racked with pools of intense pain and dull aches around it. He felt stronger and was filling up with an intense desire to kill Loki. Flexing the new muscles in his arms, he felt invigorated as his blood pumped through his body. All his senses were dramatically more acute, especially his eyesight. He started to feel invincible.

Loki was grinning at him obviously very pleased with himself. How desperately he wanted to knock that smile out of his face but he had to be patient, bide his time. He was not sure how well he could manoeuvre this new body and the pain he felt was still an obstacle.

"I hope you like your new body." Pausing briefly, he continued, "I'm afraid it's a one-way ticket. We don't do refunds here. Once transformed there's no going back."

In response, George took two faltering steps forward. Loki immediately raised his staff. "Just in case you get any revenge ideas," he laughed. George instantly felt a tightness around his neck. He went to hold his neck but found he could not move his arms. In fact, he could not move anything apart from his eyes. Pressure began building up in his lungs, he was fighting to breathe and his eyes felt like they were bulging out of their sockets, ready to pop. Blood started to trickle down his left nostril. George felt completely helpless in his grip. All thoughts of revenge disappeared – survival instincts kicked in. Unsteady on his hooved feet, he toppled over. He tried to scream out in pain as his head hit the ground with an extreme thud but no sound came from his mouth.

Loki stepped forward, bent down next to him and whispered. "I have big plans for you. Do not despair, you will learn in time that I am a fair master." With that, he raised his arms and pointed at the crowd who had been silent during the transformation. Suddenly, they came alive with cheers and nods of agreement. Bringing the staff down with a thud on the ground, he immediately released George from his paralysis. He was now aware of the rough gravel on the left side of his face digging into him. His eyes started weeping and his huge tongue lopped out of his mouth. Sprawled, out on the ground like this made him feel so vulnerable. Grunting sadly, he carefully, lifted his massive head off the ground. Slowly, he raised himself up to his knees and steadied himself before he finally forced himself to stand.

Movement in the crowd caught George's attention. He watched bewildered as a small, grey-haired dwarf walked carefully down the marble steps. Then he made his way across the arena, slightly limping, towards Loki. Holding a black notebook, he opened it up and proceeded to say, "George Layton repeat this oath after me." The dwarf paused to make sure he had George's full attention before continuing. "I swear, I will honour and obey my master's every command without question. I will protect him with my life and obey the three rules of the island on pain of death."

George tried to obediently repeat the words, pausing slightly at 'on pain of death.' He already felt he had died and hope was virtually gone. Only the thought of being able to save Dan, his beloved grandson lingered. In response, the dwarf looked at him strangely.

Gradually, George became aware of peals of laughter circulating around the arena. Loki raised his golden staff to silence them. "That's no way to welcome our newest member." Moving slightly closer to George he said, "It appears the beast is very strong in you and I'm afraid we can't understand your grunts and bellows. On this occasion, I will be perfectly happy for you just to nod and grunt in agreement with the oath."

The dwarf nodded at his master and waited for George to reply. Immediately, George felt himself go red with embarrassment, although no one else would have noticed. Lamely, he nodded and looked down at the ground.

Afterwards, the dwarf continued to read out the three rules of the island:
1. Never disobey the master's wishes they are the Law.
2. Never reveal the secrets of the island to new arrivals.
3. Never try to leave the island.

Lastly, he declared, "If you break any of these rules it will not only be yourself that suffers the consequences but anyone whom you care for on this island will also suffer." Peering over the edge of his black book, his beady eyes scrutinised George for a reaction as he said, "Do you agree to abide by the rules of the island?"

"I do," bellowed George. The dwarf was clearly unprepared for the deepness of his reply which caused him to lose his footing. Quickly, he tried to compose himself and recover his important-looking posture as he slowly closed his notebook. He bowed to his master before disappearing back into the crowd where he came from.

THE ISLAND BECOMES YOU

Smirking, Loki silenced the shrieks of delight from the crowd. "Let us welcome our newest addition to the island. George will serve as a magnificent Minotaur. I have decided that as he longs to be reunited with his great-grandson, he would best serve me by guarding the golden temple." George was strangely puzzled by this command to guard the temple and the reference to his great-grandson but he did not have to wait long for clarity. Loki's eyes narrowed as a sly smile crossed his lips and he added, "Just in case your great-grandson does make it to the golden temple you can make sure he doesn't come out alive. That is my wish and my wish is the law on this island." Pointing his golden staff at George, Loki shouted, "MY WISH IS ..."

George felt his heart collapse into pieces but he knew he had to reply or die. Still clinging to a glimmer of hope that maybe he could help his great-grandson if he bided his time, he grunted out the words, "The law."

Loki frowned, held his hand to his ear and said, "Can you repeat that please."

"THE LAW," George's grunted response thundered around the arena.

"Thank you," Loki smiled triumphantly.

Chapter 17

The rich, red, golden embers of the evening sun were just beginning to disappear as Dan reached the mountain. It stood impressively, in front of him, giant sedimentary and metamorphic rock welded together over thousands of years. From a distance, he had scanned the side of the mountain facing him, for any openings or ledges big enough for him to hide in safely during the night. One opening, a ledge a quarter of the way up, looked promising. As he got closer, he was surprised to see a rope made of knotted coconut leaves dangling down from the ledge. Time was running out so he decided he would climb up until he reached the rope. Looking at the ground below there was evidence of lots of displaced rocks, warning him to be careful during his ascent. Stopping to have a drink of water, he studied the surface, looking for good footholds. He noticed another smaller ledge just below where the rope ended. It was exactly what he was hoping for and he began to climb the rocky surface.

Loose rubble and rocks at the bottom did hinder him to start with as he struggled to find a solid foothold. Once he had bypassed these it became much easier. As he worked his way upwards towards the smaller ledge, he found his hands became sore and he acquired several grazes on his palms and fingers as he used them to haul himself up. He was nearly at the first ledge when he almost jumped and lost his footing briefly at the sound of a high-pitched screech. This was quickly followed by a whoosh of wind which alerted him to the presence of the circling harpies. Motivated by the noise he immediately hoisted himself up onto the ledge but in his haste, he accidentally, dislodged some loose stones. Holding his breath, he kept absolutely still and waited.

THE ISLAND BECOMES YOU

From high above him a pair of bright, green eyes noticed the slight movement on the narrow ledge below. She knew who it was and smiled to herself – he had managed to get further than she expected. Changing direction to the left abruptly, she led her sisters to the other side of the mountain.

Thankfully, Dan watched the harpies turn suddenly and head away in the opposite direction. Not wanting to risk another encounter he took advantage of his luck and quickly climbed up another two metres. Gingerly, he reached up and tugged at the dangling rope made from coconut leaves with his left hand. Testing it with his weight, he was glad it felt strong and secure. Letting go of the rock face with his right hand he proceeded to climb carefully up to the higher ledge. The final part of the climb seemed to take forever plus all his senses were on red alert in case the harpies returned. With huge relief he finally pulled himself onto the flat ledge, lying face down, he rested momentarily, trying to calm his beating heart before slowly standing up. Quickly, glancing back over the edge, it seemed much further up than he thought when looking up from the bottom of the mountain.

Daylight was fading fast so he headed to the shadowy corner on the left of the ledge and hoped it hid a big enough crevice for him to hide in. Sure enough, he was not disappointed. A large rock guarded the entrance which opened into a smaller chamber – quite ample for him to spend the night in comfortably. Placing his rucksack on the floor, he took out his water bottle and some berries. Once he had finished, he felt around in the semi-darkness for a clear area to lay down. Using his rucksack as a pillow, he welcomed sleep. His body was racked with exhaustion and badly needed time to re-energise itself. Dan felt some comfort that someone else must have slept here too before his eyes welded shut and sleep took over.

Dan woke after a dreamless sleep. Immediately, his waking thoughts were of George and Helena. He watched the shaft of sunlight dance along the wall of the small cave. Out of the corner of his eye, something glinted. Sitting up to get a better look, he recognised a silver strap, poking out from one of the rocks at the entrance. Scrambling, onto his feet he moved closer to the spot. As his eyes recognised the silver watch his heart sang. Picking it up, he caressed the familiar face and turned it over to confirm the words he already knew on the back, 'Dearest Helena with Love Dan.'

She was still alive, somewhere on this cruel island. A huge sigh eased from his body as he clasped the watch tightly to his relieved chest. Studying her watch more closely, he saw the time had stopped at 9:45 am. Over three hours later than when he first stepped onto the island but it did not matter now. His prayers had finally been answered, he had another big reason to keep going.

Full of renewed optimism, Dan sat on the ledge outside and looked around him. He could see the deep forest to the left and the small clearing with the waterfall and pool where he last saw George. Further away he could just make out the sandy beach. He had travelled a long way on foot since arriving on the island. His eyes wandered back to the rope made from coconut leaves. Looking closer at the knot, he smiled, it was definitely the handy work of Helena, a sheep bend, one of only five knots she had managed to master.

Lots of questions had started to fill his mind. How did Helena manage to climb up here in the first place? How long had she stayed up here? Where was she now? Brushing those questions to one side he decided to formulate a plan. Looking above him, it was too dangerous to climb any higher up the mountain. He realised his only option was to go back down and try to find any clues to where the entrance to the mountain was that Dimitri had described. He hoped Helena was up there, somewhere, already.

Placing Helena's watch in his rucksack he retraced his steps back down the mountain. At the bottom, he began searching for disturbed stones, worn surfaces or anything unusual. Standing back from the base of the mountain he tried to spot any possible outlines of a door. A few shadowy shapes caught his attention but when he got closer it was just a mixture of sunlight and different coloured rocks playing tricks on him. In desperation, he started to push against the rocks hoping it would trigger a door to open. Finally, well into the afternoon, Dan sat down on a small path leading nowhere and began to think how hopeless this plan was turning out. He wished now he had quizzed Dimitri more closely about the door entrance. All the rocks, crevices and shadows seemed to merge into one. He knew it would not be easy but the task now seemed impossible and to add more pressure he was wasting valuable time and energy. The relentless sun seemed to enjoy draining him and the nearly empty water bottle reflected this. As he contemplated what to do next a plan B started to emerge in his mind.

Gathering up what strength he had left, he climbed back up to the ledge to rest and prepare himself for what he hoped would happen later that night.

Dan was ready when he first heard the familiar high-pitched cries from the harpies. Picking up his rucksack he left the small cave and hesitated in the shadows at the back of the ledge. Was he about to do the right thing? What if it went horribly wrong? Should he wait longer and try to find the entrance to the mountain? Answering himself back, he shook his head and told himself NO! This was the only WAY!

Stepping forward he peered up at the night sky and watched the harpies dancing between the stars as they weaved in and out of each other's paths – shrieking with delight. It was time he told himself as he edged one foot forward and caressed the edge. Pausing, his foot stopped against a small pile of stones. Taking a sharp intake of breath, he pushed them over the edge. He watched as they bounced noisily, gathering speed, from one protruding rock to another before settling briefly on the small ledge below and then continuing their journey down. Making sure his rucksack was securely on his back he then felt the side of his right shoe to make sure the object was still safely concealed. Returning his gaze to the night sky, he waited.

Serena was busy watching her sisters' antics as they frolicked around and around. Every so often she cast a glance over towards the ledge and wondered if Dan was still there hiding or if he had managed to find the entrance to the mountain. She had seen him walking endlessly around the base of the mountain without much luck, earlier in the day. She hoped he had been successful. Returning her gaze back to her sisters, she laughed as Rebecca playfully clipped Sophie's wing and sent her stumbling head over heels until her other sister Diana swooped in and caught her.

Suddenly, the sound of loose stones rumbling down the side of the mountain stopped the harpies in mid-flight. Six pairs of eyes focused on the same spot. Patricia reacted immediately, screeching she began to dive down towards the ledge on the mountain. Meanwhile, Serena leapt off her rock and joined the race to get to the ledge first. She could not believe how foolish Dan was. He blatantly stood like a statue on the edge, making no attempt to hide. She knew she had to beat her sister Patricia for Dan to have a chance of surviving. Otherwise, he would share the same fate as George or even worse. She had a soft spot for the couple and wanted to reunite them so badly. Love was so precious on this island and Serena had had enough of pain and death. It was time love had a chance to triumph. Whizzing through the air she had a clear run to the ledge. However, factoring in Patricia's reaction speed and relentless determination she might just beat her. Serena could feel the presence of her sister as she sliced through the air above her. She knew she was gaining on her, using the advantage of gravity and a slight breeze to quicken her speed. Dan was almost within Serena's grasp when Patricia sensing the competition between them rolled slightly towards her sister Serena, clipping her right wing. Serena lost control briefly and had to slow down allowing Patricia to seize the opportunity to take the lead. She grabbed Dan's shoulders with her talons effortlessly and without resistance and lifted him up into the night sky. The other sisters whooped with delight except for Serena who almost crashed into the ledge behind her. Powerless, she watched her sister climb higher into the sky, parading Dan like a trophy to her sisters. She knew the master would be pleased with Patricia and reward her. Watching her sister disappear over the top of the mountain, she grimaced. All she could do now was to follow; his fate was sealed.

Dan took a deep breath and held his ground as he watched the two harpies racing to see who would reach him first. At first, he thought the flame-haired harpy had the edge but at the last moment, a foul by the raven-haired one above resulted in her winning him as the prize. He still was not prepared for the sharp penetrating pain in his shoulders as the harpy's talons tightly gripped him and hoisted him upwards. For one fleeting moment, his eyes locked with the flame-haired harpy. Her face expressed disappointment at losing but her eyes showed a flicker of sympathy. Pity, for him or for what was to come, perhaps.

The stinging pain gradually subsided as he rose higher in the sky. The raven-haired harpy could not contain her delight as she threw back her head and let out a long high-pitched screech to the stars above. Looking down at the other harpy she laughed heartily before fixing her gaze towards the top of the mountain.

Dan swivelled his head left and right and could see the other harpies were following but much higher up. The ground below was uneven, covered in shadows cast by the dimly lit moon. Ahead of him, he saw the dark outline of the ruins of an abandoned church and steeple. He decided it was now or never! He needed to get the raven-haired harpy's attention. Dan shouted up to her, "Please, please don't let go of me. It's so high up. I'm so scared of falling."

The harpy mocked him and screeched, "Shall I hold you tighter!"

Dan yelled out in pain as the talons dug deeper into his shoulder blade. "No please, I beg of you. Could you just fly lower, it's so high up here, I think I might die of fright?"

In a warm, almost soothing voice the harpy smiled and said, "If that's what you want, so be it." Without any warning, the harpy dived down towards the ground only pulling upwards at the very last minute.

After catching his breath, Dan screamed out, "Please, not again."

Laughing the harpy replied, "Ahh, but I thought all that screaming meant you were enjoying it so much."

This time as the harpy rose higher and then began to dive towards the ground again, Dan was ready. Kicking his right leg backwards he reached down for the blade concealed in his shoe. Grasping it tightly, he waited for the ground to almost reach up for him before he sliced both the harpy's shins and then stretched up to stab her left wing. Looking up, he watched her shocked face contort with pain and felt her grip loosen on his shoulder just enough for him to slip out of her hold. Her other foot managed to hold onto one strap of his rucksack. Quickly, he slid the other strap over his head and he was free. Landing with his knees bent, he immediately rolled to his left side to help absorb the impact of the ground beneath him. Scrambling to his feet, he grabbed his rucksack which the harpy had fortunately dropped beside him. Next, he was up and running, weaving his way through bushes and plants, jumping over mounds, trying his best not to trip up. Dan's heart was pumping madly, he could feel the rush of air on the back of his neck from the harpy hovering above him which spurred him on to run faster. Blind panic swept over him, this part of the plan he could not prepare for. How the harpy would react and what the terrain would be like on top of the mountain? Daring to glance upwards, he saw two more harpies flying to her aid. He heard her scream out to him below, "I shall enjoy watching you suffer at the hands of my master. Until then make the most of your freedom, it won't be long before my sisters and I catch up with you."

Seconds later, she was right, the other three harpies appeared, led by the flame-haired harpy. They seemed to be having a high-rise 'pow wow' in the sky. Although he knew he had to run, he could not tear his eyes away from the scene above. The raven-haired harpy was jostling around, trying to escape from the harpies supporting her. Eventually, the flame-haired harpy moved closer to say something to her. Then reluctantly, the raven-haired harpy headed off towards the temple city with a harpy on either side of her. Now the flame-haired harpy looked directly down at him. He knew it was time to go when her beautiful face became hideous and wizened and she let out an almighty screech and started to plunge towards him. The hunt was on!

In desperation, Dan looked ahead of him for any sort of cover or hollow to protect him. The shadowy outline of the church looked promising but it was too far away for him to reach. Looking back, towards the edge of the mountain favoured more opportunity. It was rocky, with lots of hiding places. Quickly, changing direction, he headed back towards the way he had come.

Darting in different directions, he could both hear and feel the beating wings moving closer and closer. He sprinted as fast as he could in one direction then abruptly changed. Dan knew the harpies were fast but their large wings committed them in one direction. They were not so nimble about altering direction and he was trying to use this fact to his advantage.

Trying not to look behind him, he just focused on the rocky cover in front of him. He knew without turning around that one of the harpies was dangerously close. He could almost feel her breath on his shoulder. Quickly, Dan turned to the left, he felt her outer wing clip his shoulder. The force knocked him sideways. He heard a cackle of laughter as she took off again into the sky. They were playing with him he guessed. Getting to his feet, he began running again, trying to jump over any obstacles in his path. The ground was getting more uneven and stony as he got nearer. He was so focused on his destination that he did not notice the flame-haired harpy approaching from his left side. She managed to get her talons onto his rucksack and started to hoist him into the air. Struggling with his strap, he managed to slide it off his shoulder, enabling him to fall back to the ground. The flame-haired harpy screeched in dismay and dropped his rucksack.

Briefly, gathering his breath, Dan rubbed his knees and forced his aching body to stand. This time, another high-pitched scream caught his attention.

THE ISLAND BECOMES YOU

Turning to face the oncoming blond-haired harpy, he realised there was nowhere imminent to hide. He watched her wizened face contort with glee at the knowledge she had won.

Suddenly, the sky lit up and a tremendous clap of thunder echoed around the sky. A look of shock appeared on the blond-haired harpy's face as she tried to stop herself in mid-flight and pull upwards. Reacting too late, she tried to change direction to avoid hitting Dan. Instead, she ploughed straight into some nearby bushes. Immediately, the other two harpies came to her aid. Frozen, Dan watched as the blond-haired harpy straightened her wings to make sure they were okay. Then the red-haired harpy supported her as she picked herself up. Momentarily, the injured harpy turned her head to look at Dan. Her face had softened and was covered with tiny cuts from the spiky bushes. She seemed a bit wobbly on her legs. Shaking her head, she said, "Why did he stop me?"

The red-headed harpy hesitated then replied, "I don't know sister but we must obey his wishes. Let's go and tend to your wounds." Dan was shocked, they sounded so human when they spoke.

Looking straight at him with piercing blue eyes, the blond-haired harpy yelled, "I'll get you next time!" Then she carefully extended her wings, flapped them several times and took off into the night sky with the help of the other harpies.

Completely bewildered, Dan watched them until they were a speck in the distance. Finding his rucksack still in one piece, he hoisted it over his shoulder – wincing slightly from the bruises and cuts. To the left of him was a small hollow with some rocks around it. Dan settled his exhausted body inside the mound, he expected it to start raining at any moment but nothing happened. Eventually, he relaxed enough to allow his eyes to close.

Serena closely followed her sisters back to the golden temple in the city. She was glad Dan had survived another encounter with them. She had purposely grabbed his rucksack, hoping it would slide off him so he could escape. Luckily for Dan, the master too wished for him to be set free for the time being. There was still hope for Dan and Helena to be reunited.

The warmth of the sun on his face, woke Dan up the following morning. He was surprised to still be there especially after he narrowly missed being captured by the harpies. Searching for his water bottle in his rucksack, he caught sight of Helena's watch glinting back at him. She must be close by. He so wanted to see her again.

Getting up he looked ahead of him towards the ruined church. It was possible he could make it there in a day but only if he stuck to a fairly fast pace without many breaks. Focusing on the church he tried to override how much his body ached from last night's encounter – especially his shoulders and knees. Standing there with the sun on his back, he was filled with determination to keep going and hope of finding Helena safe and well.

Chapter 18

The room was dimly lit by the shaft of moonlight coming through the narrow gap in the ceiling. Everything looked quite eerie in the semi-darkness. I waited, listening for the next thunderous rumble followed by some refreshing rain but nothing happened.

Tiredness began to pull me back down onto my makeshift pillow bed when I heard a familiar high-pitched screech overhead. Suddenly, my body was on high alert. Was I safe in this room? Should I look for somewhere else to hide? Before I had time to decide my next move, I heard something push against the door. Immediately, my gaze was fixed on the door handle as it slowly moved downwards. Grabbing the metal cross nearby, I found myself slowly trying to edge backwards towards the darkest corner of the room. Unhurriedly, the door edged open. I expected to see part of a feathered wing protrude from the gap but was shocked to see a hand appear instead. Next, a pair of legs, side-stepped carefully through the gap, attached to a body, while another hand slowly closed the door behind them. The person then collapsed to the floor, breathing heavily. Peeking from behind the cushions, I tried to catch a glimpse of the face. Partly because I prayed it was human but more importantly could it be Dan. Hopeful eyes sought out his short blonde locks, parted to the side and that infectious grin but instead my gaze fell upon dark ringlets of hair flopping over human ears.

Brushing aside my disappointment and feeling a bit braver I put my cushion down and whispered, "Who are you?"

The mop of black hair rose upwards to reveal a set of gleaming white teeth smiling back at me. "Madam, I am called Dimitri and you must be Helena!" I let out a gasp of astonishment. How on earth did he know who I was? Reading my thoughts, Dimitri replied, "I met up with Dan and his great-grandad George. Dan told me all about you. How you were both separated on the island and how he feared you had drowned or were killed by a sea monster."

To hear Dan's name being mentioned and to actually speak with another human being was too much for me. Tears of joy rolled down my face. Seeing me so distressed, Dimitri got up and tried to comfort me. I grasped his outstretched hand and stood up. His soft dark eyes, full of concern, stared at me. I responded with a big smile and a huge hug. I held on tightly for ages. It was so good to have human contact. I had never met Dimitri before but it felt so good to hold someone who had seen and spent time with my beloved Dan. He was alive! That was all that mattered. Eventually, I released him from my arms and beckoned for him to sit down on the cushions nearby. I had so many questions. Where should I begin?

The first tentative tentacles of dawn started to slither through the gap in the ceiling into our room. I could clearly see Dimitri was of Indian origin, probably in his early thirties. His clothing was ripped in places especially his shoulders which were also matted with old blood stains. My gaze lingered on his shoulders and knowingly Dimitri hunched them and winced. Looking for my water bottle I offered him a drink. Gratefully, he seized the bottle and took two long gulps from it. I then pointed to the remaining berries which he devoured in seconds. Afterwards, he looked at me apologetically but I waved his concern away and offered him some more water which he accepted.

Unable to wait any longer I asked, "What happened to you?"

He sighed before starting, "I can only thank god again for my good fortune – I have escaped my tormentor for a second time." With that, he looked upwards and made the sign of a cross.

Trying hard to hide my impatience I said, "Please continue."

"Many years ago, I arrived on this island with Dan's great-grandad. We both survived an encounter with the sea serpent who patrols this island." As he spoke, I vividly recalled the lifeless dark eyes staring back at me and I shivered as I remembered its huge tentacles grabbing my legs.

Trying to sweep those thoughts from my mind I redirected my focus on what Dimitri was saying. He talked about meeting the harpies and being carried away by one of them, though George tried his best to stop her.

THE ISLAND BECOMES YOU

Fighting an ogre and escaping from jail. Being reunited with George only to be kidnapped by a harpy again.

Listening to him I was completely mesmerised by his story. It was such an adventure with all the ingredients for a good book. Lots of near misses, encounters with monsters and last-minute escapes – very much like my own story.

Dimitri paused to take another drink. I asked him, "How did you escape their clutches for a second time and end up here?"

Slowly he smiled and said, "As the black-haired harpy carried me back towards the temple, I pretended to have given up and gave the impression I had no fight left in me. My body hung limply in the harpy's talons. I didn't protest or wiggle around. I waited until the harpy flew closer to the ground. Nearing the temple, I attacked her feet with a small pocket knife hidden in my shoe. Catching her off guard with the pain, the harpy instinctively released her grip on me. Then I was able to slide out of her grasp, I hit the ground and immediately started running for cover. There is no doubt the harpies are immensely strong and have powerful wings but their size and shape can hinder how quickly they can change direction. So, I was able to get a good head start before she turned back to find me. Also, the moon wasn't very bright so there were plenty of shadows to hide in amongst the shrubbery and trees nearby. The second harpy was committed to taking George onwards to the temple city but she said to her sister she would return and help once she had delivered George safely to the master."

I interrupted, "It's so weird the harpies have human names and are sisters. I too have encountered them on the island. One of them spoke to me about the master once being in love with her. I didn't really understand who she was referring to but I felt a deep sadness in her voice. She was very beautiful before her face changed."

Dimitri's eyes lit up in response and he asked, "Can you describe which one it was?"

"Long, flame-coloured hair, cascading in soft curls down her back. Her beautiful, emerald eyes stared at me defiantly. She was a magnificent creature. I couldn't stop staring at her. Her voice was smooth as velvet until her face transformed into an old hag and the sound from her lips became a high-pitched screech."

Nodding, Dimitri added, "Yes, I know the one you mean. I am sure they call her Serena. I think she is the most beautiful of all of them but it is hard to imagine this master could have been in love with her. Whoever he is?"

"Perhaps she was not always what she is today?" Immediately after saying it, I quickly brought my hand to my lips and wished I could erase those words. Although I was starting to feel quite comfortable sharing our experiences on the island, I was not sure about revealing everything, especially about Freya. Plus, a niggling thought at the back of my head, reminded me of Freya's words about not trusting anyone on the island.

Looking very serious, Dimitri asked, "Whatever made you say that? Has someone been telling you stories about this island? Who else have you met up with on this island?"

I did not like Dimitri's change in tone. I suddenly, felt like I was being interrogated. His dark eyes stared at me intently, searching for any clues in my body language or response. Attempting to clear the air I laughed and said, "I just thought, maybe Serena used to be happy and carefree not the sad, bitter creature she is today."

Relaxing the intensity of his stare, Dimitri seemed to accept my reply saying, "I suppose so but I'm still interested to know what has happened to you since you arrived on this island."

"Lots, but let's finish your story first. What happened next after the harpy said she would come back and help her sister look for you?"

I noticed the enthusiasm in his voice had waned as he continued, "I waited frozen to the spot, holding my breath in the small hollow while the black-haired harpy glided past me. Once she was clear, I carefully crawled over to the area she had just checked, hoping she wouldn't return. By the time her sister reappeared, she was well over by the outskirts of a small wooded area. I buried myself inside some shrubbery and prayed they wouldn't return this way. Luckily, my prayers were answered and as the sun began to appear on the horizon they took off towards the temple. Before leaving, I heard one of them shout, 'Enjoy your precious hours of freedom. There is no escape or safe place on this island – we will eventually find you again.'

"Once they had disappeared, I headed back towards this church. It took me a couple of days to get here. I made sure I was well hidden at night." Pausing, he yawned and then said, "Sorry, I haven't slept properly for two nights! Would you mind if I had a little nap? I haven't felt safe to sleep until now. You can tell me all about your adventures later."

    I watched Dimitri lean his head back on the cushion and close his eyes. "Of course," I replied. I would have loved to question him further about how Dan was but after what Dimitri had been through, how could I protest. Leaving the remainder of the water behind, Dimitri mumbled a thank you as I got up and closed the door behind me.

Chapter 19

Walking carefully through the ruined church, I headed for the fountain outside and I was pleased to see there was still plenty of water left at the bottom of it for me to drink. I even scooped up a handful of water to bathe my face and arms. Looking down at my body I was pleased to see all my wounds had healed, thanks to Freya. I wondered if I should call on her now to help me find Dan but decided against it. I knew in my heart he must be heading in this direction to follow George and maybe try to rescue him. Still, I was feeling so desperate to see his face again. Finding a shady spot on the other side of the fountain, I sat down and rested my head against the edge. I was still feeling sleepy and very soon my heavy eyes closed. Soon I was dreaming I was running towards something or someone but did not know who. I could not see their face clearly. I felt a mixture of curiosity and apprehension as I got closer. Then I heard someone shouting out my name. It was faint at first but gradually got louder. It was coming from a different direction from where I was running. In my dream, I stopped and stood still – uncertain of which way to run.

"Helena, my Helena. It is you. It must be you." This time I recognised the voice immediately. It sounded so real, I felt I could reach out and touch him. My Dan was right here, next to me. Still fully immersed in the dream, I imagined his hand brushing my hair to one side and his warm breath on my cheek. Next, I felt his soft lips on mine and I reached out to hold him and pull him closer. It was so vivid; that I did not dare open my eyes. I did not want the dream to end.

Eventually, his mouth broke away from mine, I mumbled, "Dan, please don't leave me again!"

THE ISLAND BECOMES YOU

"Helena, I promise, I will never leave you again. I love you too much." Still with my eyes firmly shut I felt his hands holding mine and lifting them gently to his face. I felt the familiar chiselled jaw and infectious grin. Raising his voice slightly, he coaxed, "Open your eyes, Helena, it's really me, not a dream." He then moved my hand to his beating heart. I could feel it pounding beneath my fingertips. It sounded so convincing; I finally opened my eyes.

Dan's beaming smile greeted me. I briefly shut my eyes again in disbelief. When I opened them, his big blue eyes were staring back at me. Loosening his grip on my hands, he allowed me to touch his face, his short blonde hair, his muscular chest and last of all his grinning mouth. Suddenly, tears started to roll down my cheeks. I managed to whisper Dan's name before his lips crushed mine. My heart pounded against his as he held me closer. My hands gripped his shoulders tighter. I was completely lost in our reunion. His lips moved from my mouth to my neck and I sighed deeply. Dan whispered, "I love you so much and I missed you terribly," as his lips caressed my skin. Closing my eyes, my hands moved under his t-shirt. I longed for the warmth of his skin against mine. Meanwhile, his hands had moved to the top of my hips and his right hand began to move slowly, upwards, teasingly under my top. Together our lips found each other again. Our tongues entwined, tasting every crevice of our mouths. My whole body responded to his touch. I sighed as he carefully manoeuvred me onto the ground. I welcomed his taut body against mine. I felt so alive with each kiss, this was definitely not a dream. I pulled him closer. His breath was hot against my neck as he whispered my name repeatedly. With urgency, his lips sought mine again. Gradually, through the mist of pleasure, I became aware of another voice calling out my name. Abruptly, the spell was broken as I realised who it was. Dan and I reluctantly broke apart from our loving embrace. Surprised, Dan whispered, "Is that Dimitri?" I nodded in response, trying hard to calm down my emotions. Sighing, Dan smiled, "We will have to put this on hold till later," as he kissed my cheek. Getting up, he grinned and added, "Perhaps we should lose each other again so we can enjoy another amazing reunion like that."

Shaking my head, I replied, "Don't even think it. You are absolutely not going anywhere without me again!"

"Don't worry Helena, I've learnt my lesson." Dan helped me up and we both peeked around the side of the fountain. We watched as a confused Dimitri wandered around shouting out my name. Holding my hand over my mouth I managed to stifle a giggle while trying to compose myself as we walked out together, hand in hand, from behind the fountain.

Poor Dimitri looked completely shocked when I first appeared, quickly followed by Dan. Dimitri stammered, "D-D-Dan, you made it?" Pausing to take in what he was seeing he then said, "How did you make it up the mountain so quickly? Did you find the secret passage?"

Dan answered with a question, "How did you manage to escape this time? When I last saw you, you looked like someone who had completely given up and was resigned to their fate."

"Ahh," said Dimitri, as he walked towards us. "That was part of my plan. The harpy wasn't expecting me to try and escape. Nearing the temple, she flew lower to the ground so I cut her ankle and she released me. It was touch and go whether I would lose her but I managed to hide in the shadows until she and the other harpy gave up and I made my way here." Pausing a moment, he continued, "I'm sorry George is still a prisoner but there is always hope he might escape too."

Dan had been observing Dimitri very closely especially his body language as he spoke about his escape. In particular, he noted how he looked down when he spoke about George and shuffled his feet about awkwardly. There was something about him that he was not sure about. He did not feel like he could trust him. Dan replied, "That is very similar to how I got here. I used the harpy to carry me to the top of the mountain then I also used a knife to cut her shins and make her release me."

Choosing to ignore his misgivings about Dimitri for the time being he instead focused on his useful knowledge of the temple city. "Dimitri, will you come back with us to rescue George?" Dan asked.

He watched Dimitri's face as he initially showed surprise then softened into a dry smile. "I'll take you as far as the temple but I fear your venture is foolhardy and impossible. Even if you did get past the guards to his cell, you would almost certainly get caught and risk your life in the arena. However, I guess, whatever I say will not stop you. It's just I cannot face the ogre again or witness my friends being ripped apart. I just want to go back to the beach. I would rather take my chances with the sea serpent and try to reach your boat. I will wait for you there."

THE ISLAND BECOMES YOU

Looking at Dan I could see both hope and despair in his eyes but I knew he would not abandon his great-grandad. Plus, with the help of Freya, we might just pull it off. I had decided to keep that encounter to myself. I was not certain about Dimitri as I had only just met him and besides, he was only planning to go as far as the golden, temple city wall. However, it would not hurt to appeal to him. "Dimitri, I understand you are scared. What about your good friend, George? He would risk his life for you. Why won't you help us more?" I pleaded.

Fixing his eyes on me, Dimitri's voice softened, "What you just said, makes me feel very selfish. You are right; I am scared but George would not give up on me." Hesitating, he said, "Yes, I will go back with both of you and rescue George."

"Thank you, Dimitri. I realise how hard it must be for you to agree to go back there, especially after what you had to do to escape," I replied.

Dan was not certain he could trust Dimitri's sudden change of heart but Helena could be very persuasive. His knowledge of the city beyond the wall was invaluable to them. However, part of him feared putting Helena's life in danger again. He had missed her so much and thinking he had lost her once would make the pain too much to bear a second time.

Looking at the dishevelled state they were both in I added, "Both of you need time to tend to your wounds and rest. You will need all your strength and resourcefulness to get through this. The sun will be setting in a few hours. Let's gather some food and water and go back to the church and rest then make plans to rescue George." Both men nodded. Dan looked down at the matted blood on his arms and legs and suddenly felt very tired. His shoulder was extremely sore and his legs ached.

I gently grabbed Dan's arm and led him back to the fountain where I carefully bathed his injuries. His eyes remained intently focused on me throughout. I had to stop the urge to smother his wounds with kisses as I was acutely aware that Dimitri was watching us. When I had finished, I beckoned to Dimitri and said, "Why don't you bathe your wounds while Dan and I collect some more berries from the back of the church."

I did sense a reluctance from Dimitri to follow my suggestion but he eventually smiled and came over saying, "I would prefer it if you bathed my wounds too."

Laughing uncomfortably, I quickly brushed his comment aside and said,

"I'm sure you can manage on your own." Out of the corner of my eye, I saw Dan grimace after Dimitri's remark. Hurriedly, I took hold of Dan's hand and led him towards the back of the church.

Once we were out of sight Dan stopped and turned to face me. Letting go of my hand he gently cupped my face and tenderly kissed my lips. "I can't bear the thought of losing you again," he murmured.

Wiping away a single tear from his face, I could clearly see all the emotion in his eyes and etched on his face. Pulling him closer, I kissed his damp cheek and said, "I love you so much, Dan. We have always been there for each other and here and now is no different. We will get through this. Fate has brought us back together for a reason. With Dimitri's help, we will rescue George and then escape from this cursed island."

Dan smiled, "You make it sound so easy when realistically this adventure we are on is thwart with danger."

"I know what you are implying but let me just say I think the odds of us succeeding are stacked more in our favour than you realise. You just have to believe we can do it and perhaps we will get help along the way." I desperately wanted to tell him about Freya but I feared Dan would laugh at me and not take it seriously. I decided it was better to bide my time and wait until we needed her help and I could prove her existence.

Dan's gaze smouldered as he began to trace the outline of my lips with his fingers, "I get the feeling you know more than you are saying but right now I have an irresistible urge to kiss you again." Placing his hands on either side of my face he pressed his lips against mine and slowly kissed me. I responded by pulling him closer. My fingers entwined in his blonde wavy hair as our kiss became more passionate. My heartbeat quickened as he edged me backwards against the side of the church and pressed his body fully against mine. Fleetingly, I noticed the roughness of the stones against my back but this was soon forgotten as I was completely swept away in the moment, all thoughts of Dimitri being nearby were removed. I cried out his name as his hot kisses trailed along my skin. While his expert hands left me breathless and wanting more.

Abruptly, Dan pulled away leaving me briefly confused until I heard Dimitri shouting as he rounded the corner, "Do you need any help with the berries?" Seeing us near the wall of the church, he stopped in his tracks and stared at us, scrutinising me in particular. I began to feel quite uncomfortable. Then he smiled warmly and said, "I see you two are getting reacquainted."

Feeling slightly embarrassed, Dan said, "Sorry we were both caught up in the moment."

Dimitri waved his hands dismissively, "Don't apologise, you've both been through a lot being apart and fearing the worst. It's only natural that you would want to show how much you've missed each other." Hesitating, he continued, "Please just warn me next time!"

Dan and I both grinned at each other. Laughingly Dan said, "We will try our best to control ourselves but I can't promise too long a gap," as he looked at me with eyes full of desire. Playfully he caressed my bottom. In response, I teasingly pushed him away and whispered, "I'll make you wait longer if you are not careful."

Dan took my hand and led me towards the berry bushes. I winced slightly; my left shoulder felt sore. I must have scraped it against the wall of the church during our passionate embrace. That was twice now Dimitri had interrupted us. I hoped there would not be a third time.

We all began picking berries but every so often my eyes strayed to find Dan. A couple of times his eyes found mine and he smiled back reassuringly as if he knew I never wanted to be parted from him again. I noticed my stomach was starting to grumble so I attempted to silence it with a few berries. Obviously, Dan noticed and teased me saying, "Save some berries for us!" We all laughed in response and then sat down together and began eating our handful of berries. They tasted delicious, very juicy and sweet. The only problem was Dan was trying to smother a laugh as he stared at my face. "You remind me of a vampire temptress with blood trailing from your lips." Immediately, I tried to rub the berry stain marks away but Dan just shook his head and said, "Let me." Carefully, he leaned across and gently licked his tongue against the corner of my mouth. Instantly, his actions sent a delightful warm shiver through my body. His mouth hovered over mine. I felt myself cry out for him to kiss me but he reluctantly looked into my eyes and then whispered "Later," before continuing to eat. However, his smouldering gaze lingered on my face. I closed my eyes and imagined him devouring my lips with his mouth. "Are you okay Helena," I heard Dan inquire, a slight hint of worry in his voice.

Opening my eyes, I beamed back a huge smile and said, "I feel absolutely fine. I'm just so happy and thankful that we managed to find each other again."

Leaning forward, I felt his arms around me as he hugged me tightly, "Me too, I hate myself for giving up hope. I should have realised our love would reunite us."

"Sorry to interrupt you two love birds but the sun is setting and we need to hide! The harpies will be out soon. Have they ever tried to come into the church Helena?"

I sighed and Dan released his grip on me. Turning to face Dimitri, I replied, "So far I have only seen them outside the church – they have never ventured inside."

"Ahh, I thought so," Dimitri replied excitedly. This is hallowed ground. The harpies won't dare to enter the church. We should be safe to stay here tonight."

Before returning to the safety of the church, Dan filled his water bottle up at the fountain. This prompted me to do the same. I followed him, standing next to him I lowered my bottle under the water to refill it. Dan purposely moved nearer so our hands touched. As his fingers brushed against mine, I felt a small electric charge race up my arm. Looking up into his eyes, he smiled and brushed his lips softly against mine before removing his bottle from the water and replacing the lid. Leaning forward again his lips brushed the top of my ear as he whispered, "We must find time to be together tonight." I nodded and smiled back. My whole body shivered in anticipation as he gently touched my cheek and then turned to follow Dimitri into the church. I remained, staring at my bottle for a few moments then my gaze moved upwards to the mermaid statue. Her face was cold and expressionless. I remembered how Freya had brought her to life only hours earlier. I so hoped with her help we would be able to rescue George and then return home safely.

Deep in thought, I moved towards the church only to be interrupted by some loose rubble bouncing downwards against the side of the building. The loose stones landed a foot from my feet, making me jump backwards. Holding my bottle above my head, I looked upwards at the church steeple but the setting sun blinded me. I thought about stepping further back to get a better look but then I heard a faint shriek-like sound in the distance which made me hurry inside instead.

THE ISLAND BECOMES YOU

Serena folded her wings back quickly; she held her breath as she watched Helena stop and peer up towards where she stood. Her left wing had brushed against some loose stones and sent them crashing to the ground. Her heartbeat raced momentarily at the thought of being discovered but luckily for her the sun setting and the angle where Helena stood must have obscured her view. Still, she had spent a whole hour mesmerised, watching the happy couple's reunion. However, seeing the other man had unsettled her. She suspected he was not who he seemed but there was no way she could let them know without revealing herself and endangering her sisters. Sighing deeply, she carefully extended her wings again and flew off towards her sisters. She would let them know; that she had not seen anything suspicious near the church.

Chapter 20

The room inside the church now seemed very cosy with three adults sharing the space. We quickly devoured the berries we had picked leaving a few for our breakfast in the morning. Dimitri seemed very quiet; I assumed his lack of sleep had caught up with him. I watched his eyes half close then his head jerked suddenly as he tried to keep his eyes open.

"Dimitri, why don't you stop fighting going to sleep and lay down on those cushions," Dan suggested.

"Sorry, I'm worried if I close my eyes I will sleep well into the next day and we need to plan for the journey back to the temple."

"Don't worry about not waking up. Go and have a re-energising nap for an hour or so and I promise we will wake you up. You will feel so much better after it," Dan replied persuasively.

"Okay, I give in but please wake me!" Dimitri got up and walked over to the cushions. He chose two then offered Dan and me what remained. Settling himself down, he laid his head on the cushion with his eyes facing us. He stared at me intently for a while, smiled and then said, "Don't get too amorous while I sleep."

Dan and I exchanged glances while Dimitri continued to stare straight through me. I found the fact he was positioned facing us quite unsettling. Even when he finally closed his eyes – I could not help but think he was still watching us. His presence and last remark seemed to temporarily dampen any amorous feelings on my part.

In the dimly lit room, Dan and I stared at each other quite bemused by the whole situation. Outside the last rays of the sun were fading fast. Slowly,

THE ISLAND BECOMES YOU

Dan stood up, holding his cushion and carefully moved a few paces away then sat down again next to the old, wooden bookcase. Putting his finger to his lips he beckoned me over. I shook my head and pointed to Dimitri but Dan waved my concern away. Shrugging my shoulders, I got up. The path to Dan was clear but I was still worried about disturbing Dimitri. I was two steps away when my cushion slipped out of my hand and landed with a small thud against the table leg. I froze and watched Dan's eyes open wider as he looked across at Dimitri. Following his gaze, I saw him mumble something and adjust his sleeping position but thankfully he did not open his eyes. Holding in a sigh, I bent down, picked up my cushion and took one large step so I was practically within touching distance of Dan. Giving my cushion to Dan, he placed it next to him and I sunk down relieved by his side. Immediately, he placed his arm around me and squeezed me reassuringly. Whispering in my ear, he said, "That was close!" I nodded and rested my head on his shoulder. I felt so safe in his arms, all my concerns seemed to ebb away. Suddenly, I felt overwhelmed with tiredness. I think Dan sensed the heaviness of my head on his shoulders. Gently lifting his shoulder so I moved my head, he patted the cushion beside him and got me to lie down. Carefully, he manoeuvred his body down beside me. One arm rested loosely on my waist while the other cupped my head and tenderly stroked my hair. The last thing I remember was Dan nuzzling my ear and whispering "I love you" before I drifted off to sleep.

Abruptly, I was woken by someone shaking me. Immediately, all my senses were on high alert. Trying to desperately focus my eyes, I recognised the hand touching my shoulder was Dan. Lifting my body up I turned towards him and tried to peer through the semi-darkness. I could see he was sitting bolt upright. I started to open my mouth to say something and he instantly brought his hand to my mouth to quieten me while his other hand pointed upwards to the ceiling.

Now fully awake I could clearly hear footsteps on the roof above our heads, moving back and forth. My body trembled. It must be the harpies. Looking over to where Dimitri had been sleeping, I was shocked to see the cushions empty. Glancing quickly around the room, there seemed to be no sign of him. Dan met my questioning gaze, shrugged, and shook his head. Carefully, I sat up fully and edged closer to Dan. He wrapped his arms around me protectively as we listened to the sound of the footsteps, stomping above us. My heart was pounding in my chest as I listened to the creaking roof. Dan held me tighter as the roof seemed to groan louder from the weight. It offered me temporary comfort but my brain was racing ahead of me. What if they found us?

Suddenly, there was a piercing shriek and a huge feathered foot with sharp talons protruded through a gap in the ceiling, sending dust and rubble crashing to the floor where Dimitri had been sleeping. I felt Dan's chest tense as I stuck my hand in my mouth to stifle a scream. Inwardly, I gasped in horror as I watched the dangling foot, frantically twisting and writhing above us. Another pair of heavy feet landed close by and slowly moved towards the gap. I closed my eyes and sank back further into Dan's arms. I heard a woman's voice ask, "Sister are you okay? Let me help you."

"Thanks, Serena, I lost my balance and placed my foot down too heavily and the roof gave way. I'm having difficulty trying to remove it."

My ears pricked up when Serena's name was mentioned and I opened my eyes. She was the harpy who first spoke to me about the master and later brushed past me while I was invisible at the fountain but did not say anything. I watched mesmerised as the huge foot jerked upwards, turned slightly and got stuck again. "Ouch," screamed the harpy.

"Let me see Rebecca. It seems to be caught on this wooden beam. I'll try and move it."

"Be careful Serena, my foot is bleeding and there are splinters of wood on it."

Trying to hide his concern from Helena, Dan checked the room again for any further hiding places – there was nothing suitable for either of them. He could hear the other harpy starting to stamp her foot down hard next to the hole that had appeared. Dan's attention was drawn to the distance between them and the door. He knew they needed to get out of the room. Once the hole was made bigger– surely the harpies would look inside the room. Hopefully, the noise and commotion would disguise their escape.

Too late the other harpy had broken the beam and with another jerk and twist the harpy's foot was finally free. Dan pressed his body as much as possible against the side of the bookcase and squashed Helena into the gap beside him. Grabbing the cushions, he placed them over their exposed limbs in an attempt to blend in. He felt Helena hold her breath as they waited.

Dan could just make out some murmuring then he saw a pair of green eyes peering down through the hole in the ceiling. Frozen to the spot, holding his breath too, he watched through a tiny gap in the cushions as the eyes scanned the room and then came to rest in the direction of the bookcase. The mouth, belonging to the eyes opened slightly and seemed to form a smile, displaying a quick glimpse of the sharp fangs hidden inside. Then it was gone. Dan took a deep, lungful breath in anticipation of having to move quickly. He felt Helena let out a silent sigh next to him. Pricking his ears, he strained to hear the harpy's response.

"It's the old study room. It's empty, apart from a table, a bookcase plus some cushions scattered around. Rebecca, take a look if you like but I think we should head back and get your foot looked at."

"But the master wanted us to look around for Helena and Dan."

"Rebecca it can wait. Besides, our other sisters are looking too. Perhaps they have already found them." Pausing briefly, Serena continued, "Can you manage to stand on your foot?"

"It's very sore, maybe a bit swollen. I think it would be better to go now."

"Okay, let me help you as you take off. Try not to put too much pressure on your foot, use my shoulder instead."

"Thanks, Serena."

The roof seemed to shake thankfully as the harpies flew off. More rubble and dust were dislodged and tumbled onto the floor. I fought an overwhelming urge to cough. I could not risk making any noise. Eventually, I had to place the cushion over my mouth and cough into it. Dan placed a reassuring hand on my back. "It's safe, they've gone," he whispered. Dan smiled and leaned towards me and kissed me on the lips. My heartbeat synchronised with his as I melted in his arms again.

We both jumped as the door began to edge open and another pair of eyes peered through the gap. I let out a deep sigh when I recognised the gleaming white smile. "That was close," Dimitri grinned. "Are you both okay?"

Dan found his voice, "Yes, it was extremely close. Luckily, they didn't see us." Frowning he added, "Where were you?"

"A noise woke me up and I decided to investigate," replied Dimitri.

"You should have woken us," Dan said with a hint of anger in his voice.

"Probably, I should have but you both looked so peaceful, entwined together in each other's arms. I just didn't have the heart to disturb you unless it was really necessary. Besides I wasn't sure what I had actually heard." Sitting down next to them Dimitri continued, "I made my way outside the church and heard the harpies flying overhead. Unfortunately, two of them doubled back towards the church so I quickly hid in the bushes outside. I saw one of them land on the roof and start walking back and forth until her foot broke through and she was trapped. Then the other harpy came to her rescue. I was so worried they would find you. It seemed ages before they finally flew off and it was safe for me to come back in."

"Do you think they will come back?" I asked hesitantly.

Dimitri replied," I think we are safe here for tonight but we need to leave here tomorrow."

Dan squeezed my hand reassuringly, "I agree, we need to press on anyway. Each day, each hour that passes leaves George in more danger!"

"Yes, but for now we need to try to rest until the morning," Dimitri replied.

"I'm not sure I could go back to sleep," I said.

"Look, I have an idea," said Dimitri. "Let me be a lookout for a few hours then Dan can replace me. That way you both can rest for a few hours knowing I am watching out for you and I promise to wake you if they come back."

"Are you sure you are up for it? You must be as tired as us," Dan queried.

Shaking his head Dimitri replied, "No it's fine, my nap revived me. I will take first watch then you can take over until the morning."

Looking at me, Dimitri asked, "Is it okay if I show Dan where I will watch from? There is a good viewpoint just inside the church, near where the altar is. He won't be long."

Dan gave me a comforting hug, followed by a peck on the lips. "Stay here, I won't be long, I promise."

Trying to sound brave, I replied, "Okay, I'll stay here and wait for you to come back."

Leaning back against the wall, I watched them both walk out of the room leaving the door ajar. Dan snuck a quick look back and smiled before disappearing from my view. I could hear the crunch of glass and wood starting to fade as they made their way nearer to the altar. Hugging my legs tightly, I could not help but look up at the sizeable gap in the ceiling caused by the harpies. I could still picture the two emerald, oval-shaped eyes staring at us. I do not know how she did not see us after our hurried attempt to hide ourselves or maybe she did. Still, we had survived another encounter. Looking back at my journey so far, I think I was much braver on my own. Having Dan with me made me worry more about my own safety and his. However, I was still determined to escape this island after rescuing George. I had never met him but he sounded so resolute and strong for surviving alone for so long and it was obvious why Dan became quite attached to him. Dimitri on the other hand came across as quite selfish at times and then tried to cover it up by becoming over-helpful. I felt quite uncomfortable in his presence and sensed him watching me too much.

Feeling a little braver, I got up slowly and carefully walked over to the gaping hole in the ceiling, making sure I avoided the loose rumble on the floor. Once underneath it, I peered upwards into the night sky. It was speckled with twinkling stars and a silvery moon. I was mesmerised by the beauty of the night sky – it was such a shame we were all stuck on this perilous island.

I was interrupted by the sound of the door edging open behind me. A strange shiver went down my spine. Pushing the sensation to one side, I turned to face a grinning Dan. He pulled the door shut behind him and stood there looking at me. His eyes moved slowly down my body, stopping at my hips before returning to my face. Taking a deep breath in he said, "You look so beautiful standing in the moonlight. I've missed you so much."

Before I could reply he walked purposely towards me, stopping just a few inches from me. I could feel his penetrating gaze full of desire burrowing deep into my eyes. The warmth of his body was tantalisingly close. His hands were pressed against his sides, it was almost as if he was trying to restrain himself from touching me. Unable to bear the suspense any longer, I reached out for him. Instantly, his lips crushed against mine. His arms were tightly wrapped around me. My body responded by moulding itself against him. Coming up for air he whispered, "I've waited so long for this," before his mouth devoured mine again. For one fleeting moment, it felt like I was kissing him for the first time. Meanwhile, his hands were reacquainting themselves with every part of my body. It was not long before his hands had expertly removed my top and were slipping down my bra straps. His lips and tongue left my mouth and began savouring all the contours of my body. His touch was like an electric charge and my body put up no resistance. I cried out, I wanted him so badly. My own hands tugged at his top. I longed to feel his skin against mine. I sighed and sought out his lips again as he deftly lifted me up and carried me back towards the bookcase. Carefully, he laid me down on the cushions. Immediately, our passion intensified and we came together as one. Sparks ignited all over my body, followed by a tidal wave of pleasure which engulfed me several times before it reached its peak and gently ebbed away leaving me breathless. Afterwards, his hands tenderly caressed my body as he planted soft kisses on my cheeks, neck and shoulders. All thoughts of harpies or Dimitri were forgotten. It was just Dan and me. We lay together, enjoying the afterglow until the small fire that still burned inside needed to be fed again. At last spent with our love making we drifted off to sleep in each other's arms.

Chapter 21

I awoke with a start, feeling slightly cold and confused as to my whereabouts. Then I smiled as I remembered our night together. Cuddling a cushion closer to my body I suddenly realised I was alone and practically naked except for the cushions strategically placed to cover my modesty. I was also aware of someone snoring gently behind me. Turning slowly, I was shocked to see the curly black hair belonging to Dimitri. To add to my embarrassment, the nearest item, my bra, was lying just next to his feet. Holding my breath, I leaned across and carefully grabbed it with my right hand while positioning the cushion in front of my chest with the other. Picking it up slowly, I underestimated the length of the strap and it brushed against his toes as I retrieved it. Still holding my breath, I froze and willed him not to move. His breathing seemed to pause momentarily before picking up its normal rhythm again. Bringing it nearer, I turned to face the wall as I fumbled with the hooks in my haste to put it on. Next, I located my t-shirt a bit further away but just out of reach. Getting onto my knees, I gradually stood up, my eyes fixed on Dimitri looking for any sign of movement. He remained in the same position so feeling braver, I stepped to the side of him, holding the cushion to hide my modesty in case he awoke. Taking another step forward, I tried to avoid standing on any loose rubble before I stretched my hand out towards my t-shirt. I felt so relieved once this item was on as it now covered me to my thighs. Moving forward again, I was reunited with my shorts. Feeling proud of my achievement so far, I stepped into my shorts and started to pull them up. Almost there, I thought, just as my balance began to teeter and my bare foot came down harder than I planned and dislodged some rubble. I winced at the sharp pain as I wobbled to gain my footing. Frozen to the spot, I stared at Dimitri, trying not to make a sound and waited for his response. Dimitri turned over and opened one eye and winked. "Don't worry, I was already awake!" I could feel my face going red with embarrassment. Quickly, Dimitri added, "I promise I kept my eyes completely shut until now!"

I was in two minds whether to believe him but he seemed quite sincere. Looking around for a safe place to sit down, I then checked my left foot. Luckily, there was only a slight scratch on the bottom of it. Reaching for my socks and shoes I started to put them on while Dimitri carried on talking. "There is no need to be embarrassed as I expected to see you together when I came back here a few hours ago. Sure, enough you were both sleeping soundly in each other's arms. I decided not to wake you so I went back to keeping a look out. However, a little while later Dan came out and joined me so I came back in here to try to get some sleep."

"So, Dan's still outside near the altar?" I managed to stumble the words out.

"Yes, but he should be back by now," he glanced up at the gap in the ceiling. "The sun is quite high in the sky." Seeing the concern written on my face he quickly added, "He's probably fallen asleep."

"I expect you are right. I'll go and check on him. Try and get some more rest, Dimitri." I was missing Dan already, especially after last night's amazing reunion.

"Okay, I'll try. I'm feeling quite exhausted now, it was a very eventful night," he yawned afterwards.

"Yes, of course, you must be exhausted after your escape. Sorry, we were rather selfish last night, thinking only of ourselves."

"Don't apologise, if you were my girlfriend, I would want to spend every moment with you too. Kissing you, touching you. It must be so awkward having me around after you have just found each other again. I'll try and give you both more privacy in future."

I really needed some air and a chance to escape this cringe-worthy conversation. Quickly, I got up and marched over to the door and smiled sweetly before saying through gritted teeth, "Thanks Dimitri, for being so understanding," then I shut the door behind me.

On the other side of the door, I took a deep breath and closed my eyes in an attempt to try to calm myself down. Yes, having Dimitri around was very difficult and his last comment did not make me feel any easier about him.

Opening my eyes, I focused on the altar. I could just about make out Dan's feet lying down on the floor. Poor thing, he must be so exhausted. Stepping carefully over the broken wood and piles of rubble, I tried not to wake him. However, as I got nearer, I began to get concerned about the position he was lying in – it did not look very comfortable. Speeding up, I dispensed with being quiet and rushed to his side. I was alarmed to see a large cut on the side of his head. The blood was now dark and congealed so it must have happened a few hours ago. Lying next to him was a piece of jagged stone with blood on one side. I knelt beside him and placed my cheek close to his mouth, for one seemly endless moment I held my breath. Relief flooded through me; thank goodness he was breathing. I could feel his warm breath on my cheek and looking down at his chest I could see it rise and fall. Gently, I held his shoulders and shook him while calling out his name. I tried again, shaking him harder and raising my voice, "Dan. Dan. Wake up! Wake up!"

Completely, focused on Dan, I had not noticed Dimitri join me. "Oh no, is he okay? I heard you shouting his name," Dimitri asked.

I looked up at him, I found it hard to focus on his anxious face as tears had started to run down my cheeks. "I don't know. He won't wake up!" I sobbed. At that moment, all I knew was I could not bear to lose him.

"Helena, please don't cry. Let me check him out. He was perfectly fine when I left him. I don't understand what happened to him."

Limply, my hands dropped to my sides and I moved backwards. I watched in slow motion as Dimitri checked his body for any other injuries, rolling him carefully on his side. Then opened his eyelids to check his pupils and called out Dan's name. Next, he tore off a piece of his shirt, grabbed the water bottle and unscrewed the lid. Wetting the material, he began to clean the blood away from Dan's head. Finally, something stirred in Dan's body, his fingers on his right hand switched. I found myself reaching out for them, I held them tightly, hoping and praying it was a sign he was about to wake up. Slowly, his eyes started to flicker and he began murmuring my name. In response, my body sighed with relief. Briefly, I smiled at Dimitri before turning my attention back to Dan. I cradled his head in my arms as I told him, "Dan, you're safe. It's me, Helena. Open your eyes. I'm here. I'll never leave your side."

His eyes were fully open now and his mouth was transformed into his infectious grin. "Helena, I was dreaming about you."

Smiling back at him, I replied, "I bet you were," and kissed him gently on the mouth.

"What was that for?" he asked.

"You had me worried earlier but you're back, you're fine now."

Dan touched the side of his head and winced, "This doesn't feel fine though. What happened?"

Suddenly, Dimitri interrupted, "What do you remember?"

Trying to sit up, I helped support Dan's back. "Dan, take it easy," I implored. "We don't know how long you were unconscious for!"

Dan smiled, "You can play nurse if you want but I feel fine, apart from a sore head." Turning to Dimitri he said, "I remember following you outside to the altar. I think I lost sight of you fleetingly and then nothing. I just remember waking up and seeing your face, Helena." I tried to smile reassuringly at him.

With a concerned voice, Dimitri asked, "So you don't remember chatting with me about our plans to return to the temple city."

Dan rubbed his head again, "No, I think I must have tripped and hit my head on something."

"Like this rock," I held up the jagged stone with blood on it."

"Yes, that looks like what happened," Dan nodded.

"So, you don't remember going back to the room and being alone with Helena?" Dimitri asked.

Dan looked at me with a smirking grin, "I think I would remember that happening!" My face crumpled. "Sorry did I forget something important? I'm sure it will come back to me," he squeezed my hand reassuringly.

Dimitri looked at me encouragingly," Amnesia, I think. Let's not push him too much. He will remember when he is ready."

"Yes, you are absolutely right." Wiping away the last of my tears. "Let's concentrate on getting you fixed up. Can you stand?" I asked trying to hide my growing concern.

"I think so," replied Dan. Immediately, Dimitri stepped forward and took hold of one arm and shoulder. Leaning on him, Dan carefully got to his feet. I supported him on the other side, holding his waist tightly. Together, we guided him past all the obstacles back to our room. Leaving them loitering by the door, I quickly went in and cleared a path to a makeshift bed I constructed out of cushions. Tentatively, Dan made his way into the room with Dimitri's help and sat down. Trying to make him more comfortable I added another cushion behind his head and got him to lay down.

"Really, you don't need to make such a fuss. I'm starting to feel much better now, apart from a dull headache. Besides we need to make plans and start our journey to the temple city."

"Wait a minute, Dan. You were probably, unconscious for quite a while and you have a nasty cut on your head. You gave us quite a scare. What you need to do is rest up, at least for today. The plans can wait until you are better," I strongly recommended.

"She's right," interrupted Dimitri. "Your health is much more important. You won't be any good trying to rescue George if you are not feeling 100% fit."

"I suppose you are right," Dan reluctantly replied. "Let me rest for a couple of hours and then see how I am."

"That's more like it. While you rest, I will prepare provisions for the journey," volunteered Dimitri. "I expect you will want to stay with him, Helena?"

I nodded and squeezed Dan's hand. Moving towards the door, Dimitri smiled and said, "Just yell if you need me, Helena." Pausing he then said, "Helena, you look exhausted, you could do with a nap too. Make sure you rest."

"Thank you, Dimitri but I want to make sure Dan's okay first."

"I'll be fine Helena," Dan smiled reassuringly. Gently, he stroked my cheek and stared at my tired face.

"You heard him, Helena, he's feeling much better," Dimitri added as he disappeared through the door.

Once he had gone, Dan sighed and patted the cushion next to him. "We could both do with a nap to recharge our batteries! Come and lay down beside me." I didn't need to be asked twice. Picking up a water bottle, I brought with me, I invited Dan to drink from it.

"Thanks," he sighed taking it from me. A few swift gulps later, he snuggled up next to me on the cushions and whispered, "I love you," before giving me a peck on the cheek. Then he laid back down and closed his eyes.

Laying, beside him I watched the steady rise and fall of his chest and was overwhelmed with a sense of relief and thankfulness. I could still vividly remember how I felt when I first found him unconscious. My heart pounded involuntarily as the emotions arose back up in my chest. I tried to blink away the tears starting to form in my eyes. I loved him so much if I lost him again – it would be utterly unbearable. The realisation of what we might face at the temple city was starting to sink in. I knew, if we had any chance of succeeding, I needed to use Freya to help us. Unable to close my eyes, I was content instead to listen and watch his breathing.

Chapter 22

Gradually, I became aware of Dan softly calling my name. Opening my eyes, I was relieved to see Dan's crinkled smile. "Sorry," I apologised. "I didn't mean to fall asleep too."

"Don't be too hard on yourself. We've all been through so much over the last few days. We need to sleep when we can."

"I know, but I was so worried when I found you. I thought …" My voice trailed off. Tears began to prickle my eyes. Dan wrapped his arms around me and hugged me tightly.

"Don't worry about me. I'm absolutely fine. In fact, after that power nap. I feel so much better."

Looking around the room, I could see the sunlight spilling through the gap in the ceiling. Concentrated in one corner, it had lots of orangey and pink hues. "Dan, I think we both must have slept well into the afternoon."

"I think you must be right Helena judging by the brightness in here. I guess we both needed that sleep. Hmmm," he said as he started to nuzzle my ear. "Talking about what we both need. Didn't we agree to carry on later with our reunion yesterday?"

I did not have the heart to tell him we had already consummated our reunion the previous night so I responded enthusiastically as he gently cupped my chin and leaned in to kiss me. Very quickly the kiss developed as his tongue began to probe inside my mouth. Pulling me nearer I wrapped my arms tightly around him. Feeling the warmth of his body against mine, sent tingling shockwaves through me. I longed to feel his skin against mine. My hands moved lower and began to pull at his t-shirt. His mouth left mine and began to weave a feathery trail of hot kisses down my neck to my exposed shoulder. I sighed as the intensity between us rapidly built up. Dan murmured, "I've been waiting too long for us to be together again. I love you so much." Abruptly, I pulled away from our embrace.

"Are you okay Helena?" Dan faltered.

Hesitating, I bit my lip, "Dan, you really can't remember what happened after the harpies' incident?"

Trying to reassure me, Dan gently stroked the side of my left cheek, "Helena please don't worry. I'm sure my memory will come back to me eventually. Look if you are still worried about me – don't be. I'm absolutely fine apart from a sore head." He laughed and then carefully touched the side of his head.

Should I tell him, we had already slept together? My mind was in turmoil. Eventually, a voice inside my head said, "Tell him later as it might upset him more if he knew!"

Clasping his hand, I squeezed it reassuringly, "Dan, I'm sorry but I can't help feeling concerned about you. It was a nasty shock finding you like that. Are you sure you're feeling much better? It's probably best that you rest some more before we get too carried away."

"Oh, but I'm enjoying it so much getting carried away. Besides we have a lot of lost time to make up." Dan smiled sheepishly. Reaching out for me again, Dan pulled me closer and kissed me. I surrendered in his arms. Very soon his body was on top of me and I was swept away by his kisses.

Suddenly, there was a knock on the door and it creaked open. Reluctantly, we broke apart from our embrace and tried to distance ourselves.

"Sorry to interrupt but the sun is starting to set. I overslept. You look like you are feeling much better Dan."

Blushing, I looked down and fumbled with my water bottle, trying to get the lid off. "Here let me," Dan swiftly took over. His fingers expertly opened the bottle lid and then casually trailed up my arm before giving me an affectionate squeeze. Looking up at him I could not resist his cheeky smile.

Before I could say anything, Dimitri excitedly made his way towards us and sat down opposite me. "Look you two, I'm so glad Dan has recovered but we need to make plans for tonight in case the harpies come back. Also, we need to make an early start tomorrow towards the city."

Dan nodded, "I agree." Looking up at the ceiling he added, "We definitely need to move out of this room tonight. The harpies could easily spot us if we stay here."

"Maybe we could make a makeshift bed in between two of the pews if we clear a space," Dimitri suggested. "Three walls still remain intact so anyone looking in will have their vision obscured."

Getting up Dan said, "Let's check it out and see if we can find a cosy spot." Grabbing his outstretched hand, I let Dan pull me to my feet. Misplacing my foot on some debris, I lost my balance momentarily and ended up in Dimitri's arms. Taking advantage of the situation, I felt his hot breath on my cheek and his hands lingered too long around my waist. I tried to disguise my disgust by casually turning my face away and laughing. Thanking him, I quickly stepped forward back into the arms of Dan. He laughed too saying, "Was it you who bumped your head?"

Without a backward glance, I let Dan guide me carefully through the rubble to find the best place. All the time, my hair stood on end and my skin prickled at the thought of Dimitri's eyes following my every move from behind. He behaved far too familiar around me; it was like he had known me far longer than a few days. Perhaps it was just he had not been near a woman for so long. Even so, I could not shake off the feeling of uneasiness. I felt it in his presence and his timing was always so perfect – interrupting us at the most opportune moments. Still, he had been like a rock and took charge when I found Dan unconscious. Maybe I was being too harsh and paranoid. Shrugging my shoulders, I decided to let my negative feelings go and concentrate on the present task.

Dan stopped abruptly and said, "Look these two pews are still intact. Let's move this one to make a V-shape so it will block any prying eyes from the window over there." Dan quickly moved to one end of the pew and I started to move to the other but Dimitri blocked my path.

Smiling he said, "Please allow me." Backing away slowly I adjusted the angle of the other pew instead.

Standing further back towards the entrance, Dan enthusiastically shouted, "Please, can you both sit down on the floor in between the pews." Silently, we both sat down. "That looks perfect from here. You're both well hidden."

Suddenly, Dimitri got up and brushed past me as he walked back towards the old, study room. "Dan, let's go back and get the rest of our things while Helena makes the area more comfortable for us." Dan saw my face and tried to look sympathetic while he followed Dimitri.

Once they were out of sight, I picked up one of the scattered prayer cushions and threw it hard against the nearby wall. I was about to throw another one when the design on the back caught my eye. Although faded, I could still make out the picture of a Knights Templar cross. I had noticed the other prayer cushion pictures mainly depicted scenes from the bible which had been lovingly sewn. This one picture stood out from the others. I remembered watching a documentary about them. Holding on to it I decided to show Dan later.

Peeking over the pews I watched Dan and Dimitri carrying the few possessions we had left on this island – two rucksacks filled with bits and pieces and some water bottles. Placing them in the pews, Dimitri returned to the room for the cushions. Bringing them back he handed them over to me. Obediently, I stood up and accepted them. He stood there watching me closely as I scattered the cushions into three equal piles. I hoped Dimitri would take the hint and opt for the furthest pile on its own thus allowing Dan and me to be close together.

"Great!" said Dan. "Now our sleeping arrangements are sorted. Do you fancy a walk around the church before it gets too dark, Helena? We could quickly collect some more berries before the sun goes down and refill our water bottles." Turning to Dimitri he added, "Why don't you get your head down first?"

"I've got a better plan," replied Dimitri as he took out a small penknife from his pocket. "I will join you outside and look for some wood suitable to make into wooden stakes to use as weapons, just in case the harpies venture too close again."

Immediately, I interrupted, "I thought you said we were safe as its hallowed ground and they wouldn't dare enter the church."

"Ah yes, I did say that but realistically the church is very derelict and has not been used for years. I think it would be good if we were better prepared for any possibility of another encounter with them."

Feeling quite vulnerable I looked over at the two pews and cushions and realised how inadequate they were defensively if the harpies attacked us. Obviously, noticing how worried I looked, Dan moved closer and placed a reassuring arm on my shoulder. Trying to sound positive, he said, "Helena, you've survived all these days alone on this island, surely you can get through one more night in this church!"

"Yes, I suppose you are right. It just seemed so much easier on my own. I didn't have to worry about everyone else and myself." Dan pulled me towards him and gave me a much-needed hug. Breathing in the scent of him, I felt so safe in his arms and for that brief moment, I forgot our predicament.

"I love you so much Helena," Dan whispered in my ear. "I won't let anything happen to you while I'm around. Just hold onto that thought."

Squeezing him tighter, I became aware of Dimitri staring at us. Begrudgingly, I released my arms from around Dan's shoulders. "Thanks, I needed that." Trying my best to avoid any further eye contact with Dimitri, I smiled at Dan and said, "Let's go for that walk now."

Smiling back, Dan replied, "Yes, you can lead the way." Holding my hand tightly, we walked out into the open and were greeted with the warm, orange glow of the sun just starting to lower in the sky. We paused to witness in the distance, the beautiful golden reflection reaching up from the temple roof to shake hands with the sun. Strangely, at that moment it did not seem such a threatening place to be travelling towards. Slowly, Dan steered me towards the berry bushes to the right. Dropping my hand abruptly, he sighed, "Hang on Helena, I'll just run back inside and get a container for the berries."

"Okay, good idea! I'll start picking some while I wait."

Once inside the church, Dan made a beeline for Dimitri. Coming up behind him he tapped his shoulder, making him turn around. In a very controlled, calm voice Dan said, "Hey Dimitri, my girlfriend needs to know she is safe here. It's only for one more night. Please stick to your first thoughts about the church being on hallowed ground. I liked that version better."

Shocked and bemused, Dimitri opened his mouth to say something but was silenced by a fist to his jaw. Making him topple backwards a few steps before regaining his balance. "What the hell was that for?" he grimaced through gritted teeth.

"I don't want to waste my time explaining. You know perfectly well why I did it. Keep your eyes and seedy hands off my girl. Don't think I haven't noticed!"

Holding his jaw, Dimitri blurted out, "I didn't mean any harm by it. She is a very beautiful woman. I know I don't have a chance with her but just looking is, okay?"

"NO, I repeat it's not okay. If I see you doing it again – you'll feel my fist again. It's only because we need your knowledge of the temple that I'm willing to let you stay with us. Once it's over, you are on your own."

Dimitri dropped to his knees and began to cry. "Please you are wrong. I want to help you find my good friend George. Please I promise, my eyes will never linger on Helena again." Pausing briefly, he continued, "In spite of what I said earlier, I'm really scared of this island and its inhabitants. It was so great to find Helena and then you joined us. The last thing I want is to be on my own again. I realise if we are to survive on this island then we need each other."

Seeing him so upset and hearing his heartfelt words, softened Dan slightly and he offered him his hand to help pull him up. "Look, I'm sorry for being so heavy handed but I've been watching how you behave around Helena and my anger built up and up only to finally spill out just now. As long as we have an understanding, I'm willing to start again with a clean slate. You are completely right; we do need each other's strengths to survive."

Getting to his feet, Dimitri wiped away a tear and shook his hand wholeheartedly in agreement. Just then they heard Helena calling out for Dan. Quickly, Dan looked around and spied his rucksack. Walking over he reached inside and pulled out a small bag. "This will do," and hurried off to find Helena.

Out of sight Dimitri smiled to himself and murmured, "If Helena was my girlfriend, I wouldn't let her out of my sight, not even for a moment, you never know what could happen!" A little later, he got up and went outside too.

Chapter 23

Over by the fountain, Dimitri bathed his sore jaw and then filled his water bottle. Out of the corner of his eye, he watched the happy couple embrace and share a long lingering kiss before finally starting to pick berries. Secretly, he wished it was his arms wrapped around Helena. Perhaps if something was to happen to Dan – he would be a shoulder to cry on and eventually maybe more … Pushing that thought to one side, he walked over to some thick bushes and using his blade began to cut off some sturdy, thick branches to use for his stakes.

The light was fading along with a slight drop in temperature. Walking over to the loved-up couple, Dimitri said, "It's best we go inside now!"

Stopping what I was doing, I looked up at Dimitri. Immediately, I noticed a vivid red mark on his jaw. I watched as he instinctively brought his hand up to shield it from me. Dan too was behaving oddly, his body seemed tense and his eyes were fixed on the ground. Sensing the awkwardness between them I pretended not to notice their behaviour or inquire about the mark. Instead, I quickly gathered up the berries and marched inside leaving them both a bit of space to sort out their differences. It was obvious something must have happened after Dan went back for the container. He was gone a tad too long and seemed overly cheerful to see me when he returned. Thinking about it, I had caught him gripping and massaging the top of his right hand earlier.

Once inside, I glanced back and saw them exchange words briefly before Dan turned and followed me in with Dimitri close behind. Settling down amongst the cushions I carried on my pretence of not noticing they had fallen out over something. Dan quickly joined me and began eating the berries we had picked. Dimitri hesitated at the entrance to the pews then said, "I'm going to work on the stakes a little longer. There is still some light near the church entrance. I plan to make the most of it."

"Here," I said, handing over a handful of berries balanced on a prayer cushion. "Eat these up. You must feel ravenous like us!"

Thanking me, Dimitri took them over to the gap where the two wooden doors used to open to welcome the congregation into the now abandoned church. Sneaking a look over the top of the pews, I watched him settle down and continue shaping the pointed ends of the wooden stakes. Saying a silent prayer, I hoped we would not see the harpies again tonight then I laid back against the cushions and sighed deeply.

"Penny for your thoughts," Dan asked me as he made himself more comfortable next to me.

"I was just wondering how much longer this ordeal will go on for. I long to be back on our boat, drinking champagne without a care in the world."

"I agree, it seems ages since we were aboard the Adventurer. I hope it's still there waiting for our return."

Spying the Knights Templar cushion, I picked it up and threw it into Dan's lap. "Changing the subject. Have a look at this cushion Dan. If you compare it to all the other cushions depicting bible stories etc. this one seems out of place."

Closely, examining the Templar cross, he nodded. "I remember the Templar knights were heavily involved in the crusades and I read the order protected ancient artefacts from being used for evil purposes. They were also linked to the Arc of the Covenant. Perhaps they knew about the existence of this island and they came here."

"You could be right I suppose. I wonder if there is a real-life Templar knight on this island …somewhere!"

Putting the cushion down, Dan snuggled up beside me. Gently, touching his head I asked, "How are you feeling? You look much better."

"Still sore to the touch. What you are really asking is do I remember anymore?" Hesitating, he continued, "I've been going over the last few moments up to when I followed Dimitri to the lookout position just inside the church but alas nothing extra comes to mind." He looked into my eyes and I found it hard to hide my concern. "Surely, a few hours missed is not the end of the world unless … something important happened. Did anything happen I should know about?"

My concern had passed onto him. Trying to reassure him, I lied and said, "I don't know what happened while you were outside the room. It's just the whole idea of you not being able to remember which worries me."

Fortunately, Dan seemed content with my response and leaned across to give me a huge hug. Nuzzling his face against my neck he planted a few kisses along my collarbone. Pulling away slightly, his arms remained loosely around my shoulders. "You know since we met up, we both haven't had the chance to talk about our time on this island while we were separated." Pausing, his face became more serious as he spoke, "I really thought I had lost you when I found the shredded remains of the yellow dinghy. It was so hard to go on without you. George was like a rock to me. He kept me going plus he gave me a purpose, to free him from this island."

"What was George like? I'm so looking forward to finally meeting your great-grandad!"

"You'll love him. He's so strong and fearless just like you would imagine an explorer of that time to be. He sacrificed so much for his passion – his dear wife and son. But it brought him such comfort to know his son survived, grew up and had a family of his own. Also, his family endured two world wars and had survived until now…" Dan paused and looked back at the cushion.

Deep down, I got the feeling Dan wished he had never pursued the same dream to find this island. Obviously, the fool-hardiness and determination not to give up had been passed down through the generations – so he did not stand a chance.

"If you hadn't pursued your childhood dream to find out what happened then you would have regretted it for the rest of your life." I was about to add, we must not give up hope when Dan interrupted my flow with a gentle kiss on my lips…

"I've had so many adventures finding my way back to you but they have all been worth it to savour the taste of your rosebud lips again," Dan whispered like a tender caress.

Pausing he pulled away again and apologised, "Sorry I keep getting distracted by your inviting lips. Please tell me your story. How you managed to survive alone on this island and how you reached the top of the mountain? Did you find the secret passage?"

So many questions! Slightly thrown by the directness of them, I found myself looking down at my hands trying to work out where to begin. A little voice in my head kept saying he would not believe your story.

Dan looked at me puzzled, during my long silence. "Don't tell me, you've got an even bigger memory problem than me," he joked.

Laughing to break the silence I shook my head. "No, it's just, so much has happened. I'm not sure where to start."

"That's easy, start at the beginning when you woke up and found me gone!"

"I was so worried when I couldn't find you on the boat."

"I realise now how stupid and impatient I was to go off on my own. I should have at least left a note," Dan added.

"Well, even if you had, I wouldn't have stayed on the boat, I would have followed you."

"So, you used the emergency yellow dinghy?"

"Yes, but as I was making my way to the shore, I had company …"

"In the shape of a sea monster!" Dan interrupted again.

"Who is telling this story? "I asked.

"Sorry! When we found the remains of your dinghy, George protected me by suggesting instead that maybe you had drowned. Much later I began to suspect you might have encountered a sea monster when we found some paintings in the cave depicting all the creatures on this island. One drawing stood out the most of a sea serpent with tentacles encircling the island.

"That sounds interesting. What else was drawn on the cave walls?"

"The sea monster appeared to guard the island and in the middle was a man in a white, golden-edged robe holding a golden staff. Above the picture of the golden temple was a beautiful woman with golden hair wearing a bright emerald necklace. She held a golden key in one hand and wore a magnificent, heart-shaped gold ring on the other. Around the island were pictures of dwarfs, giant ogres, harpies and other unusual beasts."

Immediately, I thought of Freya when he mentioned the emerald necklace. I remembered she spoke of it but she did not say anything about a golden key or a heart-shaped ring. "Perhaps this woman holds the key to escape this island," I blurted out.

"Perhaps we will find her in the golden temple and she can reveal all the island's secrets," Dan suggested.

THE ISLAND BECOMES YOU

"I guess we will have to wait and see what happens but maybe she could help us," I secretly hoped.

"We need all the help we can get," Dan replied as he gently squeezed my hand. "Please continue with your story, I promise I will not interrupt as much," he grinned sheepishly.

I laughed and said, "I wonder how long that will last!" Taking a deep breath, I continued, "Well, I survived the menacing encounter with the sea monster but I don't really know why. Its tentacles were closing in and I was hypnotised by its lifeless eyes staring down at me. Meanwhile, the tail was wrapped around the yellow dinghy which burst and flew into the creature's face. Luckily, this broke its spell over me and I was able to escape."

"Thank goodness you are here to tell the tale; I could never forgive myself if the other had been your fate. What happened next to you once you reached the island?"

"Well, unbeknown to me I clambered up a rock giant who happened to be stretched out on the beach, sunbathing, I think. He woke up and carried me to a cave on the side of the mountain where I stayed for a few days."

Dan's eyes lit up, "That's where I found your watch. I spent the night there too. I found your makeshift rope made of leaves."

"Aren't you interested in finding out more about the rock giant? I'm surprised you didn't meet him too."

Dan's eyes narrowed with concern, "Did he keep you a prisoner in the cave?"

"Definitely NO. In fact, he saved my life from a snake and a huge wolf."

"Wow, I can't believe our paths didn't cross. Apart from a few rumblings and the ground shaking a bit, we were oblivious to him. I suppose George and I spent a lot of time inside a rock cavern near the beach so we missed your encounter. Next, we ventured deep into the forest and came across some interesting human-like shrubs which could move independently and they followed a leader. Fire was our only weapon as they closed in on us. Later we stayed in an opening in the forest near a gorgeous waterfall and pool. Nearby was a small hidden cave where we slept. It was there that Dimitri found us but that night he was taken again by the harpies along with George." Dan sighed and looked away. I caught his eyes begin to glisten with tears and he rubbed them with the back of his hand. Reaching out to him, I held him close. I felt his body tense then it gave way to gentle sobs.

I rubbed his back to comfort him and waited for the compacted emotion to spill over and then eventually subside.

Finally, Dan spoke, "I can still picture myself looking up helplessly as George was carried away. I was too late to do anything. Why they had decided to leave the safety of the cave in the middle of the night was a mystery?"

"Why don't you ask Dimitri what happened that night? It might help take some of your guilt away."

"I suppose you are right but it won't change the outcome. George is stuck in a tiny jail somewhere within the walls of the temple city, waiting to face a monstrous ogre. For all we know we could be too late to rescue him!"

Tears started to appear in Dan's eyes again. Holding his face, I forced him to look at me. "Whatever happens you mustn't give up on hope. We've survived so far and we have all been reunited for a purpose. Hope makes us stronger. We will find George and the answers to the questions we seek."

Dan smiled, "That's what I love about you most. You always like to support the underdog and you never give up on me. So how did you make it to the top of the mountain?"

"Well, the giant wolf found me in the cave and the rock giant fought him to protect me. Later I was spread-eagled across a massive tree trunk which the rock giant then lifted me up on to reach the top of the mountain and safety."

"Have you seen the rock giant since?"

"Unfortunately, no. I was physically exhausted after my ordeal and I don't remember much. In fact, I don't remember how I managed to reach the church but somehow, I did. After I spent a few days convalescing here, Dimitri arrived and then you showed up."

Dan clapped, "An amazing story, I would love to meet the rock giant!"

"Me too," piped up Dimitri who was now peering over the pews at us. "We could do with his help warding off any more harpy attacks and the ogre."

"Yes, I agree. I do miss his crinkled face and strange, concerned expressions. There was definitely an understanding between us even though no words were spoken."

"Perhaps he will reappear when you most need him," Dimitri added.

"I hope he will," I replied as I pictured his stony, outstretched hand and reassuring smile. Just then, a worrying thought entered my mind. Maybe the wolf had overpowered him and he lost the battle which would explain his non-appearance.

Quickly, I calmed my doubts by focusing on how the mountain height would protect us from the huge wolf if that was the case. However, on our return journey, we would need to be careful. Going back down the mountain and past the forest. There were so many obstacles in our path to get through before we could escape this island.

"Are you okay?" Dan smiled affectionately and placed a reassuring arm around my shoulders. Squeezing his shoulder in return I nodded, "Just deep in thought about our quest."

Dan laughed, "That's a very old word to use. Makes me think of courageous knights and the round table."

"Well, strictly speaking, we are on a journey filled with adventure, monsters and a man who needs rescuing!"

"Shall I address you as Sir Helena then?"

Pushing him away playfully, I pretended to take out my sword and proceeded to place it on his shoulders and said in a commanding voice, "Arise Sir Dan!" We both fell about laughing until we noticed Dimitri's stern face looking down on us.

"Darkness is nearly upon us; we still need to prepare ourselves …" Dimitri paused as Dan suddenly stood up – their eyes locked together. Recovering himself Dimitri continued, "As I was saying, we really need to prepare ourselves for our journey to the temple city."

Cutting through the charged atmosphere I said, "We definitely need an early start tomorrow to get enough provisions and water for our journey."

Visibly, relaxing his features, Dan nodded, "Yes, there is a lot still to discuss as well."

"Come sit down Dimitri," I beckoned. "Let's eat and drink while we listen to your plans."

Awkwardness still hung in the air but all of us sitting down together helped. I found myself staring at the handful of stakes Dimitri clutched in his hand. One stood out from the others as it was much longer and wider. Following my eyes, Dimitri answered my question, "Yes, I've made one for you, just in case we need it when we enter the city. There are a few more but I left them by the doorway of the church."

It was obvious he was avoiding mentioning the elephant in the room! Yes, I might need to use them if the harpies returned tonight and actually ventured inside the church. Looking back at Dan's tense face, I wondered if their discussion earlier had been about not upsetting me further. It was almost like Dimitri was purposely pushing Dan to get an angry response but stepping back with his words just at the last minute.

Reaching to pick one of the smaller stakes, I held it aloft in my right hand to test its weight. Examining the pointed end with my fingers I marvelled how quickly Dimitri had shaped the stake using only a basic pen knife.

"It's good that you get a feel for the weapon. Perhaps tomorrow in the daylight I could demonstrate the best technique to throw it or lunge with it at your opponent," Dimitri offered.

"Sure, that sounds like a good idea. I could continue to practise on our journey to the temple so I'm prepared to use it." I felt surprisingly safer holding the stake so I found myself asking, "Do you mind if I sleep with this tonight?"

Dan gave me a puzzled look in return, then grinned, "I hope you don't plan to use it on me tonight?"

Laughing in reply, I joked, "Only if you get too close and disturb my beauty sleep."

"Can we refocus on discussing our plans for our journey to the temple city? We have an early start tomorrow and we all need some much-needed sleep," Dimitri interrupted.

"Please continue," Dan added rather subdued.

"Okay. It will probably take us two days to get there. We will need to pace ourselves on the first day in order to reach a small, rocky hollow where I safely spent one night," said Dimitri.

"Will there be room for all of us to hide?" I questioned.

"Yes, I am certain. I tested a couple of other hollows until I found the best one but I was being very picky. The one I chose would comfortably hide both of you. I'm sure you won't mind being so close together all night!" Dimitri added.

Watching his eyes closely it was almost as if he winked knowingly at us but raised an eyebrow instead. Feeling rather sick of his innuendoes I turned to face Dan and sank my exhausted head on his shoulders. "So, we will reach the temple city at the end of the second day?" Dan queried.

"Yes, but we may have to delay getting too close until nightfall to avoid being seen. There are some woods nearby where I managed to hide from the harpies."

"How will we enter the city?" I asked.

"The wall surrounding the city is extremely high with very little footings. I admit it was easier clambering over rooftops until I found one wall slightly lower than the others which luckily had vines growing on it. This allowed me to lower myself down further before I jumped into a small area of shrubs which broke my fall."

"So, your plan is to find the wall with the vines and climb up," I summarised.

"Yes, I know it sounds vague but all I can suggest is to use my own escape route backwards. Once there we may have more time to check the full perimeter and find a much better way in," Dimitri tried to sound hopeful but after looking at our sinking faces, he said in his defence. "Please remember, I was looking for the quickest escape route. I didn't have time to compare the best way out and I certainly didn't plan to come back!"

Trying to lighten the mood, Dan said, "I'm sure we will find a way into the city but we still need to discuss our plan to free George once we get there."

Leaning heavily against Dan, I suddenly felt extremely tired. Dan noticed and gently pushed some cushions together and manoeuvred himself so I could rest my head on them. Grateful, I made myself comfortable and gazed up at him. "I love you," I whispered.

Turning to Dimitri, Dan said, "Time for sleep. It's a big day tomorrow." Then Dan bent down and brushed his lips tenderly against my forehead and whispered, "Good night my love, sleep well."

Chapter 24

The last thing I remembered before closing my eyes was checking my hand was within reach of the wooden stake Dimitri had given me. Suddenly, I was in the centre of a very vivid dream. I could hear voices and someone shouting my name. I turned around and came face to face with a menacing harpy, towering over me and cackling cruelly as she pointed to one of her sisters with her outstretched wing. Terrified, my eyes dared me to look and to my horror I could see my darling Dan lying limply in her grasp, blood trickling slowly from a gash to his head. I tried to scream but I felt a strong pressure on my mouth. It seemed to be welded shut, I could not open it. Fear rapidly built up inside me, filling every crevice, forcing its way upwards towards the only exit … my imprisoned mouth. It felt like my whole being would explode. The pressure collected in my throat then started to bulge and extend upwards to my mouth but there was nowhere to escape. I was frozen to the spot unable to move except for my eyes which widened like two saucers unable to tear themselves away from Dan's lifeless body. Was he dead? I silently screamed inside my powerless body until darkness enveloped me like a favourite duvet pulled over my head – I welcomed it.

Gradually, my eyes became accustomed to the blackness and they began to recognise the outline of a familiar face. I reached out to touch him, his stubbly chin and mop of blond hair – all felt real. I heard him call my name again and this time I responded with a weak, barely audible, "Dan, is that you?"

"Thank goodness. Finally, you are awake!" he whispered back. "Sorry,

THE ISLAND BECOMES YOU

I had to put my hand over your mouth. You were making too much noise. I thought you were going to scream!"

Uncontrollable tears, flooded down my cheeks. "I thought you were dead!"

Holding me tightly, he said, "You were having a nightmare but I couldn't wake you." Then in his next breath, he whispered with a sense of urgency, "Helena, this is important. We must leave now. We are not alone!"

Quickly, my brain caught up with reality and I whispered, "Where is Dimitri?"

"He woke me and went to see what was going on but he hasn't returned yet." Pointing to the study room he said, "The noise is coming from there. We need to leave here, it's not safe!"

"But where will we go," I blindly asked.

"I've thought of that. There is an open window at the back of the church if we could reach it then maybe we could slip outside unseen." Dan offered as a solution.

"What about Dimitri?"

"We can't wait for him …" Just then Dan was interrupted by a familiar high-pitched shriek. "At least we know who are visitors are," Dan tried to joke.

Looking at my face's reaction to the sound, Dan's voice softened to say, "I know you must be scared Helena but we really need to get out of here." Giving me a quick hug, he offered me his hand and helped me up. Gripping both his hand and my stake tightly, we carefully made our way to the end of the pew. Dan briefly let go of my hand so he could crawl further round to check if the way was clear. It was only a few seconds but for me it seemed ages before I felt his comforting hand in mine again. "Ready," he squeezed my hand. "Let's try and get to the next upturned pew, ahead of us. It will give us a better view of what's going on."

I could not feel my legs, I was so scared but somehow, I managed to follow behind. Stopping every so often we checked the area around us. My eyes kept returning to the study room door. It was slightly ajar and I could hear muffled voices coming from behind it. Another overhead screech alerted us to the possibility of more harpies. My body froze to the spot. "Come on Helena, we've got to keep moving." I felt Dan lift me in his arms and carry me for the last remaining steps to the upturned pew. Cradling, my face against his chest, I held my breath. Had I had a premonition of what was to come! A cold foreboding crept across my body as Dan carefully laid me down behind the pew.

"I'm sorry, "I whispered. All of a sudden, the door of the study burst open. Peeking through a hole in the pew we both watched transfixed as one harpy's wing uncurled into its full splendour followed by the other as it squeezed through the hole that had been a door. Now it was shaped to easily accommodate the outline of the harpy. We both looked at each other, desperation etched in our eyes. The hallowed ground made no difference I thought. I turned to look at the window behind us and then back at the harpy. Even if we could make it outside, how many other harpies would be waiting for us?

Our eyes were drawn back to the harpy in front of us. I could not help admiring its magnificent feathered body, stature and splendour with its womanly qualities. Strength and power radiated from its presence but underneath there was a glimpse of the softness of a woman until its feminine features were replaced with those of an old wizened witch.

Looking closer, it was not one of the harpies I was familiar with. This one had long hair as dark as coal. The moonlight shimmered across her loose curls. Focusing my attention on her eyes they were like two piercing sapphires searching the church for any sign of us.

I gripped Dan's hand tighter as she walked nearer to the two pews. We had moved them to protect us but we had not bargained on the harpies coming through the roof of the study. I watched Dan turn to look at the window again. I knew he was trying to weigh up what to do next. Could we make our escape in time? How quick can the harpies move on the ground? Surely, their size and wings would impede them thus giving us the advantage of speed and movability.

Unfortunately, I knew at once I was so wrong with my assumption. The raven-haired harpy jumped effortlessly over several broken pews then into the middle of our strategically placed ones. She began moving cushions and rucksacks with her feet. My heart was pounding frantically in my chest as I watched her abruptly stop and her sapphire blue eyes turned to gaze in our direction. In that instant, I knew all hope was lost. Desperately, Dan pointed towards the window, gesturing for me to go ahead while he stayed behind to face her. I could not move, instead, I sank lower onto the floor and closed my eyes to the inevitability of our situation. Dan tried to shake me out of my decision. Eventually, I opened my eyes to his shocked face staring down at me. A little voice in my head said, "Don't give up now!" I could sense the harpy edging closer. Suddenly, I knew what to do. I had to believe. "Freya, please help us," I whispered under my breath. I now heard her voice counting down from 10 in my head. 10, 9, 8, 7, 6 … Turning to Dan, I whispered, "Do you trust me?"

I watched his face change from shock to a look of puzzlement then he calmly said, "Yes."

The voice in my head counted down 3, 2, 1… "Let's go now!" I uttered quietly. Standing up quickly, I held Dan's hand and ran towards the window just as the harpy lunged towards the spot where we had been hiding. Once clear of the pew, I could not resist a glance back. She had missed us and landed in a heap on the floor. Her shocked wrinkled face looked in our direction then towards the open entrance and then back towards the window. Getting up she made her decision to move quickly towards the entrance to the church.

Dan looked at me completely stunned, "Why didn't she follow us?" was written all over his face.

I mouthed the words, "Trust me," and I placed a finger on my mouth to silence him. Carefully, we crept towards the window. Using an upturned chair to elevate him, Dan went first and lifted himself up onto the window ledge. He sat straddling it as he hoisted me up. Kneeling on the sill, I waited for him to lower himself down outside before I followed him. He caught me firmly in his arms and I allowed myself to sigh briefly.

At this point we heard the harpy with raven hair talking to another harpy out of sight. "Serena and Rebecca didn't look properly last night. There are obvious signs that someone had been staying inside the church." Hesitating she continued, "It's strange, I was certain I saw someone hiding behind an upturned pew but when I pounced there was no one."

"Maybe it was just a shadow," offered the second harpy. "The moonlight reflected inside the ruined church can create all sorts of unusual shapes and darkened areas."

"I suppose you are right but I definitely smelt human scent close by."

Outside while they were speaking, I looked around for any cover as I did not know how long the invisibility spell would last for. Still quite perplexed by the whole situation Dan allowed himself to be led by me to a deep mound hidden by the berry shrubs. Lying down on the ground, Dan held me closely as we pushed ourselves into the hollow to blend in. Dan whispered, "I still don't understand why she didn't see us?"

I never replied as we heard the harpies move around from the front entrance to the side where we were hidden. Synchronised, we held our breath together and prayed they would not find us. I hoped Freya's invisibility spell would work for a while longer. I was certain Dan was trying to prepare himself for the worst. His rapid heartbeat against my back and how he held me even tighter gave it away. I wished I could reassure him it would be okay but I was not completely sure Freya's magic had worked earlier or whether we had temporarily become invisible by some fluke of light or shadows cast in the church. Still, surely, we would have been clearly spotted trying to abscond from the window. Reaching down I sought out Dan's hand and grasped it encouragingly. It helped to give me some reassurance too. At that moment, I wondered if Dimitri had managed to find a safe place to hide. He did have a habit of disappearing when the situation became dangerous and reappearing when it was all over. We would have to wait and see if history repeated itself. In the meantime, we sensed the ever-increasing closeness of each step the harpies made nearer to our hideout. They must have been practically on top of us when we heard them say, "Sister, I've lost the human scent. The berry smell overpowers it. But they must have been here earlier."

"Diane, we cannot go back empty handed for a second night. Our master will be extremely displeased."

"I know but they could be anywhere!"

"Let's go back inside the church and check for any possible hiding places."

"You're right Annette, the human scent was strongest there."

Just then I felt a strong breeze sweep over us. Momentarily, the light from the moon above us was blocked out then we felt a heavy thud hit the ground nearby.

"How nice of you to join us, Serena. I thought you were checking the ground near the temple?"

"Yes Diane, I was with Sophie and Patricia but Rebecca felt well enough to join us so I doubled back to see if you needed any help?"

THE ISLAND BECOMES YOU

"They were here. The pews and cushions have been disturbed to make a cosy place to sleep. Also, there are signs humans have been in the old, study room. It's a shame you missed these details last night!" replied Diane.

"I can assure you Diane, I looked carefully inside the room but there was a lot of dust and debris due to Rebecca's foot going through the ceiling so it's quite possible I missed something," replied Serena.

Thankfully, I became aware that Serena was gradually leading the other two harpies further away from where we were hiding.

"Well things would have been much better for us if you had discovered him. I was just saying to Diane how our lapse in recapturing him will no doubt ensure dire consequences from the master." Sighing Annette continued, "We must find him soon. The master will not tolerate any further failure on our part."

Listening to their conversation, I was extremely puzzled how they only mentioned him and not all of us. Who were they referring to? Dimitri or Dan?

"Sisters, please do not worry. We will find him. I promise. He can't have gone far. Would you like me to keep searching outside while you check the church again?"

"Alright, Serena but please make sure you don't miss anything this time!"

"Diane, I assure you it was not my intention to miss anything last night but my concern for my sister's injury prevailed over the task. Will you continue to hold that against me?"

"No, I suppose I would do the same in those circumstances but have you not noticed how obsessed the master has become about the girl. He desires all obstacles to be removed swiftly so he can continue with his plans to …"

"Shh, humans have ears – we don't know if they are within the vicinity and can hear our conversation," Serena fiercely interrupted her sister Diane.

At the mention of the girl and plans, I felt Dan tighten his grip on my hand. Questions swirled around my head; they must be referring to me. I was the only girl left on the island. What plans did he have instore for me? Perhaps his attention was to separate me from Dan again. How could the master be obsessed with me when I had never met him? Again, the same question popped into my head. Where was Dimitri?

"Sorry," her sister mumbled apologetically. "I just get so carried away."

"Well, just remember we will be in an even worse situation if the master finds out we have revealed his intentions to the humans."

"You're always so right, Serena."

"Look there is no harm done. If by some slim chance they did hear they will be none the wiser. Let's focus on picking up his scent again."

"Okay sister, we will go back inside the church and retrace our steps while you continue to check outside for any signs of him. Remember it is only a matter of time before we will find him. No one escapes for long on this island."

Chapter 25

Gradually, their voices began to fade as they probably re-entered the church. I let myself take a deep breath and allowed my body to go limp in Dan's arms. Up to this point, I must have felt very tense next to him. At the same time, I felt him let go too and his body softened against mine.

Taking another deep breath, my body at last relaxed completely in Dan's arms. I allowed myself to feel safe for just a moment. I forgot about the harpies and being trapped on this island. I was just here in the present, relishing the deep love we shared for each other. It felt so strong, I had an overwhelming urge to cry. Battling against the tears starting to form in my eyes and trying to clamp down hard on a sob about to escape from my mouth. Reality hit me like a rock, I was far from being in a safe place to allow my true feelings to surface. Danger was all around us and I had to fight with every nerve in my body to regain my composure.

Dan obviously felt the change in me – he probably realised too that there was no chance to relax. We had to think of a solution, the hollow might buy us some more time but what if Serena came back and looked more thoroughly in this area. We had to move further away from the church. Trying to twist round slightly, I let go of Dan's hand. He instantly reacted by edging back slowly to allow me room to turn to face him. His eyes reflected the concern in my face. Moving his head slightly upwards he tried to peer around the mound to pinpoint whether the harpies had moved further around the building or were in fact still there just waiting for us to expose where we were hiding.

Suddenly, a familiar voice whispered, "Dan, do not move." Dimitri had reappeared from nowhere. He was lying flat between two bushes, the leaves covered most of his body except for his protruding head. Surprisingly, I found myself relieved to see him but shocked he had got so close without us noticing.

I watched as Dimitri pointed to the church and motioned for Dan to keep down. Immediately, Dan lowered his body alongside mine again and grinned. "We're stuck here," he mouthed. I noticed Dimitri adjusted his position slightly and raised his head using the bushes for cover. Staring over in the direction of the church, I watched his head quickly bob down again. His eyes looked nervous as he pointed back at the church and then he edged backwards until he disappeared from sight. I took this cue to twist back around while Dan snuggled into my back as tightly as he could. We both held our breath, expecting at any moment for a high-pitched screech to alert the other harpies of our whereabouts.

Time slowed down; every breath seemed to last an age. Cramp began to form in my left foot, I tried to wriggle my toes within my trainers to stop it spreading. Dan held me closer and pressed his head against the hollow on my shoulder. His warm breath dampened my top.

I began to feel rather claustrophobic, the ground around me seemed to be closing in. The smell of berries was very overpowering and I desperately wanted to push Dan's body away so I could get free. Closing my eyes, I started to count to 100 then 200. I focused on each number, imagining it was a chain of links which could not be broken and our lives depended on it. Suddenly, Freya's name popped into my head, perhaps she could help again but she said I could only call on her three times. It might be a waste to use it so soon after the last one – maybe I did not need to. However, the fact I could now feel the ground shake nearby made me reconsider that last thought. They must be very nearby, practically on top of us!

"Serena, have you seen anything?" the harpy shouted. I felt the ground thud again and some soil was displaced near my head. Instantly, I closed my eyes shut to shield them from the loose debris. To my dismay, I felt a long chunk of ground fall in front of my face. Peeking upwards I could see a visible hole above me and one of the harpy's sharp talons now protruded down from it. Hovering just near my nose, I felt a terrible urge to sneeze. I nearly screamed but fortunately I felt a reassuring hand over my mouth. I realised it was Dan, anticipating my reaction to the hole above me. I could not believe how close she was! Actually, standing on the mound we were desperately trying to use to conceal our bodies. She only needed to look down or apply a bit more pressure to increase the gap and we would surely be discovered.

I was about to call again for Freya to help us when I heard Serena reply, "No, there is no trace of him." Then to my immense relief the harpy moved away from the mound just as the earth crumbled away further and the hole now easily exposed my head. Luckily for us, she continued to walk in the direction of the church, towards her sisters. I felt Dan sigh and slowly released his hand from my mouth, moving it back to my shoulder and gave me an affectionate rub. I let out a deep breath to try to stop myself becoming too overwhelmed by the enormous anxiety I had just experienced. I felt so protective of Dan. Strangely, I seemed much stronger when we were apart on the island. I knew I could not bear to watch him being captured in front of me. Still too scared to exchange words with Dan in case we were heard, I leaned back into his chest and squeezed his hand lying on my shoulder.

Together we focused our hearing on the conversation the three harpies were having. The one called Diane was getting quite irate as she screeched back at her sister, "WE MUST FIND HIM! The master will be very displeased when we report back about our lack of information concerning his whereabouts."

Meanwhile, Serena was trying her best to calm her sister. I overheard her say, "One more day won't affect his plans."

"I'm not so sure. You fully know from your own experience how severe his punishments can be even for minor setbacks."

Just then there was a high-pitched shriek from overhead. "Look sisters, Sophie is joining us!" exclaimed Diane.

"Perhaps she has good news," Serena added.

We strained our ears again to try to pick up their conversation. We felt a softer thud as Sophie landed near to her sisters but her voice was lower and it was much harder to make out what she was saying. The last thing we heard before they all took off was from Diane, "So be it, sisters. Our purpose is not to judge but obey. Let's take our leave now."

For a while, we lay there listening to our heartbeats gradually return to normal. I felt almost paralysed, unable to move in case they returned. Finally, Dan murmured in my ear, "I think it's safe to move now." Slowly, he edged away from me, allowing me to carefully wriggle around to face him. His eyes, still contained a glint of fear but mainly they showed concern for me.

"I'm fine, "I reassured him. "Are you okay?"

"Yes, but it's been so hard keeping so very still next to you when all I want to do is this." Tenderly, he touched my cheeks with his hand and leaned in to kiss me. His soft lips against mine briefly helped me forget our predicament. My love for him made me stronger. We could face anything as long as we had each other. Gently, Dan pulled away. "It's now or never!"

"Just wait a few moments more," came a voice from the bushes, stopping Dan in his tracks. Looking over I could see Dimitri staring up at the night sky. Realising we were waiting for an explanation he added, "Harpies have excellent night vision. They might be able to detect sudden movement even from that distance!" He pointed to where I could vaguely make out four moving black dots in the night sky. We all watched until the four dots disappeared over the temple.

Dan and I waited for Dimitri to get up then Dan got to his knees and reached out to help me from the hollow. My legs felt a bit shaky as I too got onto my knees. I hesitated and let Dan who was now standing, pull me up. Once we were both stood up, we brushed off loose leaves and soil from our clothes. Our eyes met; I could feel the intensity between us bubble up in my throat. I let out huge sob of relief and immediately Dan's arms were around me. I so needed that closeness it allowed me to let go. Another sob escaped from my lips followed by an endless stream of tears. I could not hold the flow back anymore, even if I tried to. The release was immense. Dan held me tighter. I felt each sob ripple through my body before escaping through my mouth. It was so long overdue. Everything I had been through; all the emotions had built up and up until this moment when they began to burst out uncontrollably. At last, the lid had been removed and the raw emotion could finally flow out. Gradually, the rate of my sobs began to subside allowing me to take a calming breath in between. Slowly, I became aware of Dan's soothing voice in amongst my tears.

"We're safe now. They've gone. Look the sun is rising." My eye sight was still blurry from all the tears but I looked up and followed the direction of his voice. There on the horizon I could just make out the faint orange glow signalling the start of a new day, a chance to begin again. I so hoped we would be successful rescuing George but deep down I knew the odds were against us but a glimmer of hope still burned brightly. I knew we could not give up. I needed to be stronger, find the reserves I had at the start of this incredible but also very frightening adventure. Looking up at Dan, I decided that this precise moment marked a turning point for me. I vowed to shed no more tears and rekindle my inner strength; I knew existed deep down in my being.

Chapter 26

George sat down against the hard, cold interior wall of the chamber that had become his prison. How he longed to see and feel the sunlight on his skin again. Instead, every day he breathed in the damp stale air of his underground tomb.

From the arena he had been escorted to his new home. Meekly, he had followed the guards, totally in shock and disbelief over what had just happened to him. They led him to the golden temple and he vaguely remembered entering a huge, ornate, golden door. After that he recalled the blurry haze of endless lit torches on the walls as he was escorted deeper into a maze of underground passages until they finally bundled him inside these now familiar four walls.

Tears trickled down his face as he stared down at the rugged hooves which used to be his feet. He had to be careful trying to wipe them away with his monstrous hands and sharp talons for fingers. Looking closer, dark blood stains had pooled around his knuckles after he had pounded for hours on the stone trap doors demanding to be released. Eventually, his cries had been answered when a smaller stone door whizzed open briefly and a bowl of bones and scraps was shoved through it before it instantly shut again. He was forced to lick up puddles of moisture from the floors and walls to quench his thirst. He was treated no better than a chained-up dancing bear, expected to perform for food scraps when his master wished it.

When he closed his eyes to try to sleep and dream his dire predicament away all he experienced was his cruel transformation repeated, again and again until he begged his body to wake him from this everlasting nightmare. Ironically, when he awoke there was no relief only constant pity drained his every thought. But the biggest fear of all! Could he bring himself to kill his great-grandson as his master had commanded?

Over in the far corner, the pile of animal bones was gaining height. How long had he been a prisoner down here? He felt incredibly hungry, the meagre scraps of meat left on the bones were pitiful and hardly touched his hunger pains. Suddenly, the stone trap door on the right side opened a foot and stopped. He was still getting used to his huge muscular body and trying to stand quickly was impossible. Finally, getting to his feet, he started to move towards the opening. To his surprise a blur of white was pushed through the gap then to his dismay he heard the stone trap door crash down again. He was about to drop to his knees when he heard a bleating sound to the left of him. He sniffed the air and now blood and fear were also mixed up in the stale aroma. Adrenalin began to course through his veins, the rush of excitement bewildered him. He was powerless to his new body's demands. He clenched his powerful fists together and slowly turned towards his meal. Vaguely, he noticed the terrified goat had its back pressed as hard as possible against the wall in the corner. Its eyes protruded with fear, completely fixated, unable to move from the monstrous creature moving steadily nearer.

George could sense the animal's distress, its heartbeat quickened and it began to almost cry like a human child. He was now within striking distance of the goat. The saliva in his mouth was dripping down his chin with expectancy. His heart was pounding too at the thought of ripping the animal apart and gorging on its fresh red blood. Suddenly, the frozen animal stopped bleating pitifully. Instead, it gazed pleadingly at George to spare its life. For one fleeting moment, George stopped and asked himself what was he about to do? How could he even contemplate doing it?

This thought disappeared completely in the blood bath that followed as he ripped through sinews and tissues like a knife cutting through butter. The last high-pitched squeal of death did not deter his blood lust as he ripped into the goat's body with his fists and attempted to quench his insatiable hunger. Grabbing huge chunks of flesh and bone and throwing them into his mouth he quickly ground them down with his enormous teeth! He could not stop himself and even licked up every drop of blood he could from the harsh cold floor. Only then did he feel satisfied, sitting back on the floor he stared at the circular red stain on the floor.

He could not believe what he had done. There had been a living, breathing creature standing there moments earlier. He knew in that instant, the beast he had become. God help Dan, if he ended up in the same room as him. He knew he had no control over his animal instincts once they kicked in. Tears began to flood down his cheeks as he imagined the blood stain on the floor was Dan's. He grieved for what he was, what he had lost but most of all for what he had become.

Chapter 27

Dan held me at arm's length and scrutinised my face for any signs of how I was really feeling. My tears had dried up. I imagined my eyes still looked very puffy but I had stopped shaking and I felt much better.

I smiled and said, "I really needed to let all that pent-up emotion out. I feel so much better now!" Not certain whether to believe me, Dan hesitated then gave me another hug.

As he held me close, he said, "We've been through a roller coaster ride of emotions since arriving on this island. It's only natural, especially after such a stressful and dangerous situation has passed for our feelings to spill over." Cupping my chin with both hands he looked straight into my eyes and said, "I can't help myself; I keep going over and over in my head what if we had been discovered. If anything had happened to you I …" His voice trailed away and he leaned in, to kiss me urgently on the lips. Immediately, I responded by pinning my body tighter against him and drawing him closer with my arms as our kiss became more passionate.

"Sorry to interrupt you both but time is pressing," said Dimitri, trying to get us to notice him. It worked. Reluctantly, we broke apart and turned around to face him, standing like soldiers ready to listen to his next order. "So glad to have your attention at last," he added sarcastically.

Jumping to our defence, Dan replied, "You can't blame us after what we went through. I can't believe we managed to evade the harpies again."

"I can't believe it too! We were just expressing how thankful we were to have survived another encounter." I noticed Dan could not hide a small smirk on his lips as I mentioned being so thankful.

Quickly composing himself Dan continued, "Let's hope our luck stays with us for the next chapter of our adventure."

"Yes, we were surprisingly lucky last night but with my help, I'm certain we will succeed," Dimitri butted in. Dan and I looked at each other and instantly fell about laughing after Dimitri's comment. He was so full of self-importance as he said it.

Eventually, I looked over at Dimitri, his face clearly showed how unamused he was at our reaction. Unfortunately, it only fuelled our laughter more until my sides ached and I could not continue. It was such a happy release of all the negative emotions I still harboured. Catching my breath, I just managed to blurt out, "Sorry," before I sank to the floor quite worn out from all the laughing. Dan sat down beside me, clutching his sides too.

A very sombre Dimitri said, "I'm so glad you found my comment so funny. I could easily walk away and leave you both to continue to the temple city on your own without any prior knowledge of the layout or what to expect inside. Therefore, cutting your chances of succeeding considerably."

Dan again leapt up to defend our actions. "We apologise again for not seeming to take this seriously enough. We just needed a release for all the terrible tension and worry we experienced earlier and the fear of being discovered. Sorry, you just sounded so … serious."

"I worry about you two. Our task shouldn't be taken lightly. It will be extremely dangerous and almost impossible to get in and out of the city without being discovered. Then there's the journey back. We only have a very slim chance of…"

"Hey, less of the doom and gloom merchant. I preferred the more serious one. We will succeed Dimitri," interrupted Dan. "Look, I realise we were acting crazy but I repeat we didn't mean to offend you. Dimitri we really need your help and guidance through the city otherwise we will waste time and make mistakes as it will be totally unfamiliar to us. You are right; we need your knowledge to have any hope of succeeding with the task ahead."

"Yes," I echoed his plea too. "We need you Dimitri, in fact, we need everyone to work together to succeed."

I watched Dimitri hunch his shoulders up and then release them before replying, "Okay I accept your apologies. Let's get organised and get going as soon as possible. The day has already begun!"

"I'll fill up the water bottles," I volunteered.

THE ISLAND BECOMES YOU

"Well Dimitri, that leaves us to start picking berries," Dan suggested

"There's also some yuca root plants I noticed while I was hiding. I will dig up some for our journey. It will give us some much-needed energy."

"Okay, I'll pick berries on my own then," said Dan. Then he stretched out his hand to pull me up from my sitting position. "Time is of the essence, my dear," Dan said playfully as he tenderly held my hand and kissed it.

"We really don't have time for any displays of affection," Dimitri snapped.

Not wanting to cause another argument and attempting to lighten the atmosphere, I replied, "You are absolutely right," trying to look serious as I looked at Dan. "We must put an end to all this frivolous behaviour."

"Alright then," Dan said begrudgingly. "Until later my lady," as he pretended to bow. Smiling warmly, I skipped off towards the church to collect our water bottles and sort out my rucksack. Dan followed me in later to collect some containers. I spied the wooden stake, Dimitri had made, still lying near the upturned pew. Remembering how strong and imposing the harpy appeared up close last night, I decided it would not have made a lot of difference if I had tried to use it. Dan saw me looking at the stake and asked, "Do you plan to take it with you? I remember you were quite attached to it last night."

"It might make a good walking stick but after last night I doubt it would have made much of an impression on the harpy's body if I had tried to use it. Their stature would make it hard to get close enough to strike them. Besides, the pointy end needs to be sharper to penetrate their solid, scaly skin and I don't have the strength needed to throw it with any conviction from a distance."

"That's a shame. You have pointed out all the negatives about it. I still think it may be useful," Dan added encouragingly.

"Perhaps I will take it with me," I relented.

Sneaking up beside me as I grabbed my rucksack. He took me in his arms and held me close. Kissing my neck, he asked, "Are you really okay, Helena? I was incredibly scared too. I thought we were bound to get discovered. Has it helped to cry? Do you feel better?"

"Stop! Stop! Too many questions. Yes, I agree with everything you said. I do feel much better and more importantly stronger."

Holding me at arms-length, he searched my face, particularly my eyes to confirm what I just said. At last, seemingly convinced, he cupped my cheeks with his hands and kissed me passionately. As the kiss continued, I pulled his body nearer and allowed myself to become completely swept up in the moment. I loved him so much and he knew me so well. It was hard to hide my true feelings from him.

Eventually, Dimitri's words about time wasting flashed up in my mind. So reluctantly I ended our kiss. "As much as I would love to carry on kissing you. We really need to focus on getting ready to go," I tried to sound convincing.

"I totally agree but one more kiss won't do any harm…" Before I could resist, his lips were purposely clamped back on mine and I did not need any persuading to respond back. This time Dan ended our kiss and hugged me tight for a few moments longer, then he whispered in my ear, "I am yours and you are mine."

Quickly, I added the word, "forever." Briefly, he squeezed me tighter before letting me go. Staring into his eyes I could easily allow myself to be pulled deeper down into those inviting blue pools but I had to resist. Forcing myself to take a step back. I bent down to grab my rucksack and said, "We both need to focus on getting ready to leave this place. Dimitri won't be very happy with us if we keep getting distracted from our tasks."

"I agree but it's so hard to resist you plus it takes my mind off what might or might not happen next." Smiling down at me he took out two more water bottles from his rucksack, passing them to me. Momentarily, our fingers touched and I felt a slight tingling sensation pass between us. Dan laughed and said, "That confirms how attracted we are to each other." Affectionately, he bent down and touched my cheek with the back of his hand then he slowly turned and walked back outside.

Collecting my thoughts and all the water bottles I followed him but once outside I changed direction towards the fountain. Bending down I took the first water bottle, removed the lid and submerged it in the water. While I put the lid back on, I stared up at the mermaid statue. Looking at the well-worn features of the yellowed marbled face, I began to wonder if I had imagined it coming to life and speaking to me. I found myself scrutinising the facial details, especially the oval eyes for any signs of life. Their gaze was fixed ahead towards the church and her stone lips were slightly parted in a half smile. Shrugging my shoulders, I returned to the task in hand and

THE ISLAND BECOMES YOU

filled the next water bottle up. However, halfway through, I became powerfully aware that someone was staring at me. I looked around, no-one was behind me or to the left of me. On my right I could see Dan had his back to me as he concentrated on collecting more berries. Further away was Dimitri using some flat piece of wood to dig up the root vegetables he had found. My eyes then looked upwards to the sky which was clear and quiet. Finally, I looked back at the statue and let out a faint gasp as her eyes were now staring down at me and her mouth was open ready to say something. My brain wanted to run and alert the others but my body refused to move. A feeling of 'Déjà vu' flooded through my body. Mesmerised, I stared up at her face and waited.

"Helena, I haven't much time. I suspect Loki may already have guessed someone is helping you."

"It was you who helped us last night," I blurted out, quite relieved.

"Yes, Helena but don't act so surprised. I told you I would help you. Remember though, you can only call on me twice more." I nodded, eager to hear what else she would say. "You must get to the temple city by nightfall on the second day and find a way in. Then you need to make your way to the golden temple."

"But first can we not rescue George," I questioned.

"Hmm, I'm not sure where he is being kept prisoner but I suspect he is in the temple. There are lots of secret passages and chambers to hold people. I would advise you to go there first. It is imperative you find a room, full of different objects collected over the years. Beware though, it is concealed well within an endless maze of corridors. There may be hidden dangers on the way. I will try my best to assist you if I can but please use my help wisely and only when your life is in danger."

"How will I know how to find this room? You mention hidden passages."

"I will try to guide you where possible and there is a small eye symbol hidden above the room you seek."

"What is so important about this room?"

"Hidden in the room is an object of great power. Once you get in the room, I will tell you what to look for." Suddenly, the mermaid's eyes darted to the right. "Promise me you won't reveal any of what I have said, even to Dan. Promise me."

"Freya, I don't understand why I can't tell him."

"Remember, what I said. Trust no-one."

"But …"

"No-one, promise me."

"Yes, okay I promise." The mermaid's lips smiled then returned to their original position.

I remained staring at her face for a while and I jumped when I heard Dimitri's voice, bellow behind me. "I saw you just staring up at the statue and wondered what had stopped you filling up the water bottles."

"Nothing in particular. I was just day dreaming about life back home," I lied. "Are you ready to go?" I asked trying to change the subject.

"Yes, it's just you holding us up." Dan joined in too. Speeding up, I quickly filled the last two bottles and handed one each to Dan and Dimitri.

"See, I've caught up. Let's get going then," I replied before they could give me any more sarcastic comments.

"Have we got everything?" Dimitri directed at Dan.

"Yes, I think so," he glanced back at the church and said, "Wait a minute," before he ran back inside.

A bemused Dimitri and I watched him go. "I thought he told me he was ready to go," Dimitri sighed. "At this rate it will be another day wasted!"

"Hey, I thought you were the one not so keen to return to the city. You seemed to have changed your tune," I joked.

Glancing down at the ground, Dimitri replied, "It was just a brief moment of insecurity. I panicked about facing the ogre again but my friend George is in danger and I would never forgive myself if I didn't try to go back and rescue him."

"I believe this island can either bring out the worst or the best in people. I hope the latter will prevail. I know from personal experience how I've managed to survive using inner strength I didn't know I possessed."

Dimitri nodded, "Yes, I do believe that too. Resilience, working together and above all not giving up will triumph over whatever obstacles are in our path."

Dan reappeared from the other side of the church, behind us. "Wow," Dan cut in, "That's some deep and meaningful stuff you two were chatting about."

"What did you go back for?" I asked.

"Dan grinned, "This!" as he brought out Dimitri's wooden stake hidden behind his back. "I really think you should take this." Studying my perplexed face, he added, "It would make a useful walking stick too."

"Okay," I said after catching sight of Dimitri's expectant face. I decided I dare not offend him by saying no. However, I was sure along the way to the city I could accidentally leave it behind somewhere. Dan handed it over to me, "Just what I could do with," I said.

"Are we ready now," Dimitri asked impatiently.

"Yes," we both shouted and spontaneously we all took part in a group hug. Breaking apart, I looked across at the temple city, shimmering in the distance. The sun was starting to climb up into the sky. I knew we really must leave. It was strange but as I took one last look at the church, I had a strong feeling I would not be seeing it again.

Chapter 28

Dimitri led the way, using his longest stake as a walking stick like me. I found mine helped to keep me balanced as I walked across the uneven ground. Dan walked by my side. As we ventured nearer to the temple city, the ground became much rockier and the vegetation sparser. We must have been walking for a few hours and now the midday heat was beginning to have an effect. With little shelter around and Dimitri's relentless march towards the overnight stop, I was rapidly becoming concerned I would not be able to keep up the pace. Dan sensed I was starting to have trouble as I began to lag behind. I watched him catch up with Dimitri and exchange a few words resulting in him abruptly stopping and turning to face me. "I think we need to stop for a rest," Dan said quite concerned. "The current pace is quite draining," he looked back at Dimitri as he said it.

Rather apologetically Dimitri replied, "Sorry, I forgot, I'm more accustomed to the heat than both of you." Staring at me he said, "Helena, you look very dehydrated and exhausted." Pointing to an isolated bush he said, "Let's sit here for a while and eat something to sustain our energy levels and replenish our bodies with water." I felt like I was taking part in a science lesson and Dimitri was trying to explain about heat exhaustion but my body gratefully sat down near the bush.

Dan quickly sat beside me and said, "You can rest your head on my shoulder and close your eyes for a bit if you want." The invitation was very tempting but I resisted as I could not trust myself to not fall asleep. Instead, I opted to drink my water and consume a handful of berries while staring at the vast empty wasteland in front of us.

Meanwhile, Dimitri found a large rock to sit on and started munching on his yuca plant. His gaze was transfixed on the golden temple ahead. It did look magnificent, a splendid golden dome, towering over the city. I wondered what wonders lay behind the unfriendly walls or what secrets it was trying to protect. I hoped we would make it beyond the hostile walls and get some much-needed answers. Deep in thought I eventually became aware of someone calling out my name. "Sleepyhead, it's time to wake up." Opening my eyes, I could not believe I had drifted off while gazing at the city. I was certain my eyes had only been drawn there a minute ago. However, Dan was quick to add, "Sorry but your 40 winks are over! Dimitri is impatient for us to get on and I don't want to risk upsetting him again."

"Sorry," I blurted out. "I didn't plan to dose off."

"I hated having to wake you but hopefully it revived you enough so you can continue our route march," Dan smirked and looked over at Dimitri who was busily spiriting away all his food and drink, ready to start walking again. Catching sight of us just sitting there watching him did not amuse him. He was about to say something but we hastily got up in readiness to continue our journey. He slowly shook his head and began to march off towards the city. I felt like I was back at school having to do exactly what my teacher said. Still, it was so nice to have Dan with me. As we hurriedly walked behind him, Dan reached out to hold my hand giving it a reassuring squeeze.

Walking along I pondered what would happen once we were inside the city. We only had Dimitri's limited knowledge of the layout based mainly on his escape route out of there. It would be under the cover of darkness but would that allow enough time to get in and out of the city? Plus, Freya had given me the task of finding a room with an eye symbol above it. Would this powerful object help me escape this island forever? I certainly had no plans to return.

Dan caught my eye, "You seem very deep in thought. Do you want to share?"

I sighed, "It's just, that I'm worrying about what we will find behind those walls and how we will avoid being discovered."

"The best thing to do is not worry. Just think about the here and now and enjoy the scenery." Afterwards, he winked at me. I could not help but laugh begrudgingly. "Besides," he added, "We will have more time tonight to talk and come up with a plan or two!"

"You mean a backup plan, if it all goes horribly wrong. After all, they will be expecting us to try to rescue George."

"Maybe," replied Dan. "However, we do have one asset though, don't we?"

"What do you mean?" I replied panicked. Surely, he did not know about Freya.

Pointing over at Dimitri, he said, "His knowledge of the city layout will help us succeed. I'm certain."

"I hope so," I replied, trying to sound confident. I just was not sure he was entirely reliable since he had a knack for disappearing conveniently when we were in danger from the harpies.

Just then Dimitri stopped, allowing us to catch him up. "Can you see the stony ridge in front of us, to the right?"

I followed the direction he was pointing with his faithful wooden stick. "Yes," I answered

"Well, that's where we need to get to before nightfall. It's where we can safely spend the night tucked away in the rocky crevices I used before."

Looking over at the gleaming sun in the sky I estimated it was about mid-afternoon. "Do you think we will make it there before it gets dark?" I asked, trying to hide my concern.

"I think if we increase our pace a bit and have fewer breaks, we should get there." I did not like the sound of fewer breaks but I kept silent.

"What about tomorrow?" Dan asked. "Isn't there a danger we could be seen as we get nearer to the temple city."

"Ahh, I've thought of that. The terrain is very rugged and hilly so we should be able to weave our way between the mounds giving us some camouflage until we get nearer to the forest area. Unfortunately, the area before the trees is quite open and exposed, therefore, we will need to wait till dusk before we make a run for cover.

"Let's worry about that tomorrow," I said. "You lead the way Dimitri."

Unfortunately, Dimitri took his role too seriously and set off again at a cracking pace. It was not long before my body responded with aches and pains in my calf muscles and feet. I longed to stop and soak my feet in some cooling water. My eyes focussed on the rocky mounds in front of us and I began to imagine they were much nearer than they were. For a while this kept me going but again, I began to drift behind. Dan snuck back a few

THE ISLAND BECOMES YOU

times to be by my side, offering words of encouragement to keep me going but eventually I abruptly stopped and sank to the ground. "Sorry," I apologised, "I need a moment to rest."

Taking my water bottle out I splashed a little on my face then I gulped some down. I heard Dimitri shout, "Stop!" Abruptly, I halted drinking in mid-flow. "Don't move," Dimitri shouted. "Don't move your hand!"

I started to twist my head to look down at my left hand, resting on the ground. My eyes locked onto Dan. I watched his face change from surprise to shock. His eyes widened and his voice was full of concern as he shouted, "Just keep looking at me Helena!"

Sheer panic bubbled up in my throat as I tried to maintain eye contact with him. My brain was full of questions. Why couldn't I look down? What was happening? I began to imagine all sorts of things. Out of the corner of my eye, I saw Dimitri move quickly to my left side. In a blink of an eye, he waved his long stake in the air and brought it crashing down within an inch of my outstretched hand. I felt the rush of air against my skin. Moving slightly further away he brought his stake down hard again and hit the ground several times afterwards.

Dan ran over and hugged me tightly. Looking at his face his eyes looked extra moist and his skin extremely pale, making me ask, "Are you okay?"

"Yes, I am now."

"What is all the fuss about?" I questioned as I started to calm down in Dan's arms.

"You can look now," Dimitri answered. Slowly, I looked back over my shoulder to where Dimitri was standing over the remains of some splattered creature. Looking down near my hand, I could make out the remains of a tail with a stinger on the end.

Instinctively, I brought my hand to my mouth and took a deep breath. "Oh no, was that …"

"A very poisonous scorpion," Dimitri finished my sentence.

Crouching down beside me he said, "I'm so sorry for scaring you but I had to act fast. It was right next to your hand and its tail was up ready to strike at any moment."

"No, don't apologise. From the size of its tail, it must have been huge! You probably saved my life."

Dan, having had time to compose himself joined in and added, "Thanks for acting so quickly. I admit I just froze at the size of it. I didn't know they grew so big!"

"Blame it on this island. Everything is cursed," Dimitri replied.

More curious than scared, I got up with Dan's help and walked over to the spot where the creature met its demise. Judging from the size of the flattened body, what was left of it must have been as big as my hand. However, the colour was almost translucent so it easily blended into the terrain around us. "Do you think there are a lot more of these creatures out here?" I asked Dimitri.

"I'm sure we would have seen a lot more of them by now. They are very camouflaged. It was only the movement of the tail as it curled up ready to strike that alerted me to its location."

"I think as long as we keep walking, we should be okay," Dan reminded us we needed to start walking again.

"Okay, let's just be more wary where we sit down in future," Dimitri obviously directed that comment at me.

The light was starting to fade and Dimitri began to panic and quickened the pace even more. My legs were crying out for a rest but I knew we had to keep going. I noticed Dan looked at me, trying to mask his concern. He said encouragingly, "It's not much further."

"How do you know," I snapped back but quickly regretted it.

"Well, if you listened," Dimitri pointed to a rocky mound ahead of us.

Looking in the distance, I could see several rocky mounds but they all looked too far away for us to realistically make it before nightfall. "Can you be more specific?" I said sarcastically, rather irritated by his earlier response, "There is more than one rocky mound." Dimitri did not respond.

Dan shook his head, "I know you are tired. We all are," he glanced up at Dimitri still marching ahead. "Well, maybe not him."

I could not help a smirk escape from my mouth as I watched Dimitri march on regardless, completely focused on his objective and not realising we had both stopped walking. Trying to compose myself I said, "Quick, we had better catch up before he notices." Closely, followed by a sigh I added, "Look, I'm sorry. My exhaustion is making me very ungrateful. You're only trying to help."

Taking my hand, Dan gave it another affectionate squeeze. Then we both managed to muster up our last reserves of energy to quickly hot-foot it after

Dimitri before he realised, we were trailing behind him. As soon as we caught up, Dimitri stopped and turned around. With his eyes on me, he said, "Well done for keeping up." I tried hard to disguise my slight panting and rising chest from him. Luckily, he then turned his attention to Dan and said, "Fortunately, you will be pleased to know it's not much further. We just need to make it to the ridge in front of us."

"How much longer will it take?" I asked.

"Another half an hour at most," Dimitri replied. Pointing ahead of him he continued, "In the distance, there are lots of bushes and rocky, hilly ground dotted about to provide excellent cover while we move closer to the walled temple city. However, we will need to wait until nightfall before making the final dash to the forest area nearby as there is very limited cover."

Surveying the area ahead, I nodded in agreement with his plan. Taking a deep breath, followed by a sip of water from my bottle I turned to a bemused Dan and said, "We had better get going then before the harpies come out!" As soon as I said it, immediately another thought entered my head. I wondered why the harpies only came out at night? Glancing over at the determined look on Dimitri's face I quickly decided not to interrupt him and save my question for later. Walking briskly behind them, I really struggled to keep up. In the end, I just focused my sight on the ridge and hoped my legs would keep going.

Chapter 29

Finally, just as dusk was approaching, we made it to the rocky mound. The hollow gap was just as Dimitri described it. There was just enough room for Dan and me to lie side by side quite comfortably. If necessary, we could squeeze together even tighter and disappear further into the back of the hollow to hopefully avoid being detected.

Dimitri chose a smaller mound opposite us but thankfully its entrance faced away from us. I was relieved he would not be staring at us all night. Brushing that thought quickly to one side, I settled down outside our mound, glad to have the chance to rest from our long-enforced march. Unfortunately, a few berries and a root vegetable were not enough to keep our energy levels high. I longed to taste a piece of chocolate or a nice sugary doughnut. Needless to say, I looked at the berries in front of me and felt quite deflated.

Reading my mind, Dan tried to tempt me by saying, "Have some of these juicy, fresh, vibrant berries, full of vitamin C and tantalising flavour. Once you start eating them you won't be able to stop." I could not help myself; my lips responded and formed a cheesy smile. Shaking my head, I found myself picking up a berry and putting it into my mouth. I closed my eyes and pretended it was a round, velvety, smooth chocolate with a raspberry, fondant centre. "See, I knew you couldn't resist my amazing sales pitch!" Dan gleamed with satisfaction.

Opening my eyes, I answered, "Surprisingly, they're not too bad. I think my stomach is just grateful for anything to fill it up." Leaning across, I rested my head on his shoulder. Dan gently kissed the top of my head and put his arm around my waist. We stayed like that for a while, chomping on our berries and looking up at the night sky. At the back of my mind though, I was poised to move swiftly into our deep hollow at the first sign of a shrill screech from overhead.

A little later Dimitri joined us and finished eating some of his yuca plant. "Tomorrow, you will be pleased to know you can have a bit of a lay-in! We must be careful as we approach the city especially when moving between the rocky hills and bushes. I will go in front to check ahead and beckon when it's safe to follow." Pausing briefly, he stared at us seriously and added, "It is extremely important you don't deviate from the path I take."

Not fully convinced Dimitri knew best, I asked, "Are you sure there will be adequate cover for us all? Remember you were fleeing from the city at speed and you were alone."

"I realise you have doubts but I assure you, I clearly remember having a choice of places to hide. Taking our time, we will get to the outskirts of the city by dusk. Then we will make a run for the safety of the trees where we can decide to pick our moment to ascend the city walls."

"What about the harpies? You said their distance vision was very good so wouldn't they notice us moving at speed?" I questioned.

"They normally come out from dusk onwards. I remember asking the young boy who gave me food in my cell and he said they sleep during the day and patrol the island at night."

"That doesn't fill me with much confidence. They could disrupt their sleep pattern at any time and come out during daylight," I replied.

"Well, I've never seen them out during the daytime since I've been a prisoner on this island," Dimitri replied, attempting to rebuke my theory.

During our conversation about harpies, I became aware of how quiet Dan was. He did not join in with the discussion or voice an opinion. It was very unlike him. We all sat in silence for what seemed ages until Dimitri eventually said, "I'm going to sleep now. I suggest you do the same – it will be a long day and night ahead of us."

As he was about to get up, Dan found his voice and said, "Wait Dimitri. I need to ask you something."

Sitting back down he replied, "Okay Dan but make it quick, I'm very tired."

"I'm not sure if it will be quick as it depends on your answer," Dan replied. I knew what he was about to ask. Reaching for his hand I gave it a reassuring squeeze. I heard Dan take a deep intake of breath before he asked, "Why did you and George leave the safety of the cave that night and what were you arguing about?"

"That's two questions," Dimitri replied. "Before I answer, I think we should move closer to the hollow to protect our location from any prying eyes."

"Fair enough," Dan answered. Releasing my hand Dan edged back further into the hollow. Taking the hint, I too shuffled back allowing Dimitri to sit alongside Dan but instead, he positioned himself in the middle of us – forcing me to move further over to the left. I did not relish the idea of sitting so close to him so I found myself pressing my back as far against the rocky hollow as I could. Luckily, Dan took the initiative to move further over to the right after seeing my discomfort written all over my face and Dimitri took the hint and moved away from me.

Dimitri looked briefly at both of us before continuing, "There's not much to say. I woke up to see George leaning over me – holding me down." Both Dan and I looked at each other quite puzzled as this did not sound like George at all. "Oh sorry, I forgot to mention I was very upset and distressed. I had a very bad dream about the ogre and George was trying to console me as I was lashing around while I slept."

"How come I didn't wake up too?" Dan asked quite baffled by what he was hearing.

"Well, I was outside the cave. I must have sleepwalked which I don't recall having done since I was a young child. Anyway, George must have woken up and gone to find me. Apparently, I was making quite a racket and he was trying his best to calm me down." Dimitri grimaced slightly and looked down before he continued, "Unfortunately, at the time I was feeling rather disorientated, probably still quite dehydrated from walking for days after my escape and still thought I was dreaming. I remember thinking George was a guard trying to capture me. Eventually, he did calm me down but too late, the harpies had been alerted by my shouting and we were both too caught up in the moment to realise what was happening until it was too late."

Watching Dan's reaction, I could clearly see he was vividly reliving the moment George was taken and was still visibly traumatised by the event. He was gripping both hands together tightly. I wished I was by his side so I could show my support. Finally, Dimitri glanced up at Dan and apologised, "I'm truly sorry George was taken from you because of me."

"No, it wasn't your fault," Dan muttered. "I just wish I had woken up earlier."

Dimitri tried to console him. "Don't beat yourself up over it. There's not much more you could have done anyway!"

"Yes, but ...," Dan tried to continue but I interrupted.

"Listen to Dimitri, it was just unfortunate it happened. But we will get him back. We just have to think positively."

Then out of the blue we all gave each other a group hug. Emotionally, we all felt quite raw and touched by the depth and honesty of how Dan and Dimitri portrayed their experiences of losing George. I even forgot my misgivings about Dimitri and believed him, whole-heartedly. We held each other for ages – deep in thought about how George was doing and our rescue attempt tomorrow. At least, I was the most confident about the outcome, knowing I could call on Freya for help. Keeping her secret was so hard, especially not telling Dan. It would give him more faith and belief we would succeed.

After a while I did begin to think Dimitri might be dragging it out too long so gradually, I began to ease myself away from the group hug and eventually, he took the hint again and moved back a bit. "Thanks for the support. We make a great team," Dan remarked happily. It was nice to see his mood improve. I hoped it would carry on until tomorrow night. However, a tinge of negativity still hung over me because of all the variable factors we had no control over. Mainly, if the harpies spotted us and whether we could find the best way into the temple city. Still, I had two more chances to ask Freya for help. I prayed they would be enough.

"Time for sleep, I guess," Dimitri said begrudgingly. "Is there room for one more in your hollow?" Seeing our stunned reaction, he laughed and said, "Only joking. Don't look so worried."

I found myself trying to laugh along with his joke to keep the team spirt going strong but underneath my body cringed at the thought of spending a night next to him. Dan perched his hand on top of mine in full support of what I was thinking. Grinning falsely, he wished Dimitri, "Goodnight."

"Try and get some sleep too," he grinned back before disappearing into his hollow.

I stared after him for ages until Dan broke the spell by planting feathery kisses on my neck. "Dan how are you feeling? Is your head still sore?"

"Stop trying to change the subject," he replied as his hands moved lower. "Can't you see I'm trying to seduce you? I've been dying to make love to you since we met up again but there always seems to be some obstacle in our way but not tonight."

I tried to hide the tenseness in my body by pushing him away playfully. It was still alarming he had no recollection we had already made love in the church two nights ago. Such a shame too as it had been an amazing reunion. Trying to sound sensible I said, "We really need to get some sleep. Tomorrow is very important and we must be fully alert and able to make decisions quickly. Besides Dimitri will hear us."

"Ahh so you've thought about doing it then," Dan replied as he poked me in the side. Leaning across to nuzzle my ear he whispered, "I love it when you try to be serious." Then he abruptly stopped and cupped my face with both hands, stared intently into my eyes and said, "Now it's my turn to be serious. I don't care about Dimitri. All I care about at this moment is how much I love you Helena and how much I want to show you, my love." Sighing, he continued, "We don't know what will happen tomorrow but we are together tonight."

Not wanting to break the intensity between us I simply nodded. He was completely right we should just focus on the here and now. Gradually, he moved his mouth closer to mine until they touched. Slowly, he kissed me. His warm lips sent delightful shivers down my body. We held each other tightly. My body responded as his kiss deepened and he parted my lips so his tongue could explore further. Willingly, I allowed him to gently push me down onto the ground, I welcomed the pressure of his body against me. Instinctively my hands clasped his back tighter. I muffled a series of moans escaping from my mouth with my hand as he expertly trailed his lips from my neck, downwards, leaving a red-hot path in his wake. I arched my back and had to stop myself from crying out as I did not want to disturb Dimitri. More importantly, I did not want Dan to have to stop. At last, our bodies moved together as one. Our rhythm intensified until I was completely overwhelmed by the full rapture of our lovemaking.

"I love you so much," Dan whispered as he covered my face with soft kisses.

THE ISLAND BECOMES YOU

I responded by pulling him closer and whispered back, "I love you too." Gazing into each other's eyes we sealed the strength of our feelings with a long lingering kiss. Content in each other's arms, we stayed like that until sleep finally beckoned.

Chapter 30

Abruptly, we were woken by someone shaking us. Twisting my head to the right my eyes locked onto Dimitri's fearful eyes. His hand was pointing upwards as he whispered, "They are circling above us." Then he added, "I'm sure they cannot see us from above but something has alerted them." I watched his eyes divert towards my naked thigh. Dan noticed and tried to cover me with his arm. I quickly decided it was not a time to be bashful and in front of an astonished Dimitri, I rose onto my knees and proceeded to reach for my shorts. His mouth dropped in aghast but he did not avert his eyes – he seemed frozen to the spot. In the end, Dan moved in front of me to protect my modesty and only then did Dimitri turn away. Slipping my shoes on swiftly, I soon joined Dimitri and Dan crouched at the entrance of the hollow looking up at the night sky.

"They do seem rather unsettled tonight," Dan answered puzzled. "I agree it does look like something or someone has spooked them." As he finished speaking the harpies suddenly darted off in the direction of the church. Automatically, a sigh of relief escaped from my lips. I gradually became aware Dan was holding my hand, gently he raised it to his mouth and kissed it. "We will always have tonight," and gazed directly at me.

Forgetting Dimitri was nearby I stared intently back at Dan, smiled and replied, "Yes."

"What about the night at the church too?" Dimitri piped up.

"What do you mean?" Dan answered and looked at me.

Unable to say anything in response, Dimitri continued, "Well, I thought you two, more than got it together that night too. Perhaps more passionately and longer than tonight." Dimitri allowed his half smile to linger purposely in my direction.

"I don't understand," Dan replied looking searchingly at me for an answer.

"Did she not tell you?" Dimitri continued to look straight at me.

"I…I …," I stammered. "I decided to wait until your memory came back."

"So, you're telling me, we made passionate love and I don't remember but he does," pointing his finger at Dimitri. "Are you sure you didn't sleep with him instead of me. Surely, I would remember!" Dan raised his voice alarmingly.

"Please Dan," tears started to stream down my face. "You hurt your head badly and I didn't want to make things worse by putting pressure on you to remember."

"But I'm sure I would have remembered that. How come he knew all the intimate details?"

Turning my head away, I choked back the emotion in my voice. "I woke up naked, you were gone and Dimitri was asleep in the room nearby," I blurted out, immediately regretting saying I was naked.

"So, you took advantage of my sleeping girlfriend," Dan grabbed Dimitri by the scruff of his neck.

"No. No," I begged Dan to stop. "You have it all wrong," I cried out. "We made love while Dimitri was on watch. We fell asleep but you must have got up later to relieve Dimitri."

"But, if that was the case, I would have asked him to sleep elsewhere, particularly if I had left you naked and asleep. What an invitation for any man!"

Tightening his grip on Dimitri's top, he hoisted him up so they stood head-to-head. Dimitri tried to grapple with him and break free but Dan held him securely in an arm lock. "Stop, both of you," I pleaded again. I shouted at Dan, "Please listen. I promise you; I made love to you and only you that night in the church. I'm sorry you don't remember."

Dan stopped in his tracks and stared at my beseeching face. Momentarily, he released his grip on Dimitri, just enough for him to get his hands in between and lever Dan backwards against the side of the mound. Dan allowed Dimitri to escape and slowly sank down to the ground. Putting his hands on his head he started to cry. "I'm sorry I doubted you. Please forgive me. I'm just so frustrated that I can't remember any of what happened after I followed Dimitri to see where his lookout position in the church was. It's all just a blank!"

Falling to my knees, I cradled his head in my arms and rocked him gently, soothing the back of his head with my hand. Out of the corner of my eye, I saw Dimitri lean against a boulder to catch his breath and check his wounds but my attention remained focused on Dan. "It's okay my love. I'm sure your memory will come flooding back. It will just take time. We are all suffering. Being trapped on this island is so stressful plus trying to avoid being captured. Please just give yourself time to catch up." I hoped these words would help to calm him down. I had never seen him so worked up before and so defensive of me.

After a while, Dan looked up and wiped the tears from his face. He attempted to reassure me he was okay with a half-hearted smile. It worked a bit so I shuffled back to give him some room to collect himself. Meanwhile, Dimitri had chosen to saunter back towards his hollow. I was worried he might not continue towards the temple city with us so I quickly got up and followed him to try to assess his mood. "Are you okay Dimitri," I asked once I had caught up with him.

"Yes," he replied rather bluntly hiding his left arm protectively.

"How's your arm?" I enquired.

"It will be fine," he answered abruptly, "but he isn't," pointing angrily over at Dan. "He nearly tried to kill me!"

"No, he didn't," I defended Dan. "Put yourself in his shoes. He has about four to five hours which he doesn't remember anything about. Then you bringing up what happened during that lost time didn't help the situation much."

Dimitri stopped and looked down at the ground, "Okay, perhaps I was a bit harsh. I suppose if I'm honest," looking up at me he continued, "I'm just jealous he has someone on this island and I don't have anyone to share this experience with."

My defensive stance softened and I asked, "Did you leave someone special behind when you joined the expedition with George."

Dimitri hesitated before answering, "Yes. I left behind my little sister. The money I was going to be paid for the trip was to support her as our parents were dead."

"I'm sorry, it must be hard not knowing what happened to her."

"Yes, I think about her every day and pray no harm came to her!"

"Hopefully her friends and other family members rallied around to help her," I tried to sound positive.

"Perhaps but most of the other villagers were poor. I doubt they had the money to take her under their wing." Sighing deeply, he then added, "I wish I had never agreed to go on this trip."

"Don't give up Dimitri. Maybe once we leave this island, we will all return to our own time zone and be reunited with our loved ones. Remember time seems to have slowed down on this island and we are trapped in a time bubble which doesn't keep pace with the outside world."

Dimitri shrugged, "I would like to believe your theory but unfortunately we won't know for certain unless we manage to leave this island."

Just then our attention was diverted towards a low rumbling sound coming from near the temple city. Looking over in the direction of the noise, I strained my eyes to focus. Annoyingly, some dark clouds were intermittently blocking out the light cast by the moon above which made it difficult to see further away. Too many shadows and the moonlit reflection of the temple blighted my view. Deciding to dismiss the sound for now I returned my attention to Dimitri and was shocked to see him prostrate on the ground with his right ear fully against the dry ground. I was about to ask Dimitri what he was doing when I felt Dan's arm on my shoulder and he beat me to it. "What do you think the noise was?" Dan asked just as puzzled as I was.

Dimitri raised his head up slightly to answer with another question. "Did you feel the ground shake slightly too?"

"Not that I remember," I answered, starting to doubt what I had actually witnessed. Had I missed the sensation – too caught up by the noise?

It was not long before the grumbling sound came again. We all looked in the same direction. This time to the right of the temple city, towards the trees. In the distance, it was hard to make out individual trees, it just looked like a solid mass with feathery outlines. The noise continued longer and slightly louder than before. Then we felt it, the ground seemed to vibrate – a low hum radiated towards us. We both continued staring, mesmerised by the sound. Dimitri was still lying on the ground, raising his head towards us again there was a sense of urgency in his voice, "Whatever it is, it seems to be moving rapidly and the vibrations are getting stronger!"

Turning my attention back to the trees I became aware of another sound, a dragging, scratching sound, followed by a clanking sound. The last sound made Dimitri stand up abruptly. I watched him cover his mouth with his hand, he stood almost paralysed watching the same spot as us.

"Dimitri! What is it?" I screamed at him.

Slowly, he turned towards me, "Oh no, it must be…" Suddenly, an almighty crashing sound interrupted his sentence. All eyes were focussed on the trees. Strangely, the trees began to part in the middle allowing the moonlight to shine through them. Then we saw it. A huge silhouette of a bulbous head, attached to a giant hairy body appeared in the gap between the trees. It was holding an object in one hand and the end was dragging through the undergrowth, ripping up plants and shrubs in its path. As it reached the outer edges of the woods it seemed to stop and stood defiantly, raising its huge arms above its head.

"Oh my god, it's…," I said. The realisation of what it was sank in immediately.

Dimitri finished my sentence. "The ogre, it has returned to fight again with me!"

I felt Dan's arm tighten protectively around me but he knew he was no match for an ogre. Finding it hard to tear our eyes away, we watched in silence as it picked up a long, snapped tree trunk. Holding it above his head, with one arm he threw it like a high-speed javelin towards us. Considering its weight, it shot through the air like the trajectory of a missile, reaching its peak height before crashing back to the ground. The impact sent seismic shockwaves radiating back to us. I felt the ground heave and I toppled over. We watched in horror and disbelief as the tree trunk ploughed through the rocky ground, finally coming to rest a few feet in front of us.

Dan was the first to speak, "We need to move. NOW!"

Finding my voice, I shouted desperately, "But where? Where can we hide from that thing? Surely, it knows exactly where we are. It threw a tree javelin at us!"

"Try and calm down," Dimitri answered. "It was just a lucky throw. Ogres can't see very well but they do have acute hearing. I can vouch for that from my previous encounter."

Suddenly, shrieks from above alerted us the harpies had returned. I cried,

THE ISLAND BECOMES YOU

"Great! The ogre might not be able to see us but they can!" I pointed upwards to the sky. Grabbing my hand tightly, Dan started to pull me back to our rocky hollow. "Stop!" I shouted. "It's too late they know where we are."

"We need to go back for our things and then make a run for it," Dan continued to lead me back towards the rock hollow.

"But where …where can we possibly go!" I cried.

Dan stood still for a moment; his eyes fixed on the ground. Then without any further hesitation he pointed towards the temple city. "That way!"

Dimitri caught up with us, "We really need to get moving. The harpies have already spotted us." As an afterthought he added, "Perhaps we should go back to the church."

"No," Dan replied firmly. "They won't expect us to carry on towards the temple city."

"But what about the ogre?" Dimitri questioned.

"Well, you said its eyesight is poor and maybe all of its thrashing around will keep the harpies away too," Dan answered.

"I suppose it might work. We don't really have any choice given our circumstances. Either head towards danger or runaway and it follows us!" I made myself agree with Dan's idea even though I was petrified.

Dimitri sighed, "Okay, but we will have to keep our movements slow. Anything too sudden will alert the ogre plus any loud noises. Its hearing must compensate for its poor sight." Turning to look at both of us he asked, "Are you both certain you want to do this?"

"Yes," Dan replied. "We've come too close to turn back."

Dan stared at me; his eyes said it all. Trying to put it into words, I held his hand tighter and said, "I love you Dan. Let's do it."

Tenderly, he embraced me. "We will survive this and rescue George," he said confidently in my ear. Only his rapidly beating heart against mine betrayed how apprehensive he was really feeling. Likewise, mine was probably beating just as fast. I squeezed him tighter, gaining extra strength from our closeness. We had to believe we would succeed or we might as well give up. Searching for my mouth he crushed it with his for an all too brief moment before releasing his grip. "I love you Helena," he murmured in my ear then he took a step back.

"Are you ready?" Dimitri asked.

"Yes," unanimously, we shouted back.

"Keep low and follow me," Dimitri cried as he turned towards the temple city.

Dan and I picked up our bags, we exchanged one last smile between us then quickly headed off behind Dimitri. Slowly, we moved from one rocky mound to another, trying to keep in the shadows as much as possible. Briefly, I crouched behind one small mound and observed the ogre twisting his head from side to side blindly trying to find us. Several times he sniffed the air. Eerily, his one main eye seemed to settle in our direction – almost convincing me he could see us before setting off again in the opposite direction. We were getting dangerously close to him; my heart was pounding in my chest but having Dan close by made me feel braver. Every so often he glanced round to check I was still there and gave me one of his reassuring smiles.

The scariest part was when we drew alongside the ogre as he stumbled about with his mallet, waving it to-and-fro, trying to swipe at its imaginary prey. Eventually, we safely moved past him. At that point, I glanced up at the sky, wondering where the harpies were. To my surprise they were nowhere to be seen.

Finally, we reached the outskirts of the open, exposed grassland before the woods. Pausing behind the last bit of bushy shrub land, we all caught our breath knowing we would need to run extremely fast to the wooded area. Thankfully, the ogre was about forty metres behind us. Dimitri joined us as we discussed what to do next. Suddenly, we heard the ogre roar in frustration. We all turned to look at him at the same time and watched him lift the giant mallet above his head. He swung it around like a shot putter does before letting it go. Unfortunately, he must have either picked up our scent or it was just lucky throw because when he released the mallet it zoomed in our direction. Immediately, Dan pushed me to one side as the flying missile struck the rock in front of us. The sheer power of it split the rock instantly in two. I could not bear to think what might have happened to us if we had not moved in time. Shocked, I felt Dan's protective arms around me, "That was close," I whispered. My eyes were drawn to Dimitri, he was lying on the ground nearby. I pointed at him. "Is he okay?" I asked.

Dan crawled over and examined him. After shaking him several times he looked up and said, "He's out cold!" Dan beckoned me over. "It looks like a piece of the split rock caught him on the side of the head. Luckily it only looks like a flesh wound but…" Staring behind, his face was etched with fear. I knew without looking the ogre had changed direction and was now heading straight for us. "We need to move now," Dan said with urgency. A faint breeze carried the ogre's foul stench ahead of him. Stealing a quick glance behind, I could clearly see its huge grotesque eye fixed directly on us. I knew it was a matter of life or death. We had to make a split-second decision about what to do with Dimitri.

"What do we do?" I blurted out.

"Let's try and lift him," suggested Dan.

"Okay, but we don't have a lot of time. We need to make a run for the trees."

"I know but there is a chance he might wake up. We can't just leave him. We've got to try." Nodding, I quickly grabbed his left arm and Dan took hold of his right. Together we attempted to lift him to his feet. He tottered halfway up, unfortunately, I did not have the strength to hold him upright as he was such a dead weight.

As he fell back to the ground, I pleaded with him, "Dimitri wake up. We must go." Now I could hear a whooshing sound, sneaking another peak I saw the ogre swinging his chain around his head. Horrified, I could see pale white human skulls glinting in the moonlight. Instantly, I remembered the bleached human skull rolling on the deck of our boat after the bird dropped it. Only now did I realise the significance of the warning.

At last, Dan made the decision for us. "We must leave him. Can you help me push him inside this rocky hollow? Hopefully, it might protect him from being seen by the ogre." Tears started running down my face as we rolled him closer to the rock and shrubs in a pointless attempt to hide him. We left Dimitri with his head and half his torso in the hollow only his feet protruded. Hastily, I broke off some leafy shrub branches and tried to cover his legs. Then I felt Dan's strong hand grab my arm and drag me up, "We've run out of time," he cried. My legs struggled to keep up the pace as Dan set off towards the line of trees. Neither of us dared to look backwards. I heard the rusty chain hit the ground behind us. I had no idea how much the ogre was gaining on us. I just focused on the towering trees ahead and the broken path of tree trunks down the middle. Next, I heard the ogre come to a thunderous halt. Then he let out a premature triumphant roar. Had he found Dimitri?

We had nearly reached the wooded area when something loud screeched past my left ear. Out of the corner of my eye, I saw the huge wooden mallet swing past and instantly strike one of the trees down like a skittle in ten-pin bowling. "Oh my god," I gasped as the huge tree came crashing down in front of us, blocking our path. "I thought they didn't have good eyesight!" I tried to joke despite fear oozing from every pore. Dan laughed hesitantly and held my hand tighter. My heart was racing. Each step the ogre took shook the ground beneath my feet making it hard to keep my balance as we darted through the tangled undergrowth. Splintered tree trunks and the barricade of tree tops made our path extremely difficult. Although my legs were exhausted and felt like lead weights, fear and adrenalin spurred me on.

Suddenly, Dan came to an abrupt halt and pulled me back. "Listen," he said. Pausing for a break, my senses caught up with me. I realised the ground had stopped shaking.

"What's happening?" I cried.

"I don't know," replied Dan. "But it's given us time to think and formulate a plan." Looking behind us through the gap in the trees there appeared to be no sign of the ogre. Unexpectedly, Dan took me in his arms and held me tight. "Whatever happens next, we will face it together. Remember I love you so much" I was about to reply when I felt a cold chill travel through my body. The hairs on the back of my neck stood on end. It was almost as if my body knew before we heard the deafening roar followed by the foul stench of bad breath that greeted us from our left. Dan dropped his arms, grabbed my hand and shouted, "RUN!"

Almost immediately, the ogre lurched forward, parting the row of trees with one mighty swipe of his hairy arm. Leaning his ugly head further forward into the gap, he sniffed the air several times. That was all I witnessed before Dan dragged me off again. Running helplessly for a few minutes, in the same direction, we finally dared to pause and look behind us. Standing in the middle of the trees, the ogre's huge eye stared down at us. Picking up the mallet it had just thrown it proceeded to wave it threateningly in the air. Then it charged towards us. Immediately, we started to run to the entrance of the wooded area. As we neared the outer edge to our horror, a familiar one-eyed, bulbous head and sharp toothy grin greeted us around the corner.

I could barely speak, "Two ogres!" I mumbled.

THE ISLAND BECOMES YOU

Dan finished my sentence, "Where the hell did the second one come from?"

Finding my voice, I yelled, "We need to change direction quickly." Running back through the trees, we nearly made it to the clearing when we heard another loud crack and another tree was sent flying towards us. It skimmed across the ground right in front of us! Thankfully, it cleared a path for us towards the temple city. Hesitating briefly, before we stepped out, I was aware of a powerful sense of being watched. Looking through the gap ahead I could now see six pairs of eyes perched on top of the temple city walls, peering down at us. "Oh my god," I screamed and fell to my knees, "We're trapped whichever way we go."

Suddenly, the name Freya screamed in my head. Burying my face in my hands, I whispered, "Freya, we need your help now!" Then in desperation I shouted, "Freya, please. NOW!"

Dan hauled me up, "Who is Freya?" he questioned.

"Sorry I don't have time to explain," I replied, trying to avoid the question and regretting my outburst.

"Okay, time to choose, ogres or harpies?" Dan asked trying to hide the fear in his voice but his eyes betrayed him. I reached up to kiss him. For a few brief seconds I forgot where we were and the awful choice we now faced.

Afterwards, we hugged each other tightly. Above his left shoulder I noticed the first crack of orange appearing on the horizon and wondered if we would survive to witness another beautiful dawn. Dan smiled and asked, "Have you decided?"

Smiling back at him, I answered, "Harpies!" Taking my hand, we both leapt out into the clearing and pelted towards a huge ivy patch growing on the walled city. We could feel and hear the ogres pounding the ground behind us but we just focused on reaching the wall.

Chapter 31

Meanwhile, Serena stood with her sisters watching the desperate scene unfold. How helpless they looked, darting from one direction to the other, only to end up facing the same foe. Her heart sympathized with them when they stood by the clearing, obviously discussing which scenario was best; the ogres or to face them. That last tender kiss touched her heart and almost made her cry. She had been routing for them to escape the dreadful sentence for venturing onto this island but now it seemed their fate would be the same as everyone else. Looking down at her own hairy talons she could still vaguely remember when she had human toes.

Abruptly, her thoughts were interrupted by someone calling out her name. She looked down at Helena and Dan running for their lives. Surely, it was not them; they were too far away. Again, she heard "Serena." It was much clearer this time and female. Definitely, not her master! She closed her eyes to focus better. "Serena, you must listen. You must save them. My name is Freya. I've been watching you help them since they arrived on this island. Please don't give up on them now when they need you the most."

"But what can I possibly do? The ogres are closing in on them!" Serena whispered.

"Fly them to the temple entrance. I will do the rest," Freya replied.

"But the master will punish me and my sisters if I interfere and go against his wishes."

"You have already disobeyed some of his rules. It's only a matter of time before he finds out. You know what path you have chosen and your sisters will forgive you. Please help them," implored Freya.

THE ISLAND BECOMES YOU

Serena looked down at the scene below. Helena had just stumbled and Dan was checking to see if she was okay. She knew she had to act quickly as the ogres were gaining on them. "Okay," she answered. "I will help them."

"Thank you," Freya's voice faded away.

Without deliberating further, Serena was in the air. She ignored the concerned shouts from her sisters below. Their orders had been to watch only, not to take part but she had made her choice to go against him. Lingering above them momentarily, a little voice inside her head said, "It's not too late, to go back!" She turned towards her bewildered sisters, half smiled and mouthed the words "I'm sorry" before descending rapidly to the ground.

Dan hurriedly helped Helena up and glanced behind him. Both ogres were on each side of them, stomping towards them. Out of the corner of his eye he saw the left ogre let out a pre-victory roar and beat its chest. Surprisingly, the other ogre came to a standstill and meekly watched. He then dropped his wooden mallet and stood there laughing, revealing a toothless grin. Both suddenly went quiet when the red headed harpy landed straight in front of him and Helena. Dan's mind was working overtime, trying to come up with a solution to their predicament. Looking from one monster to another, what should they do next? He so badly wanted to protect Helena but the whole situation had rapidly become untenable.

Unexpectedly, Dan decided to accept his fate. Looking into Helena's eyes he was surprised to still see a flicker of hope. He could not explain why but it was certainly there. Reaching out for her hands, their eyes locked together. He forgot what was going on around them and focused entirely on Helena's beautiful, green, hazel eyes. He dived into them, seeking escape from reality.

Immediately, all his senses were on high alert again. He could hear someone talking to him. "Come with me if you want to live!" beseeched the red-haired harpy. Twisting round, his attention was captured by her sparkling emerald eyes. His first thought was could he trust her or was this a trick?

Dan tried to stop me from moving forward, towards her so I brushed his doubt aside by saying, "I know this harpy. I've met her before. We can trust her." Then I pointed at the ogre on the left of us, who had begun to respond to the new arrival by swinging his chain above his gruesome head. Turning back to Dan, I cried, "We have no choice but to go with her."

"Quickly," Serena screamed at us. Taking his hand in mine, I led Dan towards the harpy. "Bend down. I will try to carry both of you. Please don't wriggle as I might drop you!" Obeying her command, I nodded to Dan and we crouched over. I felt her sharp talons grip my left shoulder and I winced with the pain as she tightened her hold. Looking across to my side I saw her close in on Dan's right shoulder. "1, 2, 3 go," I heard her say as she lifted us off the ground. Glancing back, she manoeuvred us away with just seconds to spare as the chain sliced through the ground where we had been standing.

It was obviously, extremely hard to carry both of us as the extra weight caused the harpy to lurch from side to side. She was struggling to gain height with her wings so instead she carried us along rather than upwards. As a precaution I reached upwards with my free hand and held on tightly to her feathered ankle. I noticed Dan had done the same. Below us we only just cleared the ogre's heads. They were charging along, trying to keep up with us. One appeared to be gaining on us and seemed much faster and strangely nimbler than the other. I began to panic as this ogre edged closer. Petrified, I watched helplessly as he drew level with us and began to swing his chain around as he ran. Then without warning he released it. I heard a giant whoosh through the air before it wrapped itself around the harpy's torso. A high-pitched scream protruded from her lips on impact as a life-or-death tug of war began.

Serena was trying so hard to gain height but it was virtually impossible. She saw the ogre release his spiky chain and tried desperately to lurch in the opposite direction. Too late, first one then several other spikes embedded themselves in her chest. As she tried to move and twist the ogre only pulled tighter, causing the painful spikes to dig deeper and rip her flesh. She screamed, the pain was unbearable, it was like having several hot needles in her body. Peering down, she saw Helena's distraught face looking up, etched with fear and concern. She so badly wanted to save them but the more she pulled away the tighter the ogre held her in his trap. She could barely muster the strength to overcome the pain, to keep herself in the air.

THE ISLAND BECOMES YOU

Slowly, she realised the ogre was gradually pulling her towards him. Her heart was hammering in her chest. She was beginning to lose feeling in her legs and was not certain how much longer she could hold on to them.

Suddenly, she was not alone anymore. Encircling her were the worried faces of her sisters. Rebecca and Sophie gently started to pull the spikes from her chest. Each tiny tug of a spike, left her breathless, the agony excruciating. At the same time, Diane took Dan in her grip followed by Annette who grasped Helena from her.

Meanwhile, Patricia bravely pulled on the chain, dangerously close to the furious ogre to give her sisters some slack so they could loosen it quicker. At last, the final spike was removed and she was free! Serena smiled at her sisters before her eyes glazed over and everything turned black. She welcomed the darkness; it was an escape from the pain.

From a safe distance on top of a hill, I saw the fiery red harpy, known as Serena, plummet to the ground like a bomb. Fortunately, the other harpies anticipated this and quickly assembled a canopy with their huge wings to break her fall. Carefully, they transported her over to where Dan and I were being held. Lowering Serena gently to the ground the dark-haired harpy remained by her side while the other three stood guard, bracing themselves for the ogres to attack. Periodically, they would glance back to check on their sister.

My harpy lowered me to the ground behind them. "Stay here," she commanded but I had to break free. Nimbly, squeezing between the gaps in her wing, I ran over to the flame-haired harpy.

I heard Dan shout, "What are you doing? Stay here."

I turned back to Dan who was still being held by the black-haired harpy and shook my head. "No, I have to see her."

As I approached Serena, the guard of harpies tried to stop me but the flame-haired harpy said in a shaky voice, "It's okay. Let her through." Her dark-haired sister had laid her wing tenderly across her chest. Her head was propped up on her knees. Instantly, I could tell things were grave. Her face was extremely pale, her breathing was shallow and very laboured. I could see several huge gashes on her lower torso but I suspected further deep wounds higher up on her chest hidden by her sister's wing.

Her sister turned to look at me, her face swollen from tears. She showed no resistance as I knelt beside her wounded sister. I began by saying, "I would like to thank you for helping us. I don't know why you did but we are very grateful."

Serena beckoned for me to come closer, "You have another powerful ally on this island." She paused to take a breath, "I can do no more to help except…" Turning to her other sister standing nearby she asked, "Rebecca, please do this last wish for me. Take both the humans to the temple entrance."

"Please don't ask me to do this I want to stay with you," Rebecca pleaded.

Serena smiled back, "It won't take long. Besides I'm not going anywhere soon!" Then she added, "Please Rebecca." Afterwards, she took a sharp breath in and briefly shut her eyes. The pain must be unbearable I thought.

Rebecca looked at me and then back at her sister. "Very well Serena. I will do as you ask." Stepping forward, she kissed Serena softly on the cheek, "Please hold on my dear sister. I will be back very soon."

Gently, I touched Serena's wing, "How can I ever thank you enough for what you did?"

Lifting her head up slightly, Serena replied, "Your ally asked me to help but I would have done it anyway. Since you came to the island, I have tried to help. I carried you to the church when you were too weak and several times, I diverted my sisters away so you would not be found. I…" Trying to clear her throat she began to cough.

Protectively, Rebecca interrupted, "Hush now sister. You must save your strength."

Shaking her head Serena continued, "But I have something important to say." Smiling she said, "I've seen how much you and Dan mean to each other. I have known love too." She paused as she recollected a memory then added, "I so wanted, to help you escape this cursed island."

"You've helped us so much," I answered. "I can't imagine what life has been like for you on this island. You were once human like me."

Serena sighed, "Yes, I was. A long, long time ago, I made the terrible mistake of falling in love with the master. He lied to me but once I found out who he really was I betrayed him. Afterwards, my sisters and I paid dearly for it."

The frustrated roar of one of the ogres echoed around us. "We have to go

THE ISLAND BECOMES YOU

now," Rebecca intervened. "The ogres will be here soon. I must get back in time…"

"To defend me or watch me die?" interrupted Serena.

"Please don't be cruel. I would rather stay with you than go on this fool's errand. There is no way these two humans will survive long in the temple. You know what awaits them!"

"I believe now, they will succeed where we all failed. My hope that was lost has returned. You will believe too, in time, my sister."

Another roar, closer this time panicked Rebecca. "Either we go now or not at all!"

Quickly, I got up, staring into her once bright emerald eyes I said, "Thank you for everything. I hope you find peace."

Serena tried to smile back. Then she turned to her sister Rebecca. "I love you. Goodbye my dear sister."

"Nonsense, Serena. Haven't I always been the one to look out for you? I love you so much despite your foolhardy decisions. I've always been there for you to help pick up the pieces. It's not goodbye, I will be back very soon." As she turned away and looked towards her dark-haired sister, I caught sight of a tear running down her cheek. Trying hard to control her voice she shouted, "Protect her until I get back." The dark-haired sister nodded in reply.

Bending down again I allowed Rebecca to grab my shoulders and hoist me up into the air. Looking down Serena was watching us; she smiled and then closed her eyes. She looked so peaceful – like she was sleeping. Her beautiful auburn hair cascaded around her face and almost from a distance matched the blood stains on her chest.

Soon the black-haired harpy joined us carrying Dan. Rebecca shouted, "Diane, we need to hurry. We are losing her."

"I know sister but she wishes we do this for them. So, we must." Looking down, Diane cried, "Look sister, one of the ogres is returning to the city gates."

"Yes, I see sister but the other one is still pursuing us."

"Don't worry our other sisters will protect her, they are ready for him," Diane replied confidently.

"I know they will protect her with their lives but we need to be there too. You know who they are really fighting."

"Yes," Diane nodded. "Look, the golden dome is in our sight, not long now."

I twisted my head around to try to see what was happening. I could make out the three harpies standing guard and the solitary ogre rambling on towards them. He was gradually picking up speed at the same time thrashing his mallet around in the air. Suddenly, he stopped as he reached the bottom of the mound the harpies were guarding. He waved his mallet above his head and roared loudly. Next, he began to clamber up the mound. I noticed Rebecca tighten her grip on my shoulder and I winced at the stabbing pain. Unable to tear my eyes away I watched as the ogre continued up the hill. Moving forward in unison the harpies stretched out their wings, ready for impact as the ogre began to charge towards them. Unexpectedly, the middle harpy leapt off the ground, to attack him from the air I assumed. However, to my surprise, the ogre suddenly dropped his mallet and just froze. The middle harpy now in mid-flight also froze and hovered in the air waiting for the ogre's next move. Unfortunately, that was the last glimpse I had of the harpies and Serena as Rebecca flew over the wall of the city and began their descent as they approached the golden temple.

Chapter 32

Serena felt herself drifting in and out of unconsciousness. It helped to give her some relief from the piercing pain in her chest. She was dreaming of her father and she was also aware of someone else with him. A woman in white, with long red hair like hers was smiling softly at her. Serena wanted to reach out and touch her. She felt so much love radiating from her; it overwhelmed her.

To her great annoyance, the roar of the ogre brought her back to reality. Opening her eyes, she could make out three of her sisters standing in front of her, Sophie, Patricia and Annette. She tried to call out but they did not seem to hear her. She watched them move forward together and spread their wings. Then Patricia leapt upwards but suddenly stopped in mid-flight. Patricia remained like that, hovering a few feet off the ground. Serena held her breath and waited for the ogre's bulbous, grinning face to appear.

Meanwhile, Patricia's eyes were fixed on the defiant ogre below. Finally, he took another step forward and Patricia braced herself. The ogre seemed to be focusing his one eye behind her, on her fatally wounded sister, Serena. A puzzled look appeared on its face then it returned its gaze to Patricia and her defending sisters. Was she imagining the ogre's reaction? It looked like a flash of concern shot across its ugly face. Still in shock, she watched as the ogre sank to its knees, buried his head in its huge hands and let out an almighty sob. Patricia lowered herself to the ground in between her sisters and waited. Before her very eyes, she watched the sobbing ogre transform into Loki, their master. She watched him stand up and walk towards them. Instinctively, her sisters parted to allow him past but Patricia waivered and took up her protective stance, blocking Loki from going any further. "Do you mean my sister harm?" she demanded.

Loki lifted his head; Patricia could see his eyes were bloodshot from his tears. Slowly, he shook his head and replied, "No! I can see she is gravely injured. I promise, I only wish to speak to her one last time." Tears began to trickle down Patricia's face as his words sank in. Annette wrapped her left wing around her, in an attempt to comfort her. Taking a step nearer to her sister, Patricia allowed him to pass. All three sisters turned to face their dying sister and watched Loki kneel beside her.

Serena tried to focus her eyes on the top of the mound. She waited and waited for the ogre to appear but he did not instead it was her master. Where did he come from? Then she remembered…there were two ogres! Blinking her eyes, she saw him approach her sister Patricia who stood defiantly in his way but eventually, she let him go past. She saw each of her sisters turn to face her. She smiled at each one individually then returned her gaze to her eldest sister, Patricia who was visibly very upset and Annette was trying her best to comfort her. Poor Patricia, only now did she finally show how much she loved her. Out of all her sisters, she always felt Patricia held back her emotions, especially towards Serena. She often came across as very cold and lacked sympathy.

Her attention returned to Loki, he slowly moved towards her and knelt close to her. His eyes were red and puffy which surprised her. Why would he spare any tears for her now? What they once had was over long ago. A passionate love affair built on a huge lie; the man she had loved was Loki in disguise. Besides he had made certain of destroying any remnants of their deep feelings by using his wrath to punish her and her sisters for her ultimate betrayal. Why now did he care so much? Her thoughts were abruptly interrupted by a shooting, red, hot pain within her chest. Involuntarily, she closed her eyes and screwed her face up in response – willing it to pass quickly. She knew better now though, each time the pain returned it seemed to last longer and much deeper. Her breathing was becoming more of a struggle, it was like she had to really focus to will her chest to rise and fall. As she opened her eyes again, her sight was playing tricks on her again, she now saw Anton's face smiling down on her.

"Serena my love, I've missed you so much. Everything in the past is now forgotten. I forgive you."

Through disbelieving eyes, she watched him take hold of her right hand. Her hand! It was no longer a single, sharp talon at the end of her wing. She felt him caress and kiss her left palm. "Anton," she whispered. "Is it really you? Have you finally come back to me after all these years?"

"Yes, my love," he replied, clasping her hand to his chest. "All is forgiven. I never really stopped loving you. I hoped one day our love would overcome everything and we would be reunited again."

"I wish we could be transported back to the cosy cave by the beautiful waterfall where we made love and spent such blissful time together."

"Yes, I remember the softness of your skin against mine. We were meant to be together, always."

"Why did it all go so wrong?" Serena felt tears prickling her eyes. She mourned the loss of their love, the wasted years apart and now she mourned there was no more time left, no more chances to be together. Time was ebbing away with each breath she took. His beautiful face was starting to fade around the edges – darkness was closing in. Her body was becoming very cold from her legs upwards. She started to panic, "Hold me, one last time Anton."

She felt him bury his head on her chest and place his arms around her shoulders. She bathed in his love that surrounded her and closed her eyes. She felt her sisters draw nearer too. She heard first one sister then the next say goodbye to her, gently kissing her on the cheek. "I love you very much," she heard Patricia say. She was followed by her sister Rebecca.

"You made it back in time. Are they safe?" Serena asked.

"Yes, for now," her sister Rebecca replied and gently touched her cheek and hair. "Your glorious hair!" she cried. "I will miss you terribly."

Sensing the coldness sweep further up her body towards her heart, Serena called out for Anton. "I'm here my love," he whispered in her ear. Immediately, she relaxed at the sound of his voice. She took another breath expecting the searing pain to envelop her but was pleasantly surprised how peaceful she felt.

"Anton," she whispered again. This time she felt his warm lips on her cold mouth. She smiled and tried to reach up to touch his face but her body refused to move. Instead, she felt herself float upwards, she felt free from the burden of pain. She heard one last sob from her sister Rebecca and then she saw her father's smiling face and welcomed his embrace.

Chapter 33

Both Harpies hurriedly began to set us down outside the ornate golden door of the temple. As soon as Rebecca had released her sharp talons from my shoulder, she was immediately up in the air again. I cried out, "How do we get in?"

Her brisk reply was, "Serena only asked me to take you here." Then in a flash she was gone as she disappeared over the wall. Her sister quickly followed behind, releasing Dan a fraction too soon. Unfortunately, he landed in a scrunched-up heap on the floor. Instantly, I went over to him and helped him up. I noticed he had a nasty gash on his knee.

"How come I got dumped unceremoniously while you were carefully released," he joked.

"Perhaps she likes me!" I replied. Bending down I examined his cut knee. Using a little water from my bottle I attempted to wash the dirt away. Dan winced as I did it. "I think you will survive. Just be thankful we're here now and we didn't have to climb over any walls."

Looking around, the two immense, golden doors dominated the courtyard. Slowly, walking up to them I stared at the stunning clusters of sparkling jewels which framed the edges. On each panel, there were carvings of creatures which must live on the island. Dan joined me and we both marvelled at their breathtaking, ornate beauty. Unexpectedly, our thoughts were interrupted by a familiar voice asking, "Did someone mention walls and climbing?" Turning round together, we stared up at the top of the nearby wall, Dimitri's smiling face greeted us. Dangling his legs over the edge and still holding his wooden stick he grinned and said awkwardly, "The only problem is, I managed to get up here but I think I am going to need some help getting down."

As I walked over to Dimitri, I found myself feeling quite overjoyed to see him again. I had assumed he was still unconscious or the ogre would find him. Dan limped over to join me. "Are you okay?" I asked concerned.

"I'm fine. It's nothing, just a slight sprained ankle. I will walk it out," Dan answered.

"I can't believe Dimitri made it!" I exclaimed.

"I know, he has a predictable pattern of conveniently avoiding all the action and then appears afterwards unscathed," Dan replied.

"Maybe so but he needs our help now, getting him down. Any suggestions?" Both of us started looking around for anything suitable to use. My eyes fell upon some upturned, discarded containers. Perhaps we could use them to build a tower. Just then, Dan reappeared with some rope.

"That was placed very conveniently for you!" I remarked.

"I suppose so. I'm just lucky, I guess. I found it hidden behind a bush in the corner over there," Dan replied.

"Okay cowboy! Show me how you get it up there," I pointed to where Dimitri was still sitting.

Showing off now, Dan made a loop at one end with a very impressive knot. Then he proceeded to swing it above his head. "Are you ready Dimitri?" he shouted. Dimitri sat up straighter in readiness to catch it. "Yee-hah," Dan shouted as he released it. The rope limply made it half way then slid back down the wall. "That was a practice go," Dan grinned cheekily.

I laughed and said, "Well, this time just focus on throwing it all the way!" Dan laughed too and tried again. This time the rope arched up higher and landed within reach of Dimitri's hands. Edging his way carefully along the top of the wall, he succeeded to loop the end around the next pillar and pulled it tight. Checking the tension a few times, he then managed to make his way down the rope and received a round of applause from us when he reached the bottom. Quickly, he pulled the rope taut against the side of the pillar to disguise it and buried the excess behind a flowery shrub.

"We all made it then!" I exclaimed and all of us took part in a group hug. Turning to Dimitri I tried to sound apologetic as I said, "So sorry we left you behind but we hid you the best we could." Dan nodded as I continued, "You were unconscious and far too heavy to carry and the ogre was nearly upon us." Then as an afterthought I asked, "How is your head?"

THE ISLAND BECOMES YOU

"My head is very sore but I'm fine. You don't have to apologise, you both did the best you could for me given the circumstances you were in," Dimitri replied.

"What happened when you woke up?" Dan asked.

"Well, at first, I was quite disorientated and wondered why I was lying on the ground covered loosely with branches and leaves. Then it gradually all came back to me especially when I heard the ogre roar in front of the wooded area. I saw you both running away and then quickly try to dart through the trees to avoid it, only to be confronted by a towering harpy. I took advantage of all the commotion and managed to sneak past one of the ogres as it was too engrossed chasing the other harpies. Thankfully, the other ogre gave up and returned to the city gates. I followed you both as best I could. I wasn't sure what was happening when the ogre attacked the harpy carrying you both. She looked in bad shape. Is she okay?"

"Unfortunately, I fear it is a mortal wound. She didn't have long left." I replied sadly.

"That explains why the two harpies who dropped you off didn't notice me climbing up my fateful vine. They were too focused on returning to their dying sister. How come they dropped you off here?" Dimitri asked.

"Serena seemed to have a soft spot for us," I added wistfully. She said she wanted to help us as she had been in love once, long ago."

"Didn't she say something about a secret ally on this island?" Dan directed his question at me.

Dimitri jumped in, "That would be helpful, if we knew who that was." Both sets of eyes were focused on me now.

"Yes, she did mention an ally, but I think she was referring to herself. With all the pain she was suffering, I think she was getting rather confused," I lied.

"Oh, I suppose you are right but it would have made things so much easier for us to have someone else on our side," Dan replied forlornly.

"Thinking about it. Why did the harpies bring you here and not to the cells by the arena where I was kept?" Dimitri asked me with a tone of suspicion in his voice.

"Good question! Again, it was Serena who directed them to take us here so I assume she knew where George was being kept prisoner," I answered, relieved I did not have to lie this time.

Dan looked across to the east, where a whisper of red was appearing. "Hey everyone, this reunion will have to continue later. The sun is rising, we really need to get inside the temple before anyone else is alerted to our presence," Dan said with a hint of urgency.

"You're right," Dimitri agreed. "We need to get inside before everyone wakes up."

"Who actually lives here?" I asked Dimitri.

"An assortment of creatures; dwarfs, bears and ..."

"Green bushes!" Dan added.

Dimitri did a double take, "I haven't met any of those yet!"

"Okay, enough talking. Let's go inside," I interrupted.

"Have you tried the doors yet?" Dimitri asked.

"Not really, we only just had a chance to look at them before you arrived," Dan replied.

"Let's have a closer look then," Dimitri suggested. Immediately, Dan went straight to the middle of the doors and clasped one of the two golden ringed handles. He twisted it and then leaned against the door. Nothing happened.

Stepping forward I asked, "Is it locked?" Dan tried the other handle and pushed and pulled it this time. Still no movement. Dimitri chose to ignore Dan's attempts to open the doors and remained focused on the carvings. Intrigued to see what had caught his attention I scrutinised the panels too. There were some letters or symbols running along the top and bottom of the door.

"What are these markings?" I asked.

"It's Latin," Dimitri answered.

"What do they mean?" asked Dan.

Dimitri ran his fingers along the letters and deciphered, "Beware! If your heart is pure you may enter. The truth will out. May blood and pain reign down on you if you are not?"

"I laughed hesitantly, "Well, unless you can read Latin that warning wouldn't deter you."

Dimitri turned to look at me and asked, "Does it make you have second thoughts?"

"No, I'm pure of heart," I answered back confidently although I did feel slightly perturbed by the warning. I wondered what lay behind these golden, beautifully, carved doors.

"It's still not going to help us get in," Dan reminded us.

Dimitri pointed at a wavy lined marking near the bottom left-hand corner of the door, "Look at this symbol for water. See how it is more worn away than the other symbols."

"And on the right side this heart shaped symbol is also worn," I cried out.

"Okay," said Dimitri. "Let's press them together and see what happens." Placing my thumb on the heart symbol, I waited for Dimitri to count to three and then we pressed both symbols. Suddenly, there was a loud cranking noise as something clicked into place behind the door.

"Try the handle again," Dimitri told Dan. This time he twisted the handle and the door creaked open. Bravely, Dimitri peered through the door then motioned for us to follow. In front of us, it opened into a huge foyer with brightly lit torches on both sides. In the middle were several marble steps leading up to a giant golden statue of a man in a long robe holding a staff above his head. His eyes seemed almost life like and both seemed to stare right through you. I felt quite intimidated by his gaze. He looked very powerful and strong. On his lips was a slight smirk and he appeared to be looking down on us as if we were his subjects. Behind the statue was another golden door. This time Dan peered through as he pushed the heavy door open. He let out a gasp of astonishment as he walked in. Quickly, I followed and was immediately taken back by the size and splendour of the huge, very ornate room of worship. The high ceiling was crammed with paintings of various scenes depicting gods and goddesses. Upon closer inspection, one face always seemed to be in each picture, always holding a golden staff. Below, the walls had intricate patterns of gold leaf. Golden statues of gods and goddesses adorned both sides of the inner sanctum of the temple. Rows of golden pews faced the raised golden altar. There was an elaborate golden, jewel encrusted throne positioned in front of the altar. I closed my eyes to visualise the congregation sitting expectantly, ready for 'The Master' of the island to begin his weekly sermon. Opening my eyes, I tried to take in all the breath-taking treasures packed into the temple. It was obvious who was being worshipped and paid homage to.

I was so absorbed in taking in all the magnificent detail surrounding me that I did not notice Dimitri standing so close to me. I blushed slightly and

I wondered how long he had been intently watching my reaction as I gazed in awe at the beauty of this fabulous room. Smiling he said, "I can see you are trying to soak up every inch of this amazing place of worship."

Nodding I agreed, "I can't take my eyes off it. Everywhere you look is so spectacular, the gold, the jewels, the lifelike statues and the glorious paintings; it's never ending. Whoever rules this island thinks they are extremely important and should be idolized as a supreme God; his likeness is everywhere!"

"What other thoughts do you have about this God?" Dimitri quizzed me further.

"Very vain comes to mind. I would like to know the significance of his golden staff. I guess that must be the source of his power."

"Very astute of you Helena. The golden staff features heavily on this island. Dan, didn't you see it in some cave drawings too?"

"Yes," Dan mumbled while admiring a beautiful statue of a goddess."

"Should I be jealous?" I asked.

"Sorry," blurted Dan. "It's just all the statues are so lifelike; they almost look too real."

"They do have one other thing in common – none of them are smiling. In fact, if you examine them closer you can see a tinge of sadness and maybe disbelief in their eyes," I added.

"That's interesting," Dimitri added. "I suppose there is a look of despair in their eyes. Have you noticed how their eyes seem to all be focused on the grand, golden throne which I believe is the most impressive object in this whole room?"

"That's quite unnerving, now you've pointed it out," I replied.

"Hey! You don't think they were all once alive and have been transformed into golden statues. Like in the story of 'The Lion, the Witch and the Wardrobe' when the White Witch froze all those creatures in her Ice Palace," joked Dan.

Surprisingly, Dimitri laughed with him, "Perhaps the master has a gift like King Midas and everything he touches turns to gold!"

"It's probably his staff," I piped up. "It might be the equivalent of a wizard's wand. Maybe we should steal it from him?"

Dimitri held up his fateful walking stick and waved it above his head before pointing it at Dan, trying to keep his composure he shouted, "By the power of this staff, I turn you into a golden statue." Immediately, Dan froze on the spot, pretending his stick had worked. I pulled faces at Dan trying to make him laugh. Eventually, it worked and we both crumpled to the floor giggling.

Dimitri's mood suddenly changed. He became very serious. "I think it's time we looked for George. Besides there might be guards nearby and all this frivolity might attract them to us."

"Okay Dimitri, the fun is over. Let's go back to the foyer, there were two side doors. Perhaps one of them will lead us to George," Dan replied. Reluctantly, I took one last look around the temple room interior before following them out.

The smirking golden statue greeted us. Even when the back of its head faced you it still felt like its eyes were burrowing into you, searching deep inside for all the secrets you kept hidden. "Left, or right?" Dan asked me.

Not wanting to have the final say rest solely on my shoulders, I suggested, "What about a show of hands? Everyone, close your eyes and on the count of three, raise your left or right hand." Dimitri and Dan nodded in agreement. "Okay, one, two three …" I raised my left hand then cried, "Open your eyes." To my annoyance, Dan had raised his right hand but Dimitri just stood outside the right door with both hands by his side.

I was about to voice my irritation when Dimitri announced, "Sorry but while you were talking, I noticed the left door had a huge padlock on it so I guess we can only go through the right door."

Dan went over and tried the padlock but it was definitely locked. "Damn it," Dan cried. "That's probably the way we need to go."

"Maybe but let's see where the other door takes us," I tried to sound positive. "Do you think we need to take one of those?" I gestured towards the wall torches.

Dimitri stepped forward and turned the door handle. Surprisingly, it opened easily with no creaking sound. Dan and I hesitated behind the door as Dimitri went through first. He disappeared for a few seconds then poked his head around the door, grinned and said, "All clear! We don't need torches. Follow me."

JENNIFER BARSTOW

Chapter 34

George was sat in his favourite armchair reading the paper. Looking up at his wife Maisie, sitting opposite him, she was busily sewing the hem on some new trousers belonging to their son Edward. Glancing over at his son he watched him reload and unload his wooden train. It was getting stuck on one of the bends of his railway track and he could see Edward trying his best to push it past each time but it kept on derailing. George observed him for a while and felt a twinge of pride at his perseverance. Thinking back to when he was a youngster, he would probably have thrown the train and then stormed out of the room. Instead, his son was intrigued by the problem and kept taking the train off the track, studied the underneath in closer detail and then touched the track looking for a reason why it was happening. Suddenly, he clapped his hands together then carefully picked up something small from the track. Replacing the train quickly, this time it sailed around the bend smoothly. George joined in the celebration and clapped too. Maisie looked up from her sewing and smiled.

Afterwards, George got up and sat next to Edward. His son stretched out his hand to give him one of his trains, his little face was so excited. George took the train but suddenly Edward screamed and blood started pouring out of his son's eyes and mouth then everything started to fade away. George realised he was still holding the train but when he looked down, he held a thigh bone in his hand. It was gleaming white, completely licked clean and gnaw marks ran along each side. For one horrid moment George thought he had eaten his son but gradually his mind remembered the poor goat. The pool of blood was still there along with the remains of the rope and chain which had once graced the goat's neck. Throwing the bone onto the floor in disgust, George buried his heavy head in his arm and sobbed in despair. Loud grunts and sniffs in between the tears echoed around the room.

Unexpectedly, he was distracted from his thoughts of self-pity by the sound of a trap door opening. Looking through tear-stained eyes, he was extremely puzzled as it was the larger doorway which had opened. He sat there looking beyond the doorway to the dimly lit passageway. He expected it to be a trick or someone teasing him about his freedom but it remained open – inviting him to exit. Slowly, he got up onto his hoofed feet. Hesitating, he then walked over to the entrance, all the time expecting it to shut at any time. It did not. Feeling braver he stood in front of it and pushed one arm through followed by the other then he walked out. Looking from left to right there was no one in sight. He sniffed the air around him – nothing. Suddenly, the door closed behind him. He immediately hammered and pushed against the stone door but it did not budge. He felt strangely scared, the chamber had been his home for a while now and he felt safe there. Safe from hurting anyone human. This passageway was unknown to him. More importantly, what did the master have planned for him? He had mentioned about guarding the temple from his great-grandson. This thought worried him – supposing Dan was somewhere in these underground passages. Deciding to go left he made his way along the torch lit passageway. At the end he had a further choice to go left or right. Ironically, he thought, this is some sort of maze and I am the resident Minotaur. This time when he sniffed the air, he caught a scent of something familiar. Something he had gorged himself on earlier in his cell which had left a stain on the floor. He sniffed again; the aroma was much sweeter but very faint. His heart began to pound with excitement and his palms became sweaty. The saliva in his mouth began to run down his chin. He realised sadly he had hardly any control over how his body reacted to the blood as he let out an almighty bellow. Clenching his fists tightly, his hoofed feet began to take him in the direction of the intoxicating scent.

Chapter 35

Dan held my hand as we entered the well-lit passageway. It seemed to go on forever! "We need to be careful. There are bound to be guards somewhere along here," Dan warned as he held my hand tighter.

"It's still early. Hopefully, most of them might still be sleeping," Dimitri tried to sound reassuring.

"Have you got any idea where the passageway will lead to?" I enquired.

"I'm assuming that eventually we will find steps leading underground to where George is being held." Dimitri stopped, then added, "I hope your friend Serena was confident of George's whereabouts. I hope we are not wasting our time in here."

Dan and I both looked at each other then I replied, "She gave her life for us. I trust her completely."

"Very well, let's continue," Dimitri replied.

As I walked along, I shivered slightly as my arm brushed against the cold, grey stone wall. It was a complete contrast to the elaborate golden decorations inside the temple. Up ahead on our left, we noticed a small wooden door. Remembering Freya's words, once I was close enough, I searched the top of the door for any eye symbol. Nothing.

Dimitri tried to open the door but it was locked from the other side. "It probably leads back inside the temple. I think this outer passageway runs alongside the inner chamber," said Dimitri.

"Okay, let's find out what's at the end of this long corridor," Dan decided.

Finally, we reached the end of the passageway and it continued to go left. Looking down it the corridor looked very similar to the previous one. I hoped it would not lead to a dead end. Thankfully, halfway along there was an archway on the right with stone steps leading downwards. Leaning over we could not see much as the stairs curved around and then disappeared out of sight. Carefully, I held onto the handrail and made my way down. Dimitri took the lead again and Dan and I followed. A few steps down and we all jumped at the sound of a door slamming above us. "Someone else is in the building," I whispered.

Dan nodded and pointed ahead of us. "We need to get to the bottom of these steps quickly," he whispered back. Trying to keep up with the pace as Dimitri sped on, Dan accidentally clipped the back of my heel with his foot sending me flying forward. Luckily, Dimitri instinctively braced himself as I fell towards him and his back cushioned my fall allowing me to grab the handrail and steady myself. Dan caught up with me and apologised. Wrapping his arms around me he hugged me tightly before we continued down the steps at a slightly more cautious speed. Further down, the steps became much steeper and twisting. Also, the light was becoming dimmer.

Suddenly, Dimitri came to an abrupt halt. "We're at the bottom," he declared.

"Can you see anything?" I whispered.

"Not much but there is another wall torch not far ahead. It seems to open into a room," replied Dimitri. Dan held my hand and we shuffled carefully along in the semi-darkness until we reached the flickering torch. Dominating the wall in front of us was a picture of an elaborate maze with lots of twists and turns and dead ends. In the centre, very aptly was a Minotaur head.

"So, lurking somewhere in this labyrinth is a menacing Minotaur," Dan exclaimed. Looking closer at the maze Dan pointed at one section, "These rooms at the end look promising. Perhaps George is being held there."

"I hope so," I replied. Dimitri was inspecting the archway above us.

"More symbols – what warnings do they give this time?" I asked.

"Well, it says, pick your route carefully. Take your time and don't lose your way. Watch your back or the beast will get you!" Dimitri replied.

"How very inviting," Dan said.

Pondering about what Dimitri had just deciphered made me remember something, "If I recall, in the Greek myth about Theseus and the Minotaur, he was given a ball of thread by Princess Ariadne so he could find his way out of the labyrinth."

"Yes, that would be a good idea if we had any thread to use," Dimitri shot down my thought.

"We do have some berries though," Dan piped up.

"Actually, we could use them to smear a mark on the walls to highlight where we have been," Dimitri replied excitedly.

We were interrupted by the sound of loud footsteps above us working their way along the passageway we had just come from. Holding my breath, I strained my ears to focus on the sound. Abruptly, they stopped then scarily they began to descend the grey stone steps. Dimitri dashed back to look at the maze drawing. Running back, he whispered, "We need to go left, then right, right again then left."

"Won't that lead us straight to the Minotaur," I whispered back through gritted teeth.

"No, it takes you around the middle but I can't memorise all of it," Dimitri replied.

The footsteps were getting louder, "We've run out of time," Dan gestured to the huge entrance door. Leaning back Dan gave me a quick peck on the cheek then we both followed Dimitri into the maze. Immediately, we were met with three paths to take. Without any hesitation Dimitri took the path on the left. There was no time for any discussion on the matter. The choice was made. I watched Dan squish a berry in his hand and hastily smear it on the left path's wall.

In my head, the words 'The game has begun' came to mind. Burning torches, randomly placed along the path lit the way. Glancing above, the ceilings were very high and the walls felt damp and a little moist. It was not long before we reached a fork at the end of the passageway. Immediately, Dimitri chose to go right. Again, Dan smeared the wall with the berry juice on his hand. Blindly, we followed behind as Dimitri took charge, following the initial route on the map he had memorised. Suddenly, after the last left turn, he stopped as we were met with three paths ahead of us.

"Eenie-meenie-miny-mo," I suggested.

"What about straight ahead?" Dan recommended.

Dimitri closed his eyes tightly and desperately tried to recall the picture of the maze. Shaking his head, he opened his eyes and said, "Let's hope luck is on our side from now on."

THE ISLAND BECOMES YOU

"Do you really think a Minotaur is lurking somewhere in this maze? I asked.

Dimitri raised his eye brows and answered," I wouldn't be surprised if there was one after everything else, I've seen on this island." A cold shiver went through my body as we all froze at the sound of a distant, frustrated roar.

"What direction did that come from?" Dan queried.

Trying to swallow the panic rising in me, I whispered, "I'm not sure."

Dimitri grimaced, "I wouldn't advise going right, I think there was a dead end in that direction on the map. Shall we try straight ahead as Dan suggested?"

"You don't seem very bothered by that roar," I challenged Dimitri.

"It seemed quite a way off. Besides the loudness is a good indicator of how close it is to us."

"I think it sounded pretty loud to me," I said.

"You need to remember the sound probably bounces along these long corridors so it gives you the impression the roar is nearer than it is," corrected Dimitri.

Still not feeling reassured, I replied, "Okay, let's continue straight ahead. I just hope there are no short cuts or hidden doors."

"You do have a tendency to look on the bleak side," Dimitri replied.

"I like to think of all eventualities," I corrected him.

This passageway was very dimly lit. As we felt our way along, it soon became clear the darkness was because it was a dead end. Concern swept over me as we made our way back to the three choices. Trying to sound positive Dan said, "Left it is!" He smeared a cross through the last mark and planted a new smudge on the left path.

Already, the new path looked promising as we travelled along, we could see two further wall torches ahead of us. Halfway along a further roar hit us from behind. My heart missed a beat. I silently prayed this was the correct path. I feared we would not have a chance to go back and take the third one. Whoever the roar belonged to was getting nearer to us. Dan had hold of my hand, I felt his grip harden and his pace quickened. Dimitri stopped again a little ahead of us. Please do not be another dead end I pleaded silently. This time he was looking at the stone wall on his left. Once we caught up, we could clearly see he was examining the outer frame of a doorway. The lighting was rather gloomy here as I tried to peak above the door for any eye markings. "Does it open?" I enquired.

"It's very odd," Dimitri answered quite puzzled. "There is no handle. Perhaps it might be some kind of trap door with a pulley release button nearby." He began searching the door frame for some hidden lever. Another roar from behind alerted us to the creature's closeness. This time we could hear heavy footsteps and a scraping noise.

"It's getting closer," I said. "I think we should keep moving."

"Just a minute longer," Dimitri pleaded. "I haven't checked along the top corners yet." There was a slight delay then Dimitri said triumphantly, "I've found it!"

I watched as the door juddered and began to slide upwards. Before I could protest Dimitri grabbed me and bundled me underneath the gap, closely followed by him. In the commotion Dan was caught off balance and fell to the ground. As he began crawling over to join us my last image of his face was the look of surprise when the door suddenly shut between us. "Oh no," I screamed at Dimitri. "Get it open, quickly," I ordered, desperation rising in my voice. I began pushing blindly around the outer frame of the door as I had witnessed Dimitri doing while he checked for the release button. Tears of frustration had started to run down my face. My hands were starting to feel sore from the roughness of the wood against my palm and fingers as I dragged and pushed my hands along it. Jumping up I tried to reach the top frame, being quite high it was difficult to apply much pressure on it. In my panic, I completely ignored Dimitri who was just standing behind me. Finally, turning around I challenged him, "Why are you not helping me?"

"Stop and listen," he said. Despite my deepening concern, my body instantly obeyed him. I stood in front of the door and listened. My mind took a minute or so to catch up and decipher what I was hearing. I could clearly hear the scraping sound, followed by loud footsteps making their way towards us. My heart was pounding, my eyes were now focused on our surroundings in the semi-darkness. We were inside a small chamber with two wooden doors, one to the left and one to the right of us. I heard the footsteps come to an abrupt halt. I braced myself, ready to run. My brain was still trying to make sense of it all. I looked at all three doors, unable to decide which door the creature was actually standing outside. Looking back at Dimitri, he was strangely quiet, very calm, with no emotion on his face.

Suddenly, there was an almighty roar and the stone trap door in front of us shook violently as something immensely strong began to pound against it. I teetered on my feet and took a step backwards. My mouth was wide open but no sound came out. Then I felt Dimitri's arms around my shoulders to steady me. He gently placed his hand over my mouth then turned me round to face him. My body was shaking, I allowed him to drape his arms around me as he pulled me closer. I jammed my fist into my mouth to stop me from making a noise and buried my head in his chest. I closed my eyes tightly and prayed Dan had escaped.

Eventually, the hammering on the door subsided and everything went quiet. I moved my head slightly and Dimitri released his grip on me. His face softened at the sight of my tear-stained face and puffy eyes. I must have looked a sight. Then unexpectedly, he lowered his head at an angle and kissed me gently on the lips. I did not respond. I just stood frozen to the spot. My brain was scrambled trying to make sense of what was happening. Eventually, he pulled back and searched my face for a reaction but there was nothing. All my emotion was drained, I felt paralyzed, unable to function knowing that Dan was in danger and I was not by his side. Perplexed at my lack of any reaction Dimitri shook his head and pulled me further away from the door. Then he whispered, "I'm sorry, I took advantage of you but you must have guessed by now I have strong feelings for you."

Finally, I reacted and lashed out verbally, "How dare you. Dan's only been gone a few minutes."

"At last, a response," Dimitri laughed. "I think deep down you do care for me too." Grabbing both my hands he pulled me to him and kissed me again more passionately. I tried in vain to push him away but his chest felt like a solid wall against me and his hands had me in a vice-like grip. Suddenly, my brain kicked into action so I pretended to respond back to his kiss and waited for his grip on me to loosen. Then I acted quickly, a two-pronged attack. I bit his lip and kneed him hard in the groin. Before he could respond I had wriggled free and started to run. Doubled over in pain I heard him shout, "Stop Helena, the Minotaur…" as I disappeared through the door on the left of me.

Blindly, I ran and ran through endless corridors and twists and turns until my legs gave way and I fell sobbing to the floor. Hugging my knees for comfort I desperately tried to clear my head of the fact I was now running away from two monsters. Gradually, I managed to calm down and looked around me. All the passageways seemed the same. I stood up and looked down at each end for any sign of anything or anyone following me. Pricking up my ears I was met with an eerie silence. I had no idea where I was in this huge unrelenting maze. I was trapped. I made the decision not to go back the way I had come but keep going onwards. Each time I came to a bend I listened first before slowly peering around the corner. I had lost count of the time and how many passages I had travelled down.

Suddenly, ahead of me was an object lying on the floor. My first thought was Dan but my mind quickly dismissed it as the object was too small. Creeping closer, I soon recognised the familiar straps, it was my rucksack. I must have dropped it after my struggle with Dimitri as I was running away. I realised I was right back where I started as right in front of me was the wooden door, I had run through to make my escape. Instantly, I was on my guard as I picked up my rucksack. Was Dimitri nearby? I could not see or hear anything. Trying to keep calm I slowly walked towards the open wooden door. Holding my breath just outside, I listened carefully. Taking a small wooden stake from my rucksack, I bravely peered into the room and checked behind the door. Thankfully, it was completely empty there was no sign of Dimitri.

Returning my attention to the stone doorway next to me, I presumed logically it must work the same way as the opposite side. Wracking my brains, I tried to remember what side Dimitri had found the release button on the doorframe. Was it the right or left side? Closing my eyes, I tried to picture him feeling his way around the frame. Yes, it was on the right near the top. Standing in front of the stone door I focused on the top left corner of the frame looking for any areas which looked worn. At last, I spotted a small finger width hollow and pressed it. Nothing happened. Alarmed I tried again and again but the door refused to budge. In frustration, I leant my head against the door, my hands rested on the middle of the door frame. Shocked, the trap door started to open. A thought quickly crossed my mind, perhaps Dimitri had purposely emphasised the top corner to distract us from the middle of the doorframe. He did not want us to know how to open it. Pushing that thought aside, I bravely stuck my head under the gap. The passageway looked clear both ways so I bobbed underneath. This time I was not surprised when the door closed immediately behind me. Thinking back, it was almost as if Dimitri already knew it would close so quickly after he pushed me through. Perhaps he planned to separate Dan and me all along.

Once the door had shut behind me, I felt a strong urge to look back. Four lines of scratch marks, filling the width of the door, were etched in the stone. I shivered; they were not there before I went through the door.

JENNIFER BARSTOW

Chapter 36

The shocked look on Helena's face as the door slammed shut was the last image Dan had of her. Quickly, he attempted to get to his feet but he winced with pain. Looking down, he realised the fall had knocked his gash on his knee and it was bleeding again. Ignoring his knee, he raced for the doorway and frantically started searching for the release button. He focused on the top right-hand corner where Dimitri had found it. Urging him on were the muffled cries from Helena on the other side of the doorway, desperately shouting at Dimitri to help her.

Meanwhile, the bellowing noise was getting louder and closer. He knew he was running out of time. Dan hated the thought of being parted from his beloved Helena again but a little voice in his head was telling him to run. Time was running out, the beast was closing in. He could hear its hooves, clattering down the passageway towards him. Now the voice inside his head was yelling at him to run. It was heartbreaking to hear Helena's sobs as she reacted to the beast's loud roar. Both his palms were pressed hard against the left doorframe searching for the illusive release button. Slowly, they slipped down as he leaned his head in submission against the stone door and whispered, "I love you, Helena." Then he was gone. He did not notice the patch of smeared blood he left behind on the stone door.

As Dan rounded the corner in the opposite direction of the beast, he heard it reach the start of the previous passageway. Catching his breath, he leaned briefly against the cold, stone wall and heard the beast let out an almighty roar as it reached the sliding door. He heard it repeatedly charge against the door like a battering ram. Dan hoped it would withstand the force; it was the only thing protecting Helena. Dan knew he had to keep moving but he was intrigued by the creature. After he heard huge talons scraping against the stone door, he knew it was time to go. Carefully, he made his way further up the passageway trying not to make a sound. Unfortunately, for him, he did not realise he was leaving behind a trail to follow, better than breadcrumbs and much better than thread!

Standing still, in front of the doorway the Minotaur sniffed the air again for the addictive aroma. It was strong against the door but as he turned, he could clearly smell it ahead of him. His hooves began to move again in the direction of the scent. The hunt was on!

Moving quickly but quietly, Dan reached the end of the next passageway. He again had a choice of left or right. He was worried, each step was taking him further away from Helena. Hopefully, she was safe with Dimitri and he sought comfort in the fact she too would be trying her best to get back to him. If only he had the power to see through those endless stone walls. Deciding to go right, he hoped it would lead him back nearer to her. Pausing again, just around the bend, he could hear the beast grunt and snort then sniff the air. Strangely, Dan did not feel scared, more curious to find out what it looked like so he dared himself to peek around the corner. Tip-toeing quietly, he crept closer until his feet and body were millimetres from the edge. Pressing his back hard against the wall he took a deep breath. Beads of sweat started to form on his forehead and trickled down his neck. The voice of reason in his head questioned what he was about to do as extremely foolhardy. Nevertheless, he was powerless to resist the urge to look.

Gingerly, he moved his head a fraction nearer to the edge of the wall. "It's now or never," he said to himself. In a flash, he darted his head around the corner and back again. His eyes caught a glimpse of something, something his brain could not quite comprehend in that briefest of peaks. Slowly, he sunk his head back against the wall and allowed his brain to catch up with what he had just seen. Patchy snapshots of a huge bull head with horns, a long snout and pointy ears. Long muscular legs with hooves joined to a wide rippling torso. Sharp talons and a fury mane. The most frightening thing were the large, bloodshot almond-shaped eyes that looked straight at him. Finally, his brain kicked into action and his feet began to run – he knew his life depended on it.

Once he reached the end of the passageway, he had no time to decide which way to turn, he just ran left and kept on going. Behind him he could hear the excited deep bellows, followed by the sound of hoofed feet racing down the passageway after him. Dan's heart was beating hard against his chest, he had no idea where he was going. Minutes seemed like hours as he frantically ran down the endless maze of passages. All of them looked the same to him. Pure adrenalin was keeping him going even though his legs were using up every ounce of energy left, he had to keep going. He had gone past exhaustion and was just running on fumes.

The beast inside George, allowed Dan to run aimlessly ahead, it knew given time it would catch up with him. George knew too, it was inevitable. But one small part of him dared to hope, dared to believe whatever was left of his humanity would rise above the beasts evolutionary need to tear its prey apart and gorge on the elixir of flesh, bones and blood. However, with each minute, each hour that passed the slice of humanity left in him grew fainter. Relentlessly, this thirst for Dan's blood drove him on. The beast's sense of smell was all consuming. He could smell a pin-prick of blood one hundred feet away. George had already tested this out by estimating the distance between him and a minute amount of blood Dan left on the corner of a bend while he leant against it before running on. Likewise, he could distinguish the scent of any humans from a great distance too. He had already, briefly inhaled snatches of a new human scent. Much sweeter than Dan, leading him to believe it might be Helena. The beast in him was very interested in this new smell and was torn between following the new trail or staying with Dan.

George was slightly relieved by the beast's indecision but it only delayed the final outcome for a while. He could not stop it from happening. At some point very soon, he would catch up with one of them and he knew he had barely any control over their fate.

Rounding the next corner, Dan suddenly realised he was right back where he started. He froze and felt his legs start to buckle underneath him. He knew his legs would not take him much further. The beast had left his mark on the stone sliding door. Throwing himself against the door, he reached up desperately with his hands in the right-hand corner for the release button. This was his last-ditch attempt to survive. He could now hear the beast coming around the penultimate bend and then up the previous passageway towards him. He sensed the beast had changed tactics and had slowed down to savour the chase. He must have realised Dan had stopped and there was no need to run anymore as his prey had almost given up.

Dan tried to block out his racing heartbeat and the sound of the hooves getting nearer. It was so close; that he could almost smell the stale blood on the beast's saliva. Dan felt the hairs on the back of his neck standing to attention. His hands were very clammy and sweat was dripping down his face making him blink several times to focus on his hopeless task. He knew the beast was about to arrive at the last corner. He heard it stop, grunt and sniff the air. Unable to resist Dan turned his head ninety degrees and gazed down the passageway. Mesmerised, he watched as four large sharp talons, spread out like a fan, rested on the edge of the bend. These were closely followed by a huge snout and one hoofed foot. Unable to turn away, he watched as the beast's head and body were fully revealed. Dan focused on its huge, light blue eyes; they looked slightly familiar to him. The beast too seemed to take its time as its gaze latched onto Dan. It appeared to be closely studying all of Dan's features too. Was there a small hint of a smile of recognition on the beast's lips as they both surveyed each other up and down?

Dan's survival instinct suddenly took over and he threw himself at the stone door again. Both of his hands clawed at the top right doorframe searching for the release button. Time seemed to stand still as he blindly fumbled around. He could feel his heart almost bursting out of his chest as it rested against the cold, unmovable, stone slab. Finally, dragging his eyes away from the door, Dan watched as the beast took a step forward and shook its head from side to side. Why was it hesitating? Why hadn't it just charged after him? Perhaps it preferred the chase and was just toying with him now.

George stood still at the corner and stared at his great-grandson, willing him to run. He did not know how long he could fight the irresistible urge burning within him to tear Dan apart and gorge on his flesh. The smell of his blood was so tantalisingly delicious, that it was taking all his strength and willpower to stop his body attacking Dan. His heart was pounding, relishing the thought and closeness of his next meal. But stop … this was

Dan his great-grandson; he would not be able to live with himself if he devoured him. However, the beast within him was so strong, and relentless, gradually chipping away at his willpower. A battle was raging inside him and he had no control over the outcome. The beast was extremely hungry and wanted to be fed. The taste of blood was so addictive. He longed to savour more succulent flesh, feel the sensation of crunching bones and dine on mouth-watering blood as it slid down his throat. It tasted like heaven and he so badly wanted to savour it again.

His hoofed feet moved forward unexpectedly as he pictured the cruel, horrific scene unfolding in his mind. George and the beast now stood facing his great-grandson. He saw the hopeless panic reflected in Dan's eyes as he moved nearer. George knew he was slowly losing the battle of wills – his new body was too strong to fight against for long. He watched Dan abruptly turn back to the stone door and pointlessly pound against it. He knew this because he had already tried to unsuccessfully open it earlier by charging and throwing his weight against it during his blood lust rage. The beast took another step forward. Shaking his head, he felt a strong surge of pity for his great-grandson and for himself because it was only a matter of time before the beast would win and take over. He already felt the pain and suffering that was to come. There was no escape for Dan or him.

The last slither of hope began to disappear as Dan turned fully to look at the beast. His eyes darted up the passageway ahead, perhaps he could still make a run for it but his legs were throbbing badly. How much further could he run? Leaning heavily against the stone door he stared at the beast. Its body nearly fitted the width and height of the stone passageway. The beast seemed to know Dan had all but given up as it raised his head up and bellowed long and deep.

Dan's legs felt like jelly and he was shaking badly. Transfixed he watched the beast take a step nearer then another. He could clearly see its razor-sharp smile. All at once the reality of the situation hit Dan. He closed his eyes and pictured Helena's beautiful face in front of him. He felt his left hand reach out to touch her but the image disappeared so his hand sank sadly back against the side of the doorframe. His sweaty hand spread out using the middle of the door frame for support as he waited. To his surprise, the door began to slide upwards as the weight of his body forced him down.

THE ISLAND BECOMES YOU

Immediately, he realised the release button must have been much lower down. Instinctively, his body kicked into action as he stumbled sideways and quickly slid his legs under the door.

Before his head disappeared through the opening, his eyes watched the beast's face change from being victorious to sheer bewilderment and then anger. Dan saw it roar and then charge towards him. On the other side, Dan swivelled round to face the open doorway. Edging backwards, his heart pounding, he prayed silently it would close in time. He saw the beast fall to its knees and slide across the floor in a last-ditch attempt to get to the door before it closed. Clutching his chest, Dan held his breath until the door was completely shut. Still shocked, Dan remained staring at the stone door, unable to move. At last, he sighed deeply and was about to get to his feet when he saw the bottom edge of the door lift slightly to reveal two sharp talons. Behind the door he heard the beast let out a thunderous howl and he watched in disbelief as the door gradually began to rise. Another talon appeared underneath and the door raised another inch. He knew he had to move but was frozen to the spot. The door edged up another inch as the beast bellowed with all his might. It hovered there for what seemed a few more moments, teetering. He could feel the hot breath of the Minotaur on his foot but again Dan was paralysed with fear. Eventually, the beast let out another frantic roar and the door slid down trapping a single talon. A high-pitched wail protruded from the beast and the door moved up again slightly, enabling it to free its hand. Then the door slammed shut fully. Dan could hear the beast banging against the stone door and finally he allowed himself to breathe freely. He had very narrowly escaped the beast. With renewed vigour he got up and started to run and kept on running until the lamented howls of the beast were a distant hum.

JENNIFER BARSTOW

Chapter 37

Taking a deep breath, I tore my eyes away from the deep scratch marks etched in the stone and began walking. Finally, arriving at the end of the passageway I had a dilemma. Which way did he go? I hoped against hope he had managed to outrun the beast. Closing my eyes, I used my ears and listened for any trace of sound. Was that a slight scuffling sound in the distance? I was about to go down the left path when I saw a smudge of red on the corner of the right one. My decision was made; I walked along listening acutely for any sounds to confirm I was going in the right direction. But I only heard silence and the soft sound of my shoes on the hard-stone floor. I tried to just focus my mind on finding Dan but panic was starting to bubble up in my throat. I wanted so badly to find him but I feared bumping into Dimitri again and of course the monster with the sharp claws. I clung to the hope Dan was safe and had escaped the monster's clutches.

It seemed like I had been walking for ages, then just before I reached the next bend, I found another door. At the back of my mind Freya's voice reminded me to look for the eye symbol above the door. There were no markings above it but there was a strong smell of death or rotting flesh. I began to walk past it but then I stopped to think. Maybe I should try to open it. My head was telling me to keep on moving but my heart kept shouting I should check the room. I placed my ear against the stone door – just silence greeted me. Taking a deep breath, I pushed my right palm against the middle of the frame. It opened on my first attempt. Immediately, I was hit by the stench of decay and blood. Over in the corner, I could clearly see the remains of something which had been eaten. Next to a dangling chain and collar the floor was stained with dark blood and clumps of matted red hair. I could just make out a small horn – it must have belonged to a poor goat. Quickly, I scanned the other side of the room. More chains and a pile of rotting animal bones. On the opposite wall I could make out another door with what looked like a smaller hatch to the side of it. Then thankfully, the door began to close and the smell of death began to diminish. It must be the creature's den, I thought, except for this time on the menu was us.

As I continued down the passageway, I hoped each time I rounded a corner, I would see Dan's vivid blue eyes staring back at me and not the beast. Briefly, I paused to sip some water as it suddenly struck me how thirsty I was. Still, I had to be grateful I had not come across any blood trails to indicate Dan had already encountered the beast so hopefully he was still outrunning it.

I continued to listen for noises but everything appeared to be quiet until I heard a deep bellow coming from behind me. I dropped my water bottle. I heard it clunk as it hit the floor and rolled to the side. Everything froze around me. The hairs on my arms stood to attention and on the back of my neck. I wanted to turn around but I could not. I could feel the beast's eyes burrowing into me. Why didn't I notice? Why hadn't I heard anything? Although my body was paralyzed, my brain kept functioning, analysing the situation and deciding what my best option was.

I tried to focus on what my head was yelling at me to do but everything seemed on pause. I could not move. Eventually, I heard a voice in my head shout clearly the word – RUN. Instantly, my feet kicked into action. I left my bottle and just ran. I ran and ran. My heart was pounding tightly against my chest, my adrenalin was pumping through my body, willing my legs to go faster. I no longer had time to decide what direction to choose, I just ran.

All the time I was running I strained my ears for any sign the beast was gaining on me but I heard nothing only the sound of my own feet pounding the stony corridors. Eventually, when my lungs felt they would burst and my legs refused to go on, I stopped and listened. I could only hear my heart racing and my breath coming out in quick raspy bursts. Bending over, I leant against the wall with one hand and tried to catch my breath by forcing myself to take deeper longer gulps of air. I was beginning to feel quite dizzy. At the back of my mind, I was trying to prepare myself to have to start running again if I heard the beast nearby. Realising my breath was at last slowing down back to some normality, I allowed myself to glance back down the long passageway, I had just travelled down. The burning torches illuminated the entire length. I paid particular interest to any shadowy areas, looking for any sudden movement but there was nothing. Looking around me I saw some smears of blood on the floor. Thoughts of Dan filled my head. Was he nearby? I knew I had to keep going. After checking the passageway ahead, I took a deep breath and began to run. I prayed, I was running towards Dan, not away from him.

It became a pattern, I would run and run, stop briefly to recharge and check for any sounds I was being followed before running again. I noticed the length of my running was gradually decreasing, followed by longer breaks. Physically, it was obvious, I would not be able to maintain this pace for much longer. Slowly, Freya's voice was becoming more prominent, managing to bypass the fear and survival instinct which had overpowered it. "Slow down, remember the eye symbol," I heard her say. During my next break, I contemplated this. Supposing I had already run past the room. Being in such a hurry, I had no time to scan the many corridors for a door and eye symbol. I decided I needed to slow down; I might miss signs too that Dan had passed this way. Stopping to assess myself, I realised my mouth was very parched by now and I wished I had not dropped my water bottle. Maybe I might be lucky and make my way back to where I left it. I was surprised I had not heard the beast for a while. Perhaps it was playing games with me. Lulling me into a false sense of safety only to attack very soon afterwards. Still, I also had to focus on Freya's request which might help me locate Dan too.

Continuing much slower, I paused at the next corner and checked behind me as usual. Carefully, I peered around the bend and listened. Absolute silence, apart from the sound of my breathing, slightly elevated at the thought of what I might find. I continued along the dimly lit corridor, double-checking the shadows when I came across an additional pathway leading off to the right. I found it much harder having time to decide rather than the split-second choice when I was running for my life. Contemplating both options, I looked ahead of me and then back towards the path on the right. It was dimly lit too. I wondered if it could be a dead end. The last thing I wanted was to be trapped with the beast approaching fast from the other end. While hesitating, I heard Freya's voice reminding me to look for a hidden room with the eye symbol above it. I knew I had to check every possible pathway. After several final checks in every direction, I committed myself to taking the path on the right. Halfway along, I nearly turned back as it seemed to get darker and darker. I hated the idea of not being able to see what was ahead of me. I held out my hands in front of me and continued to walk forward. Then I felt something and nearly screamed. It took all my willpower to hold it in. Slowly, my hand let go of the tuft of curly hair. My eyes made out the silhouette of a small round lump as tall as my waist and quite thick set. "I hate people touching my beard," it suddenly uttered, making me jump.

Quite taken back, I managed to reply, "I'm sorry but I couldn't see you."

"You weren't supposed to find me," he answered with a hint of annoyance in his voice. "You should have kept going down the main passageway."

"But I didn't so who are you?" I asked.

Politely, he held out his hand and said, "I'm Billiano but just call me Bill."

Before I knew it, I found myself shaking his hand and replied, "Pleased to meet you, Bill. I'm Helena. Tell me, what are you doing down here?"

"Good question. I was trying my best to hide from you. Which I was doing very well until you slowed down and noticed this passageway," he reminded me.

"Are you following me?" I asked.

Shaking his head, he cried, "No. No. I was merely attempting to get out of here before you saw me."

My eyes had grown accustomed to the darkness. I could clearly see he had a long golden red beard which almost trailed to the floor. He wore a tiny pair of spectacles across his nose and he was wearing a blue stripy shirt with brown trousers. I decided to ask him, "Can you help me find Dan?"

The dwarf seemed to ponder thoughtfully for a while before answering. I fought the urge to shake a reply out of him. "Oh yes, I remember. He passed me about an hour ago along the corridor. He was running so fast he completely didn't notice me as I pressed my body tight against the stone wall."

"So, he's still alive!" I sighed deeply.

"No," immediately my face dropped. "No, I mean yes, he was very much alive. But he had no sense of direction. He passed me twice more totally unaware, he seemed to be going in a circle." Pausing, he rubbed his beard and added, "I suppose, if you are not used to the maze, plus running at that pace, it's very easy to miss little details. I on the other hand …"

"What about the beast?" I interrupted impatiently.

"Oh, the beast was following but he didn't seem to be in a hurry to catch him. Probably waiting until he is exhausted and can't run anymore."

"Will you help me find him? You mentioned little details he missed. What do you mean by that?" I asked.

"That's two questions!"

"Well, I do have a third one. Why are you down here?"

"That's easy. My job was to let the beast out," replied Bill.

"What! So, you're responsible for our plight," I cried.

"No," he shook his head again. "I'm not responsible. I just obey what the master tells me to do."

"So, why are you still stuck down here?"

"Well, I was trying to take the shortcut back to the exit when I took a wrong turn somewhere and got lost," Bill replied.

"I got the impression you knew your way around here," I mocked.

"Considering it has been nearly 20 years since I was last down here! I think I'm doing okay," replied Bill.

"But you are still lost like I am. Perhaps we can help each other to find the way out and look for Dan." I suggested.

Bill shook his head, "I'm afraid the master won't allow me to help you find Dan."

"Why can't you help Dan?" I queried.

"The master has different plans for both of you. I'm not allowed to interfere."

"Do you do everything your master asks?"

Bill hesitated before replying, "I do now. There was a time in the past when I had a soft spot for another human and tried to help her but I only ended up making things worse for her and her family. So, I vowed never to do that again."

"So, is there anything else you could tell me without getting into too much trouble?"

"I've probably said too much already!" replied Bill.

THE ISLAND BECOMES YOU

"Could you at least answer this question. What little details did Dan miss as he was running past you?"

"Oh dear, I did say too much!" Bill replied a little upset with himself.

"Please Bill, just tell me that one thing and then you can be on your way. The master will never know," I tried to reassure him.

"Oh well, it's probably too late anyway. The master finds out everything in the end."

"Go on then, just tell me."

"If you know what to look for, there are small hidden markers along the passageways, telling you to go left or right or straight ahead." Hesitating and rubbing his beard again he added, "I think I must have mixed them up as I appear to have gone round in a circle too."

"What are these markers? I asked.

"Well, one line is straight ahead, two parallel lines mean right and three parallel lines mean left. Or is it the other way round for right and left," he rubbed his beard thoughtfully.

Rather harshly I replied, "You need to focus harder and remember. Where are the markings?"

"Hidden on the floor or ceiling somewhere before each turn." He stopped again then said, "I'm positive, it must be two lines for left and three for right that's why I went wrong. Finally, now I can get out of this gloomy, endless maze," Bill cried, pleased with himself.

"So why did you come down this path Bill, it seems to be a dead end?"

"I had to react quickly. I heard you coming and darted down here as I wouldn't have made it to the end of the passageway."

"What's down here?" I asked.

"Nothing," Bill replied very quickly. Too quickly for my liking.

"Bill," I tried to look at him sternly. "Are you sure there is nothing down here?"

"To be honest, I'm not sure. It's been so many years since I was last down here. I know there are lots of secret passages and rooms dotted about but we need to go before the beast catches our scent. If you follow me, I'll lead you out of here. I know the master would want me to get you to safety."

"I can't go without Dan," I cried.

Bill shrugged his shoulders. "It's a shame but I can't help you find him." Just then we both heard a faint roar. Looking quite agitated Bill said, "I need to go now! Are you coming with me?"

"No, I've got to find Dan and I would like to explore a bit further along this passage."

"You're a fool – especially if the beast finds you. You'll be trapped!"

"It's a risk I'm prepared to take. I need to search all the maze," I replied trying to sound brave.

"Okay, you can't say I didn't warn you." Bowing slightly, he said, "Goodbye Helena, it's been a pleasure to meet you." With that Bill turned on his heels and scooted down the passageway. Checking both ways first, he turned right and waved then carried on up the passageway.

"Goodbye Bill," I whispered after him.

Should I have gone with him I wondered but something stronger was telling me to continue up this dimly lit passage. I was torn between finding Dan and searching for the hidden room. Every few steps the passageway became even darker but I told myself I had to keep going, I might miss something important. However, deep down I was beginning to think this was pointless. Sure, enough it was not long before I reached a dead end. Frustration boiled up inside me. What a waste of time! I sank to the floor, rested my head on my knees and tried my best to conceal a few disappointed sobs. Sighing deeply, I was about to get up and start back along the dark passageway when I heard Freya's muffled voice calling to me through the wall. Getting up, I held my ear closer and listened. Yes, I could hear her calling out my name.

Using my hands, I felt along the side of the wall for a concealed door but nothing looked out of place. Remembering the eye symbol, I tried to reach higher and felt around for it. Above me was a small area which seemed smoother, I felt along further and noticed a slight groove cut into it. Using my other hand, my two fingers slid around the indentation. I checked again; it was an oval shape with a smaller circle inside it. It must be the eye symbol I had been looking for. Suddenly, I had a powerful urge to press the centre of the eye. At first, nothing happened but then slowly I heard the wall slide to the left to reveal a hidden room!

Chapter 38

With renewed vigour, the beast began to chase the new scent, stopping to snort the air every so often to check it was on the right path. George could only observe as he hitchhiked along with the beast. To his alarm, as he rounded the corner, he could see her. She was just as Dan had described her, tall and slim with lovely locks of long brown hair. She had her back to him, too engrossed in drinking her water. Obviously, her senses particularly her sixth sense had failed her. Immediately, the juices in his mouth began salivating in expectation. His eyes glazed over and his heart beat faster. Also, his legs were pumped ready to charge towards her, she would have no time to run. Pleading with his new body, he begged it to wait longer, to give her more chance to acknowledge him. His breathing became heavy in short bursts – maybe she would hear. He tried to yell, to warn her but no voice came. The beast was too strong.

Suddenly, there was excruciating pain. His head and body were wracked with it. Finally, his voice came through – he roared. Thankfully, he watched Helena drop her water bottle and then eventually she reacted. She started to run. He let out another roar, this time full of despair as he looked across at the source of his pain. Loki stood behind the other corner, just out of sight, holding the golden staff aloft and grinning from ear to ear.

Once Helena had disappeared, he spoke, "I warned you about going against my wishes. Dan is your target not Helena. If you harm one hair of her head, I will kill you."

The pain subsided briefly, to allow George to nod his head and grunt before the staff was raised again to deliver another round of intense, jaw numbing pain extending through every fibre of his body. Eventually, his body could take it no longer, he slumped to the floor and his mind welcomed the inky darkness enveloping him.

Opening his eyes, he saw the golden staff raised above him. Instantly, his body recoiled and tried to move away. "Get up," Loki commanded. "I know where Dan is. Follow me!"

Obediently, George pulled himself up. His body felt very lethargic and heavy. He also felt quite groggy and had to concentrate fully on moving one hoof in front of the other. He dared not fall behind his master and alienate him further but, in his defence, he was only acting like the beast he had become. Very soon, George began to pick up the familiar scent of blood he had originally been following. Instinctively, he raised his head and snorted. Loki stopped, looked around and smiled at him. "Good, you have picked up his scent." Gesturing back to the bend they had just passed he said, "Now, I need you to hide over there and keep completely quiet for my plan to work. I will lead Dan back this way and take the turning to the left which leads to the middle of the maze where there is only one way in or out. Once we have both gone a safe distance you can follow us. Dan will be trapped and you can claim your prize."

George found himself nodding like a robot until he mentioned 'claim your prize' and it cruelly sank in what it meant. Loki continued, "Remember if you fail to do what I ask your fate will be worse than any pain you have experienced so far. I will turn Dan into a monster like you to live on this island for all eternity." George did not miss the sly smirk on Loki's lips as he ended the last sentence. It took all of George's strength and willpower not to lunge out and hold Loki's neck in a vice-like grip. He wanted to squeeze all the life out of him but he knew how futile this was. Besides, Loki held his staff in readiness to ward off such an attack. Instead, he sobbed his heart out inwardly. What a terrible choice he had to make, either to kill his great-grandson or sentence him to a lifetime of pure mental torture, trapped in the body of a monster. Oh, how he wished, he had never left his brown, leather journal in the boat allowing Dan to piece together the location of this island and its brutal master.

"Do you understand?" Loki asked smiling triumphantly. Closing his eyes, George nodded slowly. When he finally opened them, Loki had disappeared. Reluctantly, George moved further around the bend until he was well out of sight from Dan. Resigned to his fate, he slumped his heavy body against the cold, damp walls and waited. A few moments passed and suddenly an idea began to formulate in his mind. All the festered anguish, despair and self-pity began to be replaced by a fresh glimmer of hope. He began to work on a plan. It was too late for him but maybe, just maybe he could do something to save Dan from a fate worse than death.

It wasn't long before George heard Dan's voice saying to Dimitri, "Are you sure she went this way?"

"Yes. Look, I've found her discarded water bottle."

"Let me have it please. It's still fairly full. She wouldn't have dropped it unless…"

George heard Dan's voice trail away. Quickly, Dimitri responded, "There is no sign of a struggle or anything. Don't give up hope. We will find her soon. Remember, we are all much stronger together than apart."

"You're right. I nearly lost faith before but I found her again. Did you say it was this way?" George heard Dan's footsteps change direction and start to head towards him. He could smell the stale blood on his leg. It took all his strength to fight the incredible urge to go after him. The memory of intense pain he had suffered earlier was starting to fade. Saliva was dripping down his jaw, encouraged by the thought of ripping Dan's body apart, tearing sinews and crunching down on bones. Most of all he relished the taste of warm, pulsating blood in his mouth and the strong smell of fear radiating from his prey.

Luckily for Dan, Dimitri intervened, "No Dan. I'm sure she went this way, the left path."

"Okay, let's go down here," Dan replied.

George waited for what seemed an eternity for the footsteps to fade away. Getting up slowly, he sniffed the air again and caught a slight whiff of the sweet aroma he had smelt earlier but it was in the opposite direction to where Dan and Dimitri had gone. Hesitating, his body wanted to follow the fragrant smell but he tore himself away and headed after Dan with renewed determination to end this dreadful predicament once and for all.

Chapter 39

Moving along the dark passageway, Dan felt his heart beating fast. He dreaded each new bend, expecting to see the remains of his beloved Helena lying on the cold, damp floor while the beast gorged itself on her. Trying to wipe that vivid picture from his mind he pressed onwards. Dimitri seemed so sure she came this way. He strode along the corridor full of purpose and vigour but he showed no concern about bumping into the Minotaur. Dan was a little suspicious of what Dimitri had told him earlier about what happened after they were separated. He said Helena had frantically tried to open the door after it closed but he had stopped her, making her wait until the beast had gone. Angry with him, she had eventually managed to open the doorway and without waiting for him had just run off. Dimitri had tried to follow her but he must have taken a wrong turn and instead found Dan. He brought Dan back to the last time he saw her, being so dark at the end of the corridor, he mistakenly turned right instead of left in the direction she must have gone in. However, knowing how stubborn Helena could be, he could imagine her not stopping to listen to anyone once her mind was made up. Still, it was nice to be reunited with Dimitri. It felt safer having someone else watch your back in this awful, never-ending maze.

Further along the passageway, it strangely began to get brighter. As they got nearer, Dan could make out an orange flickering glow. Uncharacteristically, Dimitri seemed slightly hesitant as he rounded the last corner, waiting for Dan to catch up rather than take the lead. Taking a quick peek, he exclaimed, "It seems to open up into a huge, round room, lit up by rows of torches on the walls."

THE ISLAND BECOMES YOU

"Any sign of Helena or the beast?" Dan asked hoping it would be the former.

"Not sure, I can't see the whole area," Dimitri replied.

Dan tried to ignore the disappointment building up at the back of his mind. Dimitri had convinced him they would find Helena very soon but that hope was dwindling away. Taking the lead, Dan walked into the brightly lit chamber. He stared at length at the room, all his senses were primed to react but there was no sound, no movement, nothing. Dan whispered, "Helena," it echoed quietly around the circular stone walls and bounced of the high ceiling. He noted the huge, dark open pit in the middle and several rows of stone steps on the right. Curious, he moved towards the dark, round pit and peered over the edge. A small, stone wall separated him from its inky black depths.

Suddenly, Dan was aware of Dimitri's presence by his side. He had not noticed him move closer. Dimitri bent right over the small wall to get a better look, placing his arm on Dan's right shoulder. Automatically, Dan grabbed the wall for support. It only came up as high as his thigh and offered little protection to stop you from toppling over if pushed. Dan wondered why that thought had popped into his head, he dismissed it hastily. Dimitri seemed to notice Dan grab the wall for safety and he straightened up. Laughing he said, "I wonder how deep the pit is?" To answer his question, he picked up a loose stone and dropped it into the pit. We listened for several seconds until eventually, we heard a loud thud as it reached the bottom.

"That's pretty deep," said Dan.

"Yes," Dimitri replied with a slight grin. "Shall we throw a torch down there and see what's lurking at the bottom?" Before Dan could answer, Dimitri had grabbed a burning torch from the wall. Hesitating as he held it over the pit, Dan could just make out some staining on the walls but before he could digest what it might be, Dimitri dropped the torch. It tumbled and bounced against the side of the dark pit before finally resting at the bottom. Dan leaned over to get a better glimpse then immediately recoiled at what he saw. Shocked, he watched Dimitri continue to stare at the crumpled pile of skulls and bones both human and animal. He seemed to be enjoying the terrible sight. Not flinching or turning away even when Dan started to back away from the pit. Dimitri remained there, staring into the pit's cruel depths until the torchlight went out.

At last Dan managed to utter, "Don't you feel anything for those poor victims?"

"How do you know they were victims, perhaps they deserved it?"

"What do you mean? It's obvious they were either killed and thrown down there or even worse pushed over the edge as some sort of sacrifice." Dan could not get over the picture in his mind of twisted bones and the painful tortured grimace on the mouths of the skulls below.

Dimitri turned fully around to face him, "It's a shame there is so much about this island you still do not know or understand. Unfortunately, …" a knowing smile appeared on his lips as he added, "You've run out of time!" Confused, Dan followed Dimitri's gaze. However, everything became much clearer, the split second after his eyes focused on the blood-shot, glowing eyes of the beast standing at the only exit to the passageway they had just walked up.

Chapter 40

Dan shouted, "We need to run now!" He turned back to look at Dimitri. The spot where he had last been standing was now empty. "How could Dimitri just vanish? I don't understand?" Dan muttered to himself. He shouted out, "Dimitri," and heard his name echo around the chamber several times before it was replaced by silence. Slowly, Dan backed away from the beast. As he moved, his eyes frantically darted from side to side looking for another possible exit. He was so desperate, that he even started to imagine doorways in any shadowy spots he found.

Meanwhile, the beast just stood there, watching him. Eventually, Dan focused his attention back on the beast. He could not help himself, he was drawn to the creature's face, particularly its light blue eyes. They looked huge and bloodshot but also seemed strangely familiar. Dismissing the thought, he concentrated on his surroundings again. Maybe somewhere there was a secret passageway which Dimitri had found. Dan looked back at the spot where Dimitri had last been, then up at the steps. This time he saw something move out of the corner of his eye. Was it a hand? Without thinking, Dan began to race towards the steps. Straight away, he heard the beast let out a huge roar and then it thundered after him.

Flying up the steps, he suddenly stopped abruptly on the penultimate step. In front of him was just a dark, grey wall slab. Convincing himself it must be a secret doorway, he jumped up the final step and began hammering on the slab with his fists trying to find a hidden lever. After a few seconds, Dan stopped, he knew deep down it was pointless to continue. Bravely, he turned to face the beast. His heart was pounding so fast in his chest he thought it would explode. He tried desperately to calm down the rapid gasps escaping from his dry mouth. The beast was closing in on him. What could he do? There was nowhere left to run!

Below him, the beast seemed to hesitate at the bottom of the stone steps then a slow grin formed on its wide, bloodstained mouth. Dan watched it slowly lick his lips with its long, thick tongue. As its smile grew, Dan could clearly see the rows of jagged teeth waiting to tear him apart. His eyes were drawn to its strong, muscular torso and rippling biceps and the two large horns on its head. Vaguely, he remembered seeing pictures of the Minotaur in books at school when they studied Greek myths. However, the pictures did not do it justice. In reality, the beast was physically so much more impressive, so much more frightening.

It took a step forward. Dan glanced left and thought about moving along the row of seats. Almost anticipating this, the beast brought his right arm crashing down against the stone seat near him. It splintered, then cracked, instantly sending a giant tremor rippling up the other steps, strong enough to make Dan fall over. Gripping the wall, Dan pulled himself up. Picking up a broken piece of stone slab, the beast threw it at Dan, narrowly missing him. Did the beast do that on purpose, just to toy with him? At that moment, Dan knew the situation was dire. There was no hope of escape. He watched helplessly as the beast took another step nearer. The beast slammed his fist down again and it picked up another broken piece of stone before hurling it at him. But this time Dan was prepared and braced himself. The beast looked at him slightly surprised he had managed to remain standing.

Dan wondered if the beast was having second thoughts, maybe he might give him a chance to escape. But alas, the beast moved another step closer, then one more. Dan's body froze, he had to fight against himself to remove his rucksack. As a last resort, he threw it with all his might at the Minotaur but it just bounced off its chest like a softball. Annoyed the beast, swiped it away with his menacing talons, splitting the bag and its contents spilled out, rolling down the steps. Dan regretted it instantly, how pointless but more importantly he saw George's precious journal fall to the ground just in front of the beast. He would now have to watch the beast destroy his treasured great-grandfather's diary before his excruciating death. Tears began to run down Dan's face as he watched the beast focus its attention on the open journal. He knew it would only be a matter of seconds before the book was destroyed and him along with it. As predicted the Minotaur bent over and raised its arm to flatten it. Unable to divert his eyes from his cherished book he waited for its cruel senseless demise. The beast looked up at Dan and then refocused its attention back on the journal. Dan watched the beast's hand come down hard and then cruelly stop, hovering a few inches from the book. It was almost as if it knew how important the book was to Dan and enjoyed the opportunity to savour and stretch out his torment. The beast's blue, bloodshot eyes came to rest on Dan's face again. There was such an intensity behind the Minotaur's eyes – Dan could not look away. They seemed to burrow deep inside him, trying to reach his innermost thoughts. A slow smile appeared on the beast's lips but this time Dan felt warmth radiating from it instead of the smugness of finally cornering him earlier. Their connection deepened further when Dan noticed a single tear glide down the beast's face, resting briefly on the side of its bulky snout before continuing down its jaw and eventually disappearing into the hairy tip of its chin. The beast tried to rub its cheek with the back of its mighty fist.

Finally, it was the beast who broke the intense connection. It closed its eyes and shook its head from side to side. Instantly, Dan stepped back, trying to brace himself for the beast's final charge but nothing happened. The beast remained there for a few moments looking down at the journal then took one step back. Immediately, Dan thought he was toying with him like a cat does with a mouse it had caught. Raising its head again, the beast stared at Dan, its face looked full of sorrow. Dan was overwhelmed by a wave of pity for him, he did not understand why but he no longer felt scared. Continuing to look at him, the beast took another step back, followed by another and another until he was back at the bottom of the steps. Dan did not know what to make of it. The beast's behaviour was so unexpected but there was also a sense of familiarity about him which Dan could not brush aside.

Suddenly, a slow hand clap interrupted his thoughts. In unison, both Dan and the beast turned to look at the source of the sound. Immediately, Dan thought it was Dimitri standing at the entrance to the chamber but the person was much taller, wearing a gold edged white robe. He cradled his golden staff in between his arms as he continued the unhurried condescending clap.

George knew who it was. He was expecting him to appear at some point, after all, he had gone against his master's wishes. It was close though, if his old journal had not tumbled out of Dan's rucksack then it would have been a different outcome. He closed his eyes; he could not bear to think of what might have happened. But the battle was not over yet, he knew he had to stay strong, stronger than he could ever imagine if he was to keep to his plan. Focusing on his master's staff he waited for the opportune moment to come.

Dan was struggling to make sense of what was happening. Why had the beast stopped his attack after seeing the journal and who was this person? Suddenly, Dan remembered. The robe gave it away. He must be the master, the ruler of the island. Dimitri had described him holding a golden staff in the arena, cave drawings depicted him and the temple had a huge golden statue of him. Why had it taken him so long to realise, shock probably, his body had gone through such an excessive amount of terror it was understandable. Still, one thing was for certain, he doubted the master was here to save him from the Minotaur.

Having got their attention, the master stopped clapping and took a firm hold of his golden staff. Dan waited for him to speak and clarify his intentions. "What a touching scene. Not how I expected it to be played out of course but it does give me the opportunity to explain the situation to your great-grandson before you decide his fate." He laughed and continued, "Unfortunately, your actions have only delayed what happens, not stopped it!"

Dan could not comprehend what the master had just said. He watched the beast roar, raise his fist in the air and take a step forward, towards the master. Unperturbed, the master simply held his staff aloft and said, "Hey don't be too hasty George, let's enlighten your great-grandson first."

The beast shook his head and looked back up at Dan. This time Dan focused on the beast's eyes. This time he did recognise them, the pale blue colour which went with the crinkled smile and grey hair – they belonged to his great-grandad, George. The slow realisation of what had happened to George spread through his body. His legs began to buckle under him, making him grip the wall for support and his heart quickened. Finally, he brought his hand up to his mouth and said, "George… it's you!"

"Finally, the penny drops! Yes Dan, this magnificent creature standing in front of you is George," the master shouted with glee.

Dan saw George attempt to smile back at him before he lowered his eyes to the floor. Dan was filled with both pity and disbelief. It was obvious now; that the old journal had saved his life. Dan could not begin to imagine the pain and suffering George had gone through and the cruelty of being forced to kill someone he loved. Just then another dark thought entered his mind. Was this going to be his fate too? Would the monster he could become be staring into Helena's eyes just before he ripped her apart?

"I guess you're thinking right now, what plans I have for you Dan. What delightful creature could I change you into? Unfortunately, your fate is dependent on George's next action. He and only he has the power to decide your fate – it's his choice. So, George, have you made your decision?"

George knew it was too late for him. His fate had been decided as he had broken one of the rules of the island but he had the power to save Dan from a cruel life changing existence. Looking back at poor Dan, he tried to smile, to reassure him but George knew he probably only saw the beast's face staring back at him not George. How could he communicate to him that it would be, okay? He was now fully in control of the beast and he would try to protect Dan at all costs. There was absolutely no way, he could kill his great-grandson so there was only one action left for him.

"Time's running out George. My patience is waning. I might be tempted to take away one of your choices," the master said slyly.

Finally, Dan found his voice. "Why do you use your power so ruthlessly against us? What do you gain from it?"

"Interesting question. I've been on this island for many years – trapped like you are. I harvest the fear from my occupants to help me increase my power. One day, I will escape but until then why not use my power for amusement. I want respect and obedience from my subjects so I must remind them of the consequences if they don't obey me. Otherwise, we wouldn't live happily on this island, everyone needs to know their place."

"So why were you put here? Why can't you escape?" asked Dan.

"I've been a prisoner on this island for nearly a thousand years. For what you ask? It was only a trivial thing. Just a dare! I never actually killed my nephew, I just wanted to win a bet with myself and find out his only weakness. My only fault was I didn't think through the consequences of my actions. I only focused on winning my bet. Still, a thousand years is way over the top to punish me. You delightful humans help make the time pass more interestingly while I plot my revenge after I escape." Pausing briefly, he added chillingly, "Unfortunately, you are both disposable but Helena, the lovely, gorgeous Helena is another matter."

Anger bubbled up in Dan, replacing the fear he was feeling. "You leave her alone," he shouted. His heart took over and, in a rush, he began to clamber along and down the stone seats towards the master. His eyes were fixed purely on him. He saw him lift his golden staff upwards but it did not deter him. It was only the body swipe from the beast that blindsided him, pushing him sideways against the stone seats. Nursing a deep cut on his arm, he stared at the beast, shocked, not knowing what to do next.

The master brought his staff back down. "Just in the nick of time George. At least now, you realise what power I have over you. Perhaps, I might change my mind about your fate George, especially if you finish off your great-grandson for me. Then I can get on with much more pleasant business." Sighing he continued, "Dan, I have wasted too much time on you already. All those delightful chats we had in the cave, in the church and on our journey here. I tried my very best to be pleasant to you even after you left me for dead when the ogre attacked us. Obviously, I had an ulterior motive. I wanted to stay close to Helena even though I suffered terribly seeing you both together. But with you out of the way, I can at last have her all to myself."

"I don't understand what you are saying. You weren't with us – Dimitri was!" Dan answered back.

"Perhaps this will make it all much clearer," the master replied. In disbelief, Dan watched as the master's face transformed into Dimitri. Turning to George the master asked, "Is it nice to see your dear friend again. He put up such a great fight against the ogre. It was such a shame when he was crushed against the wall as he tried to escape from the arena."

George's mind was in a turmoil of hell; it was so hard to control himself. He yearned to charge at his master, sink his horns into his evil body and pound him with his fists. But he needed to get closer. George noticed the satisfied look on his master's face. He also noticed he had lifted his golden staff up a bit and was staring at George's clenched fists. His master was obviously trying to goad him into attacking him. Using all his willpower, he tried to relax, unclenched his fists and stared up at Dan. His face revealed how crushed he felt knowing it had all been a huge lie.

The last secret to be revealed was too much for Dan to comprehend. His mind whizzed back to his first encounter with Dimitri and his initial gut feelings of mistrust he felt. If only, he had listened more to his body's reactions but never in a million years would he have guessed the whole extent of his deception. To be able to shapeshift and act like that person so convincingly. More frightening was his motive for doing it. Just for his own sickening amusement, he played his malicious game of pretence with people only to turn them into a monster at the end of it or worse. What about all those poor souls who had their lives extinguished down the dark foreboding pit? Was that fate intended for him – to join the hundreds of decomposing bodies already languishing down there? He became aware of George's eyes on him. It made sense now, the sorrow and sense of hopelessness eluding from the beast's eyes. He had sensed this earlier and the familiarity about his eyes. Dan could not begin to imagine the pain and anguish George was feeling, trapped inside the beast's body. Unable to control the creature's bloodlust and basic need to attack its prey. Dan tried to smile back and said, "It's not your fault George, any of this."

The master cut in, "Ahh, but it is George. You are responsible. Dan wouldn't be here if you had given up on your quest to find this island. Instead, the same dogged determination led your great-grandson here. Therefore, it is only fitting George, you should decide what happens next. So, for the last time, have you made your decision?"

George shook his head from side to side. Both outcomes were equally unbearable. An eternity for Dan, suffering inside the body of a miserable creature, forced to obey his master's bidding or to find the strength inside himself to kill his own flesh and blood. How could he possibly live with himself afterwards – being responsible for either outcome? His gaze returned to his master and he grinned to himself as he remembered there was a third option!

JENNIFER BARSTOW

Chapter 41

Stepping carefully inside the darkened room, I reached out with my hands to guide me and whispered, "Freya, where are you?"

Suddenly, the wall torches on either side of the room lit up. "That's much better. I'm over here," said Freya. It took a few seconds for my sight to become accustomed to the brightness of the room. My eyes travelled around the room, taking it all in. It was stacked with huge wooden shelves reaching up to the ceiling, adorned with endless ornaments, toys and all sorts of bric-a-brac. Sensing I was slightly distracted by all the wonderful objects on view, Freya called out again, "I'm over here."

I spun round to face her but saw nothing only rows of dolls and some glass objects. "Where are you?" I repeated.

"I'm directly in front of you. Look closer," she replied.

Taking a few steps nearer, I examined the five rows of dolls opposite me. They were made from china, wood, glass, silk and all manner of materials. Some were colourful, some plain and all different sizes. Finally, my eyes fell upon a black Russian doll with a beautifully painted face, rosy cheeks and vivid blue eyes. They appeared to stare back at me. Peering closer, I was not scared when one of the long eyelashes winked at me and the bright, red lips smiled. "Found you," I said.

"Yes, I'd nearly given up hope you would find me. We mustn't waste any more time. You need to find a golden heart shaped ring. It's hidden somewhere in this room. I can feel its power but something is blocking me from seeing its exact whereabouts."

"What will you do with the ring when I find it," I asked.

"This ring is extremely magical. It can be used to weaken Loki's power and seal the island off once and for all so no other poor soul will set foot on it and be cruelly tormented by him."

Very intrigued and wanting to know more about the ring, I asked, "How did the ring come to be on this island?"

"The ring was originally brought to this island by some brave Templar knights. They needed to take the ring to the heart of the island, where it would be most powerful. Unfortunately, Loki tricked them and stole the ring for himself. Luckily, the ring was useless to him. Only someone pure of heart can harness its power so he keeps it hidden in this room to stop anyone using it against him."

"Wow, the ring sounds incredibly important but before I start looking for it. Where is Dan? Please tell me he is still alive."

"I can still feel his strong presence on the island. He is still alive," Freya replied.

"Could you help me find him first? Then together we could help you find the ring," I suggested.

"I'm sorry but that's not a good idea. We are running out of time. I'm certain Loki will be alerted soon of our presence in this room and he will try to stop you finding the ring."

"Very well," I sighed, "Please make sure he stays safe. I will never forgive myself and you if something was to happen to him and I'm not there to help. Where shall I start looking?"

I watched the little Russian doll look behind me, "Maybe start over there and work your way systematically round to me," Freya recommended.

I began searching, moving objects, looking inside, shaking them. I found a beaten-up metal trunk and used it to stand on to reach the higher shelves. Dust was an issue, some of the objects looked very old and fragile. Many had not been touched for years so I was a little perturbed about running into a big spider along the way. Working as quickly as I could, I finished looking at the objects on the first wall of shelves and then moved to the middle. In my haste to check everything, I accidentally dropped a glass vase – it just slipped through my fingers. "Be careful Helena. You don't want to cut yourself as it might alert the Minotaur to your whereabouts," Freya warned.

"Yes, I will try to be more careful," I snapped slightly as I was starting to get fed up with searching for this elusive ring. Thinking about Dan again, I began to worry about his cut knee. "Are you sure Dan is, ok? He has a cut which might attract the Minotaur to him?"

Absently, I rested my hand on the wall behind me, through the gap in the shelves as I was thinking about Dan. Freya tried to reassure me, "All I know is he is still very much alive. Unfortunately, my power is weak in this room. I can't see where he is in the maze, I can only feel his life force."

Suddenly, the wall behind me seemed to crackle and spark into life. I jumped and quickly moved my hand away. "What is it?" I asked Freya.

"I haven't seen one of these for ages, it's a magic screen. It will show you what your heart desires," Freya replied.

Moving closer, I examined the shelves and there appeared to be a join in the middle and one further along. At the bottom of the last shelf were some wheels. Holding firmly, onto the middle wooden shelf, it groaned as I tried to wiggle it forward. Showing some resistance, I tried again, this time it moved an inch forward. I pulled again and finally the squeaky wheels moved to reveal a camouflaged flat screen, embedded in the wall. I could just make out a faint rectangular outline. "How do I turn it on?" I asked as I looked for a button or switch.

Freya laughed, "It doesn't work that way. Press the palm of your hand against it, close your eyes and concentrate on Dan." While my eyes were closed, I could feel a slight warmth on my fingertips. I opened my eyes and watched the screen come to life like a silent movie.

I recognised Dan immediately; he was stood on some steps looking down at … I gasped and held my hand to my mouth. Glaring up at Dan was the Minotaur, standing menacingly at the bottom of the steps. Nearby was another figure it looked a bit like Dimitri, wearing a robe. Eventually, I turned to the doll and pleaded, "Freya, please. You must save Dan!"

I watched the Russian doll, close its eyes and then shake its head so I knew the answer before she replied, "I'm sorry Helena but my power is suppressed by this room plus all the times I have already helped you have left me considerably weakened. I will try again to speak to George?"

"What are you talking about?" I shouted. "He's not there!"

"I'm so sorry Helena but Loki has changed him into the Minotaur you see before you. George has no choice now but to obey his master's wishes. I will try my best to reason with what is left of his humanity."

Facing the screen again, I could not believe what she had just revealed. Looking closer at the giant horns, the ringed snout, the hairy mane of hair cascading down his back, his tail and hoofed feet – he was unrecognisable. Sadly, they had set out on a quest to rescue George but he had become the very beast they were running from.

"How long have you known, Freya?" I demanded.

"Honestly, my suspicions were only confirmed when I saw him on this screen. I immediately sensed the pain and unbearable inner turmoil radiating from the beast. I was worried Loki would engineer some cruel fate for George once he was captured but I hoped you would rescue him in time."

Semi-satisfied with her answer, I returned my attention back to the magic screen and tried to make sense of what was happening. Unfortunately, there did not appear to be a volume button.

I watched helplessly as Dan tried to escape along the stone seats, unaware the Minotaur had charged up the spectator steps after him. George lunged at Dan, knocking him sideways against the seats. While Dan nursed a badly cut arm, George just stood there, towering over him. Holding my breath, I watched Dan try to get up. My whole being was willing Dan to escape. Without warning, the monster moved forward and pinned Dan either side with his muscular arms. For a while, the beast appeared to just stand there, frozen to the spot, peering down at Dan. Then to my horror the beast simply picked up Dan and carried him aloft. After an initial struggle, Dan appeared to show no resistance, resigned to his fate. I screamed at the screen, "Do something Freya. He's going to kill him."

I could not tear my eyes away as I watched George carry Dan down the steps towards the low circular stone wall. The middle of it looked dark and gloomy. I wondered if it was some sort of pit. Alarm bells started ringing in my head as George seemed to hesitate at the edge of the pit and looked across at the man, I thought was Dimitri. Why hadn't he run away, he had the opportunity to? Instead, he just moved closer to the Minotaur. I did not understand until I saw him holding a golden staff.

"Please Freya," I shouted. "Do something or Dan will die."

"I'm trying my best to focus on George and appeal to his human self but the beast in him is very strong and it's blocking me. I'm so sorry Helena."

"No! It can't end this way! How far away are they? Can I get there in time?"

"You won't make it. It's too far away!"

"So, all I can do is simply watch George throw Dan into some bottomless pit." I was crying tears of frustration and hopelessness.

"I will try again to contact George but he is not responding. I have no idea if he can hear me. Just pray Helena that it works."

At that point, I literally fell to my knees, holding my palms together. I shut my eyes and prayed for Dan to be spared. I could not bear to watch Dan die in front of me on a screen.

THE ISLAND BECOMES YOU

Chapter 42

George stared at his master and then at the golden staff. All his power originated from that staff – if only he could take it from him. Perhaps there was a way to undo all the pain and suffering he had sentenced people to over the many years he had ruled this island. George thought carefully about his next step. There was no going back once he started. George knew the master was growing impatient with him. He had to make his choice known now or his master would influence his decision and possibly change his mind.

Dan's heart was pounding, the exchange of glances between George and his master troubled him. Perhaps George was wavering and the beast was taking back control. He hoped not, his only chance of surviving depended on George. Suddenly, George let out a roar and strode towards him, leaving Dan no time to react. Pinning him on either side, Dan realised there was no escape. The beast looked down at him and licked his lips. Seconds seemed to stretch out into minutes. Pleadingly, Dan searched deep into the beast's eyes, hoping to locate George, somewhere inside. Unfortunately, all that stared back at him were two deep, unresponsive pools of blue with no flicker of emotion. Dan held his breath as the beast George had become, reached out for him and lifted him effortlessly above its head. Dan attempted to wrestle free but it was pointless, the beast only gripped him harder. Acknowledging his fate, Dan's limbs hung limply, his eyes now fixed on the ceiling above him. Every so often, a small amount of crystal buried deep in the stone reflected back a welcomed sparkle in the bleak last seconds of his life. His thoughts turned to Helena as the beast brought him to the edge of the bleak, wretched pit.

George watched his master eagerly take a step forward. "You've made the right decision George. Although, I must confess I was having great fun, imagining all sorts of creatures I could turn your great-grandson into." Pausing he grinned at Dan, "Now it is time to put Dan out of his misery. I think the big reveal has been too much for him!"

George wavered slightly; his feet seemed rooted to the spot. Sensing his reluctance, his master shouted, "DO IT NOW GEORGE. NOW!" George watched his master edge nearer and start to raise his staff. In response, George finally moved his hoof, resting it on the top of the low wall surrounding the pit.

Dan began to pray his last moments would be over quickly. The thought of lying there, broken and suffering immense pain at the bottom of the pit filled him with terror. He tried to twist his head towards George and catch his eyes, in one last ditch attempt to bring George back, to take over control of the beast. Their eyes met briefly, Dan implored, "Please George, it's Dan." However, the beast simply returned its gaze back to his master. Dan closed his eyes and waited. Disappointed tears began to well up in his eyes as his last thoughts were of Helena and how he had failed to protect her from both beasts. What he dreaded most of all, was the plans the master had for her and that she would have to face him on her own. At the back of his mind, he clung to the hope they might one day be reunited in another lifetime and place. Then Dan felt himself fall; soon the ground felt hard beneath him. He lay there hoping death would sweep him up speedily.

George acted rapidly. He dropped Dan to the floor as he strode across to his master. He noted the surprised look on his master's face as he grabbed hold of him. There was a slight delay, then he felt the familiar excruciating, searing pain throughout his body. But it was too late. George did not let go. He simply held his master tighter. One last glance at Dan, then the beast in him gave a final roar as he threw himself over the edge into the harrowing, darkness of the pit. It all happened so fast. George felt himself fall in slow motion. His life flashed before him. He saw his wife, Edward and the last person was Dan, pleading with him to change his mind. Just before the final second, he felt the gap within his arms was empty, his master had disappeared.

The impact crushed his back and broke his ribs, he felt them cutting into his chest. The pain was worse than what his master had inflicted on him. Blood bubbled up in his throat. He could not move. Opening his eyes, it was pitch black except for a white glow in front of him. "Foolish man. Do you think you can end my life so easily? It's such a shame, I was so proud of my latest creation. You've wasted your life for nothing. You haven't saved Dan; he will now take your place. Hold that thought George before you die. Your last action has sealed Dan's fate!"

George tried to speak but no words came out. He felt a warm single tear slowly slide down his cheek. Gradually, his body became numb, he could feel nothing except for the darkness closing in on him. His last thoughts were of Dan. What had he done? Just before the darkness engulfed him.

JENNIFER BARSTOW

Chapter 43

Suddenly, Dan was awake. He opened both eyes. Looking around him he realised he was lying beside the small, stone wall encircling the giant, deep pit. He forced himself up onto his knees and rubbed his head. He felt a small lump on his forehead where he must have hit the ground. He was shocked. Why wasn't he lying on a pile of human bones? Where was George? He shouted his name. Nothing, only the echo bouncing around the room. Using the wall, he pulled himself up to a standing position and peered over the edge but only an eerie blackness greeted him. A sense of urgency took over, he raced back to the wall and snatched a lit torch. Bringing it back to the pit, he hesitated and tried to prepare himself for what might be down there but it did not work. Holding the torch gingerly over the edge, he dared his eyes to look down. Lying in the middle, amongst the pile of pale, human bones was the broken, twisted body of George. In death, he had changed back into his human form. Instinctively, Dan tried to reach out to him but it was hopeless. Just to make certain, he shouted, "George." There was no response, only a deathly silence once the echo had faded away.

It was too much for Dan, the torch slipped from his fingers and he stumbled backwards. His legs gave way and he fell to the ground sobbing. He remembered their first meeting. How supportive George had been when Dan feared Helena was gone. Also, he pictured their journey to the mountain and their encounter with the bushes. Devastated, he realised the bushes had once been human too and he nearly killed one of them. He cried for them too, for him, for Helena and most of all for George. He had so badly wanted to rescue George but it was all too late. He never had a chance to. In the midst of his tears, his thoughts turned back to Helena. He had to find her before the master set his plan in place. Making himself get up, he wiped his tears away. Leaning over the wall he bowed his head and said, "I hope you find peace, George. I hope in death you are reunited with your family. I won't ever forget our time together. RIP George."

Afterwards, he shook his head at the pointlessness and sheer waste of a life. With added resolve, he walked out of the chamber exit and back towards the passageways which hopefully would lead him back to Helena. He prayed this time he would not be too late to stop the master.

JENNIFER BARSTOW

Chapter 44

The seconds passed into minutes; I still couldn't bring myself to open my eyes. I was too scared. I kept thinking if I did not open my eyes then it is not real. It was like my brain transported me somewhere else, some sort of coping mechanism kicked in. I just could not imagine my life without Dan. Gradually though, in the middle of my protective place, shut off from reality I began to acknowledge Freya's voice. "Helena, open your eyes. You need to see what's happening."

"Is Dan safe?" I heard myself say.

"Yes. Look for yourself," Freya cried.

I opened one eye to peek at the screen. I was confused. Dan was lying on the ground while George was standing on the edge of the wall holding his master. He was staring into the dark cavern below. The beast glanced over at Dan for a moment, tilted his head back and looked like he gave a final roar before he jumped into the pit.

Thankfully, soon afterwards, I saw Dan start to stir. He rose onto his knees and rubbed his head. Standing up, he shouted something then made his way to the walled edge and peered over. Next, I watched him ran back to the wall and seize a lit torch. For a few moments, he held it over the edge of the dark pit before he let it drop from his hand. Staggering backwards he fell to the ground and began to sob uncontrollably. I found myself crying with him. George was dead.

"Helena, he's safe now. You must keep looking for the ring," Freya said urgently.

Wiping away my tears I answered, "But what about Dan. I must find him him. The ring is not important anymore. Loki is dead! We saw him fall into the huge pit."

"Sorry Helena, but I don't trust what I saw on that screen. I don't believe Loki is dead or lying injured. He is too powerful. Although, he was taken by surprise, I expect he used his magic to survive."

"So, Dan isn't safe. I need to find him now and warn him." I quickly moved towards the door.

"Stop Helena! Please. You will probably get lost again trying to find him. Let me try to guide Dan here while you continue looking for the ring. Besides, I don't know how much time you have left before Loki gets here. The ring is so important. It's the only weapon we can use to stop him."

I sighed and half-heartedly returned to looking for the ring. The room was full of so many different objects. I opened several trinket boxes containing jewellery but nothing matched Freya's description of the golden, heart shaped ring. While working my way along to the last wall I said to Helena, "Are you certain this ring is definitely in this room?"

"I've used my powers several times to locate the ring and each time I have been drawn to this room. I know it's here somewhere but it's very well hidden."

Turning my attention to the last wall, I spied a small bookcase in the centre, filled with classic fiction. I ran my hand over some of the titles, Moby Dick, 20,000 Leagues under the Sea, Great Expectations, and Frankenstein. Absently, I thought, if I had more time, I would love to read Moby Dick again.

Suddenly, I heard someone shouting my name. I rushed back to the doorway and shouted, "Dan, I'm in here."

"Helena, is that you?" I heard footsteps change direction and then start to race along the dark corridor towards me. Dan fell into my arms and hugged and kissed me. "I've been so worried about you Helena," Dan murmured in my ear.

Tears rolled down my face. I was so happy to be reunited with him. "Are you hurt Dan?" I asked.

Looking down at his arms, he replied, "Just a few cuts and grazes. I will be fine." He hugged me again then asked, "What are you doing in this room?" with a puzzled look on his face.

I looked over at the black, Russian doll. Hesitating at first, I then blurted out, 'Sorry Dan, but I don't have time to explain. I need your help to find a golden, heart-shaped ring."

Dan took a step back; an astonished look clouded his face. I noticed his eyes dart around the room and then linger on the bookcase before returning his attention back to me. "What do you need the ring for?"

Freya's voice in my head reminded me that time was running out so I simply replied, "It will help us escape this island and every other poor soul trapped here. Please just help me look for it." I started walking back towards the bookcase.

"But how did you know it was here?" Dan shouted behind me.

"Because Freya told me." I put my hand to my mouth as soon as I uttered her name but it was too late.

"Who is Freya?" Dan asked. I turned round to face Dan. Realising my secret was out, there was no point concealing it anymore. My eyes automatically glanced over at the doll. I saw her mouth open and seemed to shout the word "NO." I looked back at Dan. His eyes were focused entirely on the doll.

"Freya is that you inside that doll?" I watched a very intrigued Dan, walk towards the doll.

"Freya's helped us so much. I wanted to tell you about her but she warned me not to trust anyone," I felt the need to explain myself further.

"Very wise of her," Dan replied. His eyes not moving from the doll.

Unexpectedly, Freya shouted, "Don't move any nearer." Dan hesitated briefly before he took another step forward. Confused, I watched as he reached out to grab the doll but his hand seemed to bounce off some invisible barrier. Puzzled, Dan turned to face me. Then he walked back towards me but was blocked again by some invisible force field.

"I don't understand," Dan cried out, "Help me, Helena!"

"Helena. Look at the screen!" Freya screamed.

Bewildered, I gazed up at the screen over Dan's shoulder. I gasped, at the sight of Dan walking along one of the passageways. I noticed his forehead was badly grazed from hitting his head when George dropped him on the hard-stone floor. Looking back at the Dan in the room, his face was hardly marked.

"Who are you?" I cried but I already knew the answer.

"You know who I am!" he sighed. "Helena, I fell in love with you when we first met." Suddenly, Dan's face changed into the rock giant. "I've been

THE ISLAND BECOMES YOU

following you on this island ever since." His face then changed again and Dimitri's face was staring back at me.

"Stop hiding behind the other faces. Show me who you really are?"

"I will one day, my dearest Helena but I need to tell you I did all this for you…"

Freya interrupted, "I can't hold him for much longer. Helena, you need to find the ring."

Ignoring the pleas from Loki to listen to him, I rushed over to the bookcase. Following my instincts, I immediately pulled out the Moby Dick book and opened it. The pages automatically fell open to the centre revealing a hidden compartment. Pulling back the flap revealed a small golden trinket box.

"Helena, I beg you, leave it alone. You don't know the power of the ring. Every time you use it there is a dire consequence. The ring doesn't care who is affected. It could be family member, a loved one who suffers as a result. But each time a price must be paid for using its magic."

"Ignore him, Helena, everything he says is a lie. You can't believe him after what he has done. You know what he is capable of doing. He is only trying to frighten you," Freya cried.

Picking up the beautiful golden box, I examined it closer, its reflection sparkled near the light. I looked across at Loki. Catching my eye, he pleaded, "Helena, please put the evil ring back. It will bring you so much pain if you use it."

"Pay no attention to him Helena. Quickly, put the ring on your heart finger of your left hand." Slightly hesitant, I carefully opened the box. Inside I was hit by the breath-taking beauty of the exquisite golden ring. It seemed to glow more radiantly as I removed it and placed it on my left palm. The craftsmanship was amazing, so flawless, the golden heart shape blended with perfection onto the solid gold band. I wondered how something so small could be that powerful. Just as I was about to place it on my ring finger, I noticed a faint inscription inside the ring. This troubled me, I heard the words 'evil ring' resonating at the back of my mind. I was going to ask Freya the significance of the words when two things happened simultaneously.

Freya screamed, "Put it on now!" seconds before Loki managed to break through the force field and seized the Russian doll. Then at the same time I heard Dan calling my name from the other end of the passageway leading to this room.

"Dan, in here," I yelled.

I could hear his footsteps racing down the corridor towards me. I counted the seconds before he would be in my arms again. Soon his smiling face appeared through the doorway only to change to utter shock when he also saw Dimitri holding a Russian doll. Bypassing him, Dan carried on towards me and crushed me in his arms. "It feels so good to hold you again," he murmured in my ear. Ignoring everything around us we kissed.

"How moving, the two lovers reunited!"

We both turned to face Loki. "Your plan to separate us hasn't worked," Dan replied. "Our love is too strong!"

"I can be patient. I've waited a long time to fall in love this deeply. Helena, I just need the chance to show you how strong my feelings are for you. Tell me you must have felt something for me when I was the rock giant?"

Stunned by what he was saying, I replied, "I can't believe what I'm hearing. You can't make someone love you and you certainly can't achieve it by pretending to be someone else."

"That's why we need more time to get to know each other. Your love could make me a better person. I'll prove it. I'm willing to set Dan free to go home if you would stay on this island with me Helena. Over time I'm sure you could learn to love me."

I watched Loki, who was holding the Russian doll, try to walk towards us. Fortunately, the invisible barrier was still just about holding. The thought of spending another moment on this island with him filled me with complete loathing but I briefly contemplated the thought that Dan would be safe if I agreed to his wishes. There must be another way, looking down at the golden ring in my hands I knew I had to do something. So, I put the ring on my finger.

"NO," yelled Loki.

"Love is not conditional," I yelled back at him. "If you love someone, you let them go, you don't force them to stay because it's what you want."

I could see Loki trying to fight the anger bubbling up inside him. His face was starting to go red. Loki punched through the invisible barrier with his free fist. Freya screamed, "The ring! Use the ring to escape."

THE ISLAND BECOMES YOU

Holding Dan's hand. I closed my eyes and visualised we were back on the boat, going home. I felt a warmth radiate up from my ring finger and a bright glow surrounded us. I was too scared to open my eyes. Eventually, the blinding light faded and I stood there a while longer, gripping Dan's hand, contemplating if it was safe. Gradually, I became aware of a gentle rocking motion. I knew instantly where we were. Opening my eyes, I looked across at the familiar wooden decking and mast belonging to the Adventurer. Dan was standing beside me, staring over my shoulder. "It's gone," he declared. I understood what he meant but I still turned around to look, to get closure. The island had indeed disappeared.

"I never want to see it again!" I replied.

"Me neither," Dan agreed as his left hand checked his back pocket. He was relieved, to find the journal was still there.

…

"Freya, you will pay dearly for all your meddling. I know you have used the last of your powers to stop me." Laughing he continued, "Now you are trapped here!" Lifting the small, black Russian doll high in the air he shouted, "I could so easily break you into tiny pieces but ..." He hesitated then said, "I prefer to keep you a prisoner on this island just like me!" Laughing again he added, "If you are lucky, I might pay you a visit ... perhaps once every hundred years!"

Carefully, placing the Russian doll back on the shelf he sneered, "Hope you enjoy the scenery."

He was about to walk out of the room when he heard a weak voice say, "Remember she now has the ring!"

Immediately, Loki replied confidently, "But she doesn't know its true power."

"But others do," Freya whispered back. "And in time they will find her."

"But I intend to find her first. She will be mine one day and the ring will be safely back in my possession." Smiling triumphantly, he added, "I will leave you now, all alone to reflect on the consequences of your actions. You will have an eternity to think about it!"

Slamming the door behind him, a sad silence engulfed the room. On the shelf, the small, black Russian doll closed her eyes and a single tear slid down her cheek.

Printed in Great Britain
by Amazon